# THE GOLFER'S COMPANION

## An Anthology of Golf Writing from 1457 to the Present

# THE GOLFER'S COMPANION

## An Anthology of Golf Writing from 1457 to the Present

## Compiled by Michael Hobbs

Macdonald
Queen Anne Press

A *Queen Anne Press* BOOK

This anthology Copyright © Michael Hobbs 1988

First published in Great Britain in 1988 by
Queen Anne Press, a division of
Macdonald & Co (Publishers) Ltd
3rd Floor
Greater London House
Hampstead Road
London
NW1 7QX

A member of Maxwell Pergamon Publishing Corporation plc

Design: Rita Wüthrich

**British Library Cataloguing in Publication Data**

The Golfer's companion, an anthology of golf writing from 1457 to the present
  1. Golf
  I. Hobbs, Michael, 1934–
  796.352    GV965

ISBN 0–356–15440–8

Typeset by Butler & Tanner Ltd
Printed and bound in Great Britain by
Butler & Tanner Ltd, Frome and London

# CONTENTS

# CONTENTS

# ACKNOWLEDGEMENTS

I should particularly like to thank golf book dealer Bob Grant of Grant Books, Droitwich, for his help in obtaining for me and lending, rare and valuable golf books. My publishers and I would also like to thank the following individuals, agencies and publishers for their permission to use copyright material in this book:

André Deutsch Ltd for 'A bliss like thinking of women' from *Rabbit is Rich* (1982) by John Updike.

Atheneum for 'The Haig and I', 'I remember Sammy' and 'Pinehurst revisited' from *Golfer-at-large* (1982) by Charles Price and 'Trial and error', 'It's not interesting', 'Shooting at steeples' and 'Remember the rabbit' from *Gettin' to the Dance Floor* (1986) by Al Barkow.

Al Barkow, Editor-in-Chief, *Golf Illustrated* (USA) for 'Nicklaus goes for broke' and 'Traditions in a hurry' from *Golf's Golden Grind* (Harcourt Brace Jovanovich, 1974).

Susan Calver for 'Failure of a mission' from *It was Good While it Lasted* (1941) and 'The Maestro'.

Century Hutchinson for 'No Anglo-Saxon reserve' from *Peter Alliss' Most Memorable Golf* by Peter Alliss and Michael Hobbs.

Collins for 'With time running out' and 'The car park champion' from *The Open* (1984) by Peter Alliss and Michael Hobbs.

*Golf World* for 'Beam me up, Scotty!' by Andy Totham and 'Pine Valley' by Robert Green.

Gollancz for 'Delight' from *The Good Minute* (1965) by Patric Dickinson.

Hodder and Stoughton Ltd for 'Augusta, 1980' from *Seve: The Young Champion* (1982) by Severiano Ballesteros and Dudley Doust.

For 'The game of golfe', 'Golf's goodwill ambassador', 'Two holes, six strokes', 'Billy Joe gonna do it', 'Atmosphere unparalleled' and 'Prestwick' from 'The Game of Golfe', 'Sam Snead with Hair', 'Down South' and 'The Dogged Victim' in *The Dogged Victims of Inexorable Fate* by Dan Jenkins. Copyright © 1970 by Dan Jenkins. By permission of Little, Brown and Company. Portions of this material are expanded and revised from articles that originally appeared in *Sports Illustrated* Magazine.

Mark H. McCormack for 'Could a writer get at it' and 'Head-to-head' from *The World of Professional Golf* (1968).

Charles Price for 'Hagen', '18 and 17' and 'Golf architecture, USA' from *The World of Golf* (1962) by Charles Price.

Macmillan, London and Basingstoke, for 'Strength of mind', 'Graham's great finish', 'Pebble Beach and the Open' and 'Along Carmel Bay' from *Following Through* (1986) by Herbert Warren Wind.

Moorland Publishing Co Ltd for 'The man who lost it all' and 'The necessary hero' from *Fifty Masters of Golf* (1983) by Michael Hobbs.

The *Observer* for 'Walking back to happiness' (1986) by Peter Dobereiner.

Laurence Pollinger Limited for 'The sluggers arrive' from *The Walter Hagen Story* (1957) by Walter Hagen with Margaret Seaton Heck.

Random House for 'The picture-postcard golfer' from *The Story of American Golf* (1948) by Herbert Warren Wind.

For 'A different game', 'I went home', 'Primitive courses' and 'The best bowels' from *Teed Off* by Dave Hill and Nick Seitz © 1977. Used by permission of the publisher, Prentice-Hall, Inc., Engelwood Cliffs, NJ, USA. Peter Thomson and *Golf Digest* for 'Courses that are Hell to play'.
Peter Thomson for 'Carnoustie, 1968' and 'Untidy alleys' from *This Wonderful World of Golf* (1969) by Peter Thomson and Desmond Zwar.
Phyllis Taylor for 'The death of Vardon' (1937) by J. H. Taylor and 'My first Open', and 'Devoid of natural obstacles' from *Golf: My Life's Work* (1943) by J. H. Taylor.
Jean Ward-Thomas for 'The young Thomson' from *Masters of Golf* (1961) and 'A timeless stretch of land' in *The Guardian* by Pat Ward-Thomas.
A. P. Watt on behalf of Ursula Mommens, Lady Darwin and the N.M.F Fenn Will Trust for 'A marshland of pitch' and 'The wedge' from *The World that Fred Made* (1955) by Bernard Darwin, 'Forgotten greatness' from *Golfing By-paths* (1946) by Bernard Darwin, 'The old versus the new' from *Green Memories* (1928) by Bernard Darwin, 'Into the tempest' from *James Braid* (1952) by Bernard Darwin.

Every effort has been made to trace holders of copyright. In a very few instances this has proved impossible. The publishers will be pleased to hear from any persons or organisations who are holders of such copyright and will make amendments for omissions in future editions.

# INTRODUCTION

Printed mentions of golf and depictions of golf-like games in art first appeared in the British Isles many centuries ago. The great East, or Crecy, Window at Gloucester Cathedral, which dates from about 1350, contains a roundel which shows a man swinging a 'club' at a ball. Was this golf? It's hard to say; the club looks like a modern hockey stick and the ball is far too large. On the other hand, the poise and movement of the body closely resemble that of the modern golf swing and the player stands on undulating ground, a feature of golf, unlike most other outdoor games. In the best twentieth-century style, he is making a good shoulder turn but restricting his hip movement.

The earliest written mentions of golf were three fifteenth-century proclamations by Scottish parliaments, the first of which was issued in March 1457. Subsequently, most of the references to the game were the result of prosecutions for playing golf during sermon time on Sundays. However the Stuart kings who had banned golf soon appear in a different light. James IV of Scotland is recorded in accounts of the Lord High Treasurers as having spent money on 'Golf Clubbis and Ballis' in 1503–4.

There was still a long time to go, however, before the literature of golf began to grow, though there were passing references to it in books on other subjects. The first work devoted to golf was a poem of about a dozen pages by an Edinburgh man, Thomas Mathison, published in 1743. The first prose work did not follow until 1824 with *The Rules of the Thistle Golf Club,* which contained 'An Historical Account of the Game of Golf'.

The first golf annual appeared in 1867 and in the late 1880s the flood of golf books began. At this time the first excellent golf writers, Sir Walter Simpson and Horace Hutchinson, appeared. They are well represented in this selection, as they deserve to be, for many of their thoughts on the game are still relevant a hundred years later.

The best of all golf writers is usually considered to be Bernard Darwin, who, although golf was his life's work, also wrote on boxing, cricket, Dickens and was the author of several children's books. Darwin's golf writing is rich in humour, wit, passion, nostalgia, analysis, drama – and love of the game.

The many other writers represented in this book may not have Darwin's range but they are often even more brilliant in their own fields. There are the late Patrick Campbell and Peter Dobereiner to provoke outright laughter – they never fail to entertain. At the other end of the scale there is the high seriousness of Herbert Warren Wind, who usually makes one feel that a major championship is the most important thing in the world – something you never feel in the writing of Henry Longhurst, for instance. Even more irreverent is a group of Americans which includes Charles Price, Dan Jenkins and Al Barkow.

It has been up to me to select the extracts and it is for you the reader to come to your own conclusions. Perhaps not all of the writing will suit every taste but an anthology is, by definition, a personal choice and I am confident that this book contains some of the best in golf literature from both sides of the Atlantic.

# THE APPEAL OF GOLF

*Once the appeal of golf began to gather momentum a hundred years or so ago, the trickle of golf books became a steady stream and eventually very nearly a flood. Many have tried to reach the core of the game, to define its appeal and to grasp in a phrase how it should be played. Those who came early in the field – Sir Walter Simpson and Horace Hutchinson, for example – hit most of the targets.*

## THE BEST THING IN LIFE
### A. J. BALFOUR, 1890

A tolerable day, a tolerable green, a tolerable opponent, supply, or ought to supply, all that any reasonably constituted human being should require in the way of entertainment. With a fine sea view, and a clear course in front of him, the golfer should find no difficulty in dismissing all worries from his mind, and regarding golf, it may even be indifferent golf, as the true and adequate end of man's existence.

*Although today a green is where the putting is done, the term once referred to the whole course. Scottish clubs still sometimes have a 'green ranger'. No clubs should use the term 'Greens Committee'.*
*Balfour was Prime Minister in 1902–5. His enthusiasm for golf helped the spread of the game.*

## A SMALL, ROUND WHITISH OBJECT
### JOHN STUART MARTIN, 1968

To control his own ball, all alone without help or hindrance, the golfer must first and last entirely control himself, and himself only. The little round toy sitting so alone and so still, which has so fascinated and tantalized the human animal for more than five centuries, is thus uniquely a psychic as well as physical cynosure of muscular skill and mental concentration.

At each stroke the ball becomes a vital extension, an image of one's innermost self. We remember the arching flight, the uncertain bounce, the final roll toward the hole – or away from it – as an integral whole, a unit of each digit on our scorecards. Yet from the impact of our club until the ball's arrival at its stopping spot, it is the *ball itself* that describes that whole – the airy parabola, the bounces, the linear ground track. His travelling ball is truly the player himself in motion, in the same sense that a painter's picture is himself on canvas, and a writer's words are himself in print.

We speak of eyeball-to-eyeball encounters between men great and small. Even more searching and revealing of character is the eyeball-to-golfball confrontation, whereby our most secret natures are mercilessly tested by a small, round, whitish object with no mind or will but with a very definite life of its own, and with whims perverse or beatific. Each conjunction of our own efforts and the ball's behaviour freights our memories with regret or jubilation; or, as in the rest of life, with a mixture of both in deserved proportions.

Apart from the mental and muscular efforts it exacts from us, the golf ball exerts potent aesthetic stimuli. When first taken out of its wrap of tissue or foil or plastic, it gleams with a purity more pristine, I think, than any of man's other playthings: than even a new baseball, or shotgun shell, or trout fly. Its perfect roundness, its glossy whiteness, the precision of its dimples, the tiny hallmarks etched so neatly at its poles, even its smell – nowadays so elusive as to be largely imaginary; all these are important elements of that mystique which entrances us each time we step out on a first tee.

## Naked
### MICHAEL MURPHY, 1971

Golf is first a game of seeing and feeling. It can teach you stillness of mind and a sensitivity to the textures of wind and green. The best instructional books have always said this. Golf is also a game to teach you about the messages from within, about the subtle voices of the body-mind. And once you understand them you can more clearly see your 'harmartia', the ways in which your approach to the game reflects your entire life. Nowhere does a man go so naked.

## Ever Hopeful
### SIR WALTER SIMPSON, 1887

The game of golf is full of consolation. The long driver who is beaten feels that he has a soul above putting. All those who cannot drive 30 yards suppose themselves to be good putters. Your hashy player piques himself on his power of recovery. The duffer is a duffer merely because every second shot is missed. Time or care will eliminate the misses, and then! Or perhaps there is something persistently wrong in driving, putting, or approaching. He will discover the fault, and then! Golf is not one of those occupations in which you soon learn your level. There is no shape nor size of body, no awkwardness nor ungainliness, which puts good golf beyond one's reach. There are good golfers with spectacles, with one eye, with one leg, even with one arm. None but the absolutely blind need despair. It is not the youthful tyro alone who has cause to hope. Beginners in middle age have become great, and, more wonderful still, after years of patient duffering, there may be a rift in the clouds. Some pet vice which has been clung to as a virtue may be abandoned, and the fifth-class player burst upon the world as a medal winner. In golf, whilst there is life there is hope.

*Sir Walter Simpson was not a particularly good golfer but his book,* The Art of Golf, *is one of the classics of golf literature.*

# UP TO YOU
## PETER ALLISS, 1963

The golfer has to act in cold blood. From a motionless posture he must generate a swift, sudden, powerful but rhythmic action which is complete in perhaps three or four seconds.

The final responsibility is his. It is all up to the player, the club and the ball, and no other people.

A tournament goes on for days. It is played at a dangerously high mental pressure. Golf makes its demands on the mind. A golfer is terribly exposed in almost every way. The responsibility is his and there is no way to camouflage this, no hope of jettisoning it.

# AWE
## GEORGE PLIMPTON, 1968

The game required a certain cold toughness of mind, and absorption of will. There was not an athlete I talked to from other sports who did not hold the professional golfer in complete awe, with thanksgiving that golf was not their profession. The idea of standing over a putt with thousands of dollars in the balance was enough to make them flap their fingers as if singed.

# VIRTUES OF THE GAME
## DAVID ROBERTSON FORGAN, 1898

Golf is a test of temper, a trial of honour, a revealer of character. It affords a chance to play the man and act the gentleman. It means going out into God's out-of-doors, getting close to nature, fresh air, exercise, a sweeping away of the mental cobwebs, genuine recreation of the tired tissues. It is a cure for care – an antidote to worry. It includes companionship with friends, social intercourse, opportunities for courtesy, kindliness and generosity to an opponent. It promotes not only physical health but moral force.

# THE MOST EXACTING OF GAMES
## ARNOLD HAULTAIN, 1908

Golf is more exacting than racing, cards, speculation or matrimony. Golf gives no margin: either you win or you fail. You cannot hedge; you cannot bluff; you cannot give a stop order. One chance is given you, and you hit or miss. There is nothing more rigid in life. And it is this ultra and extreme rigidity that makes golf so intensely interesting.

In almost all other games you pit yourself against a mortal foe; in golf it is yourself against the world: no human being stays your progress as you drive your ball over the face of the globe.

# IT'S VERY BAD FOR YOU
## DR A. S. LAMB

Golf increases the blood pressure, ruins the disposition, spoils the digestion, induces neurasthenia, hurts the eyes, callouses the hands, ties kinks in the nervous system, debauches the morals, drives men to drink or homicide, breaks up the family, turns the ductless glands into internal warts, corrodes the pneumo-gastric nerve, breaks off the edges of the vertebrae, induces spinal meningitis and progressive mendacity, and starts angina pectoris.

# BURNING DESIRE
## FRANK BEARD, 1970

I have some theories about what makes golf champions. The number one guys have to be almost totally self-centred. They have to possess an incredible burning for success. They have to ignore their friends and their enemies and sometimes their families and concentrate entirely upon winning. There's no other way to get to the top.

If I tried it I'd fail. I couldn't survive that constant intensity, that constant burning. I admire – hell, I envy – their ability to burn and burn and burn.

*Beard took 11 US events in the 1960s and early 1970s but was better known for his steady accumulation of cash-winnings and saw tournament golf as much the same thing as going to the office.*

# LESS INJURIOUS THAN WHISKY
## SIR WALTER SIMPSON, 1887

It is a game for the many. It suits all sorts and conditions of men. The strong and the weak, the halt and the maimed, the octogenarian and the boy, the rich and the poor, the clergyman and the infidel, may play every day, except Sunday. The late riser can play comfortably, and be back for his rubber in the afternoon; the sanguine man can measure himself against those who will beat him; the half-crown seeker can find victims, the gambler can bet, the man of high principle, by playing for nothing, may enjoy himself, and yet feel good. You can brag, and lose matches; depreciate yourself, and win them. Unlike the other Scotch game of whisky-drinking, excess in it is not injurious to the health.

Golf has some drawbacks. It is possible, by too much of it, to destroy the mind ... For the golfer, Nature loses her significance. Larks, the casts of worms, the buzzing of bees, and even children are hateful to him. I have seen a golfer very angry at getting into a bunker by killing a bird, and rewards of as much as ten shillings have been offered for boys maimed on the links. Rain comes to be regarded solely in its relation to the putting greens; the daisy is detested, botanical specimens are but 'hazards', twigs 'break clubs'. Winds cease to be east, south, west, or north. They are ahead, behind, or sideways, and the sky is bright or dark, according to the state of the game.

## GAMUT OF EMOTIONS
### ROBERT TYRE JONES, 1962

Golf has been called 'the most human of games' and a 'reflection of life'. One reason that we enjoy it and that it challenges us is that it enables us to run the entire gamut of human emotions, not only in a brief space of time, but likewise without measurable damage either to ourselves or to others.

Much has been made of the drama of championship golf, and there is no doubt that it can be intense. But within more meagre limits, ordinary everyday golf can provide the same challenge and drama. Even here, we have all the elements of a gripping experience that can be lived through to the fullest and then dismissed at the end of the day.

On the golf course, a man may be the dogged victim of inexorable fate, be struck down by an appalling stroke of tragedy, become the hero of unbelievable melodrama, or the clown in a side-splitting comedy – any of these within a few hours, and all without having to bury a corpse or repair a tangled personality.

## THE REAL MAN
### GRANTLAND RICE, 1954

Golf gives you an insight into human nature, your own as well as your opponent's. A man's true colours will surface quicker in a five dollar Nassau than in any other form of diversion. [After the game] peeled down to his shorts, a highball in one hand, an attested score-card in the other, it's hard for a man to be anything but himself.

## NEXT TIME...
### SIR WALTER SIMPSON, 1887

Although unsuited to the novelist, golf lends itself readily to the dreaming of scenes, of which the dreamer is the hero. Unless he is an exceptionally good rider, or can afford 300 guinea mounts, a man cannot expect to be the hero of the hunting-field. The sportsman knows what sort of shot he is, and the fisher has no illusions; but every moderately good golfer, on the morning of the medal day, may lie abed and count up a perfect score for himself. He easily recalls how at different times and how often he has done each hole in par figures. Why not this day, and all the holes consecutively? It seems so easy. The more he thinks of it the easier it seems, even allowing for a few mistakes. Every competitor who is awake soon enough sees the necessity for preparing a speech against the contingency of the medal being presented to him in the evening. Nor is any one much crushed when all is over, and he has not won. If he does well, it was but that putt, that bad lie, that bunker. If his score is bad, what of it? Even the best are off their game occasionally. Next time it will be different.

## DAY IN, DAY OUT
### JAMES BALFOUR, 1887

Wherein do the charms of this game lie, that captivate youth, and retain their hold till far on in life? I have known the game survive all other sports – football and cricket, shooting, salmon-fishing, hunting, and deer-stalking. Probably it owes much to the variety of its attractions. It is a fine, open-air, athletic exercise, not violent, but bringing into play nearly all the muscles of the body; while that exercise can be continued for hours. But it would be a mistake to suppose that it is only muscular exertion that is required. It is a game of skill, needing mind and thought and judgement, as well as a cunning hand. It is also a social game, where one may go out with one friend or with three, as the case may be, and enjoy mutual intercourse, mingled with an excitement which is very pleasing, while it never requires to be associated with the degrading vice of gambling. It never palls or grows stale, as morning by morning the players appear at the teeing-ground with as keen a relish as if they had not seen a club for a month. Nor is it only while the game lasts that its zest is felt. How the player loves to recall the strokes and other incidents of the match, so that it is often played over again next morning while he is still in bed! But even more does it absorb the conversation of the evening ... How each dilates on his own wonderful strokes, and the singular chances that befell him in the different parts of the green! – all under the pleasurable delusion that every listener is as interested in his game as he himself is. How he tells of his long swipes, which he is not sure have ever been equalled, and of the perfect pitch which he made with the baffy, or iron, at the approach stroke, just carrying the bunker that intervened, and narrowly escaping the whins on the left! And then the long putt – how beautifully the ball rolled over the smooth green up to the very lip of the hole.

*'Swipe' used to be the word used for a drive. A baffy was a lofted, short-shafted wood used for approach shots, turf being taken before the ball.*

## THE CHALLENGE
### ROBERT TYRE JONES, 1960

Golf has a very great and sometimes mystifying appeal to busy men. Some of its most ardent devotees are men of affairs whose lives are filled with responsibilities for making important decisions. To those who know little of golf, it is difficult to explain how a game so apparently frivolous could interest such men as these.

To those who know something of the game, there is no mystery at all. Golfers know, and have known for a long time, that when playing golf, it is almost impossible to think of anything else ... It is, therefore, the all-absorbing challenge of golf which makes it such an effective agent of mental therapy.

## DELIGHT
### PATRIC DICKINSON, 1965

I was intensely happy. I loved the wiry shiny knots of coarse grass, all the green and yellow and dun colours and the way one's boots could almost slide over it. I felt the whole scene close round me as if it were something I wore hidden against my naked skin. It clothed me secretly.

## THE MOST PLEASURE
### LORD BRABAZON OF TARA, 1956

When I look on my life and try to decide out of what I have got most actual pleasure, I have no doubt at all in saying that I have got more out of golf than anything else.

*Henry Longhurst once called Brabazon 'the universal amateur'. In these specialized times he could hardly exist – minister in Churchill's wartime government, Grand Prix racing driver, high class performer on the Cresta Run and holder of the first UK pilot's licence.*

## Best for Idiots
### SIR WALTER SIMPSON, 1887

The more fatuously vacant the mind is, the better for play. It has been observed that absolute idiots . . .play steadiest. An uphill game does not make them press, nor victory within their grasp render them careless. Alas! we cannot all be idiots. Next to the idiotic, the dull unimaginative mind is the best for golf. In a professional competition I would prefer to back the sallow, dull-eyed fellow with a 'quid' in his cheek, rather than any more eager-looking champion. The poetic temperament is the worst for golf. It dreams of brilliant drives, iron shots laid dead, and long putts held, whilst in real golf success waits for him who takes care of the foozles and leaves the fine shots to take care of themselves.

## A Few Wise Words
### HORACE HUTCHINSON, 1886

If you happen to be a really long driver, the fact will be generally admitted without your emphasizing it, to the annoyance and even peril of your neighbours, by always firing off your tee-shot the moment the parties in front of you have struck their seconds. To bear and to forbear is a necessity of golfing existence.

If your adversary is badly bunkered, there is no rule against your standing over him and counting his strokes aloud, with increasing gusto as their number mounts up; but it will be a wise precaution to arm yourself with the niblick before doing so, so as to meet him on equal terms.

Do not get into the habit of pointing out the peculiarly salient blade of grass which you imagine to have been the cause of your failing to hole your putt. You may sometimes find your adversary, who has successfully holed his, irritatingly shortsighted on these occasions. Moreover, the opinion of a man who has just missed his putt, about the state of that particular putting green, is usually accepted with some reserve.

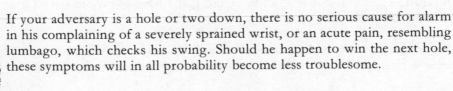

If your adversary is a hole or two down, there is no serious cause for alarm in his complaining of a severely sprained wrist, or an acute pain, resembling lumbago, which checks his swing. Should he happen to win the next hole, these symptoms will in all probability become less troublesome.

However unlucky you may be, and however pleasant a fellow your adversary, it really is not fair to expect his grief for your undeserved misfortunes to be as poignant as your own.

Try to remember, too, that a person may be a most indifferent golfer, and yet be a good Christian gentleman, and in some respects worthy of your esteem.

# DOWN IN THREE MORE
## SIR WALTER SIMPSON, 1887

The adversary who outdrives us is not difficult to deal with. If he does so on the average, he naturally gives odds, a man's driving being the usual standard by which his game is measured. If it is only when he hits them that he drives far, he is still easier to deal with. Those who hit occasional screamers, over-estimate their own game even more than the rest of golfers.

Judged by his apparent merits, the most dangerous man is he who is exceptionally good within the hundred yard radius. To estimate the comparative efficiency of men's driving is easy, but near the hole casual observation is quite deceptive. The faculty for occasionally sending the ball high in the air to land dead causes a man to be overestimated. He who, time after time, holes from a yard and a half is not necessarily a permanently dangerous adversary. It may be his own bad putting which so often renders these efforts necessary. If you are puzzled at so-and-so constantly winning, the key to the enigma will probably be found in the inconspicuous regularity with which he performs the apparently simple duty of holing in three off his iron. His approaches are not brilliant perhaps. It may even be that many of them are scuffled along the ground; but a close observation will show that they are invariably straight. Nobody is oftener past the hole than short, but the deadly player will have a good average of approaches finishing on the far side. In short, an adversary who does not seem to be playing his short game at all well, may be winning every hole because each approach is laid within 15 yards and each long putt within 15 inches – a very simple matter, which rouses no astonishment, but is perfect play nevertheless.

*In Sir Walter's day, to 'give odds' meant handicap strokes and players didn't carry a battery of approaching clubs – hence 'his iron'.*

# THE MAN WHO CAN PUTT IS A MATCH FOR ANYONE
## WILLIE PARK, 1920

Thirty years ago I coined the aphorism which heads this page. It has stood the test of time, and it is as true today as when I first made it. The statement was always the subject of much controversy, but I proved it correct by my successes in the numerous stake matches I played; and the frequency with which you will hear the sentence today, uttered with all the ring of truism and conviction, is evidence that my assertion survives the controversy and has been proved right by experience.

*J. H. Taylor later responded to Willie Park's saw: 'The man who can pitch does not need to putt'. In the first instance, Park was marketing his wry-neck design of putter; Taylor's slogan had to do with his skill at banging his ball up to the hole and making it stop there. He was striving to sell the model of mashie with which he performed the feat.*

*Later came a more persistent aphorism: 'You drive for show and putt for dough'. This was Willie Park in different words. To date, no one has equally neatly expressed the thought that without a reasonable drive you can't play the rest of the hole. As regards the sheer appeal of driving:*

# I'M THE GREATEST!
## SIR WALTER SIMPSON, 1887

There is no such being as a golfer uninterested in his driving. The really strong player seems to value his least; but this is merely because so many of his shots are good that they do not surprise him. Let it, however, be suggested that some other is a longer driver than he, and the mask of apathy will at once fall from his face, his tongue will be loosened, and he will proceed to boast.

*Horace Hutchinson, a few years later, made the simple declaration: 'If there were no driving there would be very little golf'.*

# PALLID CHEEKS
## SIR WALTER SIMPSON, 1887

When a putter is waiting his turn to hole-out a putt of one or two feet in length, on which the match hangs at the last hole, it is of vital importance that he think of nothing. At this supreme moment he ought studiously to fill his mind with vacancy. He must not even allow himself the consolations of religion. He must not prepare himself to accept the gloomy face of his partner and the derisive delight of his adversaries with Christian resignation should he miss. He must not think that it is a putt he would not dream of missing at the beginning of the match, or, worse still, that he missed one like it in the middle. He ought to wait calm and stupid till it is his turn to play, wave back the inevitable boy who is sure to be standing behind his arm, and putt as I have told him how – neither with undue haste nor with exaggerated care. When the ball is down, and the putter handed to the caddy, it is not well to say, 'I couldn't have missed it'. Silence is best. The pallid cheek and trembling lip belie such braggadocio.

# CHANGING TIMES

*The first written mentions of golf were prompted by the desire of the kings of Scotland to be ready for war with the English. They wanted their subjects to practise the military arts – specially archery – and not to waste their time at games.*

## GOLFE CRYDE DOWNE
### JAMES II OF SCOTLAND, 1457

It is decreeted and ordained, that the Weapon-schawinges be halden be the Lordes and Baronnes Spiritual and Temporal, four times in the zeir. And that the Fute-ball and Golfe be utterly cryed downe, and not to be used ... And as tuitching the Fute-ball and the Golfe, to be punished be the Barronniss un-law ... And that all men, that is within fiftie, and past twelve zeires, sall use schuting.

## GOLFE ABUSED
### JAMES III OF SCOTLAND, 1471

And that the Fute-ball and Golfe be abused in time cumming, and that the buttes be made up, and schuting used ...

## AN UNPROFFITABLE SPORTE
### JAMES IV OF SCOTLAND, 1491

It is statute and ordained that in na place of the Realme there be used Fute-ball, Golfe, or uther sik unproffitable sportes.

*During the following century golf became acceptable. The city of St Andrews, for example, in 1552 gave their archbishop the licence to rear rabbits on the links, provided this did not interfere with 'golf futball schuting' or indeed 'all uther maner of pastyme as ever thai pleis'. Golf on the Sabbath was a different matter. Various references have been found late in the sixteenth century of playing golf on this day, such as:*

## GOLF IN TIME OF THE PREACHING
### KIRK SESSION OF PERTH, 1599

John Gardiner, James Bowman, Laurence Chalmers, and Laurence Cuthbert confess that they were playing at the golf on the North Inch in time of the preaching after noon on the Sabbath. The Session rebuked them, and admonished them to resort to the hearing of the Word diligently on the Sabbath in time coming, which they promised to do.

*By this time, however, the main objection, though this varied from town to town, was to people playing golf 'in time of the preaching' rather than Sunday as a whole. Even so, many British golf clubs did not allow Sunday golf until well into this century. The ban exists today on the Old Course at St Andrews but for a different reason – to give the turf a rest.*

*Royal bans on golf were eventually lifted and the clergy, so often keen golfers themselves, may well have been influential in causing restrictions on Sunday play to be moderated, though the obstacle of cost remained. If golfing land was free and clubs inexpensive, the cost of balls meant that the working man couldn't afford to play. The arrival of the gutta-percha ball may not have opened the game to the masses but it did help to pave the way towards golf for all. In Victorian times, many poems were written about golf and this one reflects the joy felt at the demise of the expensive and flimsy feathery ball, which had been in use since about 1600.*

## IN PRAISE OF GUTTA-PERCHA
### WILLIAM GRAHAM, 1848

Of a' the changes that of late
Have shaken Europe's social state,
Let wondering politicians prate,
   And 'bout them mak a wark a'.
A subject mair congenial here,
And dearer to a Golfer's ear,
I sing – the change brought round this year
   By balls of GUTTA-PERCHA!

Though Gouf be of our games most rare,
Yet, truth to speak, the tear and wear
O' balls was felt to be severe,
   And source o' great vexation;
When Gourlay balls cost half-a-croun,
And Allan's no a farthing doun,
The feck o's wad been harried soon
   In this era of taxation.

Right fain we were to be content
Wi' used-up balls new lickt wi' paint,
That ill concealed baith scar and rent –
   Balls scarcely fit for younkers.
And though our best wi' them we tried,
And nicely every club applied,
They whirred and fuffed, and dooked and shied,
   And sklentit into bunkers.

But times are changed – we dinna care
Though we may ne'er drive leather mair,
Be't stuffed wi' feathers or wi' hair –
    For noo we're independent.
At last a substance we hae got,
Frae which for scarce mair than a groat,
A ba' comes that can row and stot –
    A ba' the most transcendent.

They say it comes frae yont the sea,
The concrete juice o' some rare tree –
And hard and horny though it be,
    Just steep it in het water –
As saft as potty soon 'twill grow,
Then 'tween your loofs a portion row –
When cool, a ba' ye'll get, I trow,
    That ye for years may batter.

Hail, GUTTA-PERCHA! precious gum!
O'er Scotland's links lang may ye bum;
Some purse-proud billies haw and hum,
    And say ye're douf at fleein';
But let them try ye fairly out,
Wi' ony balls for days about,
Your merits they will loudly tout,
    And own they hae been leein'.

'Tis true – at first ye seem to hing,
And try the air wi' timid wing –
But firmer grown, a sweep ye'll fling
    Wi' ony ba' o' leather.
Ye're keen and certain at a putt –
Nae weet your sides e'er opens up –
And though for years your ribs they whup,
    Ye'll never mout a feather.

But noo that a' your praise is spent,
Ye'll listen to a friend's comment,
And kindlier tak on the paint,
    Then ye wad be perfection.
And sure some scientific loon
On Golfing will bestow a boon,
And gie ye a cosmetic soon,
    And brighten your complexion.

24

## GUM SAVES GOLF
### HORACE HUTCHINSON, 1899

Had the gutta-percha golf ball not been invented, it is likely enough that golf itself would now be in the catalogue of virtually extinct games, only locally surviving, as stool-ball and knurr and spell.

But, as matter of history, the gutta-percha ball was invented; golf became cheap again, and with its cheapness it became popular. And this essential condition of its popularity arrived just at the time that a great wave of a rising athletic spirit was coming over all Great Britain. At the beginning of our Queen's reign [Victoria] there were scarcely any sports or pastimes that could be called popular. There was no popular interest in any game. That keen interest in athleticism which we see so strongly shown by the multitude of sporting papers, the eagerness with which football records are scanned, and the crowds that attend a cricket match, did not exist at that time. But it arose about the middle of the century, when the golf ball began to be made of gutta-percha, and the two events, the mental and the material, coinciding gave golf (which had, as the great ultimate ground of the popularity it was soon to acquire, the merit of being an extraordinarily interesting pastime) that impetus which has resulted in the legion of golf players that are in the land today.

## IMPROVING THE NEW BALL
### JAMES BALFOUR, 1887

Let us now turn to the changes that have taken place on the balls. Forty years ago, and indeed from time immemorial, the only kind of ball with which golf had been played was made of leather stuffed with feathers till it was as hard as gutta-percha. In making it the leather was cut into three pieces, softened with alum and water, and sewed together by waxed thread, while a small hole was left for putting in the feathers, which was done with a strong stuffing-iron.

The hole in the leather, which did not affect the flight of the ball, but slightly interfered with its putting quality, was then sewed up, and the ball received three coats of paint. A man could make only four balls in a day. They were thus scarce and expensive, and were not round, but rather oblong. The only ball-maker at St Andrews was Allan Robertson. The trade was hereditary in his family, as both father and grandfather had likewise been ball-makers. He was assisted by Tom Morris and Lang Willie. They worked together in Allan's kitchen, and the balls were sold at the window at the back of his house, at the corner of the Links and Golf Place. Allan charged 1s. 8d. a ball, or £1 a dozen. Gourlay of Musselburgh charged 2s. for each of his. These balls did not last long, perhaps not more than one round. They opened at the seams, especially in wet weather. Indeed, whenever the seam of a ball was cut by the club, the ball burst, and became useless. This very frequently happened, insomuch that the caddies generally took out six or eight balls with them.

About the beginning of the year 1848 balls were first made of gutta-percha. I remember the commencement of them perfectly. My brother-in-law, Admiral Maitland Dougall, played a double match at Blackheath with the late Sir Ralph Anstruther and William Adam of Blair-Adam and another friend with gutta-percha balls on a very wet day. They afterwards dined together at Sir Charles Adam's at Greenwich Hospital, and Sir Ralph said after dinner: 'A most curious thing – here is a golf ball of gutta-percha; Maitland and I have played with it all day in the rain, and it flies better at the end of the day than it did at the beginning'. Maitland came to Edinburgh immediately after and told me of this. We at once wrote to London for some of these balls, and went to Musselburgh to try them. Gourlay the ball-maker had heard of them, and followed us around. He was astonished to see how they flew, and, being round, how they rolled straight to the hole on the putting-green. He was alarmed for his craft, and having an order from Sir David Baird to send him some balls whenever he had a supply by him, he forwarded to him that evening six dozen! Sir David accordingly was one of the last who adhered to the feather balls, and did not acknowledge the superiority of the others until his large supply was finished. At first they were made with the hand by rolling them on a flat board; thus made, they were round and smooth. They were not painted, but used with their natural brown colour. When new, they did not fly well, but ducked in the air. To remedy this they were hammered with a heavy hammer, but this did not effect the object. They still ducked until they got some rough usage from the cleek or iron. This made cuts on their sides, which were not liked; but it made them fly. These cuts were easily removed by dipping them in hot water at night. I remember once playing with old Philp, the club-maker (who, by the way, was no contemptible player). I had a gutta ball, and he had a feather one. With the dislike which all the tradesmen then had for the former, he said, 'Do you play with these putty balls?'. 'Yes,' I answered. 'But does not the cleek cut them?' 'O yes,' I said, 'but if you give them a hot bath at night that puts them all right.' 'That's the mischief o't,' he replied. Yet it was soon found out that this same hot bath, while it cured the wound, spoiled the ball. I remember an amusing proof of this. I and a friend on the day before the medal played with two guttas, and they worked beautifully, so that we resolved to play with them next day for the medal. But as they had been a good deal hacked, we dipped them in hot water over-night, and removed these defects. When, however, we played off the tee next day before an assembled crowd, among whom were the ball and club-makers, both the balls whirred and ducked amid the chuckling and jeering and loud laughter of the onlookers; we had to put down feather balls next hole. The fact was, they required these indentations to make them fly. About this time it occurred to an ingenious saddler in South Street to hammer them all round with the thin or sharp end of the hammer. The experiment was completely successful, and the ball thus hammered came rapidly into use, and they were soon improved by being painted. But the ball-makers were still bitterly opposed to them, as they threatened to destroy their trade, and both Allan and Tom resolved that they would never play in a match where these balls were used. In an unlucky hour, however, Tom good-naturedly broke his pledge, and played with a gentleman as his partner who had gutta balls. When Allan discovered it he was much annoyed with Tom. Tom, when he saw this, gave up his employment under him, and opened a shop of his own, where he made both kinds of balls, and also clubs. Allan in a little time followed suit with the balls, as he discovered that he could make a dozen guttas in a shorter time than he could make one feather ball, and the sale of them increased prodigiously. After that an iron mould was invented for making these balls, and on being taken from the mould, they were indented with the thin end of the hammer. But latterly the moulds have the indentations in them, so that the ball is now produced indented and ready for being painted. The balls are made everywhere now, but some are better than others, probably because the maker takes greater pains to use good gutta-percha.

*After the introduction of the gutta-percha ball which totally displaced the feathery ball in weeks or months rather than years, the main change in golf balls was that various forms of composition were tried. The balls that resulted did not change golf drastically and for 50 years the solid ball reigned supreme – pure gutta-percha or a mixture of this and other materials. Then the Haskell, or wound, ball arrived. It was much more expensive and not as tough as the 'gutty' but went much further and was more forgiving of half-hit shots.*

# THE HASKELL ARRIVES
## HORACE HUTCHINSON, 1919

In 1899 my brother-in-law, returning from a visit to America, came down to stay and to play golf with me at Ashdown Forest, and brought with him a dozen or two of a new kind of ball which, he said, had lately been invented in the United States and was the best ball in the world. The balls were called, as he told me, Haskells. We went out to play with them. He, as it happened, played very badly, and in a very short time he was perfectly ready to go into any court of law and take his oath that they were the worst balls in the world. I had formed my own opinion of them, much more in accord with the verdict with which he had first introduced them to me than with that condemnatory one which he passed on them after two days of being off his game; but I refrained from expressing my opinion too emphatically, with the result that when he went away he said that, as for the remnant of the balls, he was not going to be bothered 'to take the beastly things away', so that I found myself the possessor of a couple of dozen or so of excellent Haskell balls – being, as he had said, in the first instance, the best balls in the world – at a time when no one else in Great Britain had such a ball at all!

It is quite true that some months previously, at North Berwick, I had been given to try, by a professional who had just returned from the States, a ball which I now recognized to be the same, in some of its essentials, as these Haskells which my brother-in-law brought over. It was the same, except for one external but extremely important essential – its nicks were ridiculously too light and slight, not nearly enough indented. So I tried that ball and found it wanting – it would not fly at all. But what I did not realize at the time was the reason why it did not fly; or, if I did realize, as one could not fail to do, that the nicks were not emphatic enough, I had not a suspicion of the merit of its interior qualities. I had not appreciated that it was an amazingly good ball if only this slight matter of its exterior marking had been attended to. I had taken no more thought or notice of it.

Armed with these new weapons I prepared to go out to Biarritz, where the annual foursome match against Pau was just impending. My partner was to be Evy Martin Smith, and as soon as I arrived I told him that we must use these new balls for the match. He strongly objected, being a firm conservative, tried the balls, with every intention of disliking them, and disliked them accordingly. The fact is that I was, at this moment, just the last man in the world to appear on any scene as an advocate of a new ball. Only a year or two before I had taken an unfortunate interest in a patent substance called 'Maponite', of which, in addition to a thousand and one other things for which gutta-percha and indiarubber are used, golf balls were to be made. And wherein exactly was the weak point about the stuff as a material for golf balls I never knew, for the trial balls that they made for us were excellent – I remember that I won an open tournament at Brancaster with them – but as soon as ever they began to turn them out in numbers they were useful for one end only – for the good of the club-makers – for they were hard stony things which broke up the wooden clubs as if one had used the clubs as stone hammers.

So I was not a good apostle of a new ball – rather discredited in fact – but I did induce Evy Smith to play with the ball finally, under deep protest, and we justified its use by winning. Meanwhile the balls were beginning to filter from America into England. It was difficult indeed to get people to appreciate their merits: the balls were not numerous, and were still hard to obtain. At Johnny Low's request I sent him one for trial. He was writing at that time in the *Athletic News*. He wrote a most amusing article about the ball – said that he had tried a stroke or two with it in his room, and had found it so resilient that it went bounding about the room like a fives ball in a squash court and finally disappeared up the chimney and was never seen again.

In fine, he gave the ball his banning, 'not because it was an expensive ball' – it is to be remembered that it was rather a shock to be asked to pay two and sixpence for a golf ball, whereas before we had paid a shilling as the normal price – 'but because it was a bad ball', meaning a ball 'singularly ill-adapted for the purpose' of golf. So difficult is it for even a clever man and wise in the royal and ancient wisdom, as Johnny Low undoubtedly is, to keep an unprejudiced judgement about any new thing.

Expensive as the ball was in the beginning, it was soon found that it was far more economical than the solid 'gutty', both because it lasted in playable condition far longer and also because it did not knock about the wooden club to anything like the same extent. But within a very short while there came such a demand for those balls, so greatly in excess of the supply, that there was a time when as much as a guinea apiece was paid for them, and numbers changed hands at ten shillings. That was round and about the time of the championships, both Open and Amateur being held that year at Hoylake, and both these championships were won with the Haskell balls.

I am calling these balls Haskells, because that is the name by which they were known and spoken of, after their American inventor, at this time. The reluctance of players to use them, and the gradual overcoming of that reluctance, had many comic incidents associated with it.

The Amateur Championship that year was full of wonders. It was won by Charles Hutchings, he being then a grandfather and 52 years of age. He knocked me out, among other better men, beating me at the last hole. And then he beat that brilliant and greatly to be regretted young golfer, Johnny Bramston. In the final he had to play Fry, and established a very big lead on him in the first round. He had about six holes in hand with only nine to play, and then Fry began to do conjuring tricks, holing putts from the edge of the green, and so on. In the event Charles Hutchings just won by a single hole after one of the most remarkable final matches in the whole story of that championship. And it is to be noted that these two finalists, who proved themselves better able than most others to adapt themselves to the new touch of these livelier balls – for nearly all the competitors used the Haskells – were extremely good billiard players. Fry had won the Amateur Championship of billiards more than once, and Hutchings was quite capable of such atrocities as a three-figure break. I think the sensitive fingers of these billiard players helped them to get the touch of these livelier balls which were so 'kittle' for the approach and putting.

After the Amateur came the Open, in which I did not take a hand, but I heard a great deal of the preliminary discussions about it. Of course, if the amateurs were difficult to convince about the merits of the new balls, the professionals, who had their vested interest in the old, and did not know how these were to be affected by the coming of the new, were harder still to convince. However, the balls were too good to be denied. Andrew Kirkaldy, a shrewd man, and one, besides, who had no interest in the sale of balls, solid or rubber cored, was one of the first and most enthusiastic converts. 'The puggy,' he declared, 'is a great ba'.' He called it 'puggy', which is Scottish for monkey, because it jumped about so. 'Ye canna' tak' 80 strokes to the roun' wi' a puggy – the puggy will na' gae roun' in 80 strokes.'

# THE CRAZE FOR LENGTH

### HARRY VARDON, 1933

The year 1902 was to prove an eventful one in the history of the game of golf. In this season a new type of ball was to make its appearance on the links. It is not too much to say that the advent of the Haskell, which was the name of this, the first rubber-cored ball, was to an enormous extent eventually to revolutionize the game. When the new ball was firmly established, golf slowly started to undergo such drastic changes that to those of us who were brought up with the gutty, it has never been the same since. This change was, as is only natural, comparatively slow. When the possibilities were realized, however, the old solid ball was doomed for ever. I personally shall always regret the passing of the gutty. In my own mind I am firmly convinced that with its passing, much of the real skill had gone for ever. Let me give my readers an instance of what I mean. With the gutty ball the game had to be thoroughly learned. No half measures would do at that period if a player was to accomplish any success whatsoever.

Let us take the case of wooden-club play. In the days of the solid ball it was necessary for the drives to be properly struck if anything approaching a good round was to be recorded. By this I mean that a half-hit tee shot would not escape the hazards which had been placed to catch an indifferent stroke, as is so frequently the case with the modern ball. Consequently correct driving was more appreciated in those days than at the present period. I hold the opinion that the proper attitude towards the art of wooden-club play is not sufficiently appreciated by the modern golfer. I will go further and say that he does not fully realize what the art of driving really means. There can be little doubt in my mind that without accuracy a golfer is not entitled to consider himself a good wooden-club player. Accuracy is the keynote of successful golf. The accurate placing of the tee shot is the art of driving. Extremely long hit balls which are badly off the fairway are nothing more or less than indifferent shots. It may at once be said that the rough grass off the fairways will prove to be sufficient punishment for this mistake. Further it may be pointed out that the rough, on a good many courses, is no better today than in the old days. This may be true. But the chief point which appears to be overlooked is the fact that the wonderful improvements in modern clubs and the more resilient ball has made recovery ever so much easier.

The advent of the rubber ball was instrumental in creating an entirely different method of striking the object. The solid ball required to be hit for carry, whereas it was quickly apparent that the Haskell lent itself to an enormous run. As this was the case golfers naturally started to hit this ball in the way they could get the maximum amount of distance which it was possible to obtain. This was the start of new methods being employed in the full shots. To gain the maximum amount of run it was deemed necessary to

play for a hook. By this means the flight of the ball was lower and the carry considerably less. The run, however, by means of the overspin that had been imparted, was twice as much, and so actually longer distances were obtained. I hold the firm opinion that from this date the essential attitude towards accuracy was completely lost sight of. This was the start of the craze for length and still more length.

*No doubt the first man to play golf gave plenty of advice to the second person who took up the game. Virtually nothing has come down to us about how people played golf in its early days apart from the diary of Thomas Kincaid. Certainly he did not intend to pass on his thoughts; like many golfers since, he was noting down his conclusions about the basics of the golf swing. Many of the musings of this young Edinburgh golfer in 1687 have been echoed by writers since.*

# THE WAY OF PLAYEING AT GOLVE
## THOMAS KINCAID, 1687

Jan 20. After dinner I went out to the golve with Hen: Legatt. I found the only way of playeing at the golve is –

1. To stand as you do at fencing with a small sword, bending your legs a little, and holding the muscles of your legs and back and armes exceeding bent or fixt or stiffe, and not at all slackening them in the time you are bringing down the stroak (which you readily doe).

2. The ball most be straight before your breast, a little towards the left foot.

3. Your left foot most stand but a little before the right, or rather it most be even with it, and a convenient distance from it.

4. Ye most lean most to the right foot.

5. But all the turning about of your body most be only upon your legs, holden together as stiff as ye can.

6. Then ye most incline your body a little forward from the small of the back and upwards; for seeing all the strenth of the stroake is from the swing of the body in turning about, then certainly the further forward you incline your body or shoulders, they most have the greater swing, and so consequently give the greater stroake; but you most not incline so fare forward as to make your stand the more unstedfastly and waver a little in bringing down the stroak.

7. You most keep your body in this posture all the time both in bringing back the club and forward, that is, you most nither raise your body straighter in bringing back the club nor incline it further in bringing down the club; but ye most bring back the club by turning your selfe about to the right hand, and that as it were upon a center without moveing your body out of the place of it, but only chainging the position of it in thrawing it about or turning it about upon that center, so that ye most cast the weight of your

body off the on leg on the other in the time you are bringing about the club: neither most you in the least turn down your left shoulder and up your right in bringing back the club thinking thereby to give the club a larger swinge and so incresse its force or to raise the ball: for it is a verie unsetled motion that throw of the body whereby you turn down the left shoulder and up the right, so that thereby you will verie often misse the ball and allmost never hitt it exactly.

8. Your armes most move but verie little; all the motion most be performed with the turning of your body about. The armes serve only to guide the club and to second and carie on that motion imprest upon it by turning of your body: therefore ye most never begin to bring about the club with the motion of the armes first, but their motion most be only towards the end of the stroak.

9. All the motion of the armes most be at the shoulder and all the motion of the legs most be at the upmost joynt at the loins.

10. You most make no halt or rest, which is slakning of the muscles of the back, between the bringing-back of the club and the bringing it forward, but bring it about with that swiftness that the naturall swing of the club requires, holding it pretty fast in your hands. In every motion the muscles that concurr to the performing at golve keep bent and stayd, which in all motions of your armes you will be helped to do by contracting your fingers, and so if there be anything in your hand you most grip verie fast.

11. You most aim directly to hitt the ball it selfe and not aim to scum the ground or strick close to the ground, thinking that then you are sure to hitt it; for this is but ane indirect way of hitting the ball, neither is it sure when the ball lies inconveniently; neither 3dly is it exact, for you will butt seldome hitt the ball exactly and cleanly this way; and 4ly it is more difficult then the other way, whereas the other way is more easie. Two, sure, 3, better for hitting the ball exactly. The way to learn this is to tie your ball at first pretty high from the ground.

12. The shaft of your club most be of hazell. Your club most be allmost straight, that is, the head most make a verie obtuse angle with the shaft, and it most bend as much at the handle as it doth at the wooping ... being very supple and both long and great.

13. Your ball most be of middle size neither too big nor too little, and then the heivier it is in respect to its bigness it is still the better. It most be of thick and hard leather not with pores or grains or that will let a pin easily passe through it especially at the soft end.

Jan 21. I thought upon the way of playeing at golve ... I found that the first point to be studied in playeing at the golve is to hitt the ball exactly; for if you hitt the ball exactly though the club have butt strenth yett the ball will fly verie farre. The way to attain this perfection is to play with little strenth at first but yet acuratly observing all the rules of poustaur and motion before sett down, and then when ye have acquired ane habit of hitting the ball

exactly ye most learn to incresse your strenth to force in the stroak by degrees, staying still so long upon every degree till you have acquired ane habit of it; neither will the knowledge of these degrees be altogether uselese afterward, for they will serve for halfe chops, and quarter chops, and for holling the ball. But then in going through all these degrees of strenth you most be verie attentive and careful not to alter that poustaur of your body or way of moveing and bringing about the club which ye observed when ye playd with little strenth: for only the reasons why men readilly miss the ball when they strick with more strenth then ordinaire is because their incressing their body and ordinare way of bringing about the club; as also it makes them stand much more unsetledly and waver in bringing about the club, and so they readily miss the ball.

## Swings and Roundabouts

### PATRICK CAMPBELL, 1951

The thing that astonishes me about golf is that 20 years after I first began to play it, I still have six separate and distinct methods of producing any given shot. The other thing that astonishes me about golf is that half of these separate and distinct methods are the precise opposite of the other three, and all of them work equally well. On – that is – their limited day.

I should have thought, after so long an apprenticeship, that one particular method would finally have risen to the top, and that with it, in the middle 80s, I should have been allowed quietly to play out my time. But no. As I stand on the first tee in the first round of, say, the Amateur Championship, at 8.30 a.m. with a nippy oblique breeze off the sea, I can strike the new ball in front of me in no fewer than six different ways, and that after a week of careful practice.

With this first shot there are three things I want to do. I want to get it off the ground. I want to be able to find it after I've hit it. And, rather specially, I want to avoid the one which shoots off the toe through the roof of the starter's tent. I might try the Hogan Crouch. I got the Hogan Crouch from looking at pictures of Ben Hogan, and with it drove the second green at Coombe Hill in March 1951. In the Crouch the knees are bent throughout the duration of the performance. The back is hollowed, and the buttocks (Hogan's word not mine) are thrust out in a sitting position. It certainly gives a feeling of exceptional power and mobility. But with the Crouch I must continue to crouch. If the knees should suddenly straighten, owing to centrifugal force, the clubhead passes over the ball, resulting in the clean miss (Wentworth, April, 1951; Stoke Poges, April, 1951; Walton Heath, April, 1951; Sunningdale, April, 1951, etc.).

The Upright Classical might be a wiser investment. I got the Upright Classical from looking at pictures of Henry Cotton, and with it nearly reached the ditch from the first tee on the first hole at Deal in a year I don't remember, because every Halford Hewitt, in retrospect, looks to me exactly alike. The difficulty with the Upright Classical is that my left leg, at impact, seems to have the rigidity and length of a telegraph pole, and a follow-through of more than a foot guarantees a permanent injury. This is the one which, incorrectly played, passes low over the heads of people not paying attention at cover point.

The Blacksmith's Convulsive has, of course, stood me in good stead before now, notably when I arose from the poker table at 9.10 one morning – previous best 6.30 p.m. to 8.15 a.m., Ballybunion, 1938 – and slashed one right down the middle, five minutes later, in a West of Ireland championship at Rosses Point. The essence of the Blacksmith's Convulsive is to seize the club so tightly that the forearms become numb, and then let drive, disregarding pivot, weight-shift and any attempt to cock the wrists. The wrists, if cocked, snap off. The value of the Convulsive is that the stroke is always completed, one way or another, before the audience have had time to observe its finer points.

The Convulsive's companion, and, of course, direct opposite, is the *Sensitive*. A French word, pronounced *Sonsitive*. The thing about the *Sensitive* is that it relaxes me right down to the ground. The club is held so lightly in the fingers, and so marked is the absence of tension, that upon my word I'm in danger of dropping off to sleep. I discovered it one summer evening at Portmarnock, in 1936. We were fooling about on the practice ground, when I had occasion to tell one of my companions that he was trying to hit too hard. 'Just drop the clubhead on the ball', I said, 'like this.' I dropped the head of a No. 5 on to the ball and it took off like a bullet, to crash full pitch through the secretary's window – as we paced it out later – 207 yards away. I could certainly use it now, except that with the *Sensitive* the backswing gives me the impression of going on for ever. I have a tendency to lose my nerve, and to wonder if the ball will still be there when, like General MacArthur, I return. Under these circumstances I'm inclined to lash out suddenly from the level of the waist, and off she goes in that special kind of hook so quick that the ball becomes egg-shaped in its efforts to take the bend.

Round about now, on the first tee in the opening round of the Amateur Championship, I often begin to wonder which hand goes on top of the club, in the grip which I am accustomed to use. But this is only a passing phase. I have more serious things to consider. Whether, for instance, at this eleventh hour, to use the Utterly Inside Out, or the Retired Colonel's Up and Down. I once played the Utterly Inside Out by accident, into the heart of the green at Calamity Corner, Portrush. There was a gale blowing from the sea. To keep the clubhead as close to the ground as possible, and thereby out of the worst of the weather, I drew it back stealthily in a half circle round my legs. I had no expectation that anything very much was going to happen, but without warning, and for the first time in my life, I felt that if we were to be fortunate some time in the future to return to the target area I was going to have a solid left side to hit against. I could actually see my left shoulder, as large as life beneath my chin. An astounding spectacle, in view of the fact that I'd never been privileged to get more than a glimpse of the elbow before. Round we came. And off he went – actually boring in from the left, to pitch downwind, check, and finish three feet from the hole. At the next, I tried it again, with the driver. We gave up looking for it almost immediately. Another couple was pressing behind. But the caddy, in that rather charming Belfast accent, said that never before in his life had he seen a shot which had travelled 270 yards without actually crossing the front of the tee.

With only a few seconds left before my name is called I decide it will have to be the Retired Colonel's Up and Down. This is the simplest style at my command. I stand in front of the ball and hold the club just firmly enough to stop it falling out of my hand – a semi-*Sensitive* – and then I pick it up and move it back and when I think I've got it back far enough I move it forward again, and if the ball, however briefly, manages to get itself tangled in the lot I do swear I'm well pleased.

But the Retired Colonel's Up and Down got me drummed out of the preliminary trials for the Walker Cup. From the first tee at Temple I knicked one so finely with the Retired Colonel, off the toe, that it would have carried away the starter's tent and the starter, if the starter and his tent had been there. As it was, it nearly felled three members of the selection committee. Discussing the technicalities of the thing afterwards, Mr Raymond Oppenheimer told me that it had seemed to him and his fellow selectors that my best prospect of making contact with the ball, as from the top of the swing, was to strike at it vertically, downwards, keeping the head well back and out of harm's way.

But now it is my turn. The die has been cast. The name has been called. After two attempts I tee up a new ball. I initiate the backswing with a slight forward press – and suddenly every one of my six systems becomes fused! From the Hogan Crouch, with a grunt, into the Upright Classical! *Sensitive* at the top of the swing! The club is lying on my collarbone! Quick – the Blacksmith's Convulsive – take hold! We're coming down. Ease her in. More. A little more. The Utterly Inside Out. Too much! I'm going to strike my hip! Quick! The Retired Colonel! The Up and Down! Level her off! I've got it! Contact! She's away! A low snakey thing, scorching the rough all along the lefthand side of the fairway. And all of 150 yards. Well, by God, that's one I haven't seen before.

# A BLISS LIKE THINKING OF WOMEN
## JOHN UPDIKE, 1982

Golf. He has taken the game up with a passion since they joined the Flying Eagle, without getting much better at it, or at least without giving himself any happier impression of an absolute purity and power hidden within the coiling of his muscles than some lucky shots in those first casual games he played once did. It is like life itself in that its performance cannot be forced and its underlying principle shies from being permanently named. 'Arms like ropes', he tells himself sometimes, with considerable success, and then, when that goes bad, 'shift the weight'. Or 'don't chicken-wing it', or, 'keep the angle', meaning the angle between club and arms when wrists are cocked. Sometimes he thinks it's all in the hands, and then in the shoulders, and even in the knees. When it's in the knees he can't control it. Basketball was somehow more instinctive. If you thought about merely walking down the street the way you think about golf you'd wind up falling off the curb. Yet a good straight drive or a soft chip stiff to the pin gives him the bliss that used to come thinking of women, imagining if only you and she were alone on some island.

*The first real instruction book was Horace Hutchinson's* Hints on Golf *(1886), rapidly followed by Sir Walter Simpson's* The Art of Golf *(1887). Far more influential, and reprinted and revised many times, was* Golf *(1890) edited by Horace Hutchinson. That was three instruction books in a short period of time, and it was only the beginning. Since then there can have been few years which have not seen the publication of one or more manuals. Some of the early books could have caused grievous bodily harm, such as the one which commanded the player to keep his eye on the ball until the completion of the follow-through (result – broken neck?). In another, the author became confused between right and left hands in advising the correct grip. Organs both tender and vital were instantly at risk.*

*Early in my undistinguished golfing career I certainly found orthodox grip advice useful. I came to the game equipped with the Don Bradman cricket bat grip. This enabled the great man to keep the ball on the ground, not what you need in golf. However, the helpful loft of golf clubs did mean that I could get the ball in the air. Some could scarcely conceal their envy that I could hit an 8-iron with low, boring flight at 180 yard par-threes. I did not reveal that my 3-iron shots hit the ground some six inches after impact, quickly fizzing and dying among the grass roots.*

*At address and impact alike, I suppose my hands were a foot ahead of the clubhead. Instead of palm to palm along the target line, one faced the sky and the other the ground. The first glance at an instruction book put me right about this. Soon I was hitting high slices like everyone else. And that's about all I have ever learned from instruction books.*

*I believe that the really significant changes in golfing technique were brought about by a very few changes in equipment. We can only speculate on the glee which may have greeted the arrival of the feathery ball, but the gutta-percha ball was welcomed because its cheapness made golf possible for far more people. The gutta-percha ball did not seem to change the way people swung the golf club a great deal, but wooden clubheads gradually became more compact and iron increasingly replaced wood for approach shots.*

*The next revolution was in the grip. The success of Harry Vardon from 1896 focused attention on his grip – one that others had used earlier – in which he overlapped the little finger of his right hand over the fore-finger of his left. But this was not crucial to the development of the game; golfers have since played equally well with the ten-finger grip, the interlocking grip and sometimes strange variations.*

*There were two far more significant changes. Enforced by the thick padded grips which helped cushion the shock of the hard gutta-percha ball, golfers held the club in their palms rather than fingers. Most players also allowed the club to move, especially in the right hand, at the top of the backswing. This helped them to make a particularly long swing, past the horizontal. On the way back to the ball they re-gripped. Today, this sounds like lunacy – it was, yet many golfers managed the feat well although they were more liable to have bad days. The change to the finger grip, where the player never lets go of the club, has been the vital change of technique this century.*

*From 1900, the Haskell, or wound, ball began to replace gutta-percha on both sides of the Atlantic. It made the game easier for the average player because fairly poorly struck shots still travelled a reasonable distance. The best players bemoaned the passing of the old ball but the greater distance the Haskell gave meant they made the change rapidly. Clubheads and technique changed in detail to prevent the ball from flying too high. The hackers were delighted that the problems of getting a ball up in the air were eased.*

*The final revolution in equipment was the introduction of the steel shaft in the late 1920s. (Jones won the 1930 British Open with hickory; Tommy Armour used steel the following year.) The consistency of the new shaft brought in the matched set and the fact that steel twisted so little made it far easier to hit full out.*

*The use of various other materials for shafts or heads since then – fibre glass, aluminium, titanium, copper berylium, carbon fibre – has sometimes been short-lived and usually of benefit only to the few. The increasing length of the golf ball and the manicuring of golf courses were far more important factors. Neither of these, however, much affects how golfers play, but does affect how well they score.*

# WALKING BACK TO HAPPINESS
## PETER DOBEREINER, 1986

A wise old editor, a man who relished a well-balanced cadence and who was well read in the superb golfing prose of Bernard Darwin and Henry Longhurst, once dropped my copy as if it might be contagious and delivered himself of some fatherly advice: 'Son, never try to compete with the real writers. Play to your strengths, such as they are, and express yourself in cat-sat-on-the-mat English. And if by chance you should survive as a columnist be sure to vary the pace. Don't go for a Hamlet every week. Throw in a really dull one every now and then.'

So be it. What is the dullest subject available? Proposed revision to the Standard Scratch Score and decimalized handicaps are soporific, nay anaesthetic, to some of us although we are forced to recognize that some people find them absorbing. To judge by my correspondence the importance of drainage in golf course design carries a high yawn quotient although I get quite misty eyed about it.

The problem, therefore, is to find a subject which is guaranteed to be universally turgid with not a single redeeming nuance of interest. And this week, by George, I do believe that I have almost literally stumbled upon one. A friend is in the habit of responding to the salutation 'How are you?' with a full medical bulletin on his current state of health.

At our latest meeting I followed the normal routine of switching all incoming conversation to the automatic answering machine and turning the optic switch to Full Glaze and then, like Sir Alexander Fleming as he was idly chucking away some culture dishes, I had this flash of enlightenment. That's it. Let us leave that thought hanging tantalizingly in the air for a moment and take a leisurely digression.

One of the occupational hazards of being a golf writer is that the job demands the reading of golf instruction books. Many years ago I absolved readers of the *Observer* of this chore by pointing out that the best use for any instruction book, including my own, was to practise swinging a golf club while balancing the book on your head. Once you mastered this feat you would be down to scratch. Since this course of action is denied to me I have had to plough through three hundred of them, probably more, in the course of a long career. Inevitably they all say the same things in different words and with different emphases. It is a terribly difficult line of work for originality.

Many authors seek to invest their books with the illusion of novelty by isolating one all-important part of the body. Ben Hogan, for example, was a great one for the last two fingers of the left hand and his moving passage about the right pinkie snugly nestling against the left pointer is a classic of golf's romantic literature.

Alex Morrison insisted that great golf flowed from the chin. Mr X, who enjoyed a considerable vogue some years ago, put his faith in the third joint of the right big toe, or the ball of the right foot in common parlance although he called it the right toe peg. The straight left elbow was a popular part of the anatomy for years although it has rather fallen from fashion in this free and easy age of doctrinal permissiveness. The master eye had its day, complete with detailed instruction on how to identify it, and Gary Player swore by propinquitous elbows.

John Jacobs had a thing about the set of the shoulders and, if memory serves, Peggy Kirk Bell wanted us all to acquire lipstick smears on the left shoulder.

The left thumb, either elongated or contracted, either on top of the shaft or alongside it, stayed in the charts for ages. Collapsing knees, sliding hips, rolling left ankles, grooves between thumb and forefinger, tilted cranium, straight spine, lively thyroid gland and right trigger finger all had their hours of glory in the spotlight as the star performers in the enactment of a good swing. Older readers may recall our competition to put the parts of the body in order of importance although we who had to go through the replies blushingly prefer to forget it.

Alert readers will have anticipated by now that I am about to make the boring revelation that I have not been myself lately. It is true. My complaint has prevented me from playing golf or, indeed, from walking any distance and that in turn has led to an unsightly degree of obesity from lack of exercise. Now what you really want is a thorough review of my symptoms and diagnosis and details of my vital functions but lack of space forbids. We must press on to the dénouement.

Suffice to say that I went right through my library of instruction books all over again, cursing those which did not have comprehensive indices, in order to refresh my memory about those parts of the body which are vital to golf. My main concern was to reassure myself about the biological bits and pieces which did not figure in the literature of the game and which, by their omission, could be considered dispensable. The search raised no alarming problems.

So, under the biblical precept that if thine eye offend thee, pluck it out, last week I had an offensive bit surgically removed, namely the end of the middle toe of the right foot. And do you know what? All those book-writing golf teachers were absolutely right not to single it out as the source of all golfing blessings because its removal does not make a scrap of difference to the swing. Mine remains a symphony of rhythm and grace and the destiny of the ball remains entirely unpredictable.

*So much for the golf swing and balls. Let's get on to what you swing with and how to hold on to it.*

## BAFFIES, RUT-IRONS AND CLEEKS
### JAMES BALFOUR, 1887

The change in the clubs has not been so important as on the balls, but some have been discontinued that were formerly used, and others have been introduced. For example, the driving putter is never now played with. It was a club with a putter head, but with a flatter angle than a putter, a shaft about the length of a middle spoon, and, though stiff, had a spring in it. It was used to play out of bents and thick grass, but as these have now disappeared, so has the club. It was convenient, too, for playing against wind.

Another club that I fear is fast getting obsolete is the baffing spoon. As golfers know, to baff a ball is to touch the turf below the ball pretty firmly when it is struck, and the ball is thus raised into the air. The baffy is a very short spoon, about the length of a putter, but spooned twice the depth of an ordinary short spoon. It is used when near the hole, and when the ball has to be lifted over a hazard or uneven ground. There are few prettier strokes in the game. The ball is tossed high in the air, and hovers for a moment, as if to choose what blade of grass to alight on, then drops, and does not run above a foot or so. It is not only a pretty stroke, but a very effective one when well played. In the hands of Captain Dalgleish, Sir David

Baird, Shihallion, or Sir Robert Hay, the baffy was a wonderful weapon. But now men have grown so fond of cleeks and irons in all shapes and sizes that it is despised. It is said that Allan Robertson introduced the use of the cleek when near the hole. If so, it is, I think, a pity that he did. It is not so pretty a stroke; it destroys the green, as some even intentionally cut the turf with it; and it is not more sure than the stroke with the baffy.

While these two clubs have gone out of fashion, two others have been introduced. One is the iron niblick, with which to play out of bunkers, or when in a hole or cart-rut. It is a heavy iron, with a short round head, and is admirably adapted for bunkers, as it takes much less sand than the ordinary heavy iron with which that stroke used to be played.

The other new club is the wooden niblick. It is a long spoon, with a very short head, plated with brass on the bottom, from which it gets its other name of the brassy. It is used for playing a cupped or bad-lying ball, or a ball on a road. On a road the brass bottom saves the club from being destroyed by the hard surface, or turned so easily as a wooden one would be. It is extremely useful, and with its short head many men can play a cupped ball as well as a ball from the tee with a play-club. No set would be complete without having both an iron niblick and a brassy.

*The very thick grips that Bernard Darwin describes helped cushion the shock of the hard gutta-percha or composition balls. As a result, golfers held the club in the palms more than the fingers. Even so, the finger grip became normal before Mr Coburn Haskell's invention. In the 1890s, however, there were still strange ideas about the golf grip.*

# A MARSHLAND OF PITCH
## BERNARD DARWIN, 1955

The grossest defect of all the clubs of those days, as seen by modern eyes, was undoubtedly in the grips. They were, as we should now think, far too thick and padded, making it harder to feel the head. That was due to the almost universal 'palm grip' with which golfers held the club, but apart from that a brand new grip of shiny yellow leather was an odious thing with an eel-like propensity for slipping out of the hand. Its only virtue was that it gave an excuse for a visit to the professional's shop to beg for a bit of pitch. Even a leather which had been broken in by use could get horribly slippery in cold weather. For many years one pocket of my golfing coat was always a marshland of pitch in which such objects as stumps of pencils were firmly embedded like flies in amber. There seems to me nothing in which the modern club has more greatly improved than this matter of the grip. When today I waggle my friends' clubs the grips feel so 'tacky', so comfortably clinging without being sticky, that I feel capable of wonderful deeds – a pleasing illusion which I carefully do nothing to dispel.

I have nothing original or entertaining to say about the balls we played with and I am mortally afraid of involving myself in an argument, even an argument with nobody, as to whether golf was a better game with a gutty ball. I am pretty sure that it was, but it is of no use to say so, as indeed it has often been said, at this time of day. Silvertown or Eclipse – that was the question in my early days and it was sometimes a difficult one as between foursome partners. I know that some of the great men, Horace Hutchinson for instance, thought the Eclipse very good in a wind and that it held its line better on the green, but to me it appeared an ugly yellow ball, that made an ugly dead sound and would not rise into the air when I hit it. I myself could not rise to a new shilling Silvertown, except on some specially opulent occasion, but a ninepenny remade was generally speaking a very good ball. What one is apt to forget about the gutty, save by projecting oneself back into the past by resolute effort, is the really appalling gash that could be made in it by a single maladroit stroke. As to a niblick shot – well, only a fool or a millionaire would take a new ball at such a hole as Cader at Aberdovey, where a topped drive meant unlimited liability in the bunker below the black-crested sandhill.

## A NATURAL TURN
### HORACE HUTCHINSON, 1890

When the club, in the course of its swing away from the ball, is beginning to rise from the ground, and is reaching the horizontal with its head pointing to the player's right, it should be allowed to turn naturally in the right hand until it is resting upon the web between forefinger and thumb.

## LET IT SLIDE
### HORACE HUTCHINSON, 1899

It is here that the great secret of a true golfing swing comes in – the 'sliding of the club in the right hand'. To any one starting in youth it comes as a second nature, but the natural inclination of the would-be golfer commencing late in life is to grip with the right hand as if his life depended upon it. Look closely at instantaneous photographs of first-class players taken when at the top of the swing, observe closely the position of the club in the right hand; it will be seen that it reposes delicately between the thumb and the first two fingers. It would almost appear that the player had lost command of the club with this particular hand, but it is not so; the muscles are simply relaxed in order to enable the club to be swung well round the neck, he has still full possession of the club, and the power behind the remainder of the hand can be applied at any moment on the downward swing. It is this sliding of the club in the right hand which is the main difficulty with all beginners; they naturally assume that to strike hard it is necessary to grip tightly. This in a sense may be true, but they cannot understand that the pressure is not applied until the club is well on its downward journey, and a tight grip with the right hand not only restricts the freedom of action on the upward swing, but also on the downward swing. Keep the club loose in the right hand, and try to play with loose joints, particularly in the knees and wrists.

## UNORTHODOX BRAID
### HORACE HUTCHINSON, 1899

Braid's is not altogether an attractive style to watch. Sound it certainly must be, or it could not execute its results; but one would not call it orthodox. A point to be noticed . . . is the comparative shortness of the swing, computed by the position of the club when at its highest. It is apparent that it does not nearly reach the horizontal behind the back – scarcely is it allowed to make more than an angle of 45 degrees behind the back. We reckon this as not enough for orthodoxy; perhaps we may regard the horizontal as about the proper standard of the classic style; it is to the horizontal that Mr Edward Blackwell – Mr Everard's *beau idéal* – approximates. Again there is a difference – and I think we see in this the reason that Braid's club does not go further back – in the grip of the right hand with Mr Blackwell and with Braid respectively. In Braid's case the club has evidently been held firmly in the right hand throughout the upward swing, and will, we may assume, be so held, no less firmly, throughout the downward swing. The club handle has not been allowed to shift at all in the grip of the fingers.

Now if you drop the book, and take up a club for a moment, you will find, I think, that, holding the club thus firmly, rigidly, and without movement, and especially if you keep the right elbow down, as Braid keeps it, it becomes very difficult to swing the club any further round behind the head than he gets it. Whereas in Mr Blackwell's case not only has the right elbow come very high up, but the grip of the right hand has evidently been relaxed to let the club, while still controlled by the fingers, go back against the web between the forefinger and the thumb. It is this permission given the club to turn thus freely in the right hand (which is not to be taken as meaning that the right hand does not still maintain a perfect control of it and keep in perfect touch with it) that gives, if we may venture on such a positive assertion, the greater freedom to the stroke of Mr Blackwell. Braid looks a trifle tied; as if certain bits of his anatomy were saying to him, 'you cannot get back any further'. Braid's fully sufficient answer is: 'I do not want to'.

*These pieces of writing have described something far more important than the Vardon grip; that is, whether one should or shouldn't hold firmly on to the club throughout the swing. Basically the Vardon grip means overlapping the little finger of the right hand*

*with the forefinger of the left which helps to make the hands work together. This grip was not invented by Harry Vardon and was nowhere near as important as the idea of maintaining the same grip throughout the swing. The Vardon grip was very popular from the turn of the century because Harry Vardon was by then recognized as the greatest player around. If James Braid was the first man to hold on all through the swing, fewer players noticed what was happening at the top of it. Always, however, the great players have been the most influential.*

*The heart of golf is the club game but it is the stars of the sport who show the average player what is possible; the experts raise standards by their example. Allan Robertson, who died in 1859, was the first golfing star. The lesson his play taught was that steady golf was better than brilliance combined with waywardness. The next evolutionary player was Young Tommy Morris, who showed that a very forceful swing could also bring accurate results. About 20 years after Morris's early death, Taylor and Ball showed that going for the flag, not merely the green, was what mattered. Harry Vardon showed that elegance of swing could combine with power and also that the so-called flat swing was not the only way to play golf. Since the turn of the century, I would argue that there have been very few changes as influential as these.*

*Writing only a dozen years after the death of Tommy Morris, James Balfour looks at lower scoring over his beloved Old Course at St Andrews. I imagine he would have thought much the same about Bobby Jones's low scoring in the 1927 Open or Curtis Strange's 62 in 1987.*

# It's Much Easier Now
## JAMES BALFOUR, 1887

From what has been said as to the changes in the links, the balls, and the clubs, it is obvious that the round ought to be done in much fewer strokes now than formerly. How many fewer it is not easy accurately to determine. Some say 20. I incline to think 15 or 16, but I believe that every year it will be done in fewer for some little time, as the course gets broader and the hazards fewer. The best gauge, perhaps, is the score at which the medal has been gained from time to time. ... Before the introduction of gutta-percha, and the change of making two putting-greens at each hole, the lowest figure at which the medal was gained was in 1834, when it was taken at 97 by Mr Robert Oliphant, while in 1839 Mr Andrew Stirling and Mr John H. Wood of Leith tied for it at 99; but these were exceptionally low; at that time it was reckoned to be very good if the medal was won at 103 or 104.

The fall has since been gradual, thus proving that it is not so much, at least, the superiority of the players now, but the comparative ease of the game. Young players are apt to think that the play is superior to what it used to be, but old men doubt this. They admit that the first-class players are more numerous than they formerly were, but they think that is because the game is played by a greater number. They maintain that there were formerly a few as good players as any of the present generation. The proportion is probably nearly the same.

After the introduction of gutta-percha balls, but before the change of the greens, the numbers fell to 98, 97, 96, at which last figure the silver cross was gained in the spring of 1850 by Mr George Condie, and in 1852 Captain Maitland Dougall, and in 1853 Mr Jelf Sharpe, each gained the same prize at the same figure – 96. But the autumn medal had never been gained under 97. I have a vivid recollection of the autumn of the year 1850, when King William the Fourth's medal was played for. The club was then just a hundred years old. The late Earl of Eglinton was captain. These was a large turn-out both of players and spectators; most, if not all, of the best players of the day were present. The weather was lovely. One of the most successful medal players of his time, now Admiral Maitland Dougall, who had gained the silver cross at 96 the year before, came in early in the day at 95, and was congratulated by every one on being sure to be the winner, and at a stroke lower than any medal had ever been gained during a hundred years before. But a little later in the day I was fortunate enough to come in at 93, and still later, to my mortification, Captain Stewart came in in 90, he thus winning the first medal, and I the second.

# From Robertson to Vardon
## Horace Hutchinson, 1899

To watch Mr Tait play, nothing appears easier than golf. There is nothing of the dash of the St Andrews school about his play, he always appears to be playing well within himself; and so I believe he is. But my impression has always been that it was not from choice, but from necessity, as he has an unruly member to look after, that dreaded right hand, and on the slightest sign of extra pressure that member is apt to assume an influence on the flight of the ball to which it has no legal claim. Occasionally it is brought into requisition, sometimes with beneficial results and sometimes to the contrary. It is an easy swing, a graceful swing, but hardly what can be called an orthodox swing, a swing apparently founded on the use and abuse of the right hand, and founded, it must be said, with extraordinarily beneficial results. A beautifully true swing is that of the amateur champion of 1895, Mr Leslie Balfour-Melville. Nothing could be cleaner and neater than the actual swing of the club itself, but owing to a certain rigidity of the muscles right through the stroke, he is apt to appear laboured, but Mr Balfour-Melville is of a sturdy build, and his golf is sturdy, and one cannot expect the freedom of a Hugh Kirkaldy from a player of his powerful physique.

Among the professionals Fernie has always appeared to me as the neatest of players. His wrist action is beautiful to watch; as quick as lightning goes the club round the neck, a quick turn of the wrist just before the club reaches its destination, and away travels the ball. It is, nevertheless, far from the orthodox, the swing of the body being sacrificed to the wrists, and in this respect bears a strong contrast to the swing of Alec Herd, which is a beautiful example of freedom of shoulder; it is Hugh Kirkaldy over again, with a tighter grip and more command of the club. Harry Vardon, like Herd, is endowed with great freedom, but, as the gentleman who is generally recognized as the best judge of the game in St Andrews remarked on first seeing Harry and Tom Vardon play in 1895, 'These Vardons are not pretty players'. And I think his judgment was not far from correct. The upward swing of the club is against all the recognized canons of tradition. The club is taken up perpendicularly, there is none of that fine circular sweep of Mr Ball or Herd. It is a style of their own, it is certainly not orthodox; but in the case of the elder brother it is almost more than effective, a fact which places it outside the pale of criticism. And so we can wander through the whole list of first-class players.

There is a refreshing crispness about the style of Andrew Kirkaldy, a calculating manner and deliberation about the play of Park which instils one with confidence, but in no single instance do they supply the ideal of the orthodox in every particular. They have their peculiarities, maybe prompted by nature, maybe prompted by that natural power of imitation which is always so noticeable in golf.

Over the Border you find your younger generation of Laidlays playing off the left leg; unfortunately, nature did not build them in the same mould as the famous ex-amateur champion, and their power of imitation has been their undoing. Similarly, at Hoylake you will find the younger generation playing off the right leg, standing what is termed open to the ball. As yet this method has not proved quite as efficacious as in the case of Mr Ball. As Mr Hutchinson once remarked, 'genius cannot be trifled with'; it can much less be imitated.

Has golf improved? The older class of golfers, who remember Allan Robertson and Young Tom Morris in his brilliant meteoric career across the golfing horizons, say nay; the younger school of golfers, whose golfing education only commenced after the passing away of these two old-time celebrities, say yea; to which the old school reply, 'How can you form an opinion? You never saw either Young Tom or Allan play.' This is only too true, and this is where lies the weakness in the armour of the arguments of the younger school; but against this they can bring forth a number of hard, stern facts which are difficult to dispute. Scores are recorded now which were never ever dreamt of five-and-twenty years ago; courses are undoubtedly kept in much finer condition nowadays, the horse mower was an unknown luxury to the ancients. Again, clubs have improved, and players have the advantage of many years of experience in connection with the manufacture of balls. But do these advantages compensate for the enormous disparity in the scores of 25 or 30 years ago and those of the present day? That is the real basis of the argument, and I am afraid that it can never be settled to the satisfaction of both sides.

My experience of the royal and ancient game unfortunately does not go far enough back to remember the days of Young Tom, as when first I began to take an interest in the game his fame was but a memory in the minds of men – a memory, however, which will never be forgotten, and golfers may come and golfers may go, but it is very much open to doubt whether any golfer will be quite the idol of the day as Young Tom was during his brilliant career, and certainly no golfer since, probably not even Harry Vardon, has shown quite the decided superiority over all rivals that he was called upon to meet as did the pride of St Andrews. It was not merely a question of one season's brilliant play, as from the very commencement of his golfing career almost to the time of his sad demise he may be said to have brooked no rivals. Naturally the question arises, whom had he to compete against? Certainly not the strength of field a professional of the present day has to meet. There were good players in those days, but they were few; probably the players who had any chance of success against him could be counted on the fingers of one hand, and that is where the difficulty of comparing his form with the Vardons, Herds, and Taylors of the present day really lies. The scores of the latter are undoubtedly far ahead of anything Young Tom accomplished, but they have had the advantage of finding greater obstacles to overcome, and that it is an advantage the past ten years' golf has plainly proved. Experience may account for a great deal of the improved form among young players, but among experienced players, those who may be said to have served their apprenticeship and been through the fire, we must look for some other cause to account for the decided improvement in the general run of the play, an improvement which has certainly taken place during the past ten years or so, and I have no hesitation in saying that it is chiefly due to increased competition, association with players of an equal or higher standard of excellence, and that consequent spirit of emulation which tends to unearth any latent talent which may be lying dormant. And it is in this respect that I think that Young Tom was placed at a disadvantage with his *confrères* of the present day. He had a certain number of opponents to meet, whom he invariably vanquished, and it is said that the greater the apparent task the more brilliant was his play; and, though I am of a contrary opinion to those who assert that his performances were equally brilliant with those of the leading players of the present day, still it is not improbable that had Young Tom been in his prime at the present moment he might have even out-Vardon'd Vardon.

# GALLOPING ALL THE WAY
## HORACE HUTCHINSON, 1899

Although the old school are fain to admit that the first-class players of the present day obtain a greater length than they did in the days of Young Tom and Allan Robertson – recent results conclusively prove that they must do –

it may be that the St Andrews celebrities in question had quite the power at their command that the leading players of the present day have, but they were apparently afraid to use it. And we have only to turn to that interesting volume by the Rev. J. G. McPherson, called *Golf and Golfers,* in which he explains the manner in which Allan Robertson played the sixth or Heathery hole at St Andrews – short of the bunkers from the tee, over the bunkers with his second and a spoon shot up to the hole side, holing in five.

Yes, Allan Robertson probably obtained as beneficial a result by his pawky play as the average of first-class players of the present day, who probably as often take five or six as four to this particular hole. But suppose during the course of these three spoon shots something came amiss – a bad lie might be sufficient – how would Allan have fared? Badly I think. Or even how would a player who followed this mode of procedure fare against, say, Andrew Kirkaldy, who habitually reaches this green with ease in two? Again badly, I think. It would be tempting providence by placing too great a premium on accuracy and superiority in the short game. No, the race goes to the swift in the days of the present, risks are taken which were never thought of in the old days. It may not be due to any superiority of talent that these risks are successfully overcome, but the ever increasing number of first-class players has had a beneficial effect in sifting the wheat from the chaff. These risks have to be taken, and unless a player can successfully overcome them he will find himself left behind in the fight for fame. Even during the past five years those who have followed the game closely have noticed an improvement in first-class play, and I have always thought that the advent of J. H. Taylor in the world of first-class golf was in a sense responsible for this improvement. His play during the championship week at Prestwick in 1893, unsuccessful as he eventually proved to be, came as a revelation to many of the older school of golfers; he played full shots up to the hole side with an amount of accuracy and apparent sang-froid which came as a revelation to them. 'Take your cleek for safety', was the old motto. Taylor ignored this safety play with wonderful results, and unearthed new possibilities in the game, which other players have unconsciously copied and have conquered, with the result that other 'Richmonds' are in the field to challenge the supremacy of 1895 and 1896. That Taylor's play has deteriorated, as many assert, I cannot believe for one moment. He can still hold his own, as he has proved on many occasions during the season 1898. But a player like Harry Vardon has, while equalling the accuracy of the Wimbledon professional, been able to produce a slight degree of extra power which has turned the scale in his favour. And watching closely the play of the first-class professional one is forced to the conclusion that it is the accuracy and power in the long game which tells in the end. Not only has a player to drive a long ball, but he has to drive consistently far, for, as one well-known professional remarked at the conclusion of the meeting at Prestwick this year, 'It is galloping all the way'. Steady, accurate golf is of no avail, it must be both brilliant and accurate; and the present generation of players, recognizing this fact, have in consequence accomplished performances which five years ago would have been considered bordering on the impossible.

# THE WEDGE
## BERNARD DARWIN, 1955

As I am writing in a sense my testament of golf I suppose I ought to make some comparison between the leading players of different generations. I shall do so in the most guarded possible manner, if only because I have never been able to make up my own mind on the subject. I remember to have asked Mr Leslie Balfour-Melville, who had played with Young Tommy Morris, whether he thought Vardon was better than Tommy had been. He did not snub me as he might, for it was a foolish question, but replied after some reflection, 'I cannot imagine anyong playing better than Tommy did'. It was a good and wise answer and I believe the right one as to any two great players of any game whom the years have kept asunder. Generally speaking, no champion can be more than the best of his time, with this proviso that now and again there arises a genius who definitely raises the whole standard of the game and compels others to follow him in gasping pursuit.

Young Tommy Morris was clearly one of these. All who saw him agreed that he was an altogether outstanding figure. There were others who might cope with him in the ordinary run of games, but when the real pinch came they could not hold him. Scores make most dangerous standards: they can be made to prove almost anything. But I cannot resist citing Tommy's great score of 149 at Prestwick in winning the championship belt for the third time running. It was, according to the calculations of contemporaries, but two over the par score for three rounds of the 12 holes. When one considers the clubs and balls with which he had to play and the relatively rough and unkempt course on which he did it, that score stands out beyond argument or criticism. He had only 16 competitors on that day, but if he had had 160 it would not in the circumstances have mattered a single jot. I am going bang against the principle that I just now laid down, but I am convinced that he was much better than those who had gone before and those who came after until nearly the time of the triumvirate.

With them came another upward surge. I believe a great amateur began it rather than any professional – John Ball, who hit full shots straight up to the pin in a way that came as a revelation. Then followed Taylor to be even more accurate, and finally Vardon, with something more of power added, a genius if ever there was one. For a little while there were two classes of people who hit a golf ball, in the one Vardon, and in the other all the other golfers. Nature enforced her invariable law; the others had to hunt Vardon and they drew closer to him, closer than ever they could have believed possible if he had not stretched them on the rack and dragged the golf out of them. Then he fell ill and was never quite the same again, so that he was caught and for a while even surpassed, but meanwhile golf had moved upward by a whole grade.

What exactly has happened since? Did Bobby Jones send the standard leaping up again and has Hogan improved on Bobby? Frankly I do not know. I could say in pious imitation of Mr Balfour-Melville, that I cannot imagine anybody hitting the ball better than Harry Vardon. J. H. Taylor, who knew his greatness if any man did, does say so. I feel – perhaps it is cowardly – that I must add the three conditional words 'up to the green'. The fact that the scores of Vardon and his rivals have been surpassed does not unduly upset me. When it comes to scores I always quote the fact that Sandy Herd, when he was a few days short of 70, holed four rounds of a good and full-sized course in an average of fours and that with a card and pencil and no charitable 'approximation'; such a score as he never did in his prime. I cannot explain it with complete satisfaction, but there is the fact that makes nonsense of arguments about scores. Today amateur golfers, good but yet not so good as to have played in international matches, have done scores that Vardon never came near to achieving. It would be merely childish to say they were as good or anything like as good as he was.

Yet what I am prepared to say is that the putting of the best golfers has definitely improved. The Americans began it and our players have tried very hard to imitate them. They have not yet quite caught them but they putt better than their predecessors. They take fewer putts in the course of a round and so down go the scores. I think, too, that on the whole they chip better from near the green and so give themselves the chance of holing more putts. The thing that I really feel sure about as an improver of scores is the wedge. I am now so long incapacitated that I have never owned a wedge: I do not really understand the art of it, but I see what it can do in a bunker and that is enough. There it has in skilful hands produced a new stroke, and it merely laughs at the sand. John Ball said that he liked to see his enemy in a bunker where he had to scratch his head to find any way out of it. Today he would see that enemy, equipped cap-a-pie with an armoury of wedges, play an easy smooth sliding shot, as it were right through the ball, and lay it as likely as not stone dead. The head-scratching comes no doubt in learning that stroke, which I would never deny is a lovely and skilful one, but once learnt it seems to perform these miracles with perfect regularity. It is this infernal machine, and I wish it had never been invented, that has in my belief made more difference than anything else, clubs, balls, green-keeping and all, and I was glad to read the other day that Tommy Armour, a great golfer who knows American golf inside out, says so, too. What a heavenly feeling it must be not to mind in the least getting into a bunker! I wish I had ever enjoyed it.

# TRIAL AND ERROR
## AL BARKOW, 1986

Then in the early 1930s, when they switched from hickory to steel shafts, I [Byron Nelson] had to start restructuring my game. I was still pronating [letting his wrist break before hitting the ball] the way you had to do with hickory because of the torque in the shaft, which would open the clubface. But steel didn't have that same torque, and I would hook the ball around a house. I had to stop the hook, so, just by trial and error – I'm going over a period of time now – I found that the more I moved laterally through the ball and kept the club and hands going in front of the ball, the straighter it would go. I could stop the pronation and carry my hands high if I stayed down and through the ball a long time and did not raise up.

See, in that day and time you pronated the hands and hit against a stiff left side. The way I taught myself to not do that, I would only practise against the wind so I could know I was moving on a lower plane through the ball. Going downwind or crosswind, the ball blew around too much. So I kept working on that, but I got too much lateral motion down below, and I was moving some up above, and I got to be the worst shanker that I guess ever lived. Because, moving the lower body laterally, and the head, too, I'd get the heel of the club into the ball first. I got so bad I would shank for weeks. And I'm not a kid now, I'm a young man. Eventually I determined, by trial and error, that if I would hit out from underneath myself, if I'd keep my head back, I wouldn't shank. The more I did that, the better I got … I had some conferences with George Jacobus … and we talked about the game and teaching. I told him I'd developed this new style of playing, and I went through the whole thing – the lateral shift and more use of feet and legs, no pronation, hands high on the backswing, staying down through the ball, low trajectory. George was from the old school, but he was a smart man and knew golf real well; he was a real long hitter and had been a pretty fair player. I asked him what he thought about all that and he said it was exactly right, that we were going to have to develop a different style of play because of the steel shaft.

There wasn't any one of my contemporaries on the tour who influenced my game, because no one was doing what I was. I've been given credit for starting this type or style of playing, but they do it better now than I did. They still use their feet and legs, but I probably overused mine some. And everybody always said I dipped into the ball. I remember Gene Sarazen said, when I first came out, that I wouldn't become a great player because I dipped. Of course, Gene hit against a straight left side, and everyone was used to seeing golfers straighten up at impact, so by comparison it looked like I dipped. Actually, I was just staying down with my body. There was a sequence of pictures of my swing in *Sports Illustrated* – the old one, not the one that is published now – and it proves I didn't dip. You can see how the head is still held back, and how the club extends. I really just stayed down and through. Even today I don't think you can improve on the position. How's a ball going to go anything but straight from there?

*Walter Hagen's supremacy in the short game was particularly noticeable because he was not a long hitter and hit more wild shots than anyone before his time or since (Ballesteros included). Even so, we can see from the piece which follows that his aim was par.*

## THE SLUGGERS ARRIVE
### WALTER HAGEN, 1957

In those early days when Harry Vardon was our pattern, we strove primarily for accuracy. We were content to get a hole in par, because par was usually good enough to win. Yet as the quality of opponents shifted, into the game of golf, just as into baseball, came the era of sluggers ... and the sensation boys. It's a sure bet that if enough of the sluggers are out there trying to make the longest drives and hitting every second shot directly for the flag, two or three or even four are bound to make it pay off and come up with amazingly low scores.

Shortly the entire field of golfers realized that winning a championship meant taking risks or letting the golfers who take the gamble walk off with the titles and the cash. They don't always win but they force the type of play, until everybody is taking desperate chances in order to pull off a miracle. In my early competitive career, a man took chances of that sort only when he was behind and the holes disappearing fast.

*The development of the steel shaft saw the end of 'early golf'. Since the introduction of steel about 60 years ago, there have been many changes in the game. Balls go further, clubs are slightly better, greens, on average, are faster, courses far better maintained. Yet whereas the Vardons, Taylors and Braids do not appear to have changed their technique to play the rubber core instead of the gutty, Byron Nelson felt he had to change his game for steel. The established players – Sarazen, for example – just found the new clubs easier to use.*

*But let's not take this look at the development of golf too seriously. I hope I haven't because, at least, I've missed out all mention of the Romans, pell-mell, chole and the golf-like activities of the Netherlands. I like this piece by Dan Jenkins because he pokes fun at a dozen or so writers and you don't need to know them to smile.*

## THE GAME OF GOLFE
### DAN JENKINS, 1970

It was a grey, drizzly day like most others in Scotland and there was I, a lonely shepherd, strolling along a swollen dune by the North Sea looking for a wee stane to hit wi' a bit crook. Clumps of heather were up to my knees and the yellow-tipped whin was up to my chest, and I was up to here with my sheep because the little dumplings had wandered away. I had this crooked stick in my hand which I normally used to keep the dumplings in line. You know. Firm left side, eye on the tailbone, slow backswing – and whap. But they were gone and I was just ambling along when I saw this chuckie stane, as it was called, this round pebble. I also saw this rabbit scrape, as it was called, through an opening in the heather and whin. So I said to myself, 'Self, why don't you take your bit crook and try to knock this here stane into that there scrape? And stay out of the heather because, boy, it'll make your hand ring.' Well, I guess I took it back a little outside because I cut a low one right into the garbage and almost never did find it, but anyhow, this is how I came to invent the game of golf a few hundred years ago.

There are those, of course, who claim that I did not invent golf in another life, nor did any other Scot. Some say the Romans did it long before me and called it *Paganica,* which I think, between you and me, sounds like a joint over an East 56th with a big tab. Some say the Dutch invented golf, or a game called *kolven,* which was similar. But no way. *Kolven* has to be a roll of veal stuffed with cheese and chives. Some say that even the French originated golf under the name of *jeu de mail,* but as any European traveller knows, this is a card game for the big players in Monaco. Actually, if the historians want to be picky, you could say that the Chinese a thousand years ago probably played a form of golf by batting a few snow peas around with chopsticks.

The fact of the matter is, golf is a Scottish game. It is naturally Scottish, as natural to our instincts as the seaside linksland is natural to the setting. It was the Scots, after all, who took the game and did something with it when everybody else was busy making crossbows. We made the courses and the clubs, the balls and the rules, the trophies and the tournaments. We invented wind and rough, hooks and slices, bunkers and doglegs, and we were just getting ready to invent the overlapping grip when Harry Vardon, an Englishman, beat us to it.

We looked at the seashores, our linksland, and said this is where the glory's at. Let the wet wind blow in from Denmark, or wherever it comes from. Let the incursions of the sea make the giant dunes and the tumbling valleys. Let the birds bring in the mixture of seeds that will grow our curious rough – the wiry, purple heather, the bulging whin, the dead fern we'll call bracken, and the green broom that does not have thorns to distinguish itself from whin, or gorse. Let the rabbits and the foxes chew out the first fairways and dig the first cups, perhaps at St Andrews where the Old Course lies today.

I don't know what the Romans, the Dutch and the French were doing around the 1450s – aside from waiting for the Bible to get printed – but us Scots were playing golfe then, and had been. At least we were when the kings would permit it, there being, from time to time, this nagging problem of national service. Had to go fight the English. Cancel my starting time.

There was this afternoon, I recall, when the game came close to being banished forever. As it happened, I was out on this moor at St Andrews trying out a new Auchterlonie driving spoon at the eleventh – the short hole, of course – when a King's guard raised up out of the whin and handed me a scroll signed by our monarch.

The scroll said, 'It is decreeted and ordained that the Fute-ball and Golfe be utterly cryed downe, and not to be used.'

'Guy never could spell', I said.

The guard pointed his crossbow at me and said that the King, Jimmy the Roman Numeral, meant business.

'The Golfe is sik unprofitabill sportis', he said.

'Pal, you got that right', I said. 'See that shepherd over there with the cross-handed grip on his bit crook? Well, he's got me out, out, out and one down.'

'Don't be abused', the guard said. 'It is statute and ordained that in na place of the realme be there Golfe in tyme cuming.'

'Look', I said. 'Smell that air. Gaze over this land. Great, huh? Who would want a guy to be hanging around a draughty castle waiting for an Englishman to scale the wall?'

'Aye', he said. 'The aire is guid and the field reasonable feir. But can ya na handle the bow for archerie? Can ya na run or swoom or warstle instead?'

'I don't know, man', I said. 'Let me put it your way. Here's the deal. I was drivin' the chuckie stanes wi' a bit stick as sune's I could walk.'

He nodded his head as if he was beginning to understand.

'Here's something else', I said. 'I happen to know that a bow-maker in Perth is fixing up a set of clubs for the King right now. Why? Because the King sneaked out the other day to see what this game was all about and the Earl of Bothwell, who plays to a cool 23, brought him to his knees on the back three at Leith. The King's getting a pretty good price, too. Like only 14 s's for the set, whatever an s is.'

The guard put down his crossbow and said, well, go ahead and play if that was the case. And by the way, he added, did I want to buy 'a dussen guid Golfe ballis?'.

'Hold it', I said. 'You got featheries?'

'Aye', he said. 'Guid featheries that cum from the Laird of Rosyth. Guid featheries stuffed with flock and wuid shavings.'

'Four s's', I said. 'And not an s more.'

'Eight s's', he said.

'They're hot, man. Six s's and we both get out clean', I said.

He went for the six – you can always strike a bargain in Europe – and disappeared back into the whin. And now that I had saved golf, I couldn't wait to try out one of the new high-compression featheries. I heeled up a good lie, and gave the shot a full body turn. Wow. Up, up, it soared – five yards, ten yard, 20 yards, and back to Earth, whatever that was, only a short rake-in from the eleventh scrape, a par-12. There is still a hole in the wind where I hit that shot, and I thought to myself, what a happy and golden time, indeed.

In a few more years, all of royalty would be playing golfe. There were rumours of Mary Queen of Scots shanking all around the fields of Seton when some said she should have been mourning the demise of Lord Darnley. Charles I got a very bad press for being in a match at Leith when the Irish Rebellion broke out. A lot of Jameses and Dukes of York were seen swinging at Musselburgh, which still claims to be the oldest layout in the world and now sits inside a race course near Edinburgh.

*Several books have been written devoted solely to putting and if we think of a few great putters it becomes obvious that their methods vary. Walter Hagen, Bobby Jones, Ben Hogan, Billy Casper, Arnold Palmer, Bobby Locke, Jack Nicklaus, Bob Charles, Gary Player, Ben Crenshaw, Tom Watson, Isao Aoki, Seve Ballesteros, Nick Faldo, Bernhard Langer ... How many different ways these had, or have, of getting the ball into the hole. One is wristy, another would push the ball at the hole with the right arm, yet another would swing both arms from the shoulders, and the great German eccentric changes his hand position from putt to putt.*

*Perhaps all they really have in common is that, when putting well, each has the clubhead square and swinging on line at impact, though I wouldn't swear even to that. One liked to have the feel of hooking the ball into the hole; others have thought they were cutting it in.*

*Overall, the change in technique from the 1920s has been to take the wrists out of the stroke and substitute an arm movement. Feeling for distance seems now to come from the upper arms rather than the fingers. But so much for technique. Isn't it a matter of the mind believing that the job is simple?*

## THE HOLE IS PRETTY BIG
### SIR WALTER SIMPSON, 1887

Although every golfer theoretically accepts it as politic to play for the back of the hole, few putt as if they thought it was. The majority treat the hole as a place more difficult to get into than it really is. They seem practically to believe that a putt one ounce too strong, or one hair's-breadth off the line, must be out. Consequently many short putts are played so timidly that they are six inches off the line, or within six inches of the goal. Now the fact is, that (from short distances) the hole is pretty big, and from all distances it is capable of catching a ball going at a fair pace. I admit that more putts of over two yards must be missed than are held, because a putting-green is not a billiard-table; but many more would go in than do if players credited holes with a little of that catching power which they really possess.

# THE MAIN IDEA
## ROBERT TYRE JONES, 1927

But as I see it, the thing that hurt my putting most when it was bad – and it was very bad at times – was thinking too much about how I was making the stroke, and not enough about getting the ball in the hole. I have always been a fair approach putter, and I am not so bad at holing out now, though not in the class of a number I could name. But I have concluded that, having acquired a fairly smooth and accurate stroke, the thing for me to do is to forget it as far as possible and concentrate on getting the ball in the cup. Which seems to have been the original object, in golf.

# IT'S NOT INTERESTING
## AL BARKOW, 1986

No one expresses much interest in the business of putting. Just about everyone complained that he would have been better, or better still, if he could have putted decently. Yet no one expounded a theory of putting, elaborate or otherwise. This is not unusual among golfers, past or present, even though putting represents almost half the strokes taken in a round by a good player, and even though everyone admits that you can't be a winner in golf without good putting. Some people explain this peculiar lack of interest by saying that putting is simply unfathomable; that there is no solution to it; that there can be no universal way to do it when you consider how totally different are the putting styles of such masters of the art as Jack Nicklaus and Bobby Locke.

There may be something to all that, but my feeling is that putting is just not as interesting as hitting full golf shots. Putting is not as complex an action, for one thing, but mainly there is the factor that the best-stroked putt in a lifetime does not bring the aesthetic satisfaction of a perfectly hit wood or iron shot. There is nothing to match the whoosh and soar, the almost magical flight of a beautifully hit drive or 5-iron. To go through all those movements of the body and get that result even once in a while is more thrilling than a hundred ten-foot putts that drop to the bottom of the cup.

# PLAYERS

*This chapter encompasses many of the great players from Young Tom Morris through to the great players of the 1970s and 1980s. Young Tom was not the first man to build a great reputation. Allan Robertson, Willie Park Senior and his father did this earlier. As time passed no one really believed that they were the equal of such men as Vardon, Taylor and Braid. Young Tom was the first man to dominate his contemporaries as surely as Hagen, Jones, Hogan and Nicklaus did in later generations. However, I make no real attempt at comparisons across the divide of the years.*

## YOUNG TOMMY'S LAST MATCH
### HORACE HUTCHINSON, 1919

Altogether they played for six whole days, two rounds a day, and all through the piece Young Tommy had the better of it. I cannot believe that in this match Arthur Molesworth did himself full justice. It is true that during the latter days snow lay on the ground, so that the greens had to be swept and the game really was not golf at all, but then it is no less true that Tommy held the advantage just as consistently in the days when real golf was to be played as on those when the snow spoilt it ... Young Tommy showed his skill wonderfully in lofting off the snowy ground to the small circles that had been swept round the holes. 'Molesworth could loft there just as well', he said, 'but Tommy, using his niblick, made the ball stay there as if it had a string tied to it, whereas Molesworth's ball was always running off on to the snow on the other side'.

\* \* \*

There was a peculiar pathos attaching to that match and Young Tommy's triumph, for it was his last. His wife had lately died, and interest in life, even in golf, had gone out for him. It was in November that he was thus beating Arthur Molesworth, and on Christmas Day of the same year he followed his young and loved wife. His memorial, recording a few of his greater victories – he was four times in succession open champion – is in the St Andrews' graveyard. Indisputable was his genius for the game; impossible to calculate is the comparison between his skill and power and that of Harry Vardon, let us say, today. Doubtless he was a far better putter, for while he was so good at all points of the game he was at his strongest of all on the green.

*Old Tom Morris was not the equal of his son as a golfer but he won the Open Championship four times. Later, he became accepted as the grand old man of golf and was active as a club and ball maker. He was greenkeeper at St Andrews for almost 40 years and designed the original layouts of many of the finest links courses in the British Isles. He was born in 1821 and died in 1908.*

# THE GRAND OLD MAN
## HORACE HUTCHINSON, 1919

There was Old Tom Morris – 'born in the purple of equable temper and courtesy', as Lord Moncrieffe, I think it is, well describes him. It would be a mistake to picture Old Tom as a witty man, or even as a clever man, unless a tact and temper that never fail be the very best kind of cleverness. But we do not find any very witty or pungent sayings attributed to Old Tom. It was his rich nature, with its perfect kindliness and charity, that made him so lovable, and such a valuable possession to St Andrews in reconciling the golfing interests, which ran with counter currents, of the town and of the club. As a peacemaker he had no equal. I, deeming myself wronged by some infringement of golfing rule or etiquette on part of another, might go to Tom – would go to him as a matter of natural course – and pour out my woes. He would listen with a charming smile in his old eyes under their bushily arching grey eye-brows, and when I had done he would take his pipe out of his mouth and say, 'Ou aye'. That was all, but it was enough to convince of his perfect sympathy. Then, from the big window of the club, or from Logan White's house on the links, I would see that wicked man, my late opponent, go up to the old man – for the scene was always that eighteenth green, just before Tom's house, where he would usually stand and smoke his old clay pipe after his two daily rounds were played – and there I would see exactly the same smile of sympathy for my opponent's recounting of his woes likewise, and at the end the pipe being withdrawn from the mouth; and I might know, though I might not hear, that precisely the same two words were being given for his sufficient consolation likewise – 'Ou aye'. So we both went away from him greatly comforted and in a disposition to make it all up again before the sun should go down on our wrath.

Old Tom was good enough to give me his friendship from the very first moment I came to St Andrews, prompted thereto, as I think, largely by a comment that one or two of the old stagers made to him that my style was not unlike Young Tommy's. I am sure that even at that time this must have been a comparison not quite just to that great young player of old, for although it is more than likely that I have cherished very many illusions in regard to my golf, I am quite sure that I have never been so deluded as to deem my style either good or graceful. But the criticism was endorsed by Tom and gave me a place in his heart. There was another point in which he gave me praise (he could give no higher) for a likeness to his talented lost son: 'Ye're like Tammie – ye'll tak' a' as much pains over a short putt as a long yin'. Anything that had to do with a short putt touched the dear old man in a very sensitive place, for he was the worst short putter, for a great golfer, that ever was. It is known that Mr Wolfe-Murray once addressed a letter to him, when on a visit to Prestwick, 'The Misser of Short Putts, Prestwick', and the postman carried it straight to Tom.

*The career of Douglas Rolland seems extremely odd to modern eyes. In a few years either side of 1890 he was probably the best player in the country but he did little to try to prove it, playing a few memorable challenge matches and competing just a few times in the Open Championship. He was second in 1884 and does not appear to have entered again until 1894 when, once more, he came in second. That was about that. Rolland later emigrated to the USA but returned to Farnborough to die in 1914, by then in his mid-fifties.*

# FORGOTTEN GREATNESS
## BERNARD DARWIN, 1946

Most of all, however, do I wish that I had watched one who never won the championship, Douglas Rolland. I caught sight of him once when his golfing days were over and he was but a shadow of his former magnificent self, crippled with rheumatism. In his erratic career he was for a while at Rye, but this was before my Rye days; he was at Limpsfield near my old home in Kent, but I had been transplanted. He came to play at Worlington and hit what was then an historic shot, a carry home in two on to the third green against a breeze with a brassy, but that was just before I had gone up to Cambridge. As far as I was concerned he was a will-o'-the-wisp always flitting out of my reach. And he must have been the best fun in the world to see because he was, as far as the long game was concerned, the best of all hitters of the gutty ball. Mr Blackwell may perhaps have been longer for individual shots, but for consistent long hitting of inconceivable fire and splendour I think all those who knew him united in putting Rolland first. Not only was it fun for the onlooker but fun for him. Mr Colt has often told me how Rolland in an ecstasy of delight over his own shot used to exclaim 'Away she sails wi' dash and spray'. I know not if this was an original remark or a quotation, and I cannot get at Mr Colt to ask him, but they are noble words to describe the flight of a great drive.

Most of all should I have liked to see Rolland on that occasion which has become part of the great golfing legend when he had to come to play an exhibition match with Tom Dunn at Tooting Bec. The legend tells how Rolland had been tasting freely of the pleasures of the town and arrived at Tooting clad in his best clothes and a hard-boiled shirt front, and with no clubs. He had apparently started with them but was like the man in the old *Punch* picture, who had not only lost his ticket but had lost the big drum. Whereupon the shirt was crumpled into greater flexibility, some clubs were borrowed, and Rolland beat the record of the course and beat poor Tom Dunn into the middle of the ensuing week. There must have been something heroic and lovable about the man who could do that, and in fact everybody adored Rolland; he had never an enemy but himself. I shall never quite get over the loss of not having seen him.

*No British golfer can rival John Ball for the number of major championships won. He totalled nine, taking the Amateur on eight occasions and the Open once, in 1890. He might have won the latter more often but competed in it only rarely.*

## A GREAT DAY FOR GOLF
### HORACE HUTCHINSON, 1919

Now all this while I have said mighty little about the Open Championship, because really the golfing world in general took little interest enough in it at that time. It was regarded as virtually an affair of the professionals. Now and then a few of us amateurs took part in it, but it was with scarcely an idea of possible success. And then, all at once, something happened, in 1890, which put the Open Championship within the possible grasp of the amateur, and therewith the general interest in that great competition became at once very much more vivid.

Johnny Ball had won the Amateur Championship that year at Hoylake, defeating Johnny Laidlay in the final. My own part in the contest was an ignominious one, for I allowed myself to be defeated rather weakly by Johnny Laidlay at the last hole after being one up with two to play. I missed a short putt at the last hole, of which the memory is still painful.

I was playing fairly well that year, notwithstanding, and went to Prestwick for the Open Championship – began by missing a very holable putt at the first hole and continued in a like vein throughout the two rounds. So that was the end of me. And then I, having finished my futile efforts, heard that Johnny Ball, who was still out, was doing terrible things. I went out to meet him, and as he reeled off hole after hole in the right figure it became apparent that bar accidents he was going to do the most terrible thing that had ever yet been done in golf – he, as an amateur, was going to win the Open Championship. Dr Purves was hurrying along at my elbow as we went, with the gallery, towards the sixteenth hole. 'Horace', he said to me, in a voice of much solemnity, 'this is a great day for golf.' It was.

\* \* \*

Johnny Ball ... continued the scoring of the right figures and accomplished the great feat, for an amateur, of winning the Open Championship. It was a win which made a difference. It seemed at once to bring the Open Championship within the practical horizon of the amateur for all years to come. It had broken a spell. Incidentally it may be noted that it put Johnny Ball's name higher than any other's had ever been, for he held the championship of the amateurs and of the professionals at the same time.

And what interested me much at the moment was the attitude of the professionals towards the result. I had expected that they would feel rather injured by seeing the championship which they had been used to regard as theirs going to an amateur. To my surprise that did not appear to disconcert them in the least. What they did resent, however, so far as resentment may be carried within the limits of perfectly good sportsmanship, was that it should be won by an Englishman. You see, it was not only the first time that it had ever been won by any other than a professional, but also the first time it ever had been won by any other than a Scot. That is a fact which will strike the reader with astonishment now perhaps, when the poor Scots must have become fairly well inured to Englishmen annexing the championship. Taylor and Vardon, to say nothing of Harold Hilton, have taught them to grin and bear it as best they may. But up to that time a Scot had ever been open champion of the game of Scotland, and Scotland did not much like another taking it.

So that was 'a great day for golf', as Dr Purves had truly said to me. It gave an added interest to all further competitions for this Open Championship; for what an amateur had once done, it seemed as if an amateur might do again, and thus the active interest was no longer confined to the professionals. The amateurs became at once something more than mere lookers on. There was only one man who did not seem to realize that Johnny Ball had done a big thing, and that was Johnny Ball. A week or so later he was playing a friendly match at Hoylake, and just as he was starting a stranger came up to him and said, 'Can you please tell me, is the open champion playing here today?' and Johnny answered, 'Yes, I believe he is'. On which the stranger started out at score over the links in search of this 'open champion', whom, presumably, he expected to recognize by some special halo set about his brow if he should come across him.

# THE MAN WHO LOVED A FIGHT
## BERNARD DARWIN, 1933

It is pleasant to be asked to write some memories of Freddie Tait, because he fell in the South African war now over 32 years ago, and one naturally begins to be afraid lest he be forgotten. To be sure, his name remains among those of the ancient and unquestioned heroes, but to most of the golfers of today he can be no more than a name. Let me try then to set down what manner of man and golfer he was, and try to explain the secret of his extraordinary fame.

In his day and in his own Scotland he was a national hero. I do not think have ever seen any other golfer so adored by the crowd – no, not Harry Vardon nor Bobby Jones in their primes. It was a tremendous and to his adversaries an almost terrifying popularity. He was only 30 when he was killed; a brave young man, like many others who were killed, a very good specimen of the plucky, cheerful, open-airish regular soldier; a thoroughly friendly creature, who made friends with all sorts and conditions of men, but not in any way possessed of an outstanding mind and character.

He was just a thoroughly good fellow who played a game very skilfully and in a cheery and chivalrous spirit. Yet, when he died, it is hardly too much to say that Scotland went into mourning, and his old friend John Low wrote a full-sized biography of him that was widely read. This is a remarkable state of things, and there was some remarkable quality about this otherwise ordinary man which, in the language of the theatres, 'got across', so that he had only to step onto the links for everyone to follow him.

There was one thing about him that appealed intensely to the Scots, namely, that Freddie was above everything else a Scottish golfer. Discussion simply ceased for him when any other course was compared with St Andrews. He stood by the old course and in the old ways. He liked the thrust and parry of match play and regarded score play as no more of a game than rifle shooting. He especially loved the foursome, and, when he played in one, was always most particular to consult his partner on any possible point of tactics. Moreover he had, as it seems to us, that almost parochial sort of patriotism which wants above everything else to see the Englishman beaten.

These were some of the things in his character that made the crowd love him, but there was further something in his manner of playing that drew them to him as a magnet. He had beyond question a wonderfully gay and gallant way with him, when playing a big match, a cheerful and brave and confident, though never swaggering, way. Attraction is always apt to be mutual and perhaps the crowd loved Freddie because he loved the crowd. He never 'played to the gallery', for there was no touch of self-consciousness, and he did not show by the movement of an eyelid that he knew the crowd was there. But he liked the tramp of the feet behind him and the squeezing his way through the serried ranks around the putting green. He liked the feeling of being in the ring because it inspired him to fight his hardest and best.

His actual shots, too, made a great appeal, because his game combined two qualities not always found together. He seemed to be hitting the ball almost gently, at any rate not nearly as hard as he could, to be playing 'well within himself'. At the same time he could, if need be, pull out a colossal shot and some of his recoveries were historic.

\*   \*   \*

Later he kept these mighty swipes for emergencies and made accuracy his aim from the tee. I ought to add here that he had no truck with any such innovations as the overlapping or Vardon grip and held his club in the old-fashioned way with the right hand noticeably underneath the shaft.

\*   \*   \*

Freddie never won the Open Championship though he was several times near the top of the list. I doubt if he ever had the mechanical accuracy quite to keep up for four rounds against the best professionals – and Vardon, Braid and Taylor were his contemporaries. He had it in him to beat any man in a match and his two chief triumphs were his victories in the Amateur

Championship of 1896 and 1898. They were won in his two distinct manners, the first by absolutely faultless golf, the second by a series of heroic recoveries following on wild shots.

I was not at Sandwich in 1896 but I did see him win at Hoylake two years later and never shall I forget his beating John Low in the semi-final at the twenty-second hole. I was a partisan of John Low that day and it certainly did seem to me that he was fighting not against a mortal man but against the devil that was in his jerkin. Two vast wooden club shots did Freddie lay so near the hole, if not positively dead, that he holed the putt. One was at the sixteenth over the cross bunker. One, even more crucial at the twenty-first, and in each case his wretched adversary had played faultlessly, whereas Freddie had made some mistakes that deserved to be fatal.

Moreover, at the twentieth he holed a great racing putt over a ridge and furrow green. That putt really was lucky, I believe, for Freddie looked a beaten man. Over those brassy shots he took plenty of pains, addressing the ball very deliberately, but he just went up to the ball and hit that putt as if in despair.

His two chief rivals were the two giants of Hoylake, Harold Hilton and John Ball. Hilton was nearly always beaten. That great little man simply could not play against him, and Freddie took perhaps some unchristian pleasure in crushing him. I remember particularly the Amateur Championship of 1898 – the first I ever saw. Hilton was open champion, in great form and on his own Hoylake. He had to meet Freddie Tait in the fourth round and all Liverpool was coming out to see the match. At lunch time I saw Freddie assiduously practising putting in front of the clubhouse. 'Is it going well?' someone asked him, and he answered with a victorious ring in his voice, 'It will be this afternoon'. It did; so much so that he won by six and five and the poor open champion crumpled sadly beneath the attack.

The other Hoylake champion, John Ball, had something the best of Freddie. He could and did generally beat him and only the most perfervid of Scots – I am English – will deny that John Ball was the greater golfer. Their most historic match was at Prestwick in 1899 – Freddie's last championship before he sailed for South Africa. He was at one time in the morning five up but he pulled down to three at luncheon and was finally beaten after a desperate struggle by John's driving a three at the thirty-seventh hole.

One must be allowed to be a little obstinate about the heroes of one's youth and I shall always maintain that this was the greatest golf match I ever saw, not by any means the most perfect in play, but the most nearly divine in point of god-like thrusts by either side. The Hoylake supporters in a body retired to the clubhouse after the thirty-sixth hole. They could endure no more and waited, with their heads presumably buried in cushions, till someone came to tell them what had happened.

*The rise of English professional golf dates from J. H. Taylor, the first of the 'great triumvirate' of Vardon, Braid and himself to emerge. Though Taylor wrote generously*

*of Vardon's greatness and considered him the supreme golfer of the generation, I wonder*
*whether Taylor would have gone down in golf history as the greatest player if he rather*
*than Vardon had won the elusive sixth Open Championship. As it is, Taylor remains*
*one of a group of players – himself, James Braid, Peter Thomson and Tom Watson –*
*who have won the Open five times. Taylor was a most interesting man and did a great*
*deal to raise the status of the professional golfer in Britain. Like Vardon and Braid,*
*his origins were humble.*

# THE 'ODD BOY'
### HORACE HUTCHINSON, 1919

It was during my time at Oxford that there came to Wellesbourne as 'odd
boy' – that is to say, to do certain odd jobs in the morning – a little, singularly
white-flaxen-haired boy from Northam village. It may seem surprising that
the coming of such a little boy to Wellesbourne should be worthy of a place
in this grave page of golfing history, and I do not know exactly what the
duties of an 'odd boy' are, but you may be very certain that he performed
them very efficiently when I tell you that his name was John Henry Taylor.
He used to do these odd jobs, whatever they were, like a champion, I am
very sure, and then he used to go down to the links and carry my clubs for
me whenever I was at home. The pay of a caddy at Westward Ho! in those
days was not exorbitant – sixpence a round, and a hard walking and sandy
round too, of 18 holes; and they had to walk down a mile and a half from
Northam village to begin to earn it. But all wages were low and all living
was cheap in North Devon at that date and the boys were glad to earn it,
particularly with a bottle of ginger beer generally thrown in of the royal
bounty of the employer. On occasions, and for valid consideration, they
would develop a spirit of independence which made money seem no object,
as in the instance, which has become historic, of the small boy throwing
down, in the middle of the round, the clubs of his master, a gallant general
officer, and making his way without a word across the Burrows. 'Where are
you going, boy?' the irate man of war shouted after him. 'I be goin' 'ome',
came the firm reply. 'There be goose for dinner.'

\*   \*   \*

We passed the time of day with him [Taylor], quite as if we were his equals,
with no notion of his future greatness. Then the Northam village players (I
hardly know whether their club was formally instituted by that date) said
they would like to play the Royal North Devon Club a match. I was put to
play Taylor. I did not think much about the job. I had hardly seen him play
a stroke before. Going to the very first hole I remember a shot of his with
a cleek: it went low; I thought he had half topped it; but it continued going.
It had seemed certain to fall into the bunker guarding the green. But it
carried that bunker and lay close to the hole. Again and again I found the

same deceptive low-flying shot going a great deal further than I had expected it to. I began to realize then that it was because of his stance, with the ball so very far back towards his right. I also began to realize that I was a hole or two down. I did not play well; really, at that date, I ought to have beaten him. But he was one up with four to play, and then I laid him a stimy. He had two for the half. But instead of putting round, as all ordinary men of experience would, he tried to loft, for the hole, with his ordinary – and his only – flat iron. He just failed: but he holed the next putt, though he was not dead. Finally he beat me – I think at the last hole – and I congratulated him, as in duty bound, adding that when he knew a little more he would not be trying to loft stimies when he was one up and had two for the half. So I said, thinking to be wise, whereas it was I really who did not know – not knowing of what Taylor, even then with a flattish iron, was capable, in the way of putting stop on the ball.

# My First Open
## J. H. TAYLOR, 1943

My reputation was on the rise, and my confidence had gained a youthful aggressiveness, so nothing remained but to see if it were justified. The championship of 1893 was held at Prestwick, so away to Ayrshire I went in September of that year. It was my first visit to Scotland and I am not likely to forget the degree of temerity which possessed me and sent me journeying north. I found my old friend Johnnie Allan installed as pro to the St Nicholas, a neighbouring club, and knew that I should find a staunch supporter and believer on the spot. I had met a few of the leading Scots pros at Westward Ho! in 1888 and soon had reason for thinking that a character for decency had preceded me. However that might be, the fact remains that they all received me with what I now think was a sort of curious suspicion as to my right to be among such a select crowd. It was my first opportunity of meeting some of the great ones in golfing history. Among the amateurs were Mr John Ball, Johnnie Laidlay, Andy Stuart, Harold Hilton, Freddie Tait and Peter Anderson. Among the pros were Willie Campbell, Willie Park, Willie Auchterlonie and Willie Fernie, and among the young fellows nearer my age were Sandy Herd, Jack White and two unknown English pros, the brothers Harry and Tom Vardon.

I rather suspect that my defeat of Andra' [Kirkcaldy] had whetted their several golfing appetites, otherwise I can see no reason why they should all have wanted to have a go at me. I took them on one by one every day for a week beforehand and emerged undefeated. I found I could drive straighter, could pitch better and could hold my own on the greens, a combination of virtues that is hard to beat. Johnnie Ball offered me a game which I accepted as a special honour. I had read and learned in my Westward Ho! days of the skill of Johnnie, for was he not one of the greatest players in the land and an old antagonist of our beloved Horace? Even in those far-off days, when he was but a youth, Johnnie Ball's skill was legendary. Hoylake people thought him unbeatable, so I was more than anxious to see him perform. I hope I am not being too presumptuous when I say I bagged him as well, but whilst doing so I formed the impression, which a long experience since has tended to confirm, that in John Ball the world has seen its most brilliant amateur golf player. And if further confirmation is needed, his successes in the Amateur and Open Championships are more than sufficient evidence, and when maintaining this opinion I do not exclude the wonderful American amateur, Bobby Jones.

# One Man in It
## HORACE HUTCHINSON, 1919

It is not very easy to find a man who, all through his golfing time, has delighted more in the storms and the rain than Johnny Ball, but I believe there is one – that same who came as a little flaxen-haired boy to our house at Northam – J. H. Taylor. He is open champion, for the fifth time, as I write, and he won that championship at Hoylake in weather as villainous, especially on the second day, as any that has generally been served out to us for the finals of the Amateur Championship. One cannot say worse of it. He had a stroke or so in hand, of the whole of his field, at the start of that second day, but the curious thing is that when the rest of the professors saw what kind of day it was, they never doubted that Taylor would win. He has a mastery over the ball in these circumstances, both in the drive and in his low and heavily cut approaches, that none other can rival – not even Vardon nor Braid themselves.

*In the one and a quarter centuries of championship golf, very few people have been recognized as the supreme player of the day by their contemporaries. The first to deserve this status was Young Tom Morris; Harry Vardon was the second.*

# Vardon Remembered
## BERNARD DARWIN, 1933

I remember very well the first time I saw him play. It was in the later summer of 1896 and he had won his first championship in the spring. I went over to Ganton, where he was then professional, for a day's golf and there by good luck was the great man driving off. He hit just the sort of drive that he always did – dead straight and rather high, the ball seeming to float with a particularly lazy flight through the air. The shot was obviously a perfect one and yet I was not quite so much impressed as I had expected to be. The style was so different from what I had been taught to admire; the club seemed to be taken up in so outrageously upright a manner, with something of a lift.

No doubt I was stupid and uneducated. So at least were other people who ought to have known much better than I, and the general impression at first could be summed up in the learned words of someone, 'These Vardons are not pretty players'. Moreover, I think his style did change a little and become both more elegant and more sound. At any rate one of his most distinguished contemporaries has told me so, adding that when Vardon first appeared he used to let his right elbow fly out a little at the top of his swing and he certainly never did that afterwards. However that may be, all the world soon became converted and by 1898 his swing was recognized not only as one of genius but also as one of surpassing ease and grace.

Well now, what were the characteristics both of his method and its results which made him so devastating a conqueror? Results are easier to tackle and I will take them first. Vardon was first of all a magnificent driver. He was with a gutty ball uncommonly long, especially down the wind, and he was very straight. Taylor had been regarded as inhumanly accurate and so he was. Now here came Vardon, who rivalled his accuracy and added to it a little something more of freedom and power. He had a gift of hitting long carrying shots and, because of his upright swing, the ball would sit down with but little run where it pitched. This gift was of enormous value through the green. The brassy was not atrophied then, there were lots of wooden club shots to be played up to the pin, and Vardon, who often played them with his driver, could and did put the ball nearer the hole than other men could with their mashies. It was his most overpowering stroke and, even if he had been a bad putter then (which he was not), it left him little putting to do.

Then, he was superb with all iron clubs. He could command great length, if he needed it, and had in particular at one time a driving mashie which was as a driver in his hand. He was beautifully accurate in all pitching shots. Taylor had got there first and acquired the reputation of the greatest mashie player in the world, but I think Vardon was just as good. He was a good approach putter and at any rate an adequate holer out, though without the touch and delicacy of the really outstanding putter.

He had a calm and cheerful temperament, the game seemed to take very little out of him and he could fight, if need be, without appearing to be fighting at all. All these were valuable qualities, but, if one thing is to be picked out that made him supreme, it was that unique power of hitting long, soaring wooden club shots up to the hole side. 'Two-shot' holes could be worthy of their name then, and given a course that had a number of them, Vardon was invincible. Other men might be scrambling on to the verge of the green and getting a certain number of fours, but he was putting for threes.

As to his style, ... Vardon certainly made no fetish of the stiff left arm. Another thing is the uniform beauty of the follow-through. Time after time he would come right through, drawn to his full height, the club right round over his left shoulder, the hands well up, the left elbow tolerably high. It was the ideal copybook follow-through and he did it every time with an almost monotonous perfection.

\* \* \*

His was essentially an upright swing in the days when orthodox swings were flat and was the more noticeable accordingly. He took the club up very straight, 'too straight' as any self-respecting caddy would have said in instructing his master. Then by way of natural compensation he flung the clubhead well out behind him and brought it down on to the ball with a big sweep. It was a beautifully free movement of one having a natural gift for opening his shoulders and hitting clean. And, of course, like the movements of all really great golfers, it was instinct with that mysterious thing called rhythm. No golfer in the world, not even Bobby himself, was ever more perfectly rhythmic than Harry Vardon.

## BROADCAST ON THE DEATH OF VARDON
### J. H. TAYLOR, 1937

By the death of Harry Vardon, the game of golf has lost one of its greatest friends and I, and many hundreds of others, a dear and valued friend. We had known each other for over 40 years. We both made our debut in the Open Championship in the same year, 1893 at Prestwick. That is a long time ago and Vardon and I have been associated as servants of the game for nearly the whole of our lives.

Vardon, as is known, learned his golf in Jersey, a favoured spot for the development of skilful players. I am often asked whom I consider to be the best golfer I ever saw, and with a lifetime of experience behind me and having seen all the great players in the last 50 years, I give it as my mature and considered judgement that Vardon was the greatest of them all.

His style was so apparently simple that it was apt to mislead. He got his effects with that delightful effortless ease that was tantalizing. It is a legend of the game that Vardon was never off the centre of any fairway in two years of play. I can scarcely subscribe to this but I do say without fear of contradiction that Vardon played fewer shots out of the rough than anyone who has ever swung a golf club.

If the test of a player be that he makes fewer bad shots than the remainder then I give Vardon the palm. He hit the ball with the centre of every club with greater frequency than any other player. In this most difficult feat lay his strength.

In addition to his wonderful skills, Harry Vardon will be remembered as long as the game lasts as one of the most courteous and delightful opponents there could ever be. I have good reason to appreciate this because Vardon and I, in the pursuit of our calling, met some hundreds of times and although I was generally unsuccessful I give it to him that when I was fortunate enough to win he gave me the fullest possible credit.

Another tribute I should like to make to my old friend. Throughout the years I knew him, I never heard him utter one disparaging remark about another player. He was at all times most anxious with his help and advice. Allied to his magnificent show, Harry Vardon will be always remembered as one of the most kindly souls who ever existed and to know him was to love him.

*Great players have always stirred their rivals to greater effort and brought about a general rise in standards. Today, the example of Seve Ballesteros has made many others realize that mechanical excellence alone is not enough. As a result, we see players trying to improve their range of shot – especially in the short game. With the death of Young Tom Morris it was 20 years before another player was so pre-eminent, J. H. Taylor. But this was not to last. In quick succession Vardon and then James Braid arrived and course records tumbled everywhere they played.*

## BRAID MAKES UP THE TRIUMVIRATE
### HORACE HUTCHINSON, 1919

In spite of this defeat by the great Harry [Vardon], whose unique greatness even then we did not at all fully appreciate, the big man in golf was still Taylor. He was still at the very top of his game. And about the same time we began to hear that there was a young fellow working as a club-maker at the Army and Navy Stores, who was capable of playing a very good game of golf. He was said to be a cousin of Douglas Rolland, the great driver, and, like him, to come from Elie, in Fifeshire. His name was James Braid. Few people knew much about him, but the few who had seen him play had the greatest opinion of his game. He was brought forward, on half-holidays when he could get away from the Stores, to play exhibition matches, and amongst these matches was one that he played against Taylor at West Drayton; and he played that great man to a level finish.

That was a result which caused a buzz of talk. The young fellow at the Stores was evidently worth watching, perhaps worth exploiting. Not very long after this the newly formed club at Romford, in Essex, found itself in want of a professional. James Braid was engaged for the post.

I had a game with him shortly after he was appointed to that job, and what impressed me about him more than anything else was the enormous distance that he could smite the ball with the cleek. I remember that this ability to get huge distances with the iron clubs was the quality that had most struck me when first I became acquainted with the game of Rolland, and I said to Braid, 'It seems to me you can drive just as far as Douglas Rolland can'. He looked at me a moment, as if in a kind of mild surprise that I should make such a comment, and said, 'Oh yes, sir, I think I can do that'.

It was an amusing answer: also it was an answer which meant a good deal, coming from a man so absolutely unable to swagger or to over-rate his own power as James Braid. I realized that we had here a great force in golf; but it was rather a long while before he made that force fully felt. Nevertheless it was there: he too had 'arrived', though it was not for a year or two that he was fated to begin the writing of his name first on the championship list. But he was there: the triumvirate was complete.

Never, as leaders at any game, were there three men so closely matched with methods so widely different. You may put that down in large measure, if you please, to the physical, anatomical differences of the three: there was Taylor, square, short, compact, stubby; there was Braid, long, loose-jointed; and there was Vardon, a happy medium between the two, and really a very finely-shaped specimen of a powerful human being. It is hardly to be questioned which of the three had the most perfect and beautiful style. Vardon lifts up his body a little, away from the ball, as he raises the club – that is a movement which we should tell a learner was apt to unsettle the aim a little. It did not upset Vardon's aim; but then Vardon was rather past the learner stage. For the rest his style was the perfection of power and ease. Taylor, with the ball opposite the right toe and every stroke played rather on the model generally approved for the half iron shot, had a style as peculiar as his 'cobby' build, and specially adapted for it. Braid swung in a loose-jointed way at the ball that did not suggest the mastery and the accuracy which he achieved. I have spoken of a kind of 'divine fury' with which he launched himself at the ball. Those were long before the days of his studies in 'advanced golf' and so on. I doubt whether he played according to any very conscious method. But the results well justified the method, or the method-lessness. For a while there was little to choose between these three great ones.

But by degrees it became evident that there was a choice: that one really was distincly better than the other two. Certainly there was a while, just before he had to go to a health resort, with a threatening of tuberculosis, when Harry Vardon was in a class by himself. For a while he was, I think, two strokes in the round better than either Taylor or Braid, and, I believe, better than any other man that we have seen.

*For the first 20 years or so in the development of American golf, standards naturally lagged far behind those set in Britain. The achievements of Willie Anderson are almost impossible to evaluate because of this but all one can do is beat whoever turns up to play. Anderson did this and no one has beaten his record of four US Opens.*

## STILL THE RECORD HOLDER
### ALEXIS J. COLMAN, 1931

As superlatives were necessary in writing of Willie Anderson living, so he merits them in this chronicle. From the first he was in the front rank. He attained greater heights than any other Scottish pro who came to dwell here, for he won four National Open and four Western Open Championships within nine years, at all times measuring skill with the best in the land. 'Anderson was the first pro of the highest class to be developed in this country', said H. L. Fitzgerald of the New York *Sun* at the time of Willie's death 19 years ago. 'How would Anderson at his best compare with Hagen and Bobby Jones at their best?' I asked Fred McLeod recently. 'As good as either one', he replied.

Strong medicine this may seem to the modern generation, which did not know Anderson.

'Conceding that Alex Smith was Anderson's greatest rival for more years than any other, in both national and western tourneys, what would you say of their relative playing ability?' I asked McLeod. He dodged.

'Willie was of the phlegmatic temperament, Alex of the nervous type', was his answer. But let Smith himself tell of this rivalry. Writing a dozen years ago, Alex said, 'In my struggles to land the Open, Willie Anderson seemed to be my Nemesis ... He was the kingpin of the pros from 1901, when he won his first Open, until 1905. He got four Open events in those five years, and although he failed to win another national championship, he annexed the Western twice after this, in 1908 and 1909. His untimely death was a blow to his friends, who looked upon him as a player most likely to set a record for Open Championships that would never be beaten.'

Anderson was the complete golfer. He excelled in all departments. One recalls his generous, sweeping strokes with the wooden clubs, his flawless long-iron shots on the flag. McLeod thinks his work with the mashie was especially his long suit. His putting was consistently good; he surveyed the line with just enough deliberation, and then, not with the quick, staccato tap of a Smith, but with a smooth, even stroke he sent the ball blithely on its way, 'in all the way'.

Sturdy, with muscular shoulders, brawny forearms and exceptionally large hands, his strokes bespoke a power and an ease akin to those of Jones. Students of rhythm and timing would have found no fault in him. His grip was an extreme interlock, the index finger of his left hand extending way through between the third and little fingers of the right, instead of allowing only the knuckle to show in that aperture. His was not the upright swing of a Vardon, but the flatter, fuller sweep of the typical Scot. Long shots to the green with the brassy – and he made much use of this club with the hard ball in his earlier years – were duplicates of his drives, far and straight.

Willie did not need any great variety of clubs. Someone asked leading pros in 1907 as to what clubs they used, and the order of their preference. Anderson regularly played with eight: driver, brassy, cleek, mid-iron, one he called a pitching iron, heavy-centered mashie, large mashie-niblick, and putting cleek. He named the driver as his favourite; then mashie, mid-iron, and brassy. These were the implements with which he showed his mastery of the game.

*    *    *

There were few exceptions to Anderson's unwillingness to take the limelight, except as his skill automatically placed him there. Probably the occasion on which he most astonished his *confrères* was on the first day of the 1901 Open at Myopia ... An officer of the club, an Englishman imbued with the spirit of old-world procedure as to the relative places of amateurs and pros, announced that the pros were to eat their luncheon in the kitchen. Willie Anderson, standing on the velvety lawn before the clubhouse swinging an iron, became so wrought-up that he lapsed into the Scottish dialect of his youth – and he was then only 21. 'Na, na, we're no goin' t' eat in the kitchen!' he exclaimed, and, whether intentionally or not, made a vicious swipe, cutting an enormous divot that flew high, before the astonished gaze of the transplanted Briton. There was a compromise; the pros ate in a tent.

*    *    *

Anderson's first bid for national honours was made that year, 1897, at the Chicago Golf Club, Wheaton, and it was then that I first saw this remarkable golfing youth of 17. He all but landed at the pinnacle on this first attempt, even though, as acknowledged by such critics as H. J. Whigham, Charles Blair Macdonald, and Tweedie at the time, the brand of golf put up by the pros was the best so far shown in America. Willie led in the morning, with 38-41-79, but a bunker at the thirty-fourth hole converted a possible three into a five, and his second round, 41-43-84, gave him a total of 163. Joe Lloyd, pro at Essex County, Massachusetts, was the only man to be feared; for, although four strokes behind at noon, he was playing much better. He had a par-four to tie Anderson; none thought he could beat him. But he did. The hole was 466 yards, and Lloyd, after a magnificent drive, sent the hard ball with his brassy to eight feet from the flag, and holed the putt – a feat justly acclaimed as one of the high achievements in golfing performance here or abroad.

'The one stroke', said Samuel L. Parrish, treasurer of the USGA, 'marks the difference between fame and oblivion'. But it didn't for Anderson ... No, it was Lloyd who thereafter was little heard from. Anderson played in 14 straight National Open Championships, 1897–1910, and finished only three times outside the money. He won four, was second once, third once, fourth twice, fifth three times, eleventh twice, and fifteenth once. In 1898 he was third, in 1899 fifth, in 1900 – the Vardon–Taylor year – eleventh. He won at Myopia in 1901, after a play-off with Alex Smith, and was fifth at Garden City in 1902.

For the next three years Anderson was undisputed potentate of the links, for he won all three National Open Championships – at Baltusrol in 1903 after playing off a 307 tie with 'Deacon Davy' Brown; at Glen View in 1904 with 303, five ahead of Gil Nicholls; and again at Myopia in 1905 with 314, two in front of his great rival, Alex Smith.

Anderson's four national victories were achieved in what may well be termed a golden age in American golf – the first half-dozen years of the century.... In the scoring game all pros and amateurs alike willingly conceded that Anderson, when right, was their master.

*It can never be decided who is, or was, the greatest golfer, but is there any question about who was the greatest personality? I think not.*

## SUCCESSFUL GESTURES
### CHARLES PRICE, 1962

Before Hagen racked up his clubs, he was to win 11 major national championships, capture 60-odd other tournaments, and play in more than 1,500 exhibitions. Like Francis Ouimet before him, Hagen was the right man in the right place at the right time. It was the jazz age, an era best put into words by F. Scott Fitzgerald, best put into pictures by John Held, Jr, and best personified by the flat-chested flappers who drank instant gin and danced the Charleston with quick-buck Johnnies during the Saturday night dances at the thousands of new country clubs such an uninhibited age demanded. Into this gaudy period stepped 'The Haig', as he was called, with the sang-froid of a Valentino, his black hair pomaded to an iridescence, his handsome features browned by the sun and the wind until they had the hue of brierwood. At the time, when most golf pros were still dressing in sack coats and brogues, Hagen began wearing silk shirts, florid cravats, alpaca sweaters, screaming argyles, and black and white shoes which he had custom-made by Oliver Moore at a hundred dollars a pair. When The Haig strolled past the verandas, he was enough to make the flappers choke on their gum.

If personality is an unbroken series of successful gestures, as Scott Fitzgerald wrote of another jazz age character, then there was something gorgeous about The Haig. It was impossible to tell what the man would do next, on or off the golf course, and most of what he did would have seemed absurd, even ludicrous, had it been done by anyone else. In an exhibition The Haig might have scrutinized the roll on a green before playing a brassy shot to it, and yet for a championship he might have holed a putt that had six breaks after only glancing at the line. At the peak of his career he once played 18 holes in 58 strokes – and another 18 in 93. One week after returning to San Francisco from a tour of the world which had netted him $23,000 in exhibition fees, a sum that somehow hadn't quite covered his expenses, The Haig was forced to sit in his hotel room for three days because he didn't have the cash to pay for his laundry.

## 18 AND 17
### CHARLES PRICE, 1962

With his record in the PGA, 'The Haig' was looked upon as almost unbeatable in match play. This reputation was bolstered considerably in 1926 when, with a hot putter, he trounced Bobby Jones in a 72 hole match in Florida by the lopsided margin of 12 and 11. Two years later, the year he finally relinquished his PGA crown, The Haig went to England with Bob Harlow to pick up the third of his four British Opens. One week before the championship, he was booked to play a 72 hole match against Big Archie Compston at Moor Park. It was the first of a series of matches Harlow had arranged for Hagen while they were there. Compston reeled off rounds of 67, 66 and 70 before walloping Hagen 18 and 17 for what should have been the most humiliating defeat ever handed one major professional by another. But not for The Haig. He laughed his way around the course, joking and waving at the spectators. After the match was over, he posed with Compston for the photographers. Hagen wore an expression on his face that would have done him justice had he been the winner. Then he climbed into his Rolls-Royce and drove away with Harlow.

Fifteen minutes passed before The Haig and an exasperated Harlow said a word to one another. Realizing that the entire exhibition schedule had now been smashed irreparably, Harlow sat steaming in silence. Finally The Haig spoke up. 'You know something, Bob?' he said, lighting a cigarette.

'What?' said Harlow irritably.

The Haig leaned back and blew into the air a column of smoke that could have inflated a bicycle tyre. Then he said, 'I can beat that sonofabitch the best day he ever had'.

## THE ART OF RELAXATION
### BOB HARLOW, 1929

If there is one expression which Walter Hagen has heard his manager use more than any other over a period of seven years of association on the road in America, Canada and Europe, it is this: 'Come on, Haig; hurry up'.

Hagan is the slowest-moving individual I have ever encountered. He can linger longer over playing a card at the bridge table than anyone of my acquaintance. If there is ten minutes to reach the theatre at something like the opening hour, Hagen can meet a friend, or stranger for that matter, in the lobby of his hotel and talk about nothing for 30 minutes.

Once Hagen gave me a good answer. He was due to start in some minor open tournament and, as usual, was taking his time about getting dressed. He does the most exasperating things. When you at last think he is all ready to leave for the course, he will take a look at the hose he has selected for the day and decide that the stockings do not look as well as he had anticipated. This means another 15 minutes while he makes a change.

On the particular occasion in question Walter was shaving and time was flying. I realized that, at the best, he would be ten minutes late at the tee. So I was being even more persistent than usual, giving him what must have been the one-hundredth lecture on not keeping his audience waiting. Of course, it did no good. This time Walter stopped, and with razor poised said, 'How do you expect me to have a smooth stroke on the green today if I start by hurrying my stroke with this razor? I can't rush around now and change my pace when I start playing golf. I want to be relaxed on the course, so I must be relaxed now.'

Of course, one might explain that he could have gotten up an hour earlier and thus had ample time to conduct his dressing and shaving according to the most suitable tempo for the day, but Hagen always has an answer and he would have said that getting out of bed the hour earlier would have been hurrying because he was not ready.

# 'COME RIGHT UP, KID'
## HENRY COTTON, 1948

I have always admired Walter Hagen very much. I liked his attitude towards the golfing world and his great financial success. I could never see the point in just becoming a club professional and remaining one, except that it was part of the qualifications for being a member of the Professional Golfers' Association.

Hagen never really trained hard, and the only time he ever practised was in his later years, when his putting left him and he was obliged to polish up his long game. My goodness! How well he played through the green; but he jerked those little putts, almost as badly as Harry Vardon did at one time, and you can't jerk little putts and win.

\* \* \*

Hagen was the only exception to the rule 'practice makes perfect', and was the only player who did not daily slog out hundreds of golf balls in those days. He told me once that if he had needed to practise like that to play golf he would have chosen some other job. Later on when staging an unsuccessful come-back he had slightly changed his tune. 'The Haig', as the press called him, loved doing himself well, and I do not think I have met anyone who had the capacity and health to enjoy so much what most of us know as 'a good time'. He loved parties, staying out late, cards; in fact, enjoying himself.

I called at Hagen's hotel to get a mashie-niblick he had promised me. I telephoned up to his room from the hall and said I had come for the club. 'Come right up, Kid', he said. He always called me 'Kid'. I went up and wandered from room to room looking for the great man in an enormous suite occupying most of a floor of the hotel, and it took me some time to find him. When I did, I found him fast asleep still clutching to his ear the telephone he had used to speak to me a few minutes before.

*What happens to aging golf heroes? In the case of Hagen there is a great contrast between the man described at his peak and in retirement. Here is Charles Price again.*

## THE HAIG AND I
### CHARLES PRICE, 1982

By 1953, the year I went to work for and to live with Walter Hagen, the legend of him had become almost Greek in its proportions, half clubhouse myth and half real man, the myth part living everywhere golf was played and the man part living nowhere anybody was precisely sure about.

Although only 61, Hagen was so utterly removed from the golf scene there were probably not a dozen people intimate with the game who even knew what part of the country he was living in, and probably not half of them knew his unlisted phone number. Even so, if you called, Hagen wouldn't identify himself until you gave him a name and a voice he could recognize instantly. Then, disarmingly, he'd ask where *you* had been. Even on the phone, Walter Hagen was the master match player.

Hagen had not played in a national championship even for old times' sake since the 1940 PGA, a title he had won five times, four in a row, all at match play. It had been 22 years since he had played in a British Open, which he had won four times, and 17 since his last National Open, which he had won twice. He had not won a mere tournament since the Gasparilla Open, back in 1935, the memory of which was hazy even to those who had played in it. But Hagen had brought it off big, scoring birdies on the last two holes. He had long since lost count of how many other tournaments he had won, but at least 60 of them had been against world-class players. In keeping with a man whose career had been so large he could not keep track of it, everyone, including his grown son, had been referring to him for years as 'The Haig', for there was something undeniably royal about him. How else could you excuse the man for not being able to remember, as he sometimes couldn't, the years he won the British Open?

Still, there was something wonderfully human about him, something that crept through the newsprint in a way it had for no other golf pro before or since and which the electronic tube today seems incapable of transmitting, possibly because, through sitcoms and wildly inaccurate documentaries, it has made implausible figures, like The Haig, so commonplace. If you brought up The Haig's name among pros past 40 anywhere in 1953, their faces would light up, as though you had mentioned some comic uncle who had made boyhood unforgettable. This would lead immediately to some outrageously apocryphal anecdote, such as The Haig showing up an hour late half drunk in a tuxedo for a national championship, and then winning it. Either that or a story of him doing something all too human, such as scoring a nine on a par-three hole, laughing all the way. Walter Hagen could do anything in golf – the more preposterous, it seems, the better. As big as the tour is today, what could professional golf give to see his likes again? They could try money. But it takes something beyond that to produce a Walter Hagen.

\*     \*     \*

When The Haig finally racked up his clubs, which was at some indeterminate date even The Haig couldn't remember, you almost had to drag him away from his hunting and fishing to be so much as a spectator. In retirement he lived in obscure villages where most of the neighbours, if they had heard of him at all, regarded him vaguely as some sort of athlete from a couple of wars ago. Here The Haig held court for those who took the trouble to find him. And there were hundreds who did, thousands more, it seemed, who would have liked to. Merely meeting the man had become a kind of golf tournament. Years later, in a hospital corridor the night before The Haig was to undergo surgery for cancer of the throat, I had to have a perfect stranger forcibly removed because he had ghoulishly persisted in taking what he thought was this final opportunity to shake the master's hand.

Typically for a man who might take three quarters of an hour shaving, The Haig spent years trying to write his autobiography with the help of newspapermen who thought they had known him. Almost all of this time had been dissipated searching for just the right title, The Haig's theory being that nobody could possibly give birth to a book without having a proper name for it. All the newspapermen had long since left the scene with near-fatal hangovers. The Haig had then tried to induce the help of Ernest Hemingway, on the excuse they had once got drunk together in Paris, but Hemingway begged off on the not illogical grounds that he knew nothing about golf. Next, The Haig tried to persuade Gene Fowler, the popular biographer (*The Great Mouthpiece; Good Night, Sweet Prince*) with whom he'd partied in Hollywood. Fowler knew it was hopeless to argue, so he agreed and then quoted a fee that meant the finished book would have to be accepted by six book clubs before The Haig would ever get a cent. The Haig told Fowler he would get back to him, and of course never did.

The Haig had now reached the bottom of the writing barrel, which is where he found me. I was 27 and had yet to write my first book. A number of my magazine articles on golfers, notably in *The Saturday Evening Post*, had been brought to his attention by his son, Walter Jr. The Haig hadn't read them, and never would, something he considered a mere oversight. But if Junior said so, then I was to be his man, or rather his boy, for I was not yet professional enough to tell immediately the difference between an auto-biographical subject and a biographical one.

The Haig was definitely not autobiographical material. Not only was he incapable of writing objectively about himself, he was incapable of writing, period, a talent he considered strictly god-given, like carrying a tune, and not worth worrying about if you weren't born with it. As a matter of actual record, The Haig seems never to have so much as written a letter. At least his son had never received one. And as if this lack of literacy were not enough, he seems never to have read anything beyond *Outdoor Life*, and this only enough to make sense out of the pictures. While I did not know it at the time, The Haig and I together would be an experience I literally would never forget, but not one that anybody would remember literarily.

As I saw it, my job would be to separate the man from the myth, to find out where the man from East Rochester, New York, had left off and where The Haig, the romantic egoist, had begun. I had already had an inkling that there had been a vast difference between the two. The Haig, for example, had been internationally credited for having taken golf pros 'into the clubhouse', meaning he had elevated their social status from servant to celebrity. But when, in preparation for the book, I interviewed the pro at the Country Club of Rochester, down the road from where Walter the boy had grown up and where he had learned to play, I was surprised to find that the pro and myself were obliged to have lunch in the kitchen.

I first met The Haig at a home he was renting at Lake Mohawk, New Jersey, a town that for its golfiness might just as well have been in the middle of Montana. That's the way The Haig liked to live – with golf at arm's length. The years had added ten inches to his waistline from his playing days, and his drinking had left his eyes baggy, his cheeks jowly, and his nose bulbous, giving him the look of a philosophical walrus. He was seated in an overstuffed armchair that had been angled into the centre of the living room, thronelike, and he was so thoroughly ensconced in it that getting out of it seemed beyond all human endeavour. But he tried and, failing, began to laugh at himself, far more than I thought the situation warranted. But, as I was to learn, The Haig was a man who could extract humour out of a nuclear accident.

In his day, The Haig had been considered the height of fashion. But now his dress had become a hodgepodge of golf-shop clichés and remnants from Savile Row that had gone out with Edward VIII. He was wearing alligator loafers with tassles, orange gym socks, cuffed flannel slacks that left him with a lapful of pleats, a silk shirt with French cuffs to which were attached links the size of champagne corks, and a florid ascot around his neck that the Duke of Windsor might have hesitated wearing on the Riviera, let alone in New Jersey.

Wrapped in a knitted coaster on the coffee table in front of him was a can of beer of some obscure brand that, I was to learn, nobody outside of Jersey City or Hoboken had ever heard of, either. It was a status symbol in reverse.

(Late, in the middle of Michigan, he would drink a local brand unheard of outside Grand Rapids.) The Haig's hands were very long and thin and surprisingly unmuscular, the way a pianist's are supposed to be but seldom are. For some reason, The Haig always held them upward, as though some poetic injustice had just taken something out of them, an analogy not too strained considering The Haig might have been the most divine putter the game has known. In them was always a cigarette, which he handled as though it were opium – and from which he could draw out more theatre than Franklin D. Roosevelt. To this day it is impossible for me to visualize The Haig without a Chesterfield between his fingers. In the 15 years I was to get to know him, I never saw him without one, not even after his larynx had been removed because of them.

With this imperial posture, I had somehow expected The Haig to have a stentorian voice. But it was not deep or loud, but high and raspy, like a falsetto that had grown rusty with age. Without his hands to help him, he couldn't have held the attention of a hotel clerk. To make matters worse, he was becoming absentminded, constantly losing his train of thought and forever forgetting momentarily the names of people he had known half his life. The result was that his speech was constantly being interrupted by embarrassing pauses, theatrical coughs, stage laughs, and assorted heh-hehs and harrumphs. While he looked like His Royal Highness, ironically he sounded like Mr Magoo.

We never discussed money or the conditions under which I would work. I just seemed to have gone to work for him automatically. One word clinched the whole deal. The Haig had waved his arm grandly about the room, indicating the tools of our now mutual trade: a tape recorder every ten feet, blank legal pads every three feet, and a newly sharpened number two pencil seemingly on every vacant foot of tabletop. 'You won't', said The Haig, pausing to take a 'toot' of beer for emphasis. 'You won't use any – heh-heh ...' and now he paused to inhale his cigarette, blowing out enough smoke to inflate a water bed. 'You won't use any of them big words, will ya? They don't sound like me.'

'Walter', I said, realizing he must have felt as though he were playing with an amateur. 'The only five-syllable word I know is *Philadelphia*.'

He threw back his head and cackled. And I knew we were on our way, The Haig and I. That too was a title we never used, for the book never got written. But I like to think today it at least had the ring of a bestseller.

One day six months later, The Haig and I were driving south to Grand Rapids from Cadillac, where he had rented a couple of cottages for us by a lake for the summer. The Haig ostensibly had hired me to help him write his autobiography, but I was fast losing any semblance of a collaborator. An utter individualist, The Haig was constitutionally incapable of cooperating with anybody at doing anything, which may explain why he was a deplorable four-ball player. (Paired with Byron Nelson late in his career in the old Inverness Four-Ball Tournament, The Haig would sometimes leave Nelson on his own for two or three holes while he repaired to the clubhouse for a quick drink or two.)

Instead of a co-writer, I was being turned into a glorified companion-stenographer, somebody to jot down the deathless details of his purple life during cocktails until he could get around to showing me how to write them properly, The Haig suddenly having materialized as a master of literary composition, this although he had never been known to write so much as a postcard. In six months, as a result, we hadn't been able to advance his life beyond his days in grade school, and he was now approaching the age of 62.

We were on our way to visit the plant where the clubs were made that bore his signature. The trip could not be called a business one in any sense, for The Haig had not stepped foot in the plant for so many years that he couldn't remember when the last time had been. The result would be that a lot of the employees of The Walter Hagen Company would be seeing him for the first time, some of whom did not know he was still alive. We were just going there because The Haig thought he ought to, now that he had moved back to Michigan from northern New Jersey. Once inside the plant, though, The Haig would soon be telling men who had been fashioning clubs for a generation how to go about it. While The Haig well knew what sort of clubs best suited him, he had actually never come closer to making one than he had as a boy serving as an apprentice to a mandolin-maker. However, that was qualification enough for a man like The Haig, who at a nightclub in New York once had taken it upon himself to tell Babe Ruth how to hit a baseball.

I was doing the driving. Although The Haig down through the years must have owned a hundred cars of some exotic make or other – Austins, Lotuses, Reos, and some even Detroit had never heard of – he preferred not to drive himself. As a result of this practice, he had made himself into an intolerable backseat driver, and he did not like the way I was handling his Buick convertible. 'Slow down!' he'd say every 15 minutes. 'We're not in any hurry.' In The Haig's eyes, anybody who drove more than 40 miles per hour was a maniac.

As we crept down U.S. 131, I couldn't help thinking of the line that had been attributed to him for so long that he had begun to believe he had coined it. 'Slow down!' the line went, 'and take time to smell the flowers.' It was alleged to be The Haig's personal philosophy. And it was. But the line was first used, in somewhat different wording, by Oscar Wilde, whom I doubt The Haig had ever read or even heard of. The last book he had read, if not the first, had been *The Rules of Golf*, his interpretations of which, all perfectly legal, had given the USGA and the R and A apoplexy.

In a play-off with Mike Brady for the 1919 National Open at Brae Burn, near Boston, The Haig had requested that he be allowed to identify his ball after if had become embedded in the bank of a bunker. Since he and Brady were the only two players on the course, and since hundreds of people in the gallery, including several USGA officials, had seen the ball socket itself, they thought his request senseless. But The Haig argued, not illogically, that it could have been a ball lost the day before, or the day before that, even.

The Haig squeezed the ball out of the bank between his thumb and his forefinger, and then began to examine it as though it were a rock somebody had sent him from the moon. After what seemed like an hour, The Haig declared the ball was his, after all. He carefully replaced it on the indentation that was no longer there, recovered for his par, and went on to win by one stroke.

The Haig was then the pro at the only club he would ever represent: brand new Oakland Hills, near Detroit, which had not quite finished its golf course. At a dinner in his honour after defeating Brady, The Haig stood up to thunderous applause and then offhandedly announced he was resigning. Before the members could fully realize what he had said, The Haig announced he had already chosen his successor for them – Mike Brady.

Charisma was not a word used in the sports pages in The Haig's day. But he had it, in spades. It was just as kinetic in those days of the biplane and the Philco as that of any of the many pros who would follow him in jets and on Sonys and for whom The Haig broke a lot of ground they have taken for granted. Compared with the hat-in-hand professionals who had preceded him, his image was incandescent. The Haig literally lit up the sports pages with a game that not too long before him had been thought by some editors to belong in the financial section.

Great golfers have always come along in pairs, much of their greatness having been achieved by beating one another. Harry Vardon had his J. H. Taylor, Ben Hogan his Sam Snead, Jack Nicklaus his Arnold Palmer. Walter Hagen had Bobby Jones, no less.

From 1923 through 1930, Jones played in 21 major national championships, passing up 11 others. The Haig played in 32, passing up nothing. In that period, Jones played in only seven tournaments that were not national championships. The Haig played in at least three hundred. Jones played exhibitions only for an occasional charity, perhaps in those years no more than half a dozen. The Haig played more than one thousand, all of them for cash. When not competing, Jones played no more golf than the average dentist, probably not more than 80 rounds a year, and this in the comparative solitude of his home club near Atlanta. The Haig, who had no home club, played every day he wasn't on an ocean liner, often twice a day, usually on a course he had never seen before, and always in front of a stampeding gallery.

Because his appearances were only two, three, or four times a year, Jones was automatically awarded centre ring in the public arena of golf. He was the star they sounded the trumpets for, the daring young man on the flying trapeze. The Haig was a fixed star, an act that ran continuously. He was a professional strong man, the strongest in the world of golf, a professional so supremely confident that he could often afford to act more carefree than the amateurs who were watching him. And, in an age when highways were today's byways and aeroplanes flew only fast enough to stay airborne, he carried this act from Cape Cod to Catalina Island, from Quebec to Mexico City, and to places where Jones would only be read about: Singapore, Buenos Aires, Johannesburg, Kuala Lumpur. While Jones, as it so happens, never played anywhere that wasn't near a major city, The Haig brought his circus-brand of golf to the backwoods of America and the hinterlands of the world.

Figuratively, the public had to crane its neck to see Bobby Jones. They could watch Walter Hagen at eye level. Spectators never thought of speaking to Jones when he was playing. They saw no reason not to speak to The Haig when he was playing. In 1914, during the last three holes of the National Open, which The Haig was winning for the first time, he smiled at a pretty girl on the sixteenth tee, struck up a conversation with her on the seventeenth fairway, and made a date with her as he walked off the eighteenth green. After The Haig, nobody would take golf *too* seriously.

I was to learn, though, that The Haig's career had not been altogether as cavalier as it seemed in retrospect. He had studiously built up a public persona, a facade of indifference in which every offhand gesture actually had been as studied as a matinee idol's. For an exhibition at ten o'clock in the morning, The Haig would get out of bed at his customary hour of 6.00 a.m., a habit he had picked up as a country boy, and then lounge around for maybe three hours. When he was positive he couldn't be on time, he would have his tuxedo unpacked by his combination valet-chauffeur-caddy, a man from Los Angeles named Clark 'Spec' Hammond, who would then roll it into a ball and throw it repeatedly against the wall to make it look as though The Haig had worn it all night. So dressed, The Haig would leap out of his Packard or Bentley, or whatever Spec happened to be driving for him that week, and trot to the first tee. Then he'd remove his coat, barrel into a tee shot, and walk down the fairway as though he had just bought the place. By the time his opponents got their minds back to golf, The Haig was handling them as though they were yo-yos. Back in the clubhouse, The Haig would order drinks for the house, at least a dozen of which would end up in his hands and most of which he would surreptitiously pour into a jardiniere or a toilet. The heavy drinking came later, after the 11 major titles had been safely stashed away.

Technically, what made The Haig such a great player had always been a mystery. He was a terrible driver, neither long nor straight. His iron play was surpassed by at least a dozen of his contemporaries. He was an atrocious bunker player who admitted he was scared to death of sand. As a putter, he was superb, but not, from what I have heard, as great as Walter J. Travis or, from what I saw, as Bobby Locke. Every pro three-putts now and then, some have been known to four-putt, and a few have putted clear off a green. Incongruously for so renowned a putter, though, The Haig may have been the first and only pro of any kind to have jabbed a putt clear out-of-bounds.

What set The Haig apart from everybody before him, if not after him, was a unique knack for getting the ball in the hole some way, somehow, at sometime when you least expected it. You couldn't chalk it up to luck, because he invented and then perfected shots that had never occurred to the tradition-minded pros he played against. In those days before the wedge, every pro played the pitch-and-run shot now and then from, say, 30 yards out. At that distance, The Haig was known to cheat the wind by using his putter – a 'Texas wedge' nobody from Texas has ever had the nerve to try. He once explained to me seven ways of getting out of sand he had developed to take the place of that hairy blast with a niblick.

Between the First World War and the Second, The Haig was the best-known golfer in the world personally, not excluding Bobby Jones, who seldom socialized with anybody other than his Atlanta cronies and who otherwise preferred the company of straight-arrow businessmen. The Haig hobnobbed with everybody: Babe Ruth, Al Jolson, Grantland Rice, A. D. Lasker, Oliver Hardy, Clarence Budington Kelland, Marshall Field, Jack Dempsey, Harold Lloyd, Ring Lardner, Charlie Chaplin, Warren Harding, Eugene Grace, the Prince of Wales. He didn't so much prefer their company as they did his, and as we drove in his car from Cadillac to Grand Rapids I began to wonder why.

Certainly, it wasn't for his sense of humour. Despite the slapstick life he led, The Haig was not verbally a funny man, his humour consisting mainly of embarrassing puns and practical jokes that never seemed to come off. At a dinner party in New York once, he was introduced to Ernestine Schumann-Heink, the famous contralto from the Metropolitan Opera. The Haig, who had never heard of her nor, surely, she of him, took one look at Mme Schumann-Heink's ample bosom and pulled off what he thought was a jewel of a *bon mot*. 'My dear', he said, 'did you ever stop to think what a lovely bunker you would make?'

On the occasion of his son's twenty-first birthday, to give another example, The Haig sent him a cable from Rangoon made up of stock messages that was 21 pages long. Unfortunately, Junior had only turned twenty.

About half an hour outside of Grand Rapids, I asked The Haig who had known him best out of all the hundreds of people who considered themselves his friend. He thought for a while, and then thought some more, until I began to think he hadn't heard me. Finally, he spoke up. The names he gave me were of a retired milkman back in hometown Rochester, a car dealer in his adopted city of Detroit, and Spec Hammond. 'Pretty soon', he added, 'it might be you.'

We eventually did become close enough to hug one another, although we mutually decided to drop the book project. (True to form, a woman got him to spill the beans in three months.) When The Haig died in 1969, Junior called me from Detroit to tell me there would be no funeral. Instead, a bunch of his cronies were going to throw a party at the Detroit Athletic Club. They thought The Haig would prefer that.

I didn't go. Like Hamlet, golf's sweet prince, I thought, deserved a grander exit than that. He was splendid. They should have carried him out on a shield.

*So far, we have seen two players who are largely unknown today – Douglas Rolland and Willie Anderson but J. Douglas Edgar is just as enigmatic a figure. Harry Vardon predicted that Edgar would become the greatest player of his day after Edgar won the 1914 French Open; many years later Tommy Armour felt that Edgar had succeeded. This man from Newcastle-upon-Tyne has a limited record, however; having reached a peak, he was murdered in Atlanta, Georgia.*

*He left an influential golf instruction book behind him,* The Gate to Golf, *in which he was perhaps the first to preach the importance of swinging from in to out.*

## SIXTEEN STROKES AHEAD
### ROBERT TYRE JONES, 1927

Then I entered the Canadian Open Championship – a bad year for everybody to enter it but the late Douglas Edgar, that strange and fascinating little Englishman who came to the Druid Hills Golf Club that spring and won the Canadian with the lowest score ever recorded for a National Open Championship in any country. He had rounds of 72-71-69-66 – 278, and he was just 16 strokes ahead of Jim Barnes, Karl Keffer and myself, who were tied for second place with 294, a decent and respectable score on the Hamilton course ... I took three putts on the seventy-second green and lost my chance for an unadulterated second place ... What a round that 66 was! I watched most of it, and Douglas was simply playing tricks with the ball, bending it out of bounds to make it come in with a great run toward the green on a dogleg hole; that sort of thing. His approaching was so good that on one green only he had a putt of more than a dozen feet. This was at number 12, a hole of three hundred yards, where he drove the green and missed a long putt for an eagle two. The gallery concluded he had blown up.

*Robert Tyre Jones is unquestionably the greatest amateur golfer ever and the only one to beat all the professionals consistently. The golden boy of his time, Jones was to suffer a painful and crippling disease for the last 20-odd years of his life. With Clifford Roberts he was the founder both of the Masters and of Augusta National.*

## THE PICTURE-POSTCARD GOLFER
### HERBERT WARREN WIND, 1948

Emperor Jones's appearance in a national tourney was the signal for five to eight thousand golfing fanatics to inundate the course and form a tense, idolatrous, noisy, frenetic, marshal-mangling gallery. Each person in the thousands wanted to touch his hero. Fans who couldn't get to the tournaments and who followed Jones's triumph by newspaper and radio felt an almost equal closeness to their hero. During the week of a national championship, the residents of every golfing community in the United States acted as if it were Atlanta. Bobby's victories were their victories, and his defeats were their defeats.

For a man who exerted so compelling a magnetism over American sports fans, Jones was an exceptionally restrained performer. He did not dramatize himself like Tilden or Hagen. He made no appeal to primitive human emotions, like Dempsey. He was no happy extrovert like Ruth. Jones's stupendous popularity – unprecedented in what had been a minor sport until he emerged – rested partially on a skill so apparent that it needed no showboating, and partially on the type of man he was.

There was a clear, cold aesthetic thrill in watching Jones hit a golf ball. The other leading players had excellent form that a duffer could appreciate, and they got results that spoke for themselves. Compared to Jones, though, they didn't look so finished. You noticed a little bumpiness in their back-swing, a vague departure from the blueprint at impact, the expenditure of brute force in the follow-through. You looked at Jones and you saw the copybook form that you and two million other American golfers were striving for. You saw a one-piece swing in which the man had somehow incorporated every 'must' your pro had enumerated – the left arm straight but not rigid on the backswing; the weight shifted from left to right going back and then gradually returned to the left side again as the club started down and the hands moved into position to unleash their power; the hit *through* the ball; the finish with the weight entirely transferred to the left side and the hands high – the million other integrated contributions of the chin, the hips, the balls of the feet, the knees, the grip, the left shoulder, the right ankle, the wrists, the eyes. If you could buckle down and remember to do all those things, then you, too, would play like Jones. No, you couldn't at that. You would always lack that something which lifted Jones above mechanical perfection. It was hard to put your finger on it. It had to do with a certain *je ne sais quoi* quality that made Bobby's swing so rhythmically singular, made it appear so effortless though you knew it was built on effort. Bernard Darwin came as close as anyone to tagging the genius of Jones when he said, without any gingerbread, that there was a strain of poetry in Bobby.

Dissected position by position, Jones's swing was, of course, not markedly different from those employed by the other stars. He did stand with his feet closer together than most of the other champions in order to facilitate the freest, fullest body turn the game has ever known. The shifting of weight is a very unglamorous facet of correct form to the average golfer. He would much rather hear that the key to playing par golf is the sturdy left elbow at contact or the machinations of the big toes. But Jones intimated that if there was any one most-important secret to his success, it was that mundane, colourless chore, the free body turn, on which the correct execution of his shots depended.

A picture-postcard golfer like Jones had few idiosyncrasies. He teed the ball on his drive opposite his left arch, a bit farther forward than most players, since he preferred to hit his wood shots at the beginning of the upswing. He teed the ball high since he inclined toward woods with deep faces about four degrees straighter than the average clubs. He was of the opinion that his pitches from 60 to 125 yards were the weakest department of his game, but none of his rivals noticed this foible. If he had a weakness, it was his periodic unsureness at fading an approach. The shots he thought he hit best were the 3- and 4-irons.

Around the golf course, Jones, who could have gotten away with vanities and eccentricities, behaved as if he were just another golfer. A few soured also-rans griped that Bobby was always given the preferred starting times at the big tournaments. This was true, but it was the doing of the USGA officials, who naturally were aware that Jones was an unrivalled drawing card. Jones's galleries were a trying lot, but no matter how deeply or how often he was disconcerted by individual gestures of love and devotion tendered at the wrong times, he never addressed a rebuking word to the offenders. His rivals were confounded by his regard for their feelings. The first word that came to Tommy Armour's mind in describing Jones was considerate.

Jones had rather simple tastes. There were stretches when he liked to be alone, such as tournament weeks. His evening ritual at these times consisted of two drinks (the first swallowed as he luxuriated in a hot tub), a relaxing dinner with Keeler and one or two other close friends, some conversation or a few chapters in a book like Papini's *Life of Christ* before retiring. But there was nothing prissy about Bobby – or Bob, as he preferred to be called. He loved the atmosphere of the locker room. He enjoyed a good story and told a good story. He used a man's language in expressing his emotions and had a nice gift for inventing phrases to describe his golf. (A hard, dangerous shot, for example, was one which demanded 'sheer delicatessen'. Bobby was an intelligent person – he had studied at Harvard for two years, after getting his BS degree in mechanical engineering at Georgia Tech, and he later prepared for his legal career at Emory Law School. He was a man of many interests, to say the least. He was a good husband, a good father, and a good son. He and his father, 'the Colonel,' got a real kick out of each other. Paul Gallico, one sportswriter who never called a spade a sable instrument for delving, wrapped up Robert Tyre Jones, Jr, as well as anyone when he said of him: 'I have found only one [sports figure] who could stand up in every way as a gentleman as well as a celebrity, a fine, decent human being as well as a newsprint personage, and one who never once since I have known him has let me down in my estimate of him'.

The American sports public didn't know the intimate personal habits of Jones, but what they saw of him was an accurate index of the man. They liked the way he acted in competition. They liked the way he looked – clean-cut, boyish and grown-up at the same time. A decade or so before they had flocked to Ouimet because he was a young American they understood and admired, and it may not be at all excessive to say that they worshipped Jones, and formed an enduring enthusiasm for the game he played, because, of all the heroes in the golden age of sport, he stood forth as the model American athlete.

# THE GREATEST YEAR
## GRANTLAND RICE, 1930

There are two features of the recent Amateur Golf Championship which blend together to make the final story. They show at last how Bobby Jones walked upon the untrod ground of a game always full of uncertainties.

The point is that in the midst of all these uncertainties Bobby Jones was never close to an uncertain turn. He almost gave the appearance of loafing through the championship, putting on pressure when he had to do so, but never crowding himself. Against Johnny Goodman at Pebble Beach last year he lost the first three holes where he started five-six-four, two over par. Against Ross Somerville, a high-grade golfer, in his first start at Merion Jones went out in 33 and finished the round four under par. There was no uncertainty about this match from the start.

\*   \*   \*

Jones started at Sandwich last May in the Walker Cup matches, and never lost a match through the closing days of September at Merion – with two medal play victories over the finest professionals in the game in between, you can see just what is meant by the one man who at last was able to lift himself above the uncertainties and inconsistencies of a game that at one time or another takes them all by the throat and leaves them throttled on the field. It has taken Bobby Jones by the throat more than once. But through his famous five-month campaign of 1930 he was at last able to shake himself loose from the grim grip that marks the game.

Just consider these cold and unbiased facts: starting early last April in the Southeastern Open at Augusta, Bobby Jones led a field of crack professionals, including Horton Smith, Gene Sarazen, Johnny Farrell, Al Espinoza, Ed Dudley and many others, by 13 strokes in 72 holes of medal play. He led a fine field at Hoylake in 72 holes through the British Open. He led a stronger field at Interlachen through 72 holes in the United States Open. He led the amateurs through 36 holes of medal play at Merion. Here you have a test of 252 holes at medal play against the finest professionals and amateurs in golf on both sides of the Atlantic. Jones finished in front at every start.

What about match play? Jones won his match at Sandwich in the Walker Cup play. He won eight matches in the British Amateur. He won five matches in the United States Amateur, making a total of 13 matches, most of them over the shorter 18-hole route, where almost anything can happen.

When you consider these two records at medal and match play and recall again how quickly golfing form and the touch of the game can grow sour and stale, you begin to get a better idea of the job he handled through this season, through the almost endless strain that started at Augusta and then ran through Sandwich, St Andrews, Hoylake, Interlachen and Merion. In any other game, this record might not be listed as such an outstanding feat. In tennis, for example, if you can beat an opponent somewhat decisively one day, you can beat him the next day – or next month. Form and touch and timing don't vary so suddenly.

But golf is a different sort of game. It comes and goes. Even with Tommy Armour's wonderful 1930 record, he lost his touch at Interlachen after opening with a 70. Even the smooth swinging Mac Smith had one or two off days in tournament play. The records of Armour and Smith were phenomenal. In some respects they reached even more brilliant heights, at their best, than anything the season showed. But for unadorned consistency, the final test along the top plateau of the game, the all-season record of Bobby Jones goes far and away beyond anything golf ever knew before. And in his final stand, where the strain is usually the hardest, there was almost no contest. It was a week of slaughter.

\* \* \*

The results were obtained with an ease and grace that were born in the system. Of the thousands of pictures taken of Bobby Jones, no one can recall an awkward pose, an awkward swing, a sign of effort beyond control.

*If one could say – without stretching emotion too far – that Jones's golf was touched by God, his last 20 years were cursed to the same extent.*

## STRENGTH OF MIND
### HERBERT WARREN WIND, 1972

In the 1960s, when Jones was confined to a wheelchair, the word went round each winter that his condition had become worse, and everyone in golf speculated on whether he would be able to attend that year's Masters. He had suffered from heart trouble since 1952, and now that, too, became increasingly debilitating. Somehow he got to Augusta each April, though by then his body had so wasted away that he weighed scarcely 90 pounds. His arms were no bigger around than a broomstick, and he could no longer open his fingers to shake hands or grasp a pen. Yet this indomitable man kept going. For many years on the day before the start of the Masters, I called in on him in company with Ed Miles, of the Atlanta *Journal*, and Al Laney, of the New York *Herald Tribune*, who was one of his oldest and closest friends. We would walk over to Jones's cottage, near the tenth tee, torn by mixed feelings – the prospect of pleasure and the prospect of sorrow.

Mrs Jones or their son Bob or his wife, Frances, would be there to greet us. There would be a few cordially jumbled minutes during which personal news was exchanged and it was computed how many people wanted Coca-Cola and whether they wanted it in a glass or out of the bottle. By this time, Jones would have appeared and would be contriving a seating arrangement that enabled him to see everyone. He never looked as bad as you dreaded he might. While his body had withered to nothing, his handsome head and features remained relatively untouched, and his mind was as good as ever. We would ask him all sorts of questions we had stored up about new golfers and old tournaments, and he would answer them with amusement and flair. You could listen to him all day; he had the same feeling for words as Adlai Stevenson, and the same wonderful self-depreciatory sense of humour. Inevitably, as the session continued you became aware that you and your friends were doing all the talking – telling Jones what you had been up to and what you thought about this and that. Jones did not bring this about by any conscious technique; he simply was extremely interested in what his friends were doing, and you felt this interest. Leaving was always hard. When he put his twisted folded-up hand in yours as you said goodbye, you never knew whether you would be seeing him again. Each year when Miles and Laney and I left the cottage, we would walk 75 yards or so – nearly to the practice green – before we exchanged a word. My God, we felt good at that moment! We were so proud of Bob Jones! There was no need to feel sorry for a man like that. If *he* could rise above his misfortune *you* could jolly well rise above his misfortune. I think that everyone who called on him responded this way.

Jones did not like his friends to talk about his illness, and they honoured his wishes as best they could. However, in writing to him shortly after the 1968 Masters to ask a favour of him, I mentioned in closing how sorry I was that he had not been well enough to go out on the course in his golf-cart and watch some of the play, as he usually did, and to attend the presentation ceremony, at which he customarily presided. In his reply, which I received the following week, he wrote, after dealing with the main subject:

> Really, I am not as far down the well physically as I appeared to be in Augusta. I picked up an intestinal virus a week or ten days before the Masters and could not shake the thing, even with a course of antibiotics. Even with that, I could perhaps have done a bit more than I did. Had I known in time that the score-card episode was going to be present, I most certainly would have appeared at the presentation, both on television and on the putting green. This happened to be the one time that I felt I should have lent the weight of whatever authority I possess to these occasions.

From that paragraph, one would have assumed that, the virus past, Jones was now back in the pink of condition.

A few days later, I received another letter from Jones. The score-card episode he had referred to in the first note was, of course, the one involving

Roberto de Vicenzo and Bob Goalby in the Masters that year. Goalby and de Vicenzo had apparently finished the tournament in a tie with totals of 277. However, de Vicenzo's playing partner, Tommy Aaron, had written down a four, and not the three that de Vicenzo had made, as his score on the seventeenth; de Vicenzo had signed the card; and, under Rule 38, Paragraph 3, de Vicenzo had to be charged with the four. This gave him a total of 278, and Goalby was declared the winner. In my account of the tournament, I had attacked Rule 38 as a bad rule. Jones had this to say:

> I find myself differing with you in your stand on the propriety of Rule 38 under modern conditions. You make the point that in an event like the Masters, with hundreds of spectators at each hole and millions more watching on television, everybody knows the score.
>
> You may recall that on two occasions in Open Championship play, I ordered a stroke added to my score. In both instances, there were several hundred spectators around the green and, in each case, I had a scorer or marker, in addition to my playing companion. Both these men on both occasions were standing within 15 feet of me. Yet each time I had to call the marker's attention to the extra stroke; and on one occasion this gentleman went so far as to appeal to the committee after the round, affirming that my ball had not moved. There is scarcely any way the spectators around the green and no way the viewers on television could know that de Vicenzo had not inadvertently moved his ball and reported the fact to Aaron between the seventeenth green and the eighteenth tee ...
>
> Believe me, I was thinking not only of de Vicenzo but of Goalby as well. Whereas de Vicenzo was the player penalized, both men were deprived of the opportunity to win the tournament in outright competition. This was as bad for one as for the other.
>
> The whole situation was tragic beyond expression. I like to think, though, that it serves one useful purpose in emphasizing the respect which golfers must have for the rule book.

I find it pleasant to quote from these letters, because they so vividly evoke Jones's personality and his manner of expressing himself. He must have been one of the great letter writers of our time. Whenever one wrote to him – and my guess is that literally hundreds of people, from Sarazen, his exact contemporary, to youngsters just starting competitive golf, did so quite regularly – he answered very promptly and with obvious thought and care. It is an understatement to say that the arrival of a letter on the distinctive heavy bond stationery he used, with its familiar Poplar Street letterhead, could make your day.

While I gather from medical authorities that it would be wrong to credit Jones with living on for years after the average person would have picked up his ball and torn up his score-card – how long anyone lives is not necessarily dictated by his will to live, they say – Jones deserves incalculable credit for how he lived out his life. Where he got the courage and energy to do all that he did there is no knowing. However, I think that Hogan put his finger on at least a part of the answer when he said, shortly after Jones's death, 'The man was sick so long, and fought it so successfully, that I think we have finally discovered the secret of Jones's success. It was the strength of his mind.'

About three days before Jones's death, when he knew he was dying, he said to the members of his family, 'If this is all there is to it, it sure is peaceful'. That is good to know. We were lucky we had Jones so long, for he had a rare gift for passing ideas and ideals on to other people. I think he probably enriched more lives than anyone else I have known. He enriched mine beyond measure.

*With the vast increase in competitive opportunities for women in the US, and increasingly in Europe, since the Second World War, it is difficult to believe in the stature of Joyce Wethered. She was undoubtedly the best woman player before the war and Bobby Jones considered her the best player of either sex.*

# THE GREATEST?
## O. B. KEELER, 1937

Bobby and his party met Miss Wethered and Miss Shaw at the airport – it was the English girls' first journey by plane, and they liked it so well they would have said they were crazy about it, had they been American girls – and at dinner that evening Miss Wethered and Bobby talked golf incessantly and she told him how Bobby Cruickshank had suggested a change in her putting grip for the American greens – the reverse-overlap; it appeared to me almost identical with that suggested to Bobby so long ago by the late Walter Travis; and Tuesday was fair, and a fine gallery turned out to see the match at old East Lake.

From the start it was easy to see that the two principal figures were 'putting out' – to employ the vernacular. I have watched many exhibition matches, but none like this one. Miraculously, Bobby's putting touch, deplorably off-colour these later years, had returned, as he laid a long one dead over the tricky Bermuda at the first green and holed a 30-footer for a deuce at the second, to put his side two up.

And Miss Wethered, hitting 240 yards into a light headwind, laid her pitch four feet from the flag at the third and holed the putt for a three, while at the 565-yard fifth, down the wind, she was level with Bobby in two great wood shots, just in front of the green, and squared with another fine wee pitch and a seven-footer, for a birdie four. Then it was Bobby again, who holed a 15-footer for a birdie three at the seventh, and pitched dead for another birdie three at the eighth; and then Miss Wethered, just short of the green with two wood shots at the 506-yard ninth, gained back a hole with an exquisite little approach that left her no putt at all.

Bobby was out in 34. Miss Wethered was out in par 36. And in the popeyed gallery people hammered each other on the back, and called attention to the fact that Bobby Jones with a 34 was just one up on the English girl. Between them they had a best-ball of 31, and while Dorothy Kirby and Charlie Yates were playing admirable golf – the 15-year-old Atlanta girl did a 41 from the back tees – the combat was between the two greatest golfers, and that was what all the gallery had come out to see, though never expecting anything so utterly dazzling as this.

And Miss Wethered, driving level with Bobby across the lake and up the long hill of the tenth fairway, squared the match for her side, and with Bobby, at the tenth. And she was square also with par of the East Lake course from the back tees, through the thirteenth, where the little Dorothy, with an exquisitely placed wood second, catching the run of the narrow apron to the bunker-surrounded green missed a four-foot putt for a birdie three that would have been a hole won all by herself, in that company!

Miss Wethered's driving was simply tremendous. The wind was coming up, and when facing it she was hitting a low, raking drive of great carry and astonishing run. And at the fourteenth, a hole of 448 yards, there was, for the moment, a half-gale coming out of the west, straight in her face. And there – well, Bobby and Charlie Yates struck off two of their best, and Miss Wethered's ball was well in front.

Against the sweeping wind Miss Wethered was flag-high with her second shot, the ball curling off to the left into a bunker. And here ensued the most whimsical play of all the afternoon.

Miss Wethered, of course, was unfamiliar with East Lake bunkers in summer, or at any other time. This was her first recovery off what looked to her as if it might be sand. She essayed a good, substantial half-blast with the niblick, and the blade, ricocheting from the sun-baked surface under a thin layer of sand, clipped the ball fairly in the back and sent it flying 50 yards over the green and the gallery, to the frank amazement of the latter and no less of Miss Wethered herself.

But she trotted down into a little valley, found the ball in a difficult place, pitched back beautifully, almost hitting the flag – and holed a 20-foot putt for a five, to be a stroke above par, while Bobby won the hole with a four.

Charlie mopped his brow. 'This is the first time', he said, puzzled, 'I ever played 14 holes as a lady's partner before I ever figured in one.' He reflected further, and added: 'Well, as long as she's carrying me around on her back, I'll just try not to let my feet drag!'

They halved the 413-yard sixteenth with four all around, Miss Wethered nearly holing a five-yard putt for a three, and Charlie, in pursuance of his announced policy, squared at the seventeenth, when Bobby's long drive was hooked to a ditch by the roadway, and Miss Wethered, for the second time on the strange Bermuda greens, took three putts.

And then came the climax of a great match. The eighteenth hole at East Lake is two hundred yards, across the lake, from a hillside tee to a hilltop green. 'I know a one-shot finishing hole is not usually well regarded', Big Bob Jones, Bobby's father, once said to me. 'But when a player stands on that tee at East Lake, with the match square, or dormie – that drive calls for all there is, in the delicatessen department.'

Miss Wethered drove first, a spoon into the wind, and her ball was dead on the line, stopping 20 feet in front of the flag. Yates' shot was the same distance from the pin. Dorothy's was short and to the right. Bobby's was shoved a bit, and his wee pitch from the side of the hill caught the slope and trickled down five yards below the hole. Dorothy came on for a four. Miss Wethered putted, and just missed a two. Charlie likewise. And the gallery pressed closer, for it was up to Bobby.

Odd, how the film spins back on the reel of memory to a certain scene, at a certain time. As I stood there watching Bobby line up that putt, I saw him again on the same green, and in the same spot, at the close of a round in the famous Southern Open, eight years before – the tournament he won from a great field, with eight strokes to spare, on his home course. And I saw him sink that putt, eight years ago, and then – well, then the roar of that faraway gallery went out under the roar of the gallery that stood all about me. For Bobby sank this putt, too. And the match was square.

Nothing devised in a scenarist's shop at Hollywood could have helped that climax. Bobby had done a par 71, on his home course. Miss Wethered, a 74. The little Dorothy, in the most distinguished company in which she will ever play, an 84. And Charlie Yates, at last travelling on his own feet in the pinch, a 76.

Miss Wethered's play was beyond praise. On Bermuda greens – more than a score of years ago characterized by one of her countrymen, Ted Ray, as 'not grawss but grapevines' – which she then saw for the first time, she had needed three putts twice, and she had been a trifle off-line with two drives. And that was all that stood between Joyce Wethered and a level 70, the first afternoon she had seen the 6,600-yard East Lake course.

*     *     *

Going down the fairway toward the sixteenth green, I was walking momentarily with Miss Wethered, and, naturally, I was complimenting her on her brilliant play. She smiled and then became suddenly grave. 'I had to play well here', she said, simply, 'Bobby arranged the match, you know. And he's said and written so many kind things about my game. And then he was ill, and then he insisted on playing ... I wish I were sure he *should* be playing, now ... It's – it's the most sporting thing I've ever known. I had to play well, at East Lake. I couldn't let Bobby down, you know.'

Yes – I knew. And I know, too, that I saw something that afternoon at East Lake that will stand out as the prettiest picture of a lifetime in sport – the two greatest golfers, playing all they knew in every shot, in generous and gallant complement to one another, in the greatest match I ever witnessed.

# The Silver Fox

## CLARENCE BUDINGTON KELLAND, 1935

Tommy Armour has a mouth like a steel trap, a nose like a ski jump, hands like the fins of a shark, and eyes which indicate he would enjoy seeing you get a compound fracture of the leg. He also plays golf. He is, in addition, a businessman.

Although it is a fact that Tommy came to this country as an amateur, he had all the qualifications necessary to elevate him to the top ranks of the professional, and among these was an acid gift of salesmanship. There are few more entertaining sights than to see Tommy go to work on a new member – or even a visitor to the shop. The first time I ever watched his methods, they were turned loose on me. I am able to speak from sad experience.

You come into the shop and meet Mr Armour. He does not fall on your neck in raptures of joy. There is little if anything of the effusive in his make-up. Instead of that, he peers at you with basilisk eyes calculating the strength of your sales-resistance and estimating your possibilities as a customer and as a human being. He snaps off a couple of Scottish consonants and then walks over to your golf bag and picks out your driver. You watch with interest. He waggles the club; he grips it; then he holds it out in front of him with a gesture so eloquent that you begin to shrivel inside your clothes and to wish you had gone to Chicago instead.

He never so much as glances at you again, but his tanned, angular face takes on an expression of such utter scorn – mixed with a trifle of sorrow – that you feel exactly as if you had been caught stealing a blanket off the baby's bed on a cold night. He puts your driver back in the bag gently – so gently! – and then walks away with dragging steps, as if there were things in the world too terrible for the human mind to consider.

If you turn then and run you may be saved; but if, as ninety-nine men out of a hundred will do, you ask what's the matter with your driver, you are lost. 'Nothing', says Tommy. 'Nothing at all.'

'It's a darned good driver', you say.

'What do ye play around in?' Tommy asks.

'Ninety', you say.

'I wonder at it', says Tommy, with just the hint of a side glance at your golf bag.

By that time you are convinced that you are unclean and unfit for human society. You are marked as an outsider, a Pariah, a leper, by that golf club. You know no gentleman would play with such a tool, and that to go out on a golf course with it is a more shameful thing than teeing up your ball in the rough.

'What's wrong with it?' you insist.

'Look at my one', says Mr Armour, and you find yourself with a club in your hands. He never says, 'Take a look at mine', it is always 'my one'. Then, saddened by so much inefficiency in the world he says pitifully, 'Who sold you such a set of clubs?'.

That will be about the finish. Presently you walk out of the shop with three new woods, a full set of irons and a putter – and a date to take a number of lessons from Mr Armour at an unpleasantly early hour when you really want to sleep. They say he is the greatest iron player of all time. Maybe. Me, I say his chief claim to fame is salesmanship.

It has been my privilege to play with him daily for weeks at a stretch. Once I played nine successive rounds with him over the exceedingly long and difficult South Course at Boca Raton. His highest score for that series was 69. And it was all under greater pressure than he has ever been in in an Open Championship, because I was his opponent, and we were playing five dollar Nassaus with me getting a stroke a hole – and his endeavour was to make a better and nobler and wiser man of me. He did.

Tommy never says an unkind thing to anybody accidentally; if he drops acid on you it is because he wants to. He never flatters, and he never falls on anybody's neck. But if he likes you you find it out. I wouldn't know just how you find it out, because he doesn't tell you, or show you. But in some mysterious, dour, ingrowing way he lets you know you are in – and then, if you are a member of the lodge in good standing, you feel honoured. For, among a number of things, Tommy Armour is a gentleman, and a judge of human critters, and a sportsman, and a conversationalist, and a drinker of beer. He makes observations. He is temperamental as a soprano with a frog in her throat, but at the same time he keeps both his feet on the ground. And, in spite of his being dour, sour, acid, vertiginous, and endowed with special and painful brands of poison, he is the sort of companion you would travel miles to sit with.

Tommy Armour is a great golfer – a superlative golfer. But he is something more than that – he is a personage. He has what it takes to stand out from the herd. There have been moments when I would like to shove an icicle through his cold heart; there have been moments when I wish his confounded Scottish consonants would split splinters off his front teeth; but for all that, at any time, I will take a long train ride to spend an evening with him. And I'm pretty choosy about whom I get shut in a room with alone for more than 15 minutes. I guess I like him.

*Great players are not necessarily great competitors. Abe Mitchell and Dai Rees were arguably the best players to fail to win the Open Championship, and Sam Snead was in the same sad position regarding the US Open, yet there is another man whose failure was even greater. In a quarter of a century of attempts, the British and US Opens and the US PGA all escaped Macdonald Smith, but at least he overcame alcoholism along the way.*

# The Sweetest Swinger

## TOMMY ARMOUR, 1935

Genius, scorned, shivering and empty-bellied in an attic; Pagliacci bellowing a laugh from his heavy heart; Mac Smith splitting ten thousand fairways and never winning a National Open Championship. Art mocks the artist.

Macdonald Smith is the master artist of golf and the art of golf has denied him national championships. This fickle and utterly irrational art has crowned as its rulers men who, as the game's artists, are merely caddies compared to the master.

I can't explain it. Mac has a remarkable competitive record. But when he wins 50 tournaments with rounds of golf played as perfectly as a tranquil dream, some fellow slugs, pats and bounces the ball for 72 holes to win just one championship and fame, because that one championship is a National Open which defies Smith.

Don't tell me that Mac hasn't a golfing temperament. He has the most ideal golfing temperament providence ever put in a man's bosom. Mac, who has seen and felt and heard Open title after Open title snatched right out of his grasp, and walked into the clubhouse calm and uncomplaining, is not the fellow to be upset when a few shots along a 72-hole route go wrong. You can't explain the mystery of Mac Smith to me by pointing out any deficiency in his game, because there simply isn't any.

Macdonald Smith's career has spanned that of three brilliant reigns in golf. When the Vardon sun was shining bright and high, Mac was great. When the blaze of Hagen was in the skies, Mac was great. When the radiance of Jones shone over the game, Mac was great. Macdonald Smith still is great.

Until he is 60 I will believe Mac Smith has an excellent chance to overcome the impudence of destiny and win a national title. Until Mac is 90 I'll be hoping that he wins the United States or British Open Championship. I've had a bet on Mac Smith in every National Open Championship he's played in. Recall, please, that the Scots wager on judgement rather than on sentiment. In my judgement Mac is the game's supreme shot-making artist.

In my heart Mac is perennial American and British National Open monarch and I know, from a very uncomfortable recollection, when frustration again put its finger on him to take a title away from him and hand it to me.

It was at Carnoustie when Mac finished five-six-five and the British Open Championship went to me. I didn't know which way to look when Mac came up to me. I knew deep in me that the title belonged to Mac. I felt very humble myself and that's not a frequent experience with me. All I could get out was, 'Tough luck, Mac'. Mac took my hand and pressed it until the fingers flattened. He smiled philosophically. 'It wasn't meant this time. Tommy m'lad, ye deserved to win.' I felt like screaming out 'Don't give it to me, Mac won it'. At no other moment in all the time I've played and won in golf tournaments, was I so depressed as when I saw Mac Smith walk into the clubhouse at Carnoustie, again the patient victim of the unkind gods of golf.

Never before – or since – in golf has there been such a gallery as there was the last day at Prestwick in the 1925 British Open. Estimates of the crowd varied. Some experts guessed it at twenty thousand; other as high as thirty thousand. Mac was due to be crowned. It was a stampeding, shoving, frantically partisan throng that came to help and witness Mac achieve his life's ambition. Instead it saw and sensed the drama of a noble man with the hand of fate tearing out his heart. Macdonald Smith, the master, took an 82. It's still unbelievable to me, that horrifying last round of Mac's.

But here I am, sympathizing with Mac Smith when he's really one of mankind most to be envied. Mac has peace in his heart. He has triumphed over ill-health and over Mac Smith. He has won more all by himself than he ever could win – or any other man could win – on any golf course.

Smith is no Caledonian tragedy even though he often has been batted back a step away from golf's heights. When you look at Mac, or at pictures of him, you may be fooled. He has the firm, dour features of an Inquisition fanatic. Inside, he's gentler and kinder than Santa Claus.

He is no glad-hander. He's shy. But he is the most courteous of hosts and listeners. He has been trapped and bounced around by fate so often himself that he is considerate and forgiving when others fall short, even though their failure may be due to causes that others consider unforgivable.

The crowd means nothing to Mac; the man, everything. Maybe it was the crowd that beat him that time at Carnoustie. It probably was the crowd that beat him out of a title at Prestwick. You'll never hear explanations or alibis for defeat from Mac. His nerves may be fighting him, but you'll never know it. He is a self-contained, high-hearted and unsurrendering fatalist.

Mac's comeback is something unique in sports. At one time he was through – through as completely and as conclusively as an athlete can be. The jitters had him. There was hopelessness in his carriage and in his eyes. He pulled himself together and thought and fought. Mac Smith won. He won something far more important than a dozen National Open Championships. He won Mac Smith.

A strange thing about it to me is that religion is said to have had a lot to do with it. Mac should be an agnostic by all the rules of human conduct. The gods have thumbed their noses at him so often he could be pardoned for thinking that he owes them no respect. If getting religion had something to do with it, you'll never know it by hearing Mac talk about salvation. He minds his own business and lets you mind yours.

Perhaps that's why Macdonald Smith, stylist of all stylists, hasn't had the effect he should have on the technique of the game. He is too retiring to be a missionary for his own ideas. Other good golfers marvel at his style and deliberately or unconsciously try to imitate it, but he never gets loquacious about how he plays, so golf writers find it easy to write about his methods.

Only his intimate friend and brother Scot, D. Scott Chisholm, among all the golf writers, has much close-up material on Mac.

The Smith swing is as bonnie as Maxwelton's braes. It's as graceful, as smooth and as apparently effortless as the swooping glide of a gull through the blue sky. Only Mac Smith can play a shot the Mac Smith way. I've not thought of it before, but that may be the reason why Mac hasn't been the author or interviewee on many golf instruction tracts.

If we all played golf like Mac, the National Open Championship could be played on one course every day in the year and never a divot mark would scar the beautiful fairway. He has the cleanest 21-jewel stroke in golf. He treats the grass of a golf course as though it were an altar cloth.

So here you have my Mac Smith, a great character who, but for the force and clarity of his own mind, might have been forgotten as a genius born to swing unsung or in contempt as a crying specimen of a frustrated man.

Open champion or not, Mac has the dignity of a true champion, the mien of a monarch and the deepest respect of all who know him. There is no luck to that and there is luck – plenty of it – in winning National Opens.

*Bobby Jones and Walter Hagen were undoubtedly the outstanding players of their time. Eugene Saraceni, who thought 'Gene Sarazen' a better handle for a golfer, ranked just below them.*

## The Cocky Little Champion
### HERB GRAFFIS, 1975

Perhaps the most famous of the youngsters who came out of the Westchester County golf nursery, and certainly an inspiration to hundreds of caddies with similar backgrounds, was Gene Sarazen. As legendary a golf figure as Walter Hagen in his own special way, the spunky, stocky Gene seems to have stalked the fairways forever and ever in his unmistakable knickers. They became his trademark long after the vogue for plus fours had died unlamented. Just like other caddies of Italian origin, though, he had to struggle while getting started in golf. In and around the New York, Boston, and Philadelphia areas, the rough, tough boys of Irish parentage had clearly staked first claim to the available caddying jobs, and other kids encroached at their peril.

However, the home professionals, almost all of whom came from Scotland and England, wisely refrained from taking sides in the caddy rivalry. They were more than willing to give a break to any boy who looked, listened, and performed well. One of them was Fred Biscelli, who was the Larchmond Country Club pro, greenkeeper, and caddy-master when eight-year-old Eugene Saraceni took that 40-minute trolley ride from Harrison to Larchmont and made his debut as a caddy in 1910. The little boy was introduced by Danny, Fred's younger brother – Gene wisely began knowing the right people early in the game.

Caddying at the nine-hole Larchmont course was dull and financially unrewarding because there wasn't enough play. In 1913, after three years when his talents hadn't filled his pockets, Gene switched to the busier Apawamis Club at Rye to give its members the benefit of his services. Golf clearly fascinated the boy; he'd practise swings and hit a ball on that four-mile walk from Harrison to his new job at Apawamis. The caddy-master at Apawamis was George Hughes, a descendant of a long line of Irish kings and not the first and most fervent of the Sarazen fans. Gaelic kids like the late Ed Sullivan were his pets. It is funny to think of little Eddie Sullivan, his bright and smiling face charming one and all around the first tee, growing up to work for years as the awkward, heart-of-gold ringmaster of the longest-running television vaudeville show on record.

As a 15-year-old, Gene went into factory work during World War I under plenty of family economic pressure. His father was a scholarly man, displaced and soured and a loser in a new land; his mother was one of those endearing women whose skillet and smile shine through the ages. An overworked teenager in a factory job, Sarazen took sick. When he beat pneumonia after receiving the last rites prematurely, he regained enough health and drive to get a job with Al Ciuci, then pro at Beardsley Park, a nine-hole pasture course at Bridgeport, Connecticut. He received no wages. The pay consisted mainly of what Gene could hustle from other golfers, and no doubt the brash, personable, highly competitive youngster more than held his own.

Al Ciuci helped Gene work out a fundamentally sound golf game, although Sarazen's grip and other elements of his technique weren't orthodox in the Scottish manner. But Gene was an experimenter from the beginning. As might be expected, Italian-Americans stuck together and Al Ciuci soon pushed his young friend onto George Sparling, a big, taciturn Scot who was pro at Brooklawn, the top club in Bridgeport. Sparling, a rather good player, wasn't eager to hire the Sarazen kid as an assistant, but when two of the club's leading members, the twin brothers Archie and Willie Wheeler, showed a favourable interest in the lad, Sparling did the discreet thing and took Sarazen on as a shop boy. The big Scot soon became impressed by Sarazen's play and mentioned it favourably, but not to Gene. That was not an uncommon attitude in those days; the pro wanted to hold his job, and eager youngsters wanted to get it. Who could blame either one? In the case of Brooklawn, Sparling knew the Wheeler brothers carried weight, and Gene also sensed that.

The kid had to do plenty of infighting to get ahead, but he knew that the odds didn't favour the nice little 'pardon-me' boys in his league. He showed that understanding again when he got a job as assistant to Ramsey Hunter, professional at the Fort Wayne Country Club, after his first winter in Florida where Bill Goebel, pro at the Charlotte (North Carolina) Country Club, and Alec Gerard, winter professional at the Lake Wales (Florida) Golf Club befriended him and gave him the chance to improve his game.

Flocks of pros went South for the winter, depending on free playing privileges at private and public courses. They hustled members for bets and playing lessons, beat the pros at host clubs out of business, and so often conducted themselves crudely and rudely as club guests that they wore out their welcome. Few of the young migrant pros were educated in the amenities – nor were they even average at reading and writing – but they were fond of playing golf in the Southland's winter sunshine instead of having to contend with hard work in the Northern winters. Besides, back home, jobs for fellows who wanted to quit as soon as spring arrived weren't easy to get.

Older professionals to whom good manners came by early training or instinct were embarrassed by the winter visitors who called themselves professionals. As a result of their thoughtless actions, what had been hospitality was replaced by limitations on the pro tourists at private clubs down South. The restrictions were undeserved and humiliating for the majority of experienced professionals who went South in the winter and whose personalities and conduct contributed to the enjoyment of the club's members and their amateur guests and pleasantly extended the service of the resident professional. And they were undeserved in the case of Gene Sarazen as well. Public relations as such wasn't stressed then, but while the screening of youngsters most likely to succeed in pro golf was taking place in the 1920s, the bright Sarazen kid was doing something to distinguish and advance himself. He was writing thank-you letters and postcards.

Sarazen was the first, and possibly still the champion, at writing to influential people who had been gracious to him. They might be amateurs who were successful businessmen, important club officials, or sportswriters he'd met here or there – all of them rated a pleasant acknowledgement. Gene was his own best press agent, and no other celebrated professional golfer ever had a busier or better one. His paperwork went ahead of him in getting pro jobs at Titusville, Pennsylvania, at the Highland Country Club, Pittsburgh, at the Fresh Meadow Country Club on Long Island, at Lakeville, and at other clubs where he has been pro in residence. The Highland job was his first big break, and he got that by showing appreciation by mail to Emil ('Dutch') Loeffler, the pro-greenkeeper at Oakmont who was the top sergeant of the noted W. C. ('Bill') Fownes, Jr, the 1910 national amateur champion who became president of the USGA.

Always a realist, Tommy Armour observed that he'd never seen Gene spend more than five minutes with somebody who couldn't do him some good. 'And that's no sin', Armour added. 'I wish I were that way myself.'

Young Sarazen's capacity for identifying himself with the right people was again in evidence when some members of the Fort Wayne Country Club who'd been impressed by his scoring paid his way to the Open at Inverness in Toledo in 1920. Inverness that year was possibly the greatest debut party in the history of American tournament golf. Playing in the National Open for the first time were Sarazen, Leo Diegel, Bob Jones, Tommy Armour, Bill Mehlhorn, and Johnny Farrell. Ted Ray of England won with 295, one stroke ahead of his travelling companion from England, Harry Vardon. Leo

Diegel, of the Lake Shore Club in suburban Chicago, tied for third with Jack Burke, one of the young Irish professionals from Philadelphia.

Sarazen should have been the first of the millionaire pros. He was willing to work for money and play all the possible angles. His club jobs weren't the sort he thought would make him rich; they demanded that he work too hard on the members' games instead of on his own. That was not for Gene. Or for Walter Hagen. It was deadly boring work. The only one of the famous playing professionals who ever did brilliantly well at a club professorial job was Armour. He found teaching – for a few hours a day – a challenge and a stimulation. Tommy was fond of both.

Gene was driven by bossiness and ambition, and a club pro job is no place for those traits to flower. So, after his victory in the 1922 National Open at the Skokie Country Club, where he registered as pro from the Highland Country Club at Pittsburgh, it was inevitable that the Sarazen career as a club professional was mutually less than agreeable. He was not yet America's sweetheart. When he'd beaten John Black, a rather elderly Scot, and Bob Jones, pride of the newborn South, by a stroke at Skokie, there were mutterings about a drive at the seventy-first hole that wasn't decisively within the premises. In 1922, when he beat Emmet French, four and three, in the final at Oakmont, Sarazen began to register as a young man who had really arrived. In 1923, when he won the PGA by defeating Hagen in two extra holes, there again was a question of an out-of-bounds shot. He was really one of the greats then, but the narrowness of his wins and his disposition to regard himself as 'picked on' instead of glorified was a soft spot in his acute sense of public relations. That was corrected eventually, when he won the British Open decisively in 1932 at Prince's Sandwich, over Macdonald Smith, by five strokes.

Then came a spectacular finish at Fresh Meadow in the 1932 US National Open, when he beat Bobby Cruickshank and Phil Perkins by three strokes. His victory in the 1933 PGA against Willie Goggin, five and four, was colourless. Both finalists were good golfers, but Willie was a 'Who's he?' and Gene had finally arrived at the top. He had mastered himself as well as the other fellows.

Mechanically, Sarazen wasn't a stylist. Psychologically, he was in command of the golf ball. In a crisis he could play better than he knew how. He had the rare quality of learning from mistakes, and he seldom made the same error twice. He was eager for publicity. Golf writers used to say that Gene would jump naked off the torch of the Statue of Liberty to get his name in the papers. He'd get an idea about an eight-inch cup for a golf tournament. That was something to talk about in the winter, but in effect, the idea was to make golf so easy that any one of a myriad clumsy slobs could win. The big cup idea was used in a Florida tournament one winter. It was a very dull bust in publicity, and Gene, a bright lad who didn't want to ride a loser, got off that hunch.

Gene was the first of the champions to criticize the architecture of a golf course. Previously, professionals had accepted courses as fields of competition they all had to play, and if any contestant thought the course had him licked at the start, he could jolly well stay away and keep his mouth shut. Gene popped off about a National Open Championship course and was knocked right out of bounds by the late Westbrook Pegler, then a hard-hitting sports reporter. Pegler wrote one of his classic barbecue columns, in which he remarked that, if the ex-caddy didn't like the course on which he was being allowed to play, with an opportunity of far higher reward than was possible by genuine work, why didn't he have the decent manners *not* to play on it, but to join the club, pay his dues, and dig into his pockets to provide money for remaking the course the way he wanted it? 'Otherwise', said Peg, 'why doesn't he shut up? He is boring.' That devastating observation ended all Sarazen criticism of championship courses. Here Gene displayed better judgement than has been shown by latter-day professionals whose snide comments on course conditions have accounted for the reluctance of first-class clubs to be hosts to tournaments.

Sarazen seemed to enjoy playing with businessmen golfers and quickly and comfortably getting them over their stage fright, regardless of what scores they were making. That valuable quality and the business sense he acquired as he grew up led him into profitable connections as a contact man for industrial organizations. Gene would play with executives of companies his employer was trying to sell, and run interference for sales engineers who were carrying the ball.

He got the itch to travel and made a couple of tours of South America and the Orient with Joe Kirkwood, the famous trick-shot artist. And he had more than the customary excursions of American professionals after their British Open working trip. His double eagle at the Masters followed by his win of the play-off against Craig Wood could have been just another one of those lucky things. It happened late on a Sunday afternoon, and the comparatively few writers covering the 1935 event, the second Masters, had virtually finished their stories when Sarazen holed an incredible 220-yard, 4-wood shot after his drive at the par-five, 485-yard fifteenth, then went on to finish in even par. The tournament itself wasn't much to write about. Without Jones playing spectacularly as the host, the competition was pretty much a Jones social affair about which the general golfing public couldn't have cared less.

Instead of the Sarazen double eagle's being given quick treatment as a substitute lead by sportswriters unhappy about having to stay through a Monday round at Augusta, it was given a big play by Alan Gould, sports editor of the Associated Press. Gould, a skilled worker, realized there was no big sports story for a Monday at that time of the year, so he made the spectacular Sarazen shot the topic that called for a ribbon head across the page. When the other reporters – a dozen or so of them – saw Gould working hard, they shrewdly guessed that Alan was building up a story that might have their editors asking, 'How come the AP made a big story out of what you handled as just another tie to be decided later?'

Gould's decision to grab the Sarazen exploit as a feature for an otherwise dead Monday, plus the continued astute plugging of Cliff Roberts, the Masters Tournament committee chairman and the canniest planner, manager, and publicist tournament golf has ever had, gave Sarazen a tremendous boost. For years he had the asset of the top ballyhoo of any one circus shot in the game.

That one stroke was the richest in golf, not only in the news space it got through the years, but in the way it kept Sarazen qualified for profitable sidelines. With only his 1958 PGA Senior title identifying him as still swinging, Gene was brought back to golf's spotlight by his job with Shell's 'Wonderful World of Golf' television series. This television golf show was the most attractive and durable golf entertainment ever aired. It combined international golf competition, scenery, close-ups of exclusive clubs all over the world, golf instruction, and even commercials that were fascinating travelogues. It was the idea of the then president of Shell Oil, and it sold the company's products. It had the rare value in television advertising of making people remember who had paid for the programme presented and what it hoped to sell.

The debonair Tommy Armour was asked to be the master of ceremonies, guide, and tutor of the deluxe golfing tour, but when he learned how much hard work, routine, and inconvenience were involved, he bowed out and said there was only one man who'd go the distance and finish chatty – that was Sarazen.

The Shell television show brought Sarazen back to life in golf. The chunky, sunny-faced veteran in the old-fashioned bloomers was unique and delightful in a simple, friendly way – not trying to be too smart, talking as though he were walking along with a rich friend, and making some mistakes that the television producer was bright enough to leave in the picture, so that Sarazen would be going along in a living room just as sociably as in a locker room.

Later, when a strenuous schedule had Sarazen showing signs of weariness and wear, Jimmy Demaret was brought in to pep up the act. Jimmy was smooth and dapper and cute to the correct degree. He kept attention on the play. The affable Demaret was known as the Bob Hope of pro golf's show business. By all accounts Sarazen and Demaret made the most entertaining, interesting, and informative sports team television has ever offered.

Gene Sarazen, on the Shell golf show, conducted his second coming as a public sports favourite. He'd had his moments when he was downright rude and abrupt, although possibly amply provoked. He was credited with the classic retort to a nuisance who hailed him just when he was about to make a shot in a tournament. 'Hey, Gene!' the man shouted. 'I'll bet you don't remember me!' Sarazen walked away from his ball, looked at the fellow, and shook his head. 'No, I don't!' he snapped, 'Why the hell should I?'. Which is exactly the reply most of us would want to come back with in a similar situation.

But then there is the classic story of how another formidable golf professional put the brusque Sarazen firmly in his place. It happened when the equally hard-nosed and outspoken Lloyd Mangrum, a relative unknown at the time but clearly a comer, was playing a practice round ahead of Sarazen's foursome. Gene was often an impatient and impulsive player, and he kept driving into Mangrum and his friends up ahead on the fairway. Mangrum stood it as long as he could, then, after either he or one of his friends had barely escaped getting beaned by one of Sarazen's powerful drives, he stalked, enraged, back up the fairway. 'Mr Sarazen', he said, glaring, 'if you do that once more, I'm going to hit a ball right down your [expletive deleted] throat!' Gene's reaction is not recorded, but it's safe to say that he knew Mangrum meant what he said and acted accordingly. However, when Gene was on the Shell television show, he was the most gracious of sports heroes. And that job brought him a connection with a Florida real-estate organization where he's probably doing more useful sales work than any other ancient athlete.

In his extraordinarily successful public relations, Gene had a genius counselling him backstage – his gracious and charming wife Mary. He had the sublime good sense to pay attention to her judgement and advice. He never was a play-around boy, and after he married his Hoosier small-town girl, Mary, he was the best of the lot, as husbands go. Sportswriters, for one reason or another, or even for no reason, were often prepared to belt Sarazen in cold type, but when they met Mary and she smiled, the hostilities were over. In his mother and his wife, Gene Sarazen had all the fan club he needed to make him great, in his own opinion. And he gradually earned a valid rating of greatness as greatness goes in sports.

*When Bobby Jones retired after his 1930 campaign it was thought that amateur golf would never see his like again. But a few years later, Lawson Little completed a feat that not even Jones had achieved in amateur golf – the winning of both British and US National Championships in the years 1933 and 1934. Little was not as effective against professionals, though, and when he joined the paid ranks he did not do as well as expected. However, he won the 1940 US Open, raising his total of majors to five.*

# MAN OF DESTINY
## BERNARD DARWIN, 1934

I am bidden to write about the chief events in the Amateur Championship at Prestwick. I will do my best but my trouble is that everything else seems very faint and far away while in front, dwarfing everything else, looms the colossal figure of Lawson Little.

No doubt you have heard long ago of all the wonderful things he did in the final at Prestwick and his ten under fours (or 13 over threes) for 23 holes, his 12 threes – more than 50 per cent – in those same 23 holes, his ten under an average of two putts per green and so on. These are eloquent statistics and I could easily provide some more, such as that if Little had given Jimmy Wallace, his poor adversary, half a stroke a hole he would still have been three up. But no statistics can convey the immense impression that he made on those of us who saw him. I am quite sure I have never seen such golf in my life, and I am equally sure that, as long as I live, I shall never admit that anybody else has played such golf again. The power and accuracy of the long game, the delicacy of the short pitches and runs among the puzzling lumps and bumps of Prestwick, the murderous putting were all equally striking. Perhaps most impressive of all was the unhasting, unresting relentless power of going on and on. Here seemed to me the beau ideal of golf played against par and not against a human adversary. I am sure that Little knew that Wallace was there because, when he was leading by untold holes, he conceded him one or two rather long putts with a gesture as generous and pretty; but regarded purely as an enemy, I do not believe he paid the least attention to him. He bent his whole mind to the task of playing each hole as well as it could be played and the more terrifying and brilliant grew his score, the less he was frightened of it and the more he concentrated on the hole immediately before him.

*Jacklin, Faldo, Lyle, Woosnam: perhaps one of these men will prove to be the most effective British player since the Second World War. To date, however, Thomas Henry Cotton is supreme among golfers born this century.*

# THE MAESTRO
### HENRY LONGHURST, 1970

When anyone asks me who is the greatest striker of a golf ball I ever saw, my answer is immediate. It is Henry Cotton. I am just old enough to have seen Harry Vardon play, but was not old enough at the time to make a fair assessment of his powers. Whatever they were, I cannot believe them to have been greater than Cotton's in the 1930s. He lifted up the nation's golfing spirit after 11 long years of American domination and, with it, the status of his own profession.

For this the Americans themselves were largely responsible. In 1928, when he was 21, he set sail for the United States under his own steam, buying his own ticket and taking with him a letter of credit for £300, which incidentally he brought home intact. He soon appreciated that the great sporting figures of the day were regarded in America almost as the aristocracy, whereas at home sport carried with it no special standing. When Walter Hagen came to England to win our championships, he stayed at the Savoy and drove up to the course in a hired Rolls-Royce. He was already 'one up' on the rest of the field. Cotton decided that what Hagen could do he could do.

I think it is fair to say that Cotton regarded himself, in his competitive days, as a kind of 'property', to be taken the greatest care of and kept in the best possible condition if it were to give the desired results. For this reason he took it to the best hotels and at lunch time, having no desire for the smoky air and, for the celebrated, the inevitable attachment of bores and sycophants to be found in the clubhouse, he changed his clothes in the car and retired to the hotel. Naturally enough, there were those who thought he regarded himself as too good for the common herd.

He developed an immense strength in his hands, and they became the focal point in his essentially simple swing. As the ball flew straight at the flag, you felt that, if you hit it in that fashion, it could hardly do anything else.

## HENRY COTTON
### STEPHEN POTTER, 1968

The most successful as a golfer, Henry Cotton, was also the most successful as a gamesman. But the Cotton gambit was a powerful one, as useful in life as it is in golf. No Unnecessary Smiling, as we might name it, is as effective as it is simple. Suddenly there was a man on our golf courses who looked serious, who looked as if he meant it, who was going to take the nonsense out of 'only a game'. Not smiling within the boundaries of the actual course is a powerful weapon. Not smiling on the green or on the tee. Not smiling when held up. Not even smiling when watching another match. Not smiling is something totally different from looking displeased. It suggests single-mindedness and concentration.

How was Cotton so successful? Remember that besides the discipline of his expression there were no untidy ends about his appearance, his personality or his game. His trousers were no less well cut than his head and his hair. For clothes and general appearance he did for English professionalism what Hagen did for American. He not only accepted Hagen's black and white outfit, he improved on it.

*At the end of the 1930s Ralph Guldahl was at the peak of his powers then suddenly he lost it all. Since I wrote this piece, I have heard various theories about what went wrong. One has it that Guldahl's action with the right wrist was at the root. Another, more beguiling, puts the blame on a book that Guldahl wrote called* Groove Your Golf, *which caused him to think deeply about his own unorthodox swing and to lose confidence.*

## THE MAN WHO LOST IT ALL
### MICHAEL HOBBS, 1983

Mary Tudor had Calais engraved upon the heart and the name of Guldahl probably features similarly for Sam Snead. The pair were tied going into the last round of the US Open at Oakland Hills and Guldahl produced a 69 to

Snead's 71. It was Snead's first season on the US tour and the first time he had played the US Open, yet he was never to come any nearer to winning it (though he lost a play-off to Lew Worsham in 1947).

Guldahl had first been heard from in 1933 when he hunted the amateur Johnny Goodman home, scoring five strokes lower in the last round but still finishing second by a stroke, after missing a fairly short putt to tie. Guldahl then virtually disappeared from the professional golf scene for a while, as the professional tour was then very different from the regularly spaced sequence of events it eventually became. A player, as in Britain, was usually first and foremost a club professional, the tour in the main a matter of winter events in the sunshine. Professionals could leave their clubs in the off season.

It is also said that Guldahl's game fell apart and that he spent the inter-vening years trying to put the pieces together again. As he had won a tour event in 1932, the Phoenix Open, coupled with a strong US Open per-formance in 1933, the latter is probably the more likely explanation. Eventu-ally, Guldahl felt that he was performing more satisfactorily and he came back as a major golfer. He won three events from part way through the 1936 season and finished only $400 behind Horton Smith as the year's leading money winner. Today I suppose a man might expect to pocket more than $300,000 for that kind of season's work. Guldahl made $8,600.

Nevertheless he was well and truly on his way. Early the next year he led Byron Nelson by four strokes going into the last round of the Masters after 69, 72, 68 but the tournament swung on the par-three twelfth and the par-five thirteenth. Guldahl went five, six, which was bad enough. Worse was that Byron Nelson recorded two, three to leap-frog into a lead which he held to the end, winning by two strokes with 70 to 76. However, it was not long before Snead's disappointment in the 1937 US Open. Snead had set a target, Guldahl knowing that he had to play from the eighth in level par to win. Guldahl promptly eagled that hole and held to par the rest of the way. His 281 total was a US Open record that stood until his contemporary Hogan broke it in 1948. More important in the evolution of major championship golf was the fact that each of his scores was good (71, 69, 72, 69). Before, the US Open had normally been won with at least one poor round in the four. In Jones's four US Open wins, for example, his worst scores were 76, 79, 79, 75. From this time on, a more rigid consistency has been required, though there have been exceptions, such as Johnny Miller's 76, 63, finish in 1973.

Guldahl played at Southport and Ainsdale in the Ryder Cup that year, winning in both foursomes and singles. In the latter, playing top for the USA, he demolished Alf Padgham by eight and seven. He earned a place in the 1939 match, which was cancelled because of war.

In 1938, he again looked a likely Masters winner, having tied with 'Light Horse' Harry Cooper but it was not to be. Henry Picard came in late to take the championship. Then came the US Open. Guldahl began 74, 70, 71 to be four strokes behind the leader, Dick Metz. Guldahl produced a closing 69 while Metz perpetrated one of the all-time collapses, a 79, but still finished second. Guldahl had become only the fourth man to take this title in successive years and only Ben Hogan has done it since.

Ralph Guldahl had just one more major championship left in him, the 1939 US Masters. Again the victim was Sam Snead. Guldahl went into the last round with a two stroke advantage but Snead came in with a total of 280, a new record for the event, after a last round 68. Guldahl got to the turn in 36, not a good enough score to win, but then came home in 33 to win by one.

That was nearly the end of Ralph Guldahl. He won two events in 1940 to take his career total to 14 and never won again. He left the tour in 1942 and had another brief attempt in 1949.

What had happened? The usual tale is that Guldahl had 'lost his swing', something not in itself unusual but highly unlikely for a golfer of his eminence, having won three major championships in just over two years and the Wester Open, little below them then in rank, three years in a row. Movie film was taken of his swing to see what faults might have developed in his method, a little difficult to tell in Guldahl's case for he always played with the rather extreme fault of falling back off the ball onto his right foot. In his good years, it hadn't mattered much.

Theories were many. The consensus was that Guldahl's swing was much the same but that the right things were no longer happening to the ball. Guldahl's explanation in later years was simple enough. He claimed that what he had lost was not his swing but his interest. He had made a name for himself and his motivation to play tournament golf was less than to live quietly with his family. The man born three months before Ben Hogan had come and gone several years before Hogan won his first major championship.

*Sam Snead won more titles – 84 – on the US Tour than any player in history. Amongst the moderns his elegance and power is rivalled only by Tom Weiskopf and Seve Ballesteros. But, despite seven major championships to his credit, he has never won the US Open.*

## I REMEMBER SAMMY
### CHARLES PRICE, 1982

Everybody called him Sammy in those days, the people out of respect for somebody handsomely homespun and the press out of duty to sports editors who would not let a given name pass when a nickname would do. And so he became 'Slammin' Sammy' Snead. Lord knows, he deserved it. The man was beautiful, almost gorgeous, this at a time when those much overused words meant something more than just out of the ordinary.

All you had to do to believe what you had read was to see him walk. His gait was like a cougar's on the scent of a doe, steady and sure, every step of it straight from the hip. He could kick the top of a seven-foot doorway and pick a ball out of the cup without bending his knees. Some people said he was double-jointed. But he wasn't. He just had a body that was – well, gorgeous.

He had just turned 26 at the time, and I was 12, bug-eyed over this game at a period in life when you were considered a sissy if you didn't deify Lou Gehrig or Bronco Magurski. I had never seen Sammy hit a shot, but he was already my unspoken idol, this pedestal he sat on having been made for me by the purple press of the day. He did not let me down when I finally got to see him play.

This event took place on the old course at Congressional near Washington, where I was growing up. Congressional was to be the Middle Atlantic scene of qualifying rounds for the 1939 Open Championship. That would be tomorrow, a Monday. But today was Sunday, and Sammy would be playing an exhibition with Jimmy Thomson, now the second longest hitter in the game, and with Horton Smith, the putter, and Wiffy Cox, the home pro. Because of the crowds, my father had to park the car near the first green. Consequently we missed the tee-off as well as the second shots. I weaseled my way toward the first ball I could see lying on the fairway. By a miracle I then considered a major one, the ball turned out to be Sammy's.

The first hole at Congressional then was a par-five. The ball was Sammy's second shot and he was about 80 yards short of the green. He was dressed in white bucks, cream-coloured slacks, a white shirt with a florid tie tucked into it, and a white cap. (The coconut straw hat with the paisley band had yet to become his trademark.) His caddy, already panting from the weight of the largest golf bag I had ever seen, reached the ball first, of course, and stood guard over it as though it were something rare on loan from a museum. Then came Sammy, with that John Wayne way of walking. He surveyed the situation, hands on hips. I could almost touch him, not difficult because he was at least 11 feet tall. He plucked a sand iron from his bag – the pitching wedge had yet to come into use – and then addressed the ball in that no-nonsense manner of his. One glance over his shoulder toward the flagstick, then that almost exaggerated forward press, and next a punch shot that was pure Beethoven. When the ball reached its apex, it looked as though it had been painted against the sky. Then it floated toward the green, did a little dance on the putting surface, and finally came to rest three feet from the hole. Even I, who had won 27 National Opens in my backyard, could not have made a sweeter shot in my imagination.

# THE MONSIGNOR AND THE POPE
## FRED CORCORAN, 1965

Coming home, we made the Grand Tour, stopping off in Rome for what Sam called an audition with the late Pope John. I suggested facetiously that

Sam might bring his putter along and have it blessed. I argued that a Papal blessing might help steer in some of those six-foot sidehill putts.

Sam was impressed. I remember we were met in the vestry of St Peter's by a monsignor whose eyebrows flitted up into his tonsure when Snead checked in with his clubs. But he turned out to be a hundred-shooter himself and he immediately went to confession to Sam about his putting problems. Sam sighed, picked up his clubs, and headed back to the car.

'If you're this close to the Pope and you can't putt', he drawled over his shoulder, 'he ain't gonna be able to do anything for me!'

*Jimmy Demaret, who died a few years ago, came close to being a great player, with three Masters to his credit and a line in clothes and repartee which tended to hit the headlines.*

## GOLF'S GOODWILL AMBASSADOR
### DAN JENKINS, 1970

From almost the instant he arrived Demaret's quipping nature, his friendliness and his passion for clothes that screamed made him golf's unofficial publicity agent. If the sports pages ever nurtured a grander cliché than 'Navy won the toss and elected to receive', it was 'colourful Jimmy Demaret, golf's goodwill ambassador'.

Demaret wore lavender, gold, pink, orange, red and aqua slacks; yellow, emerald, maroon, plaid, checked, striped and polka-dot coats; and more than five hundred hats – berets, Tyroleans, straws – importing all of it from Europe. He paid $250 for the coats as soon as he could and $125 for the slacks in an era when that kind of money could avert a bonus march. He ordered ladies' pastel fabrics from abroad and had them tailored in the US. His idea about shoes was to give a factory swatches from his slacks and have matching saddle oxfords made.

Not only did Demaret have a colour for every occasion, he also had a quip. Some of the more classic were these:

To an LA radio announcer who asked him which player on the tour had the most even disposition: 'Clayton Heafner. He's mad *all* the time.'

To a sportswriter who asked him if Ben Hogan had said much to him while they were winning the Inverness Four-Ball: 'Once I think he said, "You're away"'.

To Robert Trent Jones, the golf architect with a reputation for building monster courses: 'Saw a course you'd really like, Trent. On the first tee you drop the ball over your left shoulder.'

To Roberto de Vicenzo at the Masters: 'Play good, Roberto. I'm betting on you to be low Mexican.'

*Of all the very greatest golfers Hogan took the longest to emerge but thereafter he dominated for about 15 years. Since Hogan's retirement he has become almost a recluse but his theories on the golf swing are as influential as ever. Many consider him the best striker ever and no man has thought his way round a golf course better.*

*Three of Ben Hogan's great major championship performances have become part of golfing legend. The first of these was his win at Merion in the 1950 US Open, just over a year after his body had been smashed in a car accident. Second, again in the US Open, was his victory at Oakland Hills when he alone coped with what might then have been the world's most difficult course. Then came 1953, his greatest year when he achieved the closest approach to the modern professional Grand Slam. He won the Masters, US Open and capped the lot by winning the British Open the only time he entered.*

# THAT SMALL COLOSSUS
## BERNARD DARWIN, 1953

As long as golfers talk championship golf, 1953 will be recalled as Hogan's year. Indeed, I think it would have been even if he had not won, so entirely did that small colossus bestride and dominate the tournament.

It was Hogan who sold the tickets in their thousands to the great joy of the authorities and filled the huge park with row upon serried row of shining cars; it was Hogan who produced what was, I think, the greatest crowd of spectators that I ever saw at a championship; and it was Hogan that every single one of them wanted to watch. Hardly anyone there had seen him play before since, when he was here in 1949, he was still too ill to play, and in less than no time anyone with any knowledge of golf came back overawed and abashed by the splendour of his game.

There were to begin with certain local patriots disposed to speak of him as 'your man Hogan', and to murmur that he might do all manner of things on American inland courses, but let him wait till he comes to play over the great Carnoustie course in a Carnoustie wind. Yet even those parochial critics were soon convinced, for they knew golf and were too honest not to admit that here was such a player as occurs only once in a generation or indeed once in a lifetime. As soon as the one Scottish hope, Eric Brown, had faded away I think the whole of that vast crowd wanted Hogan to win. This is not to say that Dai Rees, the ultimate British hope, who had played most gallantly, would not have been a most popular winner. He certainly would, but the feeling that the best man ought to win – there was no earthly doubt who that was – overrode all other sentiments.

And what a wonderful win it was! He did what Bobby Jones, Hagen and Sarazen had all failed to do at the first attempt. He came here weighed down by his immense reputation, and for the first two rounds his putting was unworthy of him and he seemed to have got the slowness of the greens a little on his nerves so far as he has any nerves. Yet when he once began to take some of the chances which his magnificent iron play gave him, when the putts began to drop so that we said 'Now he's off!', and it was almost a case of in the one class Hogan and in the other class all the other golfers, it was a measure of his quality that having been hard pressed for three rounds, sharing the lead with one very fine player, and having all sorts of others hard on his very heels, he yet managed to win with something like ease.

It is an impossible task to give anything like an impression of the player to those who have not seen him, but one can perhaps pick out one or two points. Hogan stands decidedly upright with his weight rather forward on the left foot and the right foot drawn a little back. He holds his hands decidedly high, the right hand notably far over, and the right wrist almost arched. The swing is rhythmic and easy and not as long as I had expected from the photographs. The club at the top of the swing may in fact go a little past the horizontal, but if so the eye – or my eye – cannot detect it. The impressive part of the swing comes in what the books call the hitting area. Then the clubhead appears to travel with such irresistible speed that it goes right through the ball and far past it before it begins to come up again. He has, incidentally, a good deal of power in reserve, and when he really means to hit out, as he did with his two wooden clubs at the long sixth hole, his length is very great indeed. I suppose, however, it is his iron play – particularly his long-iron play – which is most striking. It is that which gives him so many chances of threes because he hits so appallingly straight. When we were all waiting behind the home green for his iron shot to the seventy-second hole and Hogan, no doubt giving the out-of-bounds on the left a wisely wide berth, finished up eight or nine yards to the right of the pin, somebody remarked: 'He's dreadfully crooked, isn't he?'. It was a true word spoken in jest. Eight yards to the left or right of the pin was definitely crooked for Hogan.

# A SERIOUS MAN
## FRED CORCORAN, 1965

Hogan never made any effort to win a popularity contest. He was a chilly, withdrawn person who didn't want anyone patting him on the back ... He preferred to walk alone. Cheers meant nothing to Ben. He looked upon hero-worshippers with little regard; and even regarded his tournament galleries with disdain.

For all this, he was one of the most honest and sincere persons I have ever known. He detested phonies. His friends were few, his intimates rare. He always preferred the company of his wife, Valerie, to anyone else.

Hogan could win under any and all conditions. He had a fierce competitive drive that was almost frightening in its intensity. And he mastered the difficult art of concentration, blanking out everything but the immediate problem – the hole he was playing, the shot he was making.

Nothing ever changed Hogan. He was the same in defeat as in victory.

He filed them both away in some mental locker box after carefully analysing them, then went right along with the business of surviving.

I had enormous respect for him and because of it could overlook the cold aloofness which at times exasperated me as a publicity-minded promoter. I never fully broke through that wall of reserve and never felt completely at ease with him. I was never sure, when he bared his white teeth in the suntanned face, whether he was smiling or unhappy. Mirth was a luxury he denied himself except on the rarest occasions, as though he were afraid it might corrode his zeal. Compete and work, compete and work ... on the practice tee and on the practice green ... then putt in the hotel room until bedtime while the others were relaxing. He even practised in the rain so he could hold his game together under these conditions. Actually, Ben didn't leave himself much time for laughter ... I can't recall him ever finding humour in anything that happened on the golf course. Golf was his business – a tough business, full of disappointments.

# THE YOUNG THOMSON
## PAT WARD-THOMAS, 1961

A summer day in 1954 was drawing to its close, and there was a greyness in the evening light, as a great crowd concentrated its pursuit on the last few holes at Birkdale. Peter Thomson was moving towards his first victory in the Open Championship and, as he stood on the sixteenth tee high up amidst the dunes and willow scrub, he knew his position in relation to the rest of the field. In those days the leaders were not sent out last on the final day, and Scott and Rees had finished some time before with totals of 284. They were enduring that awful vigil, a compound of hope and fear, that comes to those who get their blow in first. For Rees there must have been remorse as well. After a superb attacking stroke to the last hole had run just through the green he had taken three more and so had only tied with Scott. Now Thomson needed to play the last three holes in level fours to beat them, and also to make the task of Locke, who was behind him, almost impossible.

Level fours was in effect par, for the sixteenth was barely in range of two strokes, the seventeenth was a short hole, and the eighteenth required about a medium iron for the second. This made no light task but it would be considerably easier if he could get a four at the sixteenth, and that is exactly what he did. A long drive, probably the finest he had hit all day, flew past the great guardian dunes far down the fairway. The green, like most of those at Birkdale, gives an impression of gathering the second shot, because it is cloistered in a little dell of its own, but in fact it does not gather. The shot, invariably with wood, must be unerringly straight, if it is to find the green. Thomson pulled his and it came to rest in one of two bunkers on the left of the fairway, and moreover the one farthest from the hole. This meant that he had a blind pitch from sand of about 25 yards, a fearfully difficult stroke at any time, let alone at such a moment. He played it beautifully to within two feet of the hole, got his four, and one knew then with an absolute conviction that the championship was his.

It all seemed so disarmingly simple, as Thomson's golf normally is, but how easy it would have been to strike the shot a little heavy or a shade thin and then have to work for a five, or even take six. The slightest misjudgement might have cost the championship whereas he made it safe by producing a perfect stroke at the precise moment when it was necessary. Years afterwards I talked to him about that shot and his first comment, in so many words, was, 'I always remember the beautiful lie in that bunker. The ball couldn't have been placed in an easier position, slightly uphill on good sand – that's the kind of break you need to win.' This remark was typical of an attitude he had revealed earlier that day at Birkdale. I had gone out to the sixth green to wait for him, and thought as I did so how even at an Open you can find solitude.

A soft breeze was stirring in the sand grass, and it was peaceful for a while in the morning sunshine. Then the distant island fairway was filled with people as Thomson prepared to play the long blind second shot with a brassy over the towering sandhills to the green. He played, the heads of the crowd turned upwards, but the ball did not appear, and then I saw him vanish behind the tallest dune, some hundred yards short of the green. It seemed ages before the long pitch floated high to the green and finished a few feet from the hole. After he had holed the putt, and was walking from the next tee, I complimented him on a remarkable four. His first remark was, 'How lucky I was to find a good lie'.

This might not seem extraordinary to those unused to listening to first-class golfers bemoaning their luck but to me it was most unusual. Self-excuse is an ever ready companion of many golfers; to them a bad shot is caused by bad luck, but a good result is never good luck. I doubt whether many of the great players ever thought like this; it is an attitude of mind beset with danger. A refusal to accept misfortune or recognize good reveals a state of unpreparedness that eventually will betray. As a wise golfer of old once said, 'The mark of a champion is the ability to make the most of good luck and the best of bad'. Twice at least on that day at Birkdale Thomson achieved classic examples of how to make the most of fortune, and was wise enough to recognize the fact.

*    *    *

If a stranger should come upon him on an evening when he was leading in a championship, it could well be some time before the visitor realized who Thomson was. This is not because he is unduly self-depreciative or quiet, but simply because golf is not the be-all and end-all of life for him.

Neither is golf a complete expression of a personality that is more complex than at first it might appear to be. Thomson is no light-hearted boy, as some might think after watching him on the course, but a shrewd, most determined person capable of rational calculated thought who, even as a young man, had a pretty clear idea of where he intended to go. And yet his outward manner is at once attractive and charming. He gives the impression of playing golf for fun, or as a sideline to other more worthwhile activities. His attitude when talking of it resembles that of a highly observant, intelligent amateur rather than that of a world class professional. This impression of detachment is deceptive and fascinating, and unique within my experience of golfers. It could be contrived but I think not, for I believe that Thomson never has been, nor ever will be, dedicated to the game, or consumed by it as so many others are. He will never become a professional in the full meaning of the term, giving lessons, serving members, and so on, for these things are far removed from his scheme of life.

From the beginning he was blessed with great natural gifts for golf and a wonderful temperament, accepted them without question or fear, and turned them to rare capital advantage. His clearness of mind is exceptional. He has the facility of reducing things, such as the golf swing, to simple essentials. The Australian journalist responsible for transmitting articles that Thomson writes for a paper, has often told me what a pleasure it is to take copy from him, so fluently, concisely and accurately does he express himself. Few professional players of games have this talent. Although some of their expressions are undoubtedly concise, even crisply monosyllabic, they are rarely capable of lucid observant description. I often wonder how many readers of books ostensibly written by famous players, really believe that the man wrote it himself.

All these facets of Thomson's personality make for a remarkable balance in his approach to golf. If I had to choose one adjective to describe him as a person and a player it would be 'balanced' – for nothing that he does is in any sense exaggerated or unusual. When first he came to Britain in the early 1950s I was impressed by a philosophical outlook, rare in one so young, which permitted him to accept reverses of fortune without being distracted from the even tenor of his ways. So poised and assured was his manner at all times that some may have wondered whether it was assumed. It is now plain that this was not so because in all the years afterwards his serenity was disturbed but rarely and then not in moments of pressure on the golf course. That afternoon at Birkdale there was a final incident that revealed his remarkable composure. After missing the last green of all with his second shot he chipped to within five feet, and then had two for the championship. The first putt overran the hole by an inch or so, whereupon he leaned over and tapped the next one in back-handed. This seemed incredibly casual, and indeed foolish, but as he said later: 'I had both hands on the putter'. No matter, few men would have been so sure of themselves as to have done this.

Later that summer in the final of the match play championship at St Andrews Thomson met John Fallon. He had been expected to win comfortably but did not hole out as well as he might have done and Fallon, playing beautifully with, I understand, rather more at stake than Thomson, held on bravely until extra holes. Thomson was one-up going to the thirty-fourth; then Fallon holed clean across the green and the match was square; but Thomson only smiled, as if amused at what must have been, at the very least, an irritating and unexpected thrust. They reached the last green still even. Thomson putted first for his three and missed, and then came the one moment in the whole match when its destiny was out of Thomson's hands. There was nothing in the world he could do but stand and watch Fallon attempt his putt for victory. It was not long, eight to ten feet, and as he was preparing to putt, Thomson leaned on his putter and looked round at the crowd, hanging tense, eager and silent over the fences and from the windows. Our eyes met for a second and he smiled cheerfully, although a title and a fair amount of money would disappear if Fallon holed. His putt trembled on the brink and away they went down towards the Swilcan for the third time in the day. I did not follow; there seemed to be no need for I knew then that Thomson would win.

*With the decline of Hogan and Snead, US golf lacked a charismatic figure for a few years. And then came Palmer, a player made for television though unfortunate in that Jack Nicklaus came along rather too soon. Palmer's peak years were from 1958 to 1964. No further major championships came his way after his fourth Masters win in 1964, though he remained a tournament winner into the 1970s.*

# THE DOGGEDEST VICTIM
## DAN JENKINS, 1970

He first came to golf as a muscular young man who could not keep his shirt-tail in, who smoked a lot, perspired a lot and who hit the ball with all of the finesse of a dock worker lifting a crate of auto parts. Arnold Palmer did not play golf, we thought. He nailed up beams, reupholstered sofas, repaired air-conditioning units. Sure, he made birdies by the streaks in his eccentric way – driving through forests, lacing hooks around sharp corners, spewing wild slices over prodigious hills, and then, all hunched up and pigeon-toed, staring putts into the cups. But he made just as many bogeys in his stubborn way. Anyhow, a guy whose slacks are too long and turned up at the cuffs, who matches green shirts with orange sweaters, a guy who sweats so much, is *not* going to rush past the Gene Littlers, Ken Venturis and Dow Finsterwalds, the stylists, to fill the hero gap created by the further greying and balding Ben Hogan and Sam Snead. This is what most of us believed around 1960, even after Palmer had won his second Masters, even after he had begun to drown everyone in money winnings. This was a suave new godlet of the fairways, a guy out of Latrobe Dry Goods?

We were, of course, as wrong about him as the break on a downhill six-footer, as wrong as his method seemed to us to be wrong: hit it hard, go find it, hit it hard again. We knew we were wrong one day when the bogeys suddenly went away. No one understood why or how, except that Palmer willed them to. And now he had become a winner like none we had ever known. He was a nice guy, of all things. He was honestly and naturally gracious, untemperamental, talkative, helpful and advising, unselfish of his time, marvellously good-humoured; he had a special feeling for golf's history and he was honoured by its traditions; and with all of this he remained the gut fighter we insisted he be, a man so willing to accept the agonies of pressure and the burdens of fame that for a few years we absolutely forgot that anyone else played the game he was dominating and changing.

He actually started *being* Arnold Palmer in that summer of 1960, a stupidly short time ago it seems. He became the Arnie of whoo-ha, go-get-'em Arnie on a searingly hot afternoon in Denver when, during the last round of the US Open, he exploded from seven strokes and 14 players behind to win. Two months earlier he had finished birdie-birdie on national television to win the Masters and now he had created another miracle – again on national television.

Much has been written into the lore of golf of how it was that day, of the epic 65 he shot in the final round at Cherry Hills, of the day that really made him, but not by anyone who had lunched with him, kidded him, and then happily marched inside the gallery ropes with him, scurrying after Cokes, furnishing cigarettes, and hoping to put him at ease.

During lunch in a quiet corner of the Cherry Hills locker room before that round, Arnold was cheerful and joking as he ate a hamburger, drank iced tea, and made small talk with a couple of other players, Bob Rosburg and Ken Venturi, a writer named Bob Drum, and myself. He talked of no one else who might win. All he seemed concerned about was Cherry Hill's first hole, a comparatively short, downhill, downwind, par-four. It bugged him. He thought he could drive the green, but in three previous rounds he had not done it.

'It really makes me hot', he said. 'A man ought to drive that green.'

'Why not?' I said. 'It's only 346 yards through a ditch and a lot of high grass.'

'If I drive that green I might shoot a hell of a score', he said. 'I might even shoot a 65 if I get started good. What'll that bring?'

'About seventh place. You're too far back.'

'Well, that would be two-eighty', Arnold said. 'Doesn't two-eighty always win the Open?'

'Yeah', I said. 'When Hogan shoots it.'

Arnold laughed and walked out to the first tee.

For a while I loitered around the big clubhouse waiting for the leaders to go out, as a good journalist should. In the process of milling around, however, I overheard a couple of fans talking about an amazing thing they had just seen. Palmer, they said, had driven the first green. Just killed a low one that hung up there straight toward the mountains and then burned its way through the USGA trash and onto the putting surface. Got a two-putt birdie.

I smiled to myself and walked out onto the veranda and began edging my way through the spectators toward the first tee where the leader, Mike Souchak, would be going off presently. But about that time a pretty good roar came up from down on the front nine, and seconds later, a man sprinted by panting the news that Palmer was three under through three.

'Drove the first, chipped in on two and hit it stiff on three', he said, pulling away and darting off to join Arnie's Army. Like the spectator and a few thousand others who got the same notion at the same time, I tried to break all records for the Cherry Hills Clubhouse-to-Fourth Fairway Dash. We got there just in time to see Arnold hole his fourth straight birdie.

Wringing wet and perishing from thirst, I staggered toward the fifth tee, stopping to grab a Coke at a concession stand. I ducked under the ropes as an armband permitted and stood there puffing but excited. Arnold came in briskly, squinted down the fairway and walked over. He took the Coke out of my hand, the cigarettes out of my shirt pocket and broke into a smile. 'Fancy seeing you here', he said. 'Who's winning the Open?'

Palmer birdied two more holes through the seventh to go an incredible six under, working on an incorrigible 29 out. But he bogeyed the eighth and had to settle for a 30. Even so, the challengers were falling all around him like wounded soldiers, and their crowds were bolting towards him, and the title would be his. Everything would be his now. Later on, somewhere on the back nine holes, I remember sizing up a leader board with him and saying, 'You've got it. They're all taking gas.' 'Aw, maybe', he said, quietly. 'But damn it, I wanted that 29.'

There have been other major victories, as we know, and scores of lesser ones, and precisely because of him the professional tour has tripled, quadrupled in prize money. He has become, they say, something immeasurable in champions, something more than life-size, even though he has turned into his forties, the hip hurts, and a lot of other big ones have slipped away.

This is true, I think. He is the most immeasurable of all golf champions. But this is not entirely true because of all that he has won, or because of that mysterious fury with which he has managed to rally himself. It is partly because of the nobility he has brought to losing. And more than anything, it is true because of the pure, unmixed joy he has brought to trying. He has been, after all, the doggedest victim of us all.

*When Gary Player first came over to Europe to compete, some British professionals advised him to go home and find another line of work. But Player had enough ability and more desire and determination than anyone else. He won his first major title, the British Open, in 1959, and his last nearly 20 years later.*

# THE BEST BOWELS

## DAVE HILL, 1977

Gary Player: Lack of dedication has never been Gary's problem. He has done more with his natural ability than anyone else playing the game today. He works harder at golf than the rest of us – as he is always telling anyone who will listen, especially the writers.

Gary is a little man and he's tremendously proud of his superior physical condition. He runs and lifts weights and eats health foods. That's all well and good, but I get tired of hearing him brag about it. So what if he has the most perfect bowel movements on the tour?

He reminds me of a man who takes too many vitamin pills. He figures that if one is good for him, then a hundred will be a hundred times as good for him. Also Gary is a very shrewd individual. When he is pushing bananas and having them delivered to the locker room by the crateful, you can bet he has a good endorsement deal going with a banana company.

I have nothing against people like Gary who don't drink or smoke. I do resent them telling me that that's how I should live. Gary makes a lot of other players mad with his sanctimonious preachings about clean living. He likes to go on as though he's the only athlete on the tour. He's always pointing at somebody's paunch with great disdain. He overdoes it.

Weightlifting and developing all those muscles may have hurt Gary's golf some. Lifting heavy weights can shorten your muscles and tighten your back and shoulders. The golf swing is a long, stretching action. You need all the suppleness you can get to make a big turn. Lifting weights can make you as taut as a banjo string, and that isn't going to help your golf swing. Gary has great coordination and doesn't need that extra muscular development he gets from lifting weights.

His style setting up to the ball is very rigid, very tense. He is overdeveloped in the forearms and shoulders, and those muscles are extremely firm. He looks like a mechanical man. From that kind of address position it is awfully difficult for him to create the freedom of motion that marks a great golf swing. Jack Nicklaus and Sam Snead are very firm in the hands at address, but Player is firm all the way up to his shoulders.

*With the semi-retirement of Henry Cotton after his 1949 Open Championship win, British golf lacked a world-beater for 20 years. Though his peak career was short, no British player has since excelled Jacklin's achievements.*

# THE NECESSARY HERO
## MICHAEL HOBBS, 1983

When Tony Jacklin won the British PGA at Hillside in 1982 for his first win on the British mainland since 1973, this was regarded by the press as a return of the prodigal to the heights. For the remainder of the season he did relatively little; nor should too much have been expected of him. For some years, Tony Jacklin has been one of a group of very good European golfers who may be expected to win a tournament here and there. His play has not, however, justified the urge of so many to speculate at length about his chances in 'the Open starting on Thursday'. The simple enough reason is that he has not been a world-class player since around 1973 or 1974 and has been eroded by the stress of playing tournament golf for nearly 20 years. The history of US and European tournament golf is spattered with the names of those who reached their own particular peak – and were heard little of again.

For example, who are Gary Groh, Pat Fitzsimons, Tom Jenkins, Larry Ziegler and Don Iverson? Or Jimmy Kinsella, Ross Whitehead, John Garner and Norman Wood? The first group won US tour events in 1975; the second, European events in 1972. They are not failures because they have done relatively little since and neither is Tony Jacklin because he did not win more major championships after his Opens of 1969 and 1970: both, incidentally, further away in time.

Instead, he should be heralded as a British golfer who achieved, for a short space, as much as Henry Cotton in major championships. If we grant the pair equal status we have two British players whose deeds in great events have not been surpassed since the days of the great triumvirate before the First World War. Take in Europe as a whole, and there would be only Severiano Ballesteros to join them and perhaps rate higher.

Unlike these two, Jacklin's career followed a remarkably steady curve, both up and then down. He was an outstanding player by 1967 and then in both 1968 and 1969 won only one tournament. But how significant these two were. The Greater Jacksonville Open came to him in 1968, the first fully recognized event to be won in the USA by a British golfer since Ted Ray's Open win in 1920. His victory at Royal Lytham in the British Open 1969 was the first by a British golfer since Max Faulkner's Portrush win in 1951. Perhaps 1970 was his best year, as his seven-stroke margin in taking the US Open was the greatest since Jim Barnes's nine lead in 1921 and he was the first British player to win since 1920. In the meantime, no British-based player had been worth even an honourable mention, the nearest approach being Phil Perkins's joint second place behind Gene Sarazen in 1932.

At Hazeltine National, in Minnesota, Jacklin was confronted the first day of the US Open by a course which was very wet and therefore playing its full 7,151 yards. To compound the difficulties, there was a strong northwesterly wind. Jacklin came in with a 71, not normally a headline round, but this day he was the only man to break the par of 72 and found himself in a two-stroke lead. On day two the wind had dropped and better scoring was expected. (Nicklaus had taken 81, Player 80 and Palmer, with his low flight a good wind golfer, 79.) Jacklin went round in 70, a round that only Dave Hill, with 69, bettered. He was three strokes in the lead from Dave Hill.

The third day he produced another 70, one alarm coming on the seventeenth when his tee shot finished with trees blocking the route to the green. Jacklin lashed an 8-iron over, with both the height and carry to reach the green 160 yards away.

He began the last round with a four-shot lead on Hill, the next challenger a further three strokes away. Despite the lead, he had to conquer the temptation to play safe, which often enough leads to over-caution and sudden panic if shots begin to seep away. Jacklin did have a crisis: after six holes he was one under par but then went over on two successive holes. On the ninth, his birdie putt was far too strong and would have been several feet past but he had the luck to hit the back of the hole, his ball hopped in the air – and went in.

By now, Jacklin was in a trance-like state, a cocoon of concentration when only making the next shot exists, the world shut off. As he played the last hole he had a six-stroke lead, sent a 4-iron to the green and, for good measure, holed a long putt. He was the first Briton to hold the British and US Opens at the same time.

In America, Jacklin did not go on to build a formidable career. He had joined the US tour in 1967, when he still had to consolidate his name in Britain, and for some time it had been fun. As the years passed, competing in a foreign land and incessant motel life lost appeal. He had one more tournament victory, the 1972 Greater Jacksonville Open, the last event won by a British player until Peter Oosterhuis's 1981 Canadian Open. In the years from Ted Ray's US Open win in 1920, there have been five wins in important US events, three of them going to Tony Jacklin. (The other, is Henry Cotton's win in the 1948 White Sulphur Springs Invitational, not a PGA-recognized event.)

But despite his success in America, where he won some $300,000, his performance in the British Open are the real barometer of his career. He first featured in 1967, coming in fifth, seven strokes behind Roberto de Vicenzo at Hoylake and the following year at Carnoustie was amongst the leaders until an 80 in the final round dropped him to eighteenth place, ten behind Player.

Then came his glory at Royal Lytham, his fellow protagonists Bob Charles, Peter Thomson, Roberto de Vicenzo, Christy O'Connor and Jack Nicklaus – all except O'Connor previous and recent winners of the championship.

Jacklin began with a 68 to excite British hopes, Bob Charles, champion in 1963, making the running with a 66. The New Zealander followed with a 69 to lead Jacklin's 36-hole total by three strokes. Also well up were

O'Connor (71, 65 – one behind Charles); Thomson (71, 70); Wolstenholme and Moody (70, 71); and Casper (70, 70).

On the third day, Casper, Wolstenholme and Moody were gone. Charles and O'Connor fell behind with 75 and 74 respectively; Thomson held steady with another 70, while Vicenzo strode up the field with a 66. At the end of the day, after a 70, Jacklin held the lead. His score had been saved with some superlative bunker play (a very strong area of his game) towards the end of his round. On the fifteenth he got out to a foot from the hole, birdied the sixteenth after an immense drive and then hooked into a gully behind bushes off the next tee. After his second shot he was still in the rough and then put his next into a greenside bunker and came out to just over a couple of feet and holed for a one over par-five. On the last he drove into a heavy lie in the right rough and with his second was bunkered on the right of the green, but came out to three feet to par the hole.

His 208 total put him two ahead of O'Connor and Charles, three better than Vicenzo and Thomson; Nicklaus had made a move with a 68 but at five in arrears had far to go.

Jacklin and Charles were paired for the last day. By the fourteenth, Jacklin still had his two-stroke margin and on that hole increased it to three. Both dropped strokes on the fifteenth and parred the sixteenth, while Jacklin saw a shot of his lead go on the next when he took three putts after being short with his first from 11 yards. He went into the last with a two-stroke lead but if Charles should birdie ...

Jacklin hit a huge drive to carry the threatening bunkers on the eighteenth and hit his second to about three yards, with Charles a little further away, also in two. When Charles could not quite succeed with his longer putt Jacklin was champion.

The following year, as holder of both US and British Opens, he made a startling beginning to the defence of his British title at St Andrews, three weeks after he had won at Hazeltine National. On the first, he wedged to four or five yards and holed the putt and repeated the birdie on the next from about five foot. Two pars followed before he two-putted the 567 yard fifth for another birdie. On the seventh he hit a long drive onto a bunker lip but played a deft pitch and run from an uncomfortable stance to four feet and holed. The climax to the first half came on the ninth. He played a 1-iron from the tee at this 359 yard hole and followed with a 9-iron to the green which bounced once, bounced again and dropped into the hole for an eagle. Jacklin was out in 29, perhaps the best start made in a major championship by anyone, anywhere. He birdied the next, parred the eleventh and his drive to the 312 yard twelfth would have reached the green but was diverted by a scorer at the approaches. He 'only' parred the hole – failure after what had gone before – and then the rains descended on the parched course. On the 560 yard fourteenth he hit a good drive but came off his 4-wood second shot, perhaps distracted by a cry of 'Fore', and cut it into a bush. At this point the course was under water and play was suspended.

The next day, he bogeyed the hole and also the sixteenth and seventeeth, finishing in 67; an excellent score but not the marvel that had been in prospect. After two rounds, he was level with Nicklaus on 137, both one worse than Lee Trevino. After day three, Jacklin and Nicklaus were still level, joined by Doug Sanders, leaving Trevino with a two stroke lead.

On the final day, winds gusted up to 60 mph and many of the last day qualifiers scored in the high 70s, Trevino with 77 amongst them and Jacklin also, with a 76 and fifth place behind the play-off between Nicklaus and Sanders.

The following year at Royal Birkdale Jacklin was once more in the thick of it, producing rounds of 69, 70, 70, 71 for the third place, two behind champion Trevino and one behind 'Mr Lu' from Taiwan. He was not overly disappointed because he did not feel he had played well.

Tragedy was to follow in 1972 at Muirfield, perhaps twice. He began 69, 72 to Trevino's 71, 70, while a highly motivated Nicklaus (he had won both the Masters and US Open that season) was after the Grand Slam and had begun 70, 72.

The third day, Jacklin played finely for his 67, the high point being an eagle on the 558 yard fifth hole. He established a lead over Trevino early on. But Trevino's finish was breath-taking and must have taken the wind from Jacklin's sails. He finished with five consecutive birdies but more remarkable than the card scores was the manner of accomplishment. On the fourteenth he holed from five yards; on the fifteenth from twice that distance and on the 188 yard sixteenth was bunkered, thinned his explosion shot but struck the flag on the second bounce and down and in went his ball; he reached the par-five seventeenth in two and two-putted for another; on the last, he sent his second shot through the green but holed a long chip shot. Where Jacklin might have held a comfortable lead at the end of play, he was a stroke behind.

The final day was closely contested by Trevino and Jacklin, though Nicklaus became a major factor from six strokes behind. He birdied six of the first 11 holes and at one point had edged into the lead. After Jacklin birdied the fourteenth, there was a three-way tie. Nicklaus then dropped a shot on the sixteenth and failed to birdie the seventeenth, finishing with a magnificent 66 that should not have been quite good enough to beat either Trevino or Jacklin.

As Mary Tudor had her Calais, Jacklin has his seventeenth at Muirfield, a hole which some argue changed the whole course of his career. He drove long and straight while Trevino was bunkered and still behind Jacklin's drive after his recovery. Trevino then hit a 3-wood short of the green and into long grass, while Jacklin hit his second to within a short pitch of the green. Trevino had hit his fourth shot through the back. He would have to struggle for a six. Jacklin pitched up a little short of the flag while Trevino, recognizing defeat (he had just said: 'That's it. I've thrown it all away.') carelessly selected a chipping club, gave a glance at the hole – and ran his ball in for a five.

Jacklin had now to hole his putt to take the lead. He putted firmly – too firmly – and was about three feet past. When he missed the return the championship was Trevino's, unless he faltered on the last. He didn't. Jacklin dropped another shot to finish third, behind Nicklaus.

Each year from 1967 onwards, Jacklin had contended for the Open. Indeed, if we stretch credulity, he could have won them all. But Muirfield in 1972 was the end for him as far as major championships are concerned. He has never since featured, other than momentarily.

In the years that followed, Jacklin was considered by most to be the best striker of a golf ball in Britain and many on both sides of the Atlantic considered him the most reliable long driver that there was. As recently as 1982, he was only a dozen yards shorter in European tour averages than the leader, Greg Norman. He despaired increasingly of his putting and his wedge and short iron play suffered from the pressure of feeling he had to get such shots close to the hole for his putter was going to lose, not save, strokes.

There are many who have argued that success spoiled Tony Jacklin. Wealth poured down upon him, bringing a Rolls-Royce and a country mansion in the Cotswolds, and the lad from Scunthorpe was well satisfied, not having that supreme appetite to be the greatest golfer in the world. Others claimed that the demands on his time from his manager Mark McCormack for money-making engagements left him tired and with insufficient time to practise. Perhaps, but the Palmers, Players and Nicklauses thrived on the same diet.

My own feeling is that few golfers, except the very greatest, stay at the top for long. With seven or eight years as a very superior golfer indeed, Tony Jacklin showed himself more of a master than any British player since the great triumvirate, with the sole exception of Henry Cotton.

*I believe that Jack Nicklaus will eventually be recognized as the greatest performer since the era of the Parks and Morrises because of his 20 major championships and the level of competition he faced throughout his career. But even Nicklaus is not a complete golfer. Many people have felt, for instance, that he usually plays too cautiously and Trevino is just one contemporary who has pointed out that Jack is relatively poor at the short pitch and from sand.*

## NICKLAUS GOES FOR BROKE
### AL BARKOW, 1974

At Muirfield the plan was to leave his great mace, his driver, in the bag, use it only sparingly. He would not need it much. The fairways were fast-running, and the ball would roll substantially after landing. And old Muirfield has so many ageless, unplaned little knobs poking up to freckle its surface that no one can be sure which way a ball will bounce off them, especially with the harder-hit driver. So Nicklaus would use his 1- or 2-iron, or 3-

wood, to get a softer descent and to keep the ball out of the long grass. He could afford the loss of distance. He was using the smaller British ball, and with any ball could hit those shorter clubs as far as most men hit their drivers. Muirfield was a lady to be not assaulted but caressed.

Thus he played for the first three days – restrained, conservative petting. It was taking much of the buff off the polish of promise that had begun the week, but that was Nicklaus's way. He won with massive, relentless, all-front sweeps, not the commando raids of Arnold. Yet this time the plan was not working. That is, it was and it wasn't; Jack was only one shot behind the lead after 36 holes, but his plan had been devised for windy weather, not without a century of good reason, and it was calm – calm and warm. Almost as if he believed reality would conform to his plan, on the second day of play he had overdressed and had to shed a woollen turtleneck sweater.

Muirfield was not cooperating, and neither were some of the golfers, two of whom approached old Muirfield as though she were a young harlot with her pants down. In the third round, Lee Trevino and Tony Jacklin shot 66 and 67 respectively. A 'piece of cake', Jack said of the course, but he stuck to his diet and had a third-day 71. With one round to go, he was six shots behind Lee, five behind Tony, both formidable champions themselves. Would Jack scrap the plan he had so doggedly held to? He would have to, wouldn't he?

On the first hole of the last round came the answer. The first hole at Muirfield is possibly the toughest on the course, a long par-four played through a narrow alleyway slinking between mother's grabby arms. Jack had been using his 1-iron from the tee, but now, with his back to the wall, he pulled his bludgeon driver from his bag. When he took the cover from its head, it was the dragon slayer unsheathing his mightiest sword. A bright metallic click in the open air of Scotland and the ball was away – long, long. Gone was the little controlled fade. The ball had the more natural draw at the end of its trajectory. The night before, Nicklaus had told friends, 'What the hell. I'm going for broke. I either shoot 82 or 62.' The game was on.

He parred the first, playing a short-iron second shot. At the next, a short par-four where he had also been playing his iron from the tee and using an 8-iron for his approach, he again bared his driver. With it he mauled the ball to within 30 of his own steps from the green. He had little more than a long chip shot left, and he played it well – to within ten feet. He birdied. At the third, again going to his big stick where he hadn't before, he nearly drove the green. Another birdie. He was now into what was to be one of the most absorbing, impassioned 11 holes of golf this writer and many another had ever witnessed.

With every shot Nicklaus played, both the jaded and the initiates to golf were burbling more and more with excitement and running after the big blond, who himself had begun to exhibit the current he was generating. For a big man, Nicklaus has a short stride, making him appear to be walking faster than he really is. But now the step did have more ginger, and he was difficult to keep up with. Always a courteous golfer, at one point Nicklaus showed some impatience at having to wait for his playing partner to hit a shot. Perhaps it was more surprise. It seemed he didn't realize that in fact there was another person playing golf with him. The fellow was Guy Hunt, a little-known English professional, and to his credit he played fine if unnoticed golf in the eye of the tornado.

No one could keep up with Jack's storm of birdies, either, and as he completed the ninth hole with another birdie, his fourth of the day, and dashed to his rooms in the Grey Walls hotel just behind the tenth tee to have his daily mid-round 'relief stop', he had drawn into a tie with Jacklin and Trevino. 'Bloody marvellous!'. 'Keep it up, Jacko, I got me a fiver on you, mate!' were some cries from the gallery.

A fine, low-running 6-iron approach at the tenth set up another birdie, which he got, and a big smile came over his face. Coming from six back, he had the lead, was five under par going for the moon. At 11 Jack pitched his second shot to within six feet of the cup. Another birdie coming up. Hot damn, he may get his 62. There was palpable silence around the green as Nicklaus prepared to putt. He stood over the ball stock still, a block of heavy concentration. But an instant before he would take the club back, with the timing of a desperate hustler there came a tremendous roar from afar. Not too far. The ninth hole, to be exact. Trevino and Jacklin were paired together and on that hole at the time. One of them had just done something big. It was more than a birdie. The roar had a deeper resonance, was more sustained. The scream of an eagle. The ninth is a par-five reachable in two, and eagleable. We learned soon after that Trevino had indeed chipped in ... for a three, an eagle. Nicklaus stepped away from his ball, reprepared himself.

All quiet again, and Jack was once more just ready to stroke his putt when yet another howl came from the ninth green, this with an even greater, throatier gusto since it was for the British hero, Jacklin, who holed a long putt for his own eagle. No one knew better than Nicklaus what had transpired two holes away. Jack knows the scream of an eagle. Again he stepped away from his ball, this time shaking his head. He half smiled and said, 'Geez'. Those who heard the remark could not help but smile. The man wasn't all computerized birdie maker after all.

But back to business. That little putt. He would need it now to hold a tie with Trevino. After those two interruptions, did the putt get a few feet longer, the hole smaller? We would now see the stuff of which Nicklaus was made. Steel. He again set himself, deliberately. He eased the putter back as only Nicklaus seems able when under pressure – slowly. He eased the blade through, and the ball went dead into the hole. The roar at that matched at least one of the preceding.

Then, dimly at first, later more noticeably, we could see that Jack had lost, or had decided to back away from, his aggressive stance. With the lead, he reverted to his conventional form, letting others make the mistakes. He went back to using safe irons from the tees. He had birdie chances at 13, 14, and

15, but missed. The putts had not been hit with quite the same authority as before. The thrill was ebbing. At 17, a par-five he could have reached with a 3-wood and an iron, he did use his driver. Strange, because here he didn't really need it. And he hooked it badly into deep grass on the slope of a fairway bunker. He played out far short of the green, but hit a fine 6-iron to within 12 feet of the hole – a birdie chance. The putt slid by, and as he waited crouched beside the green for Guy Hunt to putt out, Jack's head hung weighted down as if by a stone, his body elastic gone limp.

Still, he was not out of it. Trevino and Jacklin were only one shot ahead of him, although they had the seventeenth to play and you had to expect at least one of them to birdie the hole. So why not recharge himself for one more big play at 18? It is a strong par-four that Jack had been playing with a 1-iron from the tee and another to reach home, which meant it was also a very long hole. He should go for the driver here, I thought, shorten the test as much as possible, and enhance the chance for a birdie by leaving only a short iron to the green.

But no, he didn't. He played a 1-iron and a 5-iron. All right. The second shot was 35 feet or so from the cup. Not a real birdie chance, but surely he would give it a good run. Again, no. He left the putt short – *short*. He said later that he played a 1-iron from the eighteenth tee because of the percentages. He wasn't that confident with his driver (hadn't used it enough all week), and he played for a sure par on the grounds that the other fellows would still have to play the hole. If neither birdied 17, Nicklaus didn't want to bogey the last hole and lose the tournament should Trevino or Jacklin also bogey it. This is also why he didn't charge the last putt.

A Kantian critique of pure reason – good golf sense, good management. Then Trevino chipped in at 17 to save par, and after seeing that, Jacklin three-putted from inside 20 feet to fall out of contention. Trevino, who grew up in the discomfort of a fatherless, poor home, to whom management meant seeing the piece of cake and taking without hesitation, bashed his driver on 18, stroked an easy 7-iron to the green, and walked away with the title by one stroke over Jack.

When it was over, I could not help feeling that Nicklaus had somehow betrayed the deeper spirit of competition, that on the final hole he might have revived that brief but galvanic 11-hole departure from character and torn head-on into the last hole with all he had. Sure, his great success in golf comes from careful control of his mental and physical powers, but he had shown a flash of daring, a blood-and-guts Nicklaus transported beyond common sense. It had worked, and it was good. But he didn't do it again, and as I drove slowly back to Edinburgh through a Sunday twilight, I felt a selfish disappointment at being deprived of a memorable sporting moment.

*Dave Hill is no sycophant which makes his respect for Nicklaus the competitor and Nicklaus the man the more striking.*

# A DIFFERENT GAME
## DAVE HILL, 1977

I would like to see Jack Nicklaus win the Grand Slam – the four major tournaments in the same year – for the simple reason that he is capable of doing it. It's his one remaining goal and I hope he fulfils it. I ought to hope he fulfils it soon. Maybe then he would feel he had no more worlds to capture and would retire and leave the tour to us mortals.

Nicklaus is playing a different game than the rest of us. Any year he doesn't win two major tournaments has to be a bad year for him in his own mind. Jack would rather win one major title than five lesser ones. He knows he'll be remembered by the number of major championships he wins. Sam Snead has won 28 more championships than Ben Hogan, but Hogan always ranks ahead of Snead when you're debating greatness because Hogan won all the big ones.

As good as Hogan was, I don't think he or anyone else is close to Nicklaus as an all-time great. Nicklaus has much more physical equipment than Hogan had and he's maturing into just as good a strategist. Jack hits the ball so well that people don't appreciate that he thinks his way around a golf course better than anybody else on the tour today.

Jack's still a young man, in his thirties. Hogan was only beginning to do his thing well at that stage of life. Nicklaus is pacing himself, playing only 20 to 25 tournaments a year, and I expect him to be beating everybody in 15 years. He could be another Sam Snead if his desire holds up. He's building a unique busines empire and he has to keep winning to make it go. That's a keen incentive.

When Jack is playing well, nobody beats him. Not Tom Weiskopf or Johnny Miller or me or anybody else. He knows it and we know it. We don't talk about it in those terms, but we accept it as a fact of life. I'm not saying the rest of us have written ourselves off against Jack. He's human, and if he's a little off and I play up to my capacity and make all my putts, I can beat him. But he has to be almost mediocre to lose.

He's the only man on tour who can make two or three straight bogeys and then turn his round right around with two or three quick birdies. It all starts with his tremendous tee ball. He has more accurate length than anyone else. We have several players who can move the ball 300 yards off the tee. Jim Dent can hit it 350 with a three-quarter swing. Larry Ziegler, Bobby Nichols, Eddie Pearce – all of them can hit it a ton. The difference is that Nicklaus can hit it far and consistently straight and carry the ball higher. He's having some lower-back problems that seem to be costing him a little power but not that much.

He beats you to death on the par-fives. They're damn near eagle holes for him. On most courses he can count on birdieing at least three of the four par-fives, and he's going to make some eagles hitting the green in two. On a lot of par-fives he can hit a driver and a middle iron. On a long course like Firestone – which is generally considered a great test but is too dull by my standards – he has to be a huge favourite. On the second hole, for instance, a par-five that doglegs left, I'll hit a driver and 3-wood and be short of the green. He can cream his driver over the trees at the corner of the dogleg and have an iron to the green. If we were in a play-off, I'd feel like walking straight into the clubhouse.

Nicklaus has an advantage on longer par-threes because he hits his long irons so high that he can drop them softly on the green when I'm hitting a 3-wood that will hit and run. A high ball isn't good – except when Nicklaus hits it. He can hit the ball high and still hold it on line in the wind. The ball doesn't sail or hang up on him.

On par-fours he has an edge because he can carry the fairway trouble with his high driver shots. The bunkers and water hazards are out there 250 to 260 yards, where most pros drive the ball. Nicklaus flies the ball over all that trouble. He flat air-mails it. Recently we played a course that is typical. The par-fours were bunkered left and right and everybody was playing in between the bunkers. Nicklaus simply flew the fairway bunker that was on the shortest route to the green.

The only way to equalize these conditions between Nicklaus and me would be to stagger a series of fairway bunkers from 250 on out to 280 yards and taper them into the fairway so that he would have to contend with the same number of hazards as everyone else. Make the first two bunkers shallow and the last two deeper. Or if you're talking about a lateral water hazard, extend it farther towards the green and cut it out into the fairway more so that the farther you hit the drive the greater the risk you run. None of this would affect the playability of the course for the average golfer – he'll be driving the ball short of the trouble. Then Nicklaus would have to work for his distance the same as everyone else.

Another thing about Jack's driving. He can afford to let out because he's stronger out of the rough. Long grass doesn't bother him the way it does us shorter players. He can go for the green where another player can't do anything but chop the ball back to the fairway. That's why he's particularly tough in the US Open. The US Golf Association grows dense rough everywhere you look; but you don't see Nicklaus losing many strokes in the rough.

Nicklaus's power swing is the modern action. It's right for him, but I think thousands of average players are making a mistake trying to emulate Jack's swing, especially his overly upright plane. He forces the club up and out of a natural 45-degree plane on his backswing, letting his right elbow fly out away from his body. For the average player that's disaster. For Jack it works to give him a bigger swing arc because he is able to make well-timed adjustments at the start of his downswing.

Jack is a body player. He uses the big muscles. He's a hitter, not a swinger. He creates tremendous torque on his backswing by turning well with his upper body but resisting with his legs. Then on the downswing he uses his legs mightily. He is the ultimate legs player. His unusual physique has all but dictated that he build a swing on strong leg action. His secret, physically, is that he's four inches short of normal in the thighs and upper arms for a man of his girth. He's 5 feet 11 inches and 185 pounds. His thighs are massive; they're 29 inches around, which just happens to be my waist size. He has me in the thighs by a foot! The man is abnormally built, and that has a lot to do with his power.

He has his swing so well grooved that he gives the appearance of being almost mechanical. His movements appear to be programmed. He may not be the most elegant looking swinger on the tour, but he stays in good balance through the ball and there is a great freedom of motion in his swing.

His finesse is underrated. His putting touch on fast greens is unbelievable. He rolls it so well from 20 feet. I'm better on slow greens because I don't have a nice fluid stroke. When I can rap the ball, I can get it on line. My stroke isn't a smooth, repeating stroke, and on slow greens you can get away with making a little different hit every time. On fast greens you can't, and on fast greens he is the best. And he's the best lag putter, getting long putts from thirty to a hundred feet to within 'gimme' distance of the hole. He wouldn't three-putt a supermarket parking lot.

I wouldn't rate Jack the best putter in the world overall because he doesn't put that much pressure on his putting. He hits so many greens in regulation figures that he doesn't have to sink a lot of putts to beat you. I will say that if I had to have somebody putt a 20-footer for everything I own – my house, my cars, my family – I'd want Nicklaus to putt it for me.

Jack can't tell you why he makes so many crucial putts, except he works harder on them mentally. It's painful watching his concentration. He can stand over a putt for 40 seconds before he pulls the trigger. If I did that, I'd freeze. It would drive me up the wall. But he isn't aware of the time passing.

A friend of Jack's told me something that points up his unusual power of concentration. Few people realize that Jack smokes two packs of cigarettes a day. He's almost a chain smoker. But he doesn't smoke while he's playing – maybe because he's afraid he'll be a bad influence on young people – and he concentrates so hard on his golf that he doesn't miss smoking!

Does Nicklaus have a weakness? He has a glaring weakness. From a hundred yards in to the green he is one of the poorer wedge players on the tour. He is very weak pitching the ball with a three-quarter swing. A player like Lee Trevino is much better at these shorter finesse shots than Jack.

The three-quarter shot is a feel shot. Jack has no feel in his pitch shots and sand shots. It certainly is something he could learn – but his idea of how to play a pitch shot is wrong in my opinion. His full swings are correctly based on leg action. Whenever he's playing bad golf he thinks it's because his legs aren't moving enough on the downswing. They start forward before his hands finish going back.

He tries to play short shots the same way, and you can't. You don't play those little shots with your legs, you play them with your hands. Your legs do move some, but you don't drive them hard toward the target. Jack tries to feel a 30-yard pitch shot through his legs when he should feel it through his hands. He treats a pitch shot too much like a power shot and that's why he isn't a good wedge player. It's why he doesn't win as much on shorter courses.

How is Jack as a playing partner? One of the best. He is exceptionally courteous and friendly; he always has been, despite his public image as a somewhat aloof, cold person. He always thinks to compliment you on a good shot, and has something pleasant to say when there's a wait on the tee. His galleries aren't as boisterous as Arnold Palmer's always have been, but they get bigger every year with more people coming to appreciate his ability, and he goes out of his way to see that they don't bother you. Often he will let you putt out first even though it's his turn. That keeps the gallery from running to the next tee.

As well as Jack has played recently, I don't think he's struck the ball as well the past six years as he did the six years before. But he's learned to accept it and he uses his head much better. As a strategist I can't imagine anyone but Hogan ever comparing with Jack. He almost never stops thinking during a round. He's always driving the ball at a small target, not just down the centre. He doesn't let a bad shot bother him – as soon as he believes he understands what he did wrong, he turns his entire attention to the next shot. He can manoeuvre the ball. He likes to play a fade for control, but can draw the ball from right to left if he wants to. At Augusta he draws his drives because it's a right-to-left course. Most players can play only one way or the other.

He's a great playing partner, but I hate to be paired with him down the stretch in a tournament if we're both in contention because his power makes you feel so inadequate. You tend to start pressing to hit it as far as he does, and then you're off your game. He's a slow player but faster than many others. He walks very fast; he's slow over the ball. Other than that, he's a model partner.

It's funny about the superstars' personalities off the course. The fans assume that Arnold Palmer is great company and Nicklaus is a bore. Arnold has much more charisma on the course; he can look at you if you're in the gallery and you think you've been friends, or lovers, for life. Arnold has more expressions than a French mimic if he misses a shot, and the fans feel for him. Jack is changing, but he's essentially still the opposite of Arnold as a public personality: serious, all business.

But off the course, Jack is much more fun as a dinner companion than Arnold, or at least that's been my limited experience. I don't dine regularly with either Arnold or Jack, but I find Jack a stimulating man who can talk about many subjects. Arnold is fun but he seldom thinks about anything but golf. I understand he has only a dozen books in his house – and they're all golf books. Jack enjoys interesting people who aren't in golf. He's not funny, but he has a little dry wit. He's straightforward. If something's bugging him, he says so, but he doesn't hold grudges.

We had dinner at La Costa one night during the Tournament of Champions and it was one of the most pleasant evenings I have had. Both of us are amateur wine buffs and we drank and discussed good wine. Jack has started his own wine collection and I intend to start one. When the wine steward started to pour the wine without letting it sit open for several minutes, we straightened him out. Jack talked about his changing business ventures and how the demands on him are growing. I think he thoroughly relishes his bright new image, and I don't blame him at all. He joined the tour as the big fat boy who had been raised with a silver 7-iron in his mouth, and one of the first things he did was upset Palmer, everybody's hero, in the 1962 US Open at Oakmont. He didn't like to talk to the press and, since the press likes to be catered to, that cost him. I think he eventually would have won over the fans anyway – it's hard to dislike the best player in history – but he speeded the process a few years ago when he lost a lot of weight, let his hair grow, started dressing better, and developed into a good interview for the writers. All of a sudden Jack Nicklaus was sexy, of all things.

# TOURNAMENTS

*The majority of tournament reporting is done in haste. Play has just ended; there is a deadline imminent; eight hundred words have to be typed and phoned in to the office.*

*Good writing can sometimes be the result but the journalist is often confined to reciting what he thought were the key happenings of the day. So, we tend to start off with the simplification: 'Faldo holes four-foot putt to win Open' or 'Italian stopped his ball going out of bounds', as Hagen once claimed of Sarazen.*

*Bernard Darwin had a very different approach. He concentrated on what he had seen. And, if he was often in the wrong place at the wrong time, that couldn't be helped. The scores would have to tell that part of the story.*

*Sometimes, too much detail can be a draw-back. The reader feels buried under an avalanche of birdie putts, double bogeys, and the lengths and numbering of holes. Even so, the best writing about golf events is usually recollected in tranquility and found in magazines and books.*

## COULD A WRITER GET AT IT?
### MARK McCORMACK, 1968

What an achievement it would be to set forth, properly and for all time, the glories of a golf tournament, the subtleties of mood, the severity of the strain, the infinite complexity and pure simplicity that taken together make up what I think is the most stimulating sporting event of all. The stuff is there, to put it bluntly. I wish a writer could get at it so that forevermore, to cite one benefit, the galleries that fill courses, drawn as they are by the smattering of the drama they are knowledgeable enough to see, would be able to savour the true richness of the game and its demands. The sport deserves such a piece of literature someday. I once offered this notion to a golf writer of considerable repute. He pondered it for a moment and then gave me an answer that struck me as fair enough. He said such a story would take as much time, effort, and research as the chronicle of a battle, and therefore would not be worth it. That kind of art, he said, deserves a life and death issue. He is probably right.

*The first championship at Muirfield was highly controversial. The town of Musselburgh, where the event was due to be held was furious. The Honourable Company had moved their home to Gullane and taken the championship with them. The players themselves were none too pleased. They thought the new course was very poor. It was to be many years, not until the late 1920s, before Muirfield began to approach the status it has today.*

## Muirfield's First Open
### DAVID SCOTT DUNCAN, 1893

According to time-honoured precedent the Open Golfing Championship, the event *par excellence* of the golfing season, fell to be held last year over Musselburgh links. But with the exodus of the Honourable Company of Edinburgh Golfers from the 'honest town' to Muirfield, the council of that venerable company, whose turn it was to manage details, in their wisdom decreed that the championship should accompany them eastwards. Of course, as one of the three promoting clubs the Honourable Company were strictly within their rights in changing the venue, but we question the wisdom of the change. Muirfield is an excellent private course – in fact, we know of none better – and the putting greens are magnificent; but there is a sameness about the 18 holes, and they are not such a reliable test of golfing ability as the nine holes at Musselburgh. Then its inaccessibility, situated as it is about four miles from the nearest railway station, is an undoubted drawback in some respects, albeit this much may be said, that the players are not hampered by large followings.

On the other hand, we have nothing but praise for the general arrangements. The imposition of an entry fee is a move in the right direction, and will go far to deter vainglorious players from entering and cumbering the field. The increase in the prize-money was a welcome surprise to the professional candidates for honours, and the extension of the competition over two days, and 72 holes, was a decided improvement on the conditions which formerly obtained, and reduced the chances of a snatch victory to a minimum. If we except Mr J. E. Laidlay and Douglas Rolland, every player with any pretensions to championship form (and, be it confessed with bated breath, many with none) figured in the entry list of 66; and the hundred or so followers of the royal and ancient game who journeyed from Edinburgh on the morning of Thursday 22 September, the opening day, went prepared to have a thorough treat. And so they had; for the play, if scarcely up to the extraordinary pitch of excellence attained at the Musselburgh tournament the previous week, was well above the average of previous championships, and the lovely weather put the players and onlookers alike on the best of terms with themselves.

The scratching of half a dozen players necessitated a slight alteration in the draw. This was soon fixed up, and Mr B. Hall Blyth, who controlled matters at the starting point, got the first couple dispatched punctually at half-past ten.

*   *   *

At the outset Mr John Ball and Willie Park drew the bulk of the spectators after them, and both gave an excellent account of themselves. The amateur champion's driving was straight and true, and his approaching perfect; but a stroke or two was dropped here and there on the putting green by being short. Still, the excellence of his golf was testified to by his score of 75 for the first round. Park was occasionally off the line with his tee shots, but he never failed to recover any little advantage thus lost, and his 78 was a record of steady play.

Other good scores among the early couples were 76 by D. Anderson, Jr, 77 each by A. Herd and Hugh Kirkcaldy, and 78 by Mr Hilton; but it was well on in the day before Mr Ball was ousted from premier place. This honour fell to Mr Horace Hutchinson, whose return to his very best form was welcomed by all. Like Park's, his driving was a little faulty in line, but his iron approaches were peculiarly telling, and his score of 74 must rank as one of his best efforts. Davie Brown, of Malvern, although far from well, registered a very steady 77 in Mr Hutchinson's immediate wake, these being the lowest returns for the first round. Andrew Kirkcaldy and Archie Simpson were somewhat disappointing, and so was Mr A. M. Ross, who had been carrying everything before him in Gullane and district, but he had singularly bad luck meted out to him. Naturally Mr Hutchinson had a large following in the second round, and he kept up his good form right to the end, where, in missing a simple looking putt for a five, he made his only bad mistake, and with a 77 he headed the field by three strokes on the day's play. Park and Herd also kept up their charter for steadiness with 77 and 78 respectively; but Mr Ball fell off a little, and, returning an 80, tied with Park and Herd for second place. An 83 dropped Hugh Kirkcaldy somewhat; but, with a 75 and 76 respectively, [Tom] Vardon and Sayers improved their positions considerably, and were still well in the running, in fact, the day's play left the issue extremely open, and any one of the first dozen seemed quite likely to win.

The draw for the second day was entirely different from the first – a really good idea.

\*     \*     \*

Of the more likely candidates, the first to attract attention was Mr Ball, who, partnered by Douglas M'Ewan, drew a large proportion of the spectators with him. For the nine outward holes his game was nearly perfection, perhaps his only mistake being in approaching at the fourth hole; and, keeping up the same form coming home, his 74 put his backers, whose name was legion, on the best of terms with themselves. For a time no one came near this figure, but at length Hugh Kirkcaldy handed in a very fine 73 – the best up to this point on either of the days. Out in 38, he came home in one less, three threes helping him considerably. Meanwhile it was known that the erstwhile leader, Mr Hutchinson, for whom Mr A. J. Balfour was acting as marker, had not only lost his advantage, but placed himself comparatively out of it. Beginning badly by pulling his tee shot into the wood which bounds the course to the first hole, bad luck dogged him throughout, and at the close of a disastrous round his figures totalled 86. With a steady 77, marred by a six to the ninth hole, where he topped his drive and foozled his second, Herd still kept second place; and a really good 74 somewhat improved J. Kay's position. But it was left to Mr Hilton to provide the sensation of the round. A grand tee shot to within a yard of the pin enabled him to get down in two at the first hole, and from here on to the home hole he showed the most brilliant golf, and holed out in 72 amidst general applause, thus taking second place to Mr Ball. A little behind him came Willie Park and Mr Mure Fergusson, who each registered 80, faulty putting on the second green, and two strokes lost in the bunker at the fourteenth hole, being responsible for Park's falling away.

The last round saw more chops and changes among the six leaders – Mr Ball, 229; Mr Hilton, 231; A. Herd, 232; Hugh Kirkcaldy, 233; J. Kay, 234; and Willie Park, 235. Of these Mr Ball led the way, and although off the tee and through the green he showed no falling off, he was frequently short in his long putts, and with a 79 his aggregate was 308, thus furnishing a cue to the others as to what they had to beat. Hugh Kirkcaldy preserved his good form of the forenoon, and driving to the last hole had a five to beat Mr Ball; but he pitched into the ditch guarding the green with his third, and, although he made a grand recovery, it took him six, and so he dead-heated with the amateur champion. Herd, a couple or two behind, had also a similar figure to head the poll, but he missed an easy putt, and was consequently bracketed level with the other two. From the rear, however, came such glowing accounts of Mr Hilton's progress, that nearly everyone rushed to where he and his partner, Jack Ferguson, then were, and with an enthusiastic and ever increasing following they made their way home. At the turn Mr Hilton had drawn level with Mr Ball, and, forging steadily ahead on the home coming, he had 20 to tie with four holes to go. A three and five to the next two gave him 11 to win driving to the second last green. Here Jack Ferguson created a sensation by getting down in two, but when Mr Hilton's ball found the bottom in one more, all was over, bar accidents. A six to the home hole completed a grand round, played with the greatest confidence and dash, and, amidst general cheering, Mr Hilton was hailed as champion for the year. With a fine free style, he is one of the most rapid players we have ever seen, taking little or no time to judge his shots; and his partner, Jack Ferguson, who likes plenty of time, seemed thoroughly glad when the round was over. Nor did Mr Hilton's success end with the championship, for he also secured a special prize, value £5, given to the compiler of the lowest round, his first round of 72 on the second day being one stroke better than the best effort of Hugh Kirkcaldy, the previous champion. Needless to say, Mr Hilton was loudly cheered when he received the champion cup and accompanying gold medal at the hands of Mr Alex Stuart, captain of the Honourable Company of Edinburgh Golfers; and in briefly returning thanks, he spoke of the excellent condition of the green, and hoped he would be able to play there again on some future occasion. Mr Hilton is the second amateur who has secured the Open Championship, his mentor, Mr John Ball, Jr being the other.

Thus, within the short space of two years, we have seen the two distinguished Hoylake amateurs succeed, where all Scotch amateurs have failed, in vanquishing the pick of the professional players, and so carrying the blue ribbon of golf south of the Tweed. In them Hoylake has two sons of whom she may justly feel proud, and, with English professionals like [Tom] Vardon and More coming rapidly to the front to assist them, Scotland will indeed require to look to her laurels at her own peculiar game. Still, it is international trials of strength like these that will bring added popularity to an already popular event, and, with Scotland now fairly on her mettle, this year's meeting at Prestwick should see a rare good fight for supremacy between the sister countries. Needless to say, after the severe test of two days' golf, there was not the semblance of a fluke about Mr Hilton's win, and although through sheer bad luck he has never yet succeeded in enrolling himself as amateur champion, he has, at the second time of asking, secured the more important sister event. Mr Hilton is pluck personified, and his dashing play was in pleasing contrast to the more cautious mode of the professionals. But, of course, with an amateur in the Open Championship, it is *aut Caesar aut nullus,* and this may account for the difference.

## MY FIRST AMATEUR
### BERNARD DARWIN, 1946

Freddie Tait not only won that championship but was by far its most dramatic figure. There were two Freddie Taits. There was the one who had swept through the championship of two years before at Sandwich, having the hardest part of the draw, encountering one famous player after another and knocking their heads off, murdering Harold Hilton in the final. That one could play beautiful faultless golf, making none of his traditional recoveries because none was needed. The other Freddie could be extraordinarily erratic for so great a player, in need of all the recoveries in his bag, and it was this one who was chiefly on view at Hoylake. His long game was all awry, and though his swing looked as graceful and easy as usual, the ball went to very odd places, and only a real genius for getting out of them, together with some of that fortune that favours the brave, pulled him through.

As I remember it now, everything in the championship seemed to be working up to a grand climax, the meeting of Tait and Hilton in, I think, the fourth or fifth round. From the start it was clear that they were foredoomed to meet. All Hoylake and all Liverpool hoped that now, when Harold was Open Champion and on his own course, he would not only win the Amateur at last but would conquer once and for all the weakness which always beset him when he had to face his Scottish rival. He was playing well, he had won his early matches with ease, and the crowd poured out to see the match and did not, I fancy, do its hero much good by many preliminary pats on the back, which were meant to be encouraging.

136

Harold looked uneasy and Freddie full of confidence. I remember seeing him practising at the putting holes inside the chains and white posts in front of the clubhouse. A friend asked after his game and he replied cheerfully: 'All right except this part of it, and that'll be all right by the afternoon'. So it was, for not only did he put away his eccentric mood in the long game but his putting seems in the recollection to have been devastating. Neither began very well, but Harold putted dreadfully on the second green and lost a hole which he looked as if he were going to win. At the fourth, the Cop, Freddie holed a good putt to be two up and all was over. Only one other shot do I recall, a long putt which Freddie holed on the Briars green. I can see him thrusting forward his right foot in a most characteristic movement, just as the ball is going in. The match ended at the Rushes, the thirteenth, and it was a sad procession that took its way back to the club. A perky little Cockney golfer, long since dead, with a 'quiff' of hair, who looked like a drawing of Phil May's, said to the defeated champion: 'Well, Harold, I don't think you ever will win this championship'. As an example of sympathetic tact, the remark left something to be desired.

*The American and British Amateur Championships have been largely killed by the riches of the professional game. To win one is a stepping stone to playing for money. Even so, it isn't so many years since these championships were as closely followed as an Open and received far more space than a run-of-the-mill tournament. In 1927, for instance, when the first Ryder Cup match was played in America, Bernard Darwin stayed at home to report the Amateur Championship.*

*This next piece recalls John Ball's last victory – 24 years after his first.*

# THE OLD VERSUS THE NEW
## BERNARD DARWIN, 1928

A terrible battle was that at Westward Ho! in 1912, when Mr John Ball beat Mr Abe Mitchell, then still an amateur, at the thirty-eighth hole. Mr Ball had begun that championship meeting in one of his apparently lazy moods. He had played downright ill in the international match, which was that year played entirely by foursomes; after that he had improved and fought his way into the sixth round when he met Mr F. S. Bond, and Mr Bond, playing uncommonly well, appeared to have the match at his mercy. I think he was five up with seven to play when Mr Ball began to spurt. Two holes were lopped off, but even so Mr Bond was dormy three. The strain was telling on him, however, and Mr Ball was playing like clockwork, holing no long putts but sticking ruthlessly to the perfect figure.

And so all those three holes dropped away and the nineteenth as well and Mr Ball miraculously survived. He beat Mr Angus Hambro comfortably in the semi-final, and there he was, yet again in the final of the championship. Meanwhile Mr Mitchell, though he had one or two close runs, was yet looking all the time like a winner. He had had a good deal of experience since he had appeared raw and fresh from his native Ashdown two years before at Hoylake, and the long course suited his tremendous driving. He was not then the accurate player that he is now; in particular he had not mastered the controlled iron shot which is such a feature of his game; but, as far as pure length was concerned, I am inclined to think that he was longer than he is today and he always was a neat pitcher with a mashie. There were certain holes at Westward Ho! that year which he seemed to be able to reach with a drive and an iron, while no one else reached them in two shots of any kind. That he could beat Mr Ball for length was certain; beyond that no one could prophesy.

\* \* \*

It came on wet and stormy at Westward Ho! and while this exactly suited the dogged genius of Mr Ball, it did not suit his adversary, who had some difficulty in holding his wet clubs; he lost something of his length of driving and with it his one distinct advantage.

There was, as I think, another factor worth mentioning, and that was the behaviour of a section of the crowd. There trooped out of Bideford a body of spectators who knew very little about golf, but appeared to be imbued with a violent and wholly inappropriate 'class' feeling: there was a working man in the final and they had come to see him win. Not content with this reasonable partisanship they fanned themselves into a still warmer flame by imagining Mr Ball, as the typical capitalist, trampling on the honest workman. Their behaviour was at once venomous and absurd. It was utterly repugnant to Mr Mitchell, whom they supported, and did him no good and probably a great deal of harm. As to Mr Ball, if it had any effect on him at all, it was to harden his resolution and make him set his teeth even more tightly. To make him angry is the way to make him win.

At the end of the first round youth was three up on age and three holes should surely take a lot of getting back, against superior length on a very long course. I remember to have been told, whether truly or not I do not know, that Mr Ball himself made a prophecy at this point: it was that if he could hold his man for the first three holes after lunch he might just about be able to do it. These first three holes, with the wind blowing as it was, gave the long driver an advantage; and the prophecy, if it was made, was an astute one. In fact Mr Ball did better than hold his own in those three holes, for he got one back; he had the turn of the luck at the short hole and was now not only within striking distance but right on his enemy's heels. That enemy, however, had plenty of fight left in him, and the match went on with thrilling ups and downs till it was all square with three to play. On the sixteenth green Mr Ball with a putt for the half was laid what looked the deadest stymie that ever was laid, the adversary's ball on the brink of the hole and no apparent way round – no, not a ghost of a one. Mr Ball looked at his opponent with a smile, half quizzical, wholly good-natured, and there are not many people who could smile at such a moment. Then he settled down to his putt and, with an aluminium putter of all unlikely clubs, played the shot at exactly the dead strength and by some miracle holed it.

All square with two to play, and then Mr Ball missed his second to the long seventeenth and Mr Mitchell was dormy. Both of them were over the black and oozy burn in two, neither was quite dead in three. I imagine each ball lay four or perhaps five feet away. Mr Mitchell had to play. This for the championship! No doubt the putt looked horribly long to him at that moment. He pushed the ball out to the right of the hole, and made a gesture of stifled despair. Mr Ball rapped his in, right at the back of the hole, and the crowd rushed out across the burn again. The nineteenth was marked by two splendid recovering shots, Mr Ball from a bunker on the right, Mr Mitchell from a watery ditch on the left (it was the Alps at Prestwick over again), and the hole was halved in five. At this point I raced away down the fairway of the second hole in order to see the second shots. One ball came right down the middle of the course: that was Mr Ball's. There followed a long pause: no second ball came. What on earth had happened? Clearly some tragedy had overtaken Mr Mitchell, but what could it be? 'The match is over' – the word was passed along and we rushed back bewildered. Mr Mitchell had topped his ball into a ditch and in trying to get out had hit the ball on to himself. Mr Ball had won his eighth championship. Will any man ever win so many again?

*One year later one of the most significant championships ever was held and the USGA is commemorating it by taking their Open to Brookline in 1988 on its 75th anniversary.*

# Local Boy Makes Good
## MICHAEL HOBBS, 1976

Miller, Trevino, Nicklaus, Weiskopf, Player: these are the biggest names in international golf in the mid-1970s. All except one are American. In 1913 the names were Vardon, Taylor, Braid and Ray. All were British, and all played most of their golf in the British Isles. When any one of them ventured overseas it was to show the natives how the game should be played. If they all competed in a championship, the question was which of them would come first.

Harry Vardon made his second exhibition tour of the US in 1913, accompanied by Ted Ray, the 1912 British open champion. Wherever they went, crowds flocked. Was not Vardon incomparably the greatest player the game had yet seen? Even today his swing is still thought of as the most graceful and easy the game has known. His accuracy gave birth to a host of stories. He could place a brassy shot as near the pin as a modern master with a wedge. It was said, and widely believed, that he could not play the same course twice in a day without experiencing a problem that never faced other players. The second time round his tee shots at the par-fours and fives were said to come to rest in the divots left by his second shots of the morning round.

Ted Ray was an attraction of a different kind. True, he did not quite rank with the great triumvirate, as they were called, of Vardon, Taylor and Braid, because his record in the British Open was inferior to theirs, but of these figures of the dim golfing past he, more than anyone else, had something of the crowd appeal that Arnold Palmer was to have in the 1950s and 1960s. Not for either of them a steady progress down the centre of the fairway and arrival at the fat of the green. The ordinary golfer could identify with Ted Ray. His ball also frequently came to rest behind trees, in bunkers and wide in the rough. But the similarity ended there. Ted, like Arnold Palmer, was a player of great power. His swing was not pretty – some called it a combination of lurch and heave – but he did smash the clubhead into the ball. And if not too large a sapling lay between him and it, he could deal with that as well. So golfing galleries gasped as his ball soared over trees and out of bunkers or flew up out of the rough accompanied by prodigious turves.

In September 1913, the Englishmen interrupted their tour to call in on the US Open Championship at the Country Club. Gathered to meet them was a host of hopeful, rather than confident, Americans – whatever they may have said for the benefit of the press. Many were not native-born but, like Jim Barnes the Cornishman, and Macdonald Smith, a Scotsman, had emigrated to the money and better status enjoyed by the professional golfers of the US. There was, however, 'Hagin, a home-bred American of whom no one seems to have heard much', as Bernard Darwin of *The Times* put it. It was a name that would soon be well known on both sides of the Atlantic, and in a day or so Darwin had got his spelling right. Walter Hagen already thought he was as good as anyone, though he had not yet made up his mind whether to concentrate on golf or baseball. His performance in this his first national tournament decided him, but much of the field was of poor quality – Darwin commented, 'Many of the players supply irrefutable evidence that the word "professional" is not always synonymous with "good"'.

The 36-hole qualifying was split into two days. No one was much surprised when Vardon led the first day's qualifiers on 151 and Ted Ray led the second group, but three strokes better. Already, some of the Americans must have been wondering which of the two Englishmen would win. Hagen felt he had not disgraced himself with 157 and a young American amateur with the unlikely name of Francis Ouimet had made the best use of his local-boy knowledge to total 152. He had probably burned himself out and the 72 holes of the championship proper were yet to begin.

The scores followed a predictable pattern for the first two rounds, at which point Vardon and Wilfred Reid, another Englishman, led on 147, followed by Ray on 149, after a tournament-best round of 70; the Anglo-Americans Macdonald, Smith and Barnes were on 150. And then came the first native

Americans, Hagen and Ouimet. Ouimet was still there after the third round and was tied for the lead with both Vardon and Ray on 225.

In the final round Ray faltered to a 79 but he was the leader in the clubhouse. The rest of the field would have 'only' 304 to beat.

Never a good putter in his later years, Vardon played well through the green but also returned a 79. Barnes, Smith and Hagen faded out over the second nine. Hagen's last fling for the title had contained a wealth of variety. He had begun, six, five, seven against a par of four, four, four. During practice he had studied Vardon's swing. His own was not going well, so he would try Vardon's to see if that would work better. An eagle two followed at the next and then a birdie. Much better. He then birdied the sixth and parred the seventh.

Hagen now seemed back in contention but thought he had again put himself out of it when he dropped shots at each of the next two holes to turn in 40. However, he then heard that Vardon and Ray were doing no better. They turned in 42 each. The three were level with nine holes to go. On the thirteenth Hagen had a medium-length putt to go into the lead, but it slipped by. The fourteenth finished his chances. Ahead, Vardon and Ray had both birdied it, and Hagen decided to risk a brassy from the wet turf; it fizzed along the ground for just a few yards. Next he went for the green with a long iron and hooked it. In the end there was a seven to go down on Hagen's card and the three strokes dropped here to Vardon and Ray were the final margin between them.

Meanwhile, Ouimet seemed headed for not much better than 90. He took 43 to the turn and then dropped two more strokes on the par-three tenth. He parred the next and then dropped yet another stroke on the twelfth. He had to cover the last six holes in two under par and the course was playing long and near-water-logged. On the thirteenth he chipped in for a birdie. He had to struggle for his pars on the next three holes and with two holes to go had to find a birdie on one of them. He got it with a downhill, sidehill putt of some five yards on the seventeenth. He had only to par the last hole to tie with Vardon and Ray. He did so fairly comfortably. It was a story too unlikely to have been given space in a *Boys' Own*. The 20-year-old local boy had tied the English multi-champions. It was as if today a two-handicap golfer matched, say, Miller and Nicklaus stroke for stroke.

Francis Ouimet was almost an unknown, though he did hold his state's amateur championship and had reached the semi-final of the US Amateur. He awoke on 20 September 1913 to newspaper fame, but at the course there were few takers at the 10-1 odds against his beating Vardon and Ray in the 18-hole play-off.

Francis went over to the practice ground and hit some warm-up shots out to his ten-year-old caddy Eddie Lowery, until he was told that Vardon and Ray were awaiting him at the first tee. The first crisis of the day concerned Eddie. Francis was stopped by a friend, a golfer of experience, who offered to caddy for him. Obviously his advice might be useful during the pressures of the day. He told the friend to get Eddie's agreement which the boy refused to give, even when he was offered a bribe. When Ouimet saw tears coming into his eyes he said, 'Eddie's going to caddy for me'.

In a steady drizzle that followed hours of heavy rain Ouimet, Vardon and Ray drew straws for the honour. Ouimet teed off first. 'Be sure and keep your eye on the ball', Eddie Lowery advised. Francis put his drive safely down the middle and felt some of the tension drain away. In the heavy conditions none of them could reach the 430 yard par-four in two, and three fives went down on the cards. Vardon and Ouimet parred the second and third, where Ray dropped a stroke. Ted was playing erratically. After pushing his drives off the first three tees, he hooked at the fourth hole.

The fifth brought Francis Ouimet his first crisis of the round from his first real error. He sliced his brassy second out of bounds. Without a change of expression he dropped another ball and put it on the green with the same club. He got down in two more and in fact each of the players took five. (At the time, the penalty for going out of bounds was just the wasted shot rather than the later more severe stroke and distance.) Francis had lost no ground. It was one turning point.

Vardon birdied the next, which put him a shot up on Francis and two on Ted Ray. By the eighth they were all level. Francis hit a mid-iron dead at the flag and holed from about 18 inches. Vardon had a par-four and Ray holed a long one for a birdie. They all had par-fives at the ninth, so at the halfway stage their cards read as follows:

```
Ouimet   38 (5, 4, 4, 4, 5, 4, 4, 3, 5)
Vardon   38 (5, 4, 4, 4, 5, 3, 4, 4, 5)
Ray      38 (5, 4, 5, 4, 5, 4, 3, 3, 5)
Par      36 (4, 4, 4, 4, 4, 4, 3, 4, 5)
```

Not great scoring certainly but every shot was all carry.

At the 140 yard tenth Ouimet took the lead for the first time. All three hit the green but Vardon and Ray three-putted. On the twelfth Ouimet had the chance of gaining two shots on Vardon and Ray but he was short with his birdie putt while they were taking bogey fives. Vardon then birdied the next to pull himself back to only one shot behind Ouimet.

The pressure now began to tell. Each player faltered on the fourteenth. Vardon hooked off the tee, recovered well, and then hooked his approach. Ray pushed his long second well out to the right. Ouimet failed to benefit, as he topped his second, but played a good iron to the green and the hole was halved in par-fives. Ray was lucky on the next hole. His tee shot was flying well into the rough when it struck a spectator and ricocheted back on to the fairway. Perhaps upset by the man's anger, he failed to take advantage of his good luck, and took a six, to the par-fours of the others. Four behind Ouimet and three behind Vardon, he was now more or less out of the hunt and emphasized this by three-putting the short sixteenth.

It was clearly now Vardon v Ouimet as they teed up on the seventeenth, a dogleg. One shot behind, Vardon took the risk of aiming for the angle of the dogleg, hoping to set up a short pitch to the green. He hooked into a bunker where he had no shot at all to the green and a five was inevitable. Francis had driven straight and followed with a mid-iron about 20 feet past the pin. If he could just ease his putt up to the hole, the championship would be in his pocket. His putt died on the lip – and toppled in.

The eighteenth became almost a formality. Vardon took a dispirited six and Ray's birdie came far too late. Francis was on in two and putted about 4 feet short. The coma of calm in which he had played throughout now deserted Ouimet as he grasped the size of his achievement. His knees and elbows trembled. He paused for a second or two and then got it into the hole. A 72 to Ray's 78 and Harry Vardon's 77. Their scores over the last nine, against a par of 3, 4, 4, 4, 5, 4, 3, 4, 4, were:

Ouimet   34 (3, 4, 4, 4, 5, 4, 3, 3, 4)
Vardon   39 (4, 4, 5, 3, 5, 4, 3, 5, 6)
Ray      40 (4, 4, 5, 4, 5, 6, 4, 5, 3)

American golf never looked back. True, Ted Ray took the US Open in 1920 but no Englishman was to do so again for 50 years. Ouimet had foreshadowed the coming mastery of men such as Hagen, Sarazen and Jones and had shown that the best Britons could be beaten by a young man of 20 who, to be unkind, was only a good golfer – never again did he play quite as well as in that September of 1913.

*Harry Vardon, J. H. Taylor and James Braid were involved in most of the Opens between the mid-1890s and the First World War. Taylor was the one who coped best with bad weather.*

## INTO THE TEMPEST
### BERNARD DARWIN, 1952

I have woken up to two other terrible mornings in championship weeks, those of Cotton's championship at Carnoustie in 1937 and Reg Whitcombe's at Sandwich in the following year, but 1913 was, I think, worse than either of them. It was hard to walk against the wind without turning tail now and then for a rest, and as to hitting against it – well, I take two eloquent statements from J. H.'s autobiography. The first hole at Hoylake that bends its way round that dreadful field of out-of-bounds memories is said in the books to measure 435 yards in length. It took J. H. two full shots with wood to reach the corner of the field, then another wooden club shot and a long run-up put him near the hole and down went the putt for five. Poor light-weight Michael Moran who had been on his heels the day before began with a ten. The third hole is longer, 480 yards: it took J. H. three full shots, a 60 yard run-up and a putt for another five. He went round in 77 and if ever there was a better round played in a tempest I have never heard of it. In the afternoon, when the wind had ever so slightly abated he had a 79, containing his tremendous three at the Briars, where his driving-mashie shot nearly knocked the pin out of the hole and he lay dead for a three. He won with 304 against Ray's 312, and the glory of the Briars still dazzles my sight.

*Though Taylor and Braid continued to play well for several years after the First World War, they were by then into their fifties. The result of the 1914 Open Championship did much to settle the placing of Vardon, Taylor and Braid in golf history.*

*Vardon and Nicklaus remain the only players to have won any major six times.*

## THE SIXTH OPEN
### HARRY VARDON, 1933

This championship was to prove one of, if not the most, memorable events in my golfing career. I think I am right in stating that it will go down in golfing history as one of the greatest contests in the annals of the game. There were several reasons for this. Possibly the chief one was the fact that Taylor and I, who occupied the two leading positions at the outset of the final day's play, were paired together. As it happened, the outcome of the championship resolved itself into a duel between the two of us. With one round left to be decided it appeared certain that either Taylor or myself would triumph. Thus it was to be a hand to hand fight. The crowd, too, was enormous. It was estimated that there were nearly five thousand people following us in the morning round. In the afternoon, however, this figure must have been doubled, as special trains came from Glasgow and other places bringing heavy additions at frequent intervals. Actually how many onlookers were present in the afternoon it would be impossible to state. I do know there were far too many to make things pleasant. It was an experience I would not care to go through again. This is by no means any reflection on those officials responsible for the management of this huge gathering that assembled on the famous Ayrshire links in an endeavour to witness the concluding stages of the championship. It would be impossible to bestow too much praise on the officials of the Prestwick Club for the admirable methods which they adopted to control this enormous crowd. For all that, it was indeed a trying ordeal. I do not think the average golfer has the slightest conception of what a leading player undergoes under these circumstances. He is battling to win the highest honour in his profession. As a start 72 holes of medal play is not only a severe test of golfing skill, but is also a stern nerve test as well. With the huge, excited crowd surging all around him, in their endeavour to be so placed as to have a view of the following stroke, it is only natural that the player should come in for a good deal of buffeting about. It may come as a surprise to many people to know after a big tournament my ankles and shins are black and blue. This is caused by the kicks received from those anxious to find a position in which to see something of the play. When I have struck my ball it is absolutely essential for me to at once give my club to my caddy so as to prevent it from being broken by the rushing crowd. Consequently, as I walk along in the midst of this multitude, I am pushed, elbowed and kicked as I make my way to my ball. Possibly if the spectators realized I was one of the players they would show a little more consideration. At least half of them do not realize that they are in any way interfering with one who is at the time, anyway, an object of attraction. Why should they? I am moving forward in the best way I can, in exactly the same way as they are. Consequently, as I am not carrying a club, there is nothing to show I am not a spectator. It will be readily realized under these circumstances that to attempt to produce one's best golf, with the additional nerve strain which competing in a major tournament is bound to produce, is indeed more of an ordeal than can be imagined by those who have not experienced it. There is another reason why this championship was to prove such a memorable one. Jimmie Braid, J. H. Taylor and I had all gained five victories, and as was only natural, were all extremely desirous of being the first to score the sixth success. Thus when 'J. H.' and I, with the championship practically resting between us, were drawn together on the last day for the concluding 36 holes, additional interest was added to the outcome of the result.

There is yet another factor which may have been taken into consideration. Taylor, Braid and I had all been exhibiting good form, and with such notable golfers as Ray, Duncan, Massy and Herd, to mention a few, all possessing chances of securing the coveted honour, the event was looked upon as having a somewhat open appearance. It is true many critics had predicted my success owing to the fact that I had been playing exceedingly good golf, and so they stated, had displayed such form at Cruden Bay which they appeared to consider ranked with the golf I had been able to produce in the days when at the height of my form. There was, too, additional interest to the event by the entry of Francis Ouimet, who had defeated Ray and myself in the American Open Championship the previous year. The usual qualifying test had to be undergone before a start could be made with the championship. This was a wearisome business and took place over the Troon and Troon Municipal course. On the opening day one-half of the competitors played 18 holes at Old Troon, while the other half played their first round on the Municipal links. On the following day this order was reversed. The qualifying rounds were favoured with splendid weather, in fact throughout the whole of the meeting the weather conditions were excellent. Prestwick was a very different course at this date than it had been six years previously on the last occasion on which the Open had been held there. Back tees had been made at many holes and the alteration at the ninth had put an extra 40 yards both to that hole and the tenth. The total length of the course had been increased by over five hundred yards. In addition to this a large number of new bunkers had been put in, and it was thought that Prestwick would prove to be a stiff test of golf for this meeting. I have always considered the Ayrshire links to be a fine test of the game, and my impressions of some of the outstanding holes may prove interesting to my readers. On the outward half the third, which is known as the Cardinal, is one of the finest holes to be found on any links. The length of this hole is 492 yards. A good straight tee shot is required if the famous hazard, from which the hole is named, is to be carried with the second stroke. The green is long and narrow and any player getting home in two shots may well be satisfied with both his length and his accuracy. The fifth, a one shot hole of 196 yards, with the Himalayas to be carried, is a splendid type of one-shotter. Number nine, measuring 493 yards, was in this championship an extremely testing hole. Many new bunkers had been put in for the big event and anyone steering clear of these hazards with his full second shot was not only exceedingly accurate but fortunate as well. On the homeward journey the eleventh and long twelfth are good, while at the fifteenth, a hole of 325 yards, a very accurate tee shot is necessary if trouble is to be avoided. The seventeenth, called the Alps, is possibly the most notable hole at Prestwick. The length of this one is 383 yards. A good straight drive will enable the player to be in a position for the second shot which has to be played over the formidable hazard which guards the green. Sound accurate golf is required on this fine testing course which is in every way a fitting one on which to hold the Open Championship.

The weather was perfect as my partner, Gordon Lockhart, and I set out for the opening round. I played extremely well that morning, and reaching the turn in 36 and completing the homeward journey in one over fours, was a splendid start in my endeavour to secure my sixth victory in the premier golfing event of the world. Actually my score of 73 which, incidentally, constituted a record for the altered course, might have been a couple of shots lower. I had missed holeable putts on each of the first two greens. Owing to the prolonged drought they were exceptionally fast and, as the event continued, became almost like glass. However, I was well satisfied, not only with the card which I had handed in, but also with the form I had displayed. I was driving a long straight ball and my iron shots were entirely satisfactory. After the two opening holes, I had no complaint to make about my putting which was sound rather than brilliant.

I distinctly recall one hole with which I was pleased. This was the Cardinal, where, after a good tee shot, I placed my second about six or seven yards from the flag. Although I did not hole my putt for a three, those two full wooden club strokes were as well and accurately struck as any I have ever hit in my life. One stroke behind my score came Jimmie Braid, J. H. Taylor and E. Whitcombe. Francis Ouimet was, I understand, experiencing trouble in the control of his wooden clubs and his card of 86 practically put him out of the running at this the very outset of the competition. In the second round I started away in fine style with a couple of threes, but the greens were now fast becoming extremely difficult, and I slipped several putts. I reached the turn in 38, and an incoming score of 39 gave me a card of 77 for the round.

My play had been as good with all clubs as in my first 18 holes. It is true my score was four strokes higher than in my opening round and that I had wasted several shots on the putting greens. This apparent failure was not so much the result of bad putting as the extreme keenness of the greens. Putting throughout this championship was exceedingly difficult. My total of 150 for the 36 holes placed me in the leading position, one stroke ahead of J. Ockenden. His 76 added to his 75 in his first round, gave him an aggregate of 151. J. H. Taylor occupied third place one stroke further behind. Jimmie Braid, after his good score of 74, experienced considerable difficulty with his holing out and an 82 gave him a total of 156. Abe Mitchell, who was competing in his first Open Championship as a professional and who was at this period attached to the Sonning Club, returned an aggregate of 154, made up of two steady rounds of 76 and 78. On the same mark as Mitchell was J. D. Edgar, who was professional in Northumberland, and Tom Williamson, of Nottingham. Reggie Wilson led the younger school of professionals and by his cards of 77 and 76 was fast making a name for himself as many competent critics had predicted would be the case.

The final day's play will ever live in my memory. I set out on that memorable day with a lead of two over my great rival, J. H. Taylor. The third round in a championship is always considered the testing one. On this occasion it was certainly a thrilling one. I continued to play well and reaching the turn in 37 to my opponent's 38 was now leading him by three strokes. There are two holes on the outward journey which I shall always remember. One was at the seventh, a hole of 287 yards. Both my opponent and I hit excellent tee shots. When we arrived at our respective balls I found it was mine which was just short, while my opponent was comfortably on the green not far from the hole. This gave him a splendid opportunity of securing a two, which I may say he was quick to take advantage of. As I did not lay my run up sufficiently close to enable me to get a three he had reduced my lead from four to two strokes. The other hole which I recall was the ninth, where with two really excellent wooden club strokes I was home and had a putt for three. Although I failed to hole it, I gained a further shot, as J. H. was trapped in one of the numerous bunkers which had been put in at this hole. Taylor is well known for his sterling fighting qualities. I had played with him on so many occasions that I was well aware of this characteristic. On many occasions I have had cause to admire the dogged determination with which he faced adversity. Never was this quality more in evidence than in this third round at Prestwick. J. H. found more than his fair share of trouble during that trying morning play. That he eventually returned a score of 74, and gained four strokes on the round after being three behind at the end of the first nine, was a performance worthy of his great reputation as a golfer and a fighter. Although my opponent gained five strokes on me in the inward half I did not in any way play badly. I dropped a stroke here and there which no doubt I should not have done, and Taylor was quick to seize his opportunities. At the tenth I found a bunker on the left hand side of the green from my brassy shot, while at the following hole my long iron up to the pin was a little pulled and was also bunkered on the left-hand side of the green. At these two holes my opponent, by recording a couple of fours, was able to recover three strokes, thus wiping out the lead I had secured over him at the turn. The eleventh hole is one I am never likely to forget. I have already stated that my ball was bunkered off my iron shot. Owing to the excessively hot weather the sand in the hazard had become very fine and dry. My ball was so completely buried that at first we were unable to find it. Eventually it was located and Johnnie Laidlay, who was acting as umpire, had to scrape some of the sand away in order to enable me to see the top of the ball. As soon as this was done the fine sand immediately closed over it again and I played this stroke more with a sense as to where the ball was located than actually knowing its exact position. It was a testing ordeal coming as it did when my lead was fast disappearing. However, I managed to get the ball out, but required a six for the hole. As the result of some fine play on the part of my opponent and a further slip or two on my part during the remaining holes of the round, I had not only lost my advantage, but was two strokes behind with 18 holes left to be played.

Although it is now over 18 years ago, my recollections of the final round are distinctly vivid. As I write, the scene of the first tee as Taylor and I started out for the concluding stage of this remarkable championship is as plain as if it had taken place a matter of weeks instead of years ago. The spectators formed almost a solid wall from the left of the teeing ground to the hill in front of the first green, as Taylor, who had the honour, drove off. The excitement was intense and it was obvious that my opponent and I were in for an exceedingly trying ordeal. I have frequently been asked what my feeling were when, at the conclusion of the third round, such a dramatic change had taken place. At the ninth hole I was leading J. H. by three strokes. When we had holed out on the home green he had gained no fewer than five shots on the inward half, thus giving him a two stroke advantage. As I went into lunch my view of the situation was this. I had played two shots which were just a little off line and had been well and, no doubt, properly punished for my errors. I had also dropped a stroke or two which, under the circumstances, was possibly only to be expected. My opponent had taken the opportunities which I had given him and great credit was due to him for so doing. All the same, I knew in my own mind I was playing well. That I had been guilty of a few slips was only part and parcel of the game. I was hitting the ball well and fully expected to give a good account of myself after lunch. I can truthfully say I thought I was going to win the championship even though I was two strokes behind. Prestwick was a very severe test of golf on this occasion and any slips which a player made were, as had been the case with me, promptly punished. I did not anticipate committing these mistakes in the afternoon, and felt convinced if my opponent gave me any chances I should be able to take them. After his display in the forenoon, it was not unreasonable to think that he might drop a shot or two during the course of the round, as his fine effort under the existing conditions must have taken a good deal out of him. This, then, was how I reviewed the situation. I partook of a hearty lunch so as to be fortified for the forthcoming struggle. At the opening hole Taylor increased his lead to three. Owing to the extremely dry conditions which prevailed the first was a difficult hole. The second shot, which was a pitch over a bunker, had of necessity to be played to carry on to the green. As the latter was exceedingly fast it was extremely difficult to prevent the ball from over-running, especially as no chances could be taken in cutting it fine with the possibility of being caught in the hazard. My approach was a little too strong, and three putts being required, a six was recorded. My opponent also missed a short putt, a five going down on his card. Thus at the very outset I had lost a further stroke. It has always been accepted that my opponent lost the championship at the fourth hole, where a series of disasters terminated in his taking a seven. I personally have always held the opinion, although it was the 'burn' which actually ruined my opponent's chance of winning the championship, that it was the previous hole, which was a more important factor than was generally realized. We had halved the short second, which brought us to the famous Cardinal with Taylor still retaining his lead of three strokes. I have already described this hole. By the aid of a fine tee shot, and a really excellent second which I played with my brassy, I had placed my ball on the green within reasonable holing distance for a three. J. H. did not get home in two, and took a five. Although I did not hole my putt, I secured an easy four, and reduced the deficit against me to two. I feel convinced the two shots which I played at the third that afternoon were to a big extent instrumental in gaining for me my sixth victory in the premier event. My opponent's experience at the following hole, unfortunately for him, virtually decided the issue, as against the seven which he required, I recorded a par-four. The position at this stage had certainly undergone a complete change. Two holes previously J. H. was in possession of the comfortable advantage of a three stroke lead. As we walked off the fourth green his lead had been wiped out, and he was one stroke behind. There was, too, another aspect to be considered. A breakdown such as had occurred to Taylor was sufficient, for a little time anyway, to have a damaging effect upon him. There is no one in the history of the game with such a deserving reputation as a courageous fighter as my old friend and great rival. Even he may be readily excused under the circumstances for being badly shaken. The enthusiasm at this point was intense. The huge gallery of spectators, although admirably controlled by the stewards, appeared to surge all around us in their attempt to witness the play at the following holes. After gaining another stroke at the Himalayas, I slowly forged ahead, and at the turn held an advantage of three strokes. My score for the outward half was 39, which, considering the extraordinary circumstances under which we were playing, and taking into account the six which I had required for the first hole, was very steady going. It may be of interest to state that from the second to the ninth I had seven consecutive fours. On the homeward journey I continued to produce steady, accurate golf, and gave my opponent no opportunity to reduce my lead. I was not guilty on this occasion of finding the bunkers by the green at either the tenth or the eleventh. At both these holes I secured the correct par figure. With three holes left for play I was in the commanding position of five shots to the good. At the sixteenth Taylor holed out in a splendid three, while I slipped a stroke and took a five. Fine effort as this was on the part of my opponent, it made little difference to the outcome of the contest. We both finished with two steady fours and I may safely say I will never forget the scene at the conclusion of this round. My score for the 18 holes was 78, which gave me an aggregate of 306 for the 72 holes. This return was three strokes ahead of Taylor's total, which was 309.

As soon as I had holed my last putt on the home green a rush was made by a large section of the gallery to see Abe Mitchell who, it was rumoured, had an outside chance of tying with my aggregate. At the end of the third round there were few players who had any chance of overtaking either Taylor or myself, unless a serious breakdown in our final round occurred. As I have related, Taylor experienced this unfortunate occurrence, and while I had played steadily my 78 had left a remote possibility that some player who was still battling away on the course might yet create a tie. As a matter of fact, J. L. C. Jenkins, who had occupied third position at lunch by the aid of a splendid score of 73, had finished his fourth round before Taylor and I. A card of 83 had ruined any opportunity he may have had. Harry Simpson had also been an early starter and his total of 310 was the leading one until our cards were handed in. Simpson had played fine steady golf throughout the event. Arnaud Massy and Mitchell were the only two left to be considered. The Frenchman had apparently, early on, put himself out of the running. Mitchell, however, had been playing excellent golf, and a rapid calculation showed if he could finish in two under fours for the four remaining holes which he had still to play he would tie with the leader. This feat, although by no means impossible, was considered improbable. All the same a huge crowd witnessed his tee shot at the fifteenth hole, which as it turned out spoilt his chance. He was bunkered off his drive and failing to get out in his initial effort required a six. A five at each of the two following holes and a score of 79 placed him in fourth position with Tom Williamson, who had returned an aggregate of 312. J. L. C. Jenkins was the leading amateur, tying for eighth place with P. L. Gaudin with a total of 315. This was a very creditable performance on the part of the new amateur champion. Thus ended a remarkable championship which gave me the distinction of gaining my sixth victory in the premier golfing event of the world.

It was a proud occasion for me, and although I had gained many notable victories during my career I can safely say there was no success which I had achieved that gave me such utter satisfaction as my victory at Prestwick.

# Hagen's Fifth PGA
## Fred Corcoran, 1965

A typical Hagen story is an account of his match with Joe Turnesa at Dallas in 1927. Hagen was the master of applied psychology and always said he liked the head-to-head character of match play. He said he always knew exactly where things stood.

On this occasion, Walter arrived at the clubhouse 30 minutes late and was sharply scolded by the tournament officials. Hagen knew he was wrong. He apologized humbly and hurried off to dress.

On the first three holes he grandly conceded putts of varying lengths and Turnesa quickly went three up. Then Hagen said, 'There, that makes up for the 30 minutes I was late. Now we'll play...'

Well, the match rocked along until they reached the seventeenth hole – the thirty-fifth of the match – and Joe had a fairly easy putt. But Hagen made no gesture of conceding it. In fact, he was elaborately helpful to Joe in lining it up. Joe missed it and the match was all even.

They came to the last hole and Hagen put his second shot off to the right in some tall grass, partially screened off from the green by trees. Turnesa was in good position in the middle of the fairway. Walter studied the line of flight, paced back and forth several times, tentatively drew three or four clubs from his bag. Then he turned and waved Turnesa back into the gallery.

'Joe', he called, 'I may have to play this safe.' Later he chuckled, 'I could have driven three Mack trucks up to the green through those trees'.

Then he settled down and played his shot, sticking the ball within 12 feet of the flag. Turnesa, kept waiting and watching this strange performance, finally stepped up to his easy shot and dunked it in the trap flanking the green – and Walter had won his fifth PGA championship.

Curiously, Hagen's grandstand performance thoroughly delighted Turnesa, as it did the gallery. One of the remarkable things about Walter Hagen was the fact that, even in their defeat, his opponents all had tremendous affection for him. In fact, Turnesa tells this story with complete admiration for Hagen.

*Though the Walker Cup has normally been dominated by the USA, many individual matches have been closely contested. In the 1930 match this single seemed to be in the bag for Great Britain and Ireland, but ...*

# A VISITATION FROM GOD
## FRANCIS OUIMET, 1933

A wonderful match was going on just behind us, and Tony and I finished just in time to see Don Moe, the American, hole a 30-foot putt on the twelfth green to square his match with Bill Stout, the Englishman. I could not believe the match was even, because I knew Moe was four down in the morning, and when Stout started three, three, three after luncheon, he had run his lead to seven up. Yet here was Moe even. What had happened? Moe had won seven of the next nine holes. He had gone out in 32. It was remarkable golf on a stiff test. They battled on. The thirteenth was halved. On the fourteenth, a very long and hard par-five hole, Moe planted a brassy shot on the green in two and won the hole to take the lead. The fifteenth, another long one, went to Stout.

Both reached the green on the short sixteenth. Stout put his long putt stone dead. Moe was short with his and had to drop an eight-footer for a half. The seventeenth likewise saw the two still even, and they headed for the final hole just where they started in the morning after 35 holes of brilliant playing. Stout is a terrific hitter and he hammered a mighty drive down the fairway. Moe followed with one just a few yards behind. The last hole at Sandwich is about 460 yards long, and since the wind is invariably against the player, it is very seldom reached in two shots. I had seen Jones and Wethered with two full wooden shots fail to get home.

Moe had to play first, and I was amazed to see him pick out a number 2-iron. I did not think he had a chance of getting home. He hit that 2-iron on the nose and the ball actually carried to the green on a dead line for the flag. It hopped in the air and rolled for the pin. It barely missed the marker and stopped three feet from the hole. Never have I seen a more wonderful iron shot in my life, taking into consideration the tenseness of the competition and what it meant. A roar of approval went up from the crowd surrounding the green, a token of real admiration for a fighting American. The British sporting public are excellent sportsmen. They naturally hoped Stout would win, but their feelings were smothered when Moe played his spectacular stroke. Stout pulled his ball to the left of the green, but, unless he placed his ball alongside Donald's, it mattered little. In the morning Stout had got round in 68; Moe's three gave him a 67, a stroke under the course record.

In the locker room after the match, the British and American players were changing their shoes. In the group was Bill Stout, and he gazed out of a window not sadly but in meditation. Then, during a lull in the conversation that ran through the room, Stout got up, moved over to Don Moe, and said, 'Donald, that was not golf, that was a visitation from God'.

# THE BRAIN WHIRLING
## BERNARD DARWIN, 1931

There is some judgement but a great deal of luck in seeing the important things at an Open Championship, and it was wholly luck that made me see the most crucial of all incidents in Armour's last and victorious round at Carnoustie.

There is one point on the links where everyone forgathers. It is close to the ominous wood of black firs into which luckless people may hook the ball at the short eighth hole. Here the seventh, eighth, twelfth and thirteenth holes all more or less converge, and here I was standing on the last afternoon, rather dizzy in the midst of a whirlpool of rumours. Along came Armour to the twelfth hole and hit a magnificent brassy shot right onto the middle of the twelfth green, which very few players could reach in two. Rumour, which turned out for once not to be lying, said that his score was two under fours. That was just about good enough to win, even though he had started five shots behind Jurado, and clearly he must be watched.

He struck his long putt perfectly and the ball slipped past the edge of the hole not more than two feet away. Then he took rather a long while and missed the two-foot putt by a good two inches. To the next, the short thirteenth, he played a poor tee shot and the ball ended off the green, rather fortunately not in heather or sand. Armour came up to play his chip and it was clear that his emotions had almost beaten him. He waggled and he looked up at the hole with a quick turn of the head, and he went on waggling and looking until no one else could bear to look at him. If he misses this one, I thought to myself, he is done; but he waited until he could settle down, he laid it nearly dead and he holed the putt. The crisis was past and he went on playing lovely golf to the end.

In the evening I told him that I had seen those two holes, and he agreed that they had settled the issue. No one could believe, he said, what a blow that short putt missed had been; there he was playing beautifully and then came this sudden, staggering shock. If, he added, his tee shot to the thirteenth had found trouble, as it well might, he was 'gone', and, even when it did not, he felt he simply could not play the next shot because his brain was whirling like a mill-race and he was thinking and thinking about everything in the whole world except the business in hand. Our Open Championship was the one thing he wanted to win, and he felt himself on the verge of throwing it all away.

One could almost see him thinking all these things, and I have told the story at length both because I hope it is rather interesting and because it shows the kind of golfer that the new champion is. He is full of imagination, a bundle of quivering nerves kept fiercely under control, and this is the kind of temperament that either breaks a player of games or makes him terribly formidable. As a striker of the ball, except sometimes when it is dead at the holeside, Armour is truly magnificent. I do not believe that Taylor or Vardon at their best ever gave themselves so many possible putts for three with their iron shots as he does, and his style is the perfection of rhythm and beauty. From the beginning of the week I bored all our small party at the hotel by telling them that Armour was the best player in the field, and I am not likely to recant now.

A man may be the best player and still he cannot win the championship unless the luck be with him. Armour unquestionably had the luck of the weather, and at the end of the first two days he said that, having had the luck, he had missed the chance of getting away with a substantial lead. The wind blew pretty hard on Wednesday morning and Thursday afternoon. It lulled on Wednesday afternoon and Thursday morning. Sarazen and Farrell had to play their first round on Wednesday morning and their second on Thursday morning; Armour and Jurado had to do exactly the opposite, and while their advantage cannot be exactly computed in strokes it was a very real one. Had matters been the other way round, either Sarazen or Farrell might have won. As Gene said, 'You have to take the breaks', and they did not have them.

The last three holes at Carnoustie with the wind blowing from the east (which is not the normal way or the best way for the course) make up just about the most testing and perilous finish in all golf. Consequently there were several tragedies enacted there. If Alliss could have done the last two in four and five he would have tied with Armour's score, and he took five and six with a dreadfully superfluous shot out of bounds at the last. Then there was Macdonald Smith. This was the supreme effort of a golfing lifetime on his own native heath; he had pulled round splendidly from a bad start in his first round and he was playing like clockwork in his last. He wanted three, four, five, par golf, to beat Armour, and could afford to lose one stroke and yet tie with him. He lost four strokes in two holes and finished five, six, five. I saw the six at the seventeenth, without his ball touching any form of hazard, and I felt rather as if I had gone to see a man hanged. Finally, and most poignant of all, was Jurado's tragedy, also at the seventeenth. He wanted a four and a five to win, and it seemed as if he could hardly fail to get the two fives to tie, for the seventeenth down the wind, though not an easy four, is quite an easy five. One thought of all sorts of mistakes he might make but one never dreamed of the one he did make, when he popped the ball into the burn off the tee, more or less in front of his nose. It was terribly sad, for he is a splendid little man (he does not weigh ten stone) and had played splendidly courageous golf, full of smiling excitement but always keeping control of himself. I wish these horrid things were not inevitable in championships.

Yet another tragedy, of course, had happened earlier in the day, and that was the breakdown of Cotton in his third round, when British hopes of his winning were very high. Cotton today is a great golfer, and I think his time will surely come but a championship only comes once a year, and he that will not when he may, etc. The technical cause of his downfall was, as it seemed to me, that he was getting on the wrong side of the hole; he was sparing his approaches down the wind going out with the result that he left himself long down-wind putts. Continually to lay these dead is desperate work; he left himself too much to do, and when the ensuing five-foot putts went astray his game began to disintegrate. No doubt there was a more general cause, too, namely, that though Cotton has tried hard to school a naturally rebellious temperament, he has not yet wholly succeeded, and when things went wrong he could not quite stand the strain. It is this control that he has to practise now, for his hitting of the ball is just about good enough for anything or anybody.

# Failure of a Mission
## HENRY LONGHURST, 1941

There is only one way to travel, believe me, and that is first-class at the expense of Lord Beaverbrook. That is how I went to the United States for the second time.

Being in pretty good form at the time (with the pen, I mean; journalists have their on and off periods just like anyone else), I was invited to record for the *Evening Standard* the activities of the 1936 Walker Cup team, who were to play the Americans at Pine Valley early in September, and at the same time given a roving commission to cover anything else that might appear to be of interest.

No journalist ever had a more welcome assignment. To be sent at all was a compliment that had been paid, I believe, only to one golf correspondent before – naturally Mr Bernard Darwin. Incidentally, a member of the team fell ill, Mr Darwin took the last place – and won his match. I suspect that the same thing very nearly happened to me, but we needn't go into that.

Of a million golfers in Britain it falls to a tiny percentage to make the Walker Cup pilgrimage to America. Some of the best would give a year's income for the experience. I was getting it for nothing. Couldn't be better.

We set out in an atmosphere of bitter controversy. We were to travel on the *Transylvania* which, if it docked to schedule, would still leave the team less than a week for practice. The *Queen Mary,* recently put into service, was sailing at exactly the convenient time. Why not the *Queen Mary?*

However, last-minute intrigues failed to get the team transferred to the *Queen Mary,* and so one dark night we converged one by one upon an unprepossessing Glasgow quay and groped our way on board the good ship *Transylvania.* (Three or four months ago I shed a nostalgic tear over the news that she had been sunk while serving as an auxiliary cruiser.)

We were an odd assortment. Whether the team were the ten best golfers in Great Britain I'm not prepared to say, but geographically representative they certainly were – and for that reason I had my doubts as to whether they would not very soon be falling out among themselves.

Harmony on these outings depends largely, as you'll agree if you've taken part in one, on the captain. Our captain – I say 'our', for although I was not officially attached to the team I was at once invited to consider myself as such, despite the last-minute assurance of the secretary of the R and A that it was 'against all precedent' to have a Walker Cup team contaminated by journalists – our captain was a 39-year-old Midland practitioner, Dr William Tweddell.

A reserved, amiable fellow was Tweddell, all for a quiet life. I doubted his ability to hold his miscellaneous crew together without friction. After all, he had nothing closer than a nodding acquaintance with any of them, and their ages, their interests and outlook on life, their incomes, even their accents, were as divergent as could be. I could see them, as the half-empty *Transylvania* bored its leisurely way across the Atlantic with a load of Middle West sightseers, getting on each other's nerves, or worse, breaking up into cliques.

We were, as I say, a motley crew – four Scotsmen, an Irishman, a Lancastrian, a Midlander, three Londoners (stockbroker, undergraduate, and schoolboy), and the official scribe. Of the Scots, Hector Thomson, by virtue of his amateur championship, was reckoned our leading golfer, with Jack Maclean a close second. Golf was their abiding interest. Gordon Peters was another fine Glasgow player, though more catholic in his tastes, while the irrepressible Morton Dykes, who had played rugby football for Scotland, was by that time a purely weekend golfer. He earned his place on his play in the championship a few weeks before, yet he confessed that he had really had no intention of playing in it. He only entered, he said, because it was at St Andrews – and he always enjoyed a week at St Andrews.

The Irishman was Cecil Ewing, a bespectacled giant from Sligo with a mighty drive and strong political principles. Harry Bentley, with his typically Lancastrian shrewdness and gay philosophical wit, was the 'character' of the party.

Alec Hill, Laddie Lucas, and John Langley represented the pampered south – and the old school tie. When the selectors had left a couple of places open till the championship results were known, Hill, a semi-finalist, got one of them. He, too, was the purest weekend golfer (a compliment, this), and had gone to St Andrews for no better reason than that a friend of his cancelled his room in the hotel at the last moment, and so left it available for Hill. Rather 'thin on the top', this pillar of the London Stock Exchange looked the oldest member of the party. He was, in fact, 28. We found that we had much in common.

Lucas at the time of his selection was in his second year at Cambridge and was to be captain the following year. He had the physique of an athlete, had been captain of cricket and football at Stowe, and was probably the best left-hander in the world at that time.

If Lucas, chosen while still an undergraduate, was *rara avis,* Langley was *rarissima.* He was chosen during his last holiday from Stowe, before ever he went as a freshman to Cambridge. Indeed, he was the youngest player ever chosen by either side.

Well, for two days we felt our way cautiously, each on his best behaviour, especially in the presence of the headmaster, Bill Tweddell. A comparatively insignificant incident broke the ice on the second night out. The headmaster had a second glass of *kümmel* to his dinner.

Golfing excellence, unlike excellence in most other games, goes hand in hand with alcohol, as many an open and amateur champion has shown. Incidentally, Harry Vardon had the last word on this subject. When, during the last war, a woman asked him to join the temperance movement, he replied: 'Moderation is essential in all things, madam, but never in my life have I failed to beat a teetotaller'.

We arrived in New York and berthed insignificantly beside the *Queen Mary.* She had come in on the previous day, having left six days after us, and had broken the record. It was all rather galling.

Everyone who plays golf has heard of Pine Valley, few have had the luck to play there. I look on it as the greatest of all inland courses, the perfect examination of the golfer's physical and psychological powers. It was cut at spectacular expense from some virgin forest slopes 15 miles below Philadelphia, and such is Pine Valley's challenge to the conceit of American golfers, such is the legend of its defiance to mere man, that the club has two thousand country members, some of them living three thousand miles away.

The singular difficulty of Pine Valley is easily described. It has no rough, in the accepted sense of the term, and no semi-rough. Your ball is either on the fairway, in which case it sits invitingly on a flawless carpet of turf, or it is not. If it is not, you play out sideways till it is. In a week's golf, including the Walker Cup match, I saw no single recovery shot, as we use the expression. You don't make 'recoveries' at Pine Valley, except of course from the sand traps – you merely push your way into the undergrowth and endeavour to knock your ball out through the bushes to where it ought to have been in the first place.

The sand bunkers are desert wastes left bare and unraked round the greens. Small bushes grow in them, and no one is expected to smooth out his footprints. The greens, like the fairways, are perfect – once you get there. Par is 70 – with two long holes that no man has ever reached in two, and four short holes.

One of these, the fifth, may be the greatest golf hole in the world. Green and tee are on a level, 225 yards apart, but between the two lies a vast depression, with a lake full of turtles and other unlikely creatures. The green itself, long and narrow, slopes sheer away on the right, and a ball that misses the green bobbles merrily down until stopped by a tree trunk. On the left a gravel pit gnaws its way into the green. To ensure a satisfactory level of casualties the club committee are in the habit of placing the flag far back in the left-hand corner.

I never forgot this fifth hole after our 1930 visit to Pine Valley. On the voyage across I enlarged upon its terrors to the team, none of whom had seen it before. The time came at last to play it once again. 'I've waited six years for this shot', I observed – and nothing shall stop me from telling the rest of the story. The drive flew straight for the flag – just enough 'draw' to keep it from slipping down into the forest on the right, not enough to take it into the gravel pit. It finished, amid murmurs of applause, my own perhaps the most audible, nine feet from the hole; and the putt ran gently in for a two. Nothing much mattered after that. I was out, very cocksure, in 34 – but let no man rejoice at Pine Valley till the last putt is safely bottled in the hole. It took me 41 to get home.

They'll lay odds of anything up to ten to one against the ordinary scratch golfer breaking 80 in his first round at Pine Valley, and they are rarely known to lose. There's a tradition at the club – I know of no parallel – that the cup of misfortune must be drained to the dregs, and no man shall pick up his ball midway to save the ultimate ignominy of revealing his score. Each hole carries its legend of tragedy to some victim or other. Roger Wethered's name, for instance, will always be linked with the eighth, a mere drive and a pitch – though what a pitch! The plateau green is microscopically small and pretty well surrounded by sand. Poor Roger, going strongly at the time, pitched in the sand. Thence he went to and fro, from sand unto sand, and holed out in 11.

One partner of mine completed the shortest hole on the course in 23. Laddie Lucas was another who fell. Like so many left-handed players he was liable to spells of inaccuracy. He started 'spraying' his tee shots, as the Americans say – and Pine Valley is no place for the sprayer. In three rounds that I played with him before the match his lowest total was 94 – a score which in England, even at the age of 20, he probably had not taken once in the past six years.

It was in one of these rounds that his caddy made an observation that will cling to Lucas to the end of his days. He and the caddy had already spent most of their time in the woods when at the seventh hole Lucas hit another wild, curving slice that soared away over the forest. 'Watch it', he cried 'Watch it!'

'You don't have to watch 'em,' said the caddy, 'you gotta listen for 'em.'

Incidentally, while we are talking of caddies – here is an 'It couldn't happen here' story. I was standing one evening at the bar of the roadhouse a mile or two from Pine Valley in which I stayed for the match, when I fell into conversation with a good-looking young American, attired in 'faultless evening dress' and accompanied by an equally elegant young woman with corn-coloured hair. After the inevitable comparisons of conditions in Great Britain and the United States, we fell to talking of the prospects for the Walker Cup match and the performances of the various players in practice.

He had been there during the day, it seemed, and was thoroughly familiar with the contestants on both sides. He criticized their style with an obvious knowledge of the game, and later events bore out his judgement in picking Gordon Peters as one of the best of our team.

Next day I saw him again on the course. He was Morton Dykes's caddy.

Both the Walker Cup teams were lodged in the Pine Valley clubhouse, and it wasn't long, if the truth be told, before the suspense, the solitude, and the pine-scented stuffiness of the atmosphere began to get on the nerves of the British side.

Tweddell in these circumstances made an ideal captain. He combined firmness with his natural amiability, and his reward was the lifelong friendship and respect of ten fellows from all walks of life whom he scarcely knew before. The loyalty of the team (not always, I may add, a feature of such outings) broke down Tweddell's innate reserve, and he made a great hit with the Americans. One night at a roadhouse, when the team's identity became known, Tweddell was dragged to a spotlighted microphone and made a speech that had two or three hundred people standing on chairs to applaud. I fancy he'd never have backed himself to do such a thing when he left Glasgow.

The American team turned up at Pine Valley soon after ourselves and it was amusing to hear that two of them, Scotty Campbell and Harry Givan, had travelled farther to reach the club than we had. They had come from Seattle.

It didn't take long to realize that all these young full-time American golfers were not only a cut above our own full-timers in the shape of Thomson and McLean, but could give fifty yards in a hundred to weekend amateurs like Tweddell, Hill, Dykes, and Ewing, who played golf largely for their own amusement. They were suitably impressed, but not the least frightened, by the course. Its tightness only accentuated their superiority. To ask some of our team to play round Pine Valley was like sending a boy for a scholarship when he could not pass a common entrance exam.

The Americans were captained by Francis Ouimet (pronounced 'we met'), one of the gentlest and most respected personalities in the game, who had earned immortality 23 years previously when, as an ex-caddy of 19, he beat Harry Vardon and Ted Ray in the play-off for the United States Open Championship at the Country Club, Brookline.

I suppose their best player was Johnny Goodman, a tough, ruthless little fellow from Omaha with an astonishing facial resemblance to Lord Mandeville – well aware of his own ability and with no hesitation about rubbing it in.

'Good shot!' cried a spectator ecstatically. 'I'll say!' said Goodman. Three years before, at the age of 24, he had won the United States Open, starting with a 66 and finishing with a string of fours and threes.

Four of their side hailed from the South, and wickedly good players they were too: Ed White, from Texas, slim and dark with humorous film-star eyes; Walter Emery, of Oklahoma City, a big, happy-go-lucky fellow of infinite jest; Reynolds Smith, from Dallas, stocky, dark, and determined; and Charles Yates, a wise-cracking happy-go-lucky young protégé of Bobby Jones down in Atlanta. So infectious, incidentally, were Yates's high spirits that two years later he accomplished the unprecedented feat of standing on the steps of the Royal and Ancient clubhouse at St Andrews after the Walker Cup match and inducing the crowd to accompany him in 'A Wee Doch and Doris'.

The voices of this quartet intrigued their British visitors, who had not heard the like except in the movies and had hardly believed it then. Their average age was 23, which in golfing maturity is equivalent perhaps to 30 over here. They chewed stubs of cigars and let forth a barrage of wise-cracking good humour. Emery had a broad-brimmed hat and needed only a lasso hanging from his golf bag to complete the picture.

The remaining Americans were George Voigt, an old campaigner at 39; Johnny Fischer, of Cincinnati, long-legged, shock-headed, and nervously reticent, a truly magnificent golfer; and amiable George Dunlap, New York 'socialite' and an old friend of mine, who was already beginning to suspect that 69 round golf courses were not the end-all and be-all of life.

When the great day arrived, it was seen that the two captains, though each had had a 70 in practice, had left themselves out of the teams. Ouimet remarking characteristically: 'Waal, I've been at this game a long enough time to give these young boys a chance to get some of the nice things of golf'. Lucas was dropped, inevitably, from our team, Dunlap from theirs.

We had a lovely day for the match, warm and easy, and the remoteness of Pine Valley kept the crowd down to people genuinely anxious to see the golf. No sightseers; no peanuts. I am afraid I had come to the conclusion before the start that if the match were to be played under identical conditions ten times we should be lucky to win it once. I think most of the team knew it too. We buoyed ourselves up with the hope that this might be the tenth time – but it wasn't long before we saw that it was going to be one of the other nine. I don't think that collectively a better team than these ten young Americans ever played in a Walker Cup match.

Tweddell, on the principle of not putting his two best eggs in one basket, split up the Thomson-McLean partnership, putting Bentley to play top with Thomson and Langley second with McLean. Peters and Dykes were third, Hill and Ewing fourth.

Incidentally, it was simple enough for the spectators to tell the teams apart. Every one of our side except Bentley wore the 'national costume' of white shirt and grey flannel trousers. Bentley wore a pair of trousers that had already been 'written up' by every American correspondent. A spectator had come up to him and remarked with a knowing air: 'It's easy enough to tell you're English by the cut of your trousers'. Harry's reply was: 'Yes, they're good, aren't they? I bought them in Clementon the other day for a dollar sixty-nine!' It was quite true.

By lunch-time our four pairs were five down, one down, one up, and four down respectively. By half-past three in the afternoon I knew I was going to have to cable home a score-card of four noughts out of four.

Thomson and Bentley had been one up on Goodman and Campbell after ten holes in the morning – and then the deluge. They lost six holes out of the remaining eight and were five down. Mclean and Langley, temperamentally ill-fitted to each other as it turned out, held on well enough to be only one down to Reynolds and White. Our third pair played some magnificent golf and were round in 73 against 75 by Yates and Emery, which gave them the only hole on the credit side of the balance. Hill and Ewing, bringing up the rear, lost the last two holes to Givan and Voigt and finished four down, seemingly outclassed.

Luncheon and mint juleps revived our spirits – I can still hear the old coloured servants offering their inevitable first course of 'cantelupe, rasspberries, or snapper soup' – and we consoled ourselves with much wishful thinking, to use the current cliché, regarding the second and third pairs.

For 13 holes in the afternoon Thomson and Bentley were only two over fours, but there was no arguing with Goodman and Campbell. They won two more holes and the match by seven and five. Worse was to come. Langley and McLean, full of hope, lost the first four holes and were scuttled almost before they were launched. Poor McLean, he lived for golf. I recall his saying: 'I have been playing serious golf for 11 years and I have been a good many down without losing heart. This is the first time I have had my spirit really broken.' They lost by eight and seven.

So it seemed that if we were to save anything from the wreck, enough at any rate to preserve any interest in the morrow's play, Peters and Dykes had to win at number three. What a match that was! And what a hero was Peters! They began, unpromisingly enough, with three fives, and were lucky not to lose more than the single hole by which they had led. It was Peters who turned the scale by slamming an iron shot to within a couple of feet at the fourth. At the sixth he holed a 12-footer. When I said that I saw no 'recovery' shot played at Pine Valley, I was wrong. I saw one. It was played by Peters at the seventh and I remember it well. The hole is, I suppose, one of the most architecturally perfect long holes in the world. The drive has to be placed on the left-hand side of an island of turf between the woods. The second has to carry 120 yards of sand and scrub to a second island. The third has to pitch on a green which is itself surrounded by sand. The hole is about 580 yards long.

Dykes hooked their second shot, thus to all intents declaring a minimum of six, but Peters, up to his knees in grass among the poplar trees, hacked their ball on to the green and followed it up by lofting it into the hole from seven feet over a stymie.

Some more wild shots by Dykes lost them the eighth and tenth and at the eleventh the Americans had such luck as I never did see. Emery hooked his drive round his neck into the forest and we heard it clattering about among the trees, when suddenly it was seen to ricochet high into the air and fall on the fairway. Yates hit a glorious spoon shot to within seven feet of the flag, when by rights he should have been crawling about on all fours in the undergrowth, and Emery, of course, holed the putt for a three. They went on with another three at the twelfth and suddenly, instead of three down, found themselves one up.

Peters banged another long iron shot to the pin at the fifteenth and they won it with a four – the hole is 605 yards long, over a lake and then uphill all the way; so far as I know, no man has ever reached it in two – and Dykes came in with a fine second from an awkward place at the seventeenth, and an equally awkward putt for a half. All square with one to play.

I trembled for poor Dykes, for the last drive is played from a considerable height down to a fairway sloping from left to right and bounded by every kind of horror, but he came up trumps and the ball was seen, amid gasps of British relief, to finish in play. It never entered anyone's head that the Americans would take more than four, and so Peters was left with his last iron shot, over the lake and up to the plateau green between the trees. It had to be high – not easy from a downhill lie – and it had to be long. I stood beside him as he played it, and can certify that it was both. 'Marvellous', said I. 'Aye – trembling with bravery!' he said.

So Peters and Dykes halved their match, and their half point, it seemed, was to be the extent of our ration from the four matches. Hill and Ewing had lost three of the first six holes to be seven down, and frankly neither I nor anyone else paid much further attention to them. It did not seem to matter very much whether they lost by 12 and 11, or 13 and 12.

When Hill holed a four-yarder with his old aluminium putter to win the long seventh in four, he can scarcely have dreamed that he was starting one of the most astonishing 'come-backs' in Walker Cup history. But so it proved. He holed another good one on the ninth, and Ewing ran down a ten-yarder for a two on the tenth. Back to four down.

The Americans exploded from a bunker to within one inch of the hole on the eleventh, but Hill kept things going with a seven-footer. He had another for a 'birdie' three at the twelfth and the next they won easily. Only two down now, and the Americans clearly shaken. Such treatment was unusual from English golfers. At this critical moment Hill played an excellent stroke to the island green at the fourteenth. To see the British ball sitting serenely on the green below would have made Voigt distinctly uneasy – but, alas, Hill had taken the wrong club and his ball sailed over the green and fell with a splash into the lake beyond. Three down with four to play.

Young Givan, showing distinct signs of strain, went into the trees at the long fifteenth, though in the end Hill had to hole from four yards to win it. Ewing in turn found the forest at the next, but Givan obliged by doing likewise and Britain won the hole. We had a perfect four at the seventeenth and, thanks to a slice by Givan, won it. All square with one to play.

Givan with the brilliance so often born of depair hit a beauty to within ten feet of the eighteenth, while Ewing's was every inch of 15 yards away. Could he and Hill get this ball down in two between them, and could Voigt fail with his ten-footer?

The answer was yes. Hill judged the long one to a nicety, and Voigt, going boldly for the hole, overran by three feet. Not for a hundred dollars would I have changed places with Harry Givan as he tried to sink that putt. In deathly silence he pushed it nervously towards the hole. It toppled in at its last gasp.

So two halves left us something to play for in the singles after all, and after the gloom of mid-afternoon there was something approaching jubilation in the camp. Alas, it took no time at all on the following morning to see that these Americans, if some of them were fallible in foursome play, to which they were unaccustomed, were quite unbeatable once they were on their own. I won't go into details. Suffice to say that at luncheon the British positions in the eight matches were two down, all square, two down, eight down, three down, four down, two down, five down. A melancholy catalogue. Yet our first three performers, Thomson, McLean and Ewing, had had scores of 74, 73, and 75.

In the afternoon there was no holding the Americans. Goodman polished off Thomson by nonchalantly rolling in a five-yard putt at the thirty-fourth. Campbell put paid to McLean with three threes in a row. Fischer, three under fours for 11 holes, saw Ewing off the course to the tune of eight and seven. Yates, most devastating of the lot, beat Dykes by as much. His afternoon figures are worth quoting, bearing in mind the course on which they were played. They were: 4, 4, 4, 3, 3, 4, 4, 4, 4, 3, 3.

Langley could do nothing at all with White, though his swing remained polished and smooth to the end. Only Bentley and Peters made any sort of impression. Peters went gallantly round in 72 which, jointly with Goodman's morning round, was the lowest score of the day, but he only won two holes back from Emery and that was just one too few. And so it was left to Bentley to hole a putt of one yard before the assembled multitude to credit Britain with a solitary half out of eight matches. He was round in 76.

The British side of the scoreboard looked like a daisy chain, with 12 noughts one beneath the other. I settled down to cable the mournful tale and felt more than ever convinced that I should never live to see the Walker Cup won by Great Britain.

# TWO HOLES, SIX STROKES
### DAN JENKINS, 1970

The Byron Nelson of 1937 was barely 25-years-old, tall, slender, nervous and usually outfitted in starched dress shirts with the cuffs turned up twice on the order of a pharmacist. But he opened that championship with a 66, the lowest round Jones and his friends had seen in the tournament. Nelson's lead slowly dribbled away to a more experienced Ralph Guldahl, and on the last day, with nine holes to play, Byron trailed by three strokes.

Guldahl was playing one hole ahead of Nelson, who was paired with Wiffy Cox, and when Byron reached his drive down the tenth fairway it was just in time to see Guldahl take a birdie putt out of the cup. 'If I don't get a birdie here, I'm four behind with only eight to go', Nelson thought to himself. 'I wonder what second money is?'

Without thinking much more about his predicament than that, Nelson hit a good shot into the tenth green and saw it spin up close for a short birdie putt. He made it, and Wiffy Cox said to him, 'Kid, I think that's the one we need. It'll show Ralph he can't shake you, and there are plenty of holes left.'

Both men got par-fours at the long, dangerous eleventh, but when Nelson reached the twelfth tee, the crowd, he noticed, was scurrying over to him in mad droves, jamming around him. And he thought he heard someone talking about Guldahl taking a double-bogey five on that dandy little water-logged par-three.

'My adrenalin really got going', Nelson says. 'I suddenly realized I'd been playing negative golf for two days.' Nelson, somehow was seized by aggressiveness. He splintered the flag with a 6-iron at the twelfth and dropped the ten-footer for a birdie two. Wiffy Cox did a little dance.

Now, up ahead on the par-five thirteenth, Guldahl, reeling from Nelson's pursuit, gambled on a second shot to the green, plopped it into Rae's Creek and took a bogey six. Then Nelson, almost in a dead run, whomped a spoon over the creek and off the left edge of the green, whereupon he took a 3-iron and gently chipped in a 50-foot eagle three.

In just two holes Nelson had gone two–three to Guldahl's five–six, and it was all over.

'I really didn't realize the importance of it at the time', Nelson says. 'It was quite a while before I remembered I'd played the first four holes of the back nine four under. In those days, the money was the main thing, the *only* thing I played for. Titles were something to grow old with.'

# WITH TIME RUNNING OUT
## PETER ALLISS AND MICHAEL HOBBS, 1984

Undeterred by the international tensions of the Berlin Airlift and the slaughter in India and Pakistan, an excellent field gathered at Muirfield for the 1948 Open. This time there was a potentially very strong American contingent, which included the man who had three months before equalled the four-round Augusta record in winning the Masters – Claude Harmon, he of the strange backswing and shut face. Lawson Little was back again and so was Frank Stranahan, refreshed by having taken the Amateur Championship at Royal St George's without being extended in any round. So also were two Americans of Scottish birth: Bobby Cruickshank, who had lost a play-off for the 1923 US Open, thus giving Bobby Jones his first major championship; and Jimmy Thomson, one of the most prodigious hitters of all time. He played round with Fred Daly, no mean hitter himself, in the qualifying rounds and usually outdrove Daly by 50 yards and more, yet failed to qualify.

Henry Cotton was particularly keen this year to add a third title to his record, for his time was running out. He decided that the main threat came from the South Americans. He played a lot with them in practice, feeling that if he could beat them he could beat anyone. The two principals were the charming, stick-like Mario Gonzalez, then an amateur but now professional at Gavea, Rio de Janeiro (with a son Jaimé on the US tour) and, making his first entry, Roberto de Vicenzo, who was to feature centrally in the championship for many years. Observers quickly noted the beauty and power of his hitting and Bernard Darwin thought he 'gave more aesthetic pleasure than any other man in the field'. Some accolade indeed from a man whose judgement over a 50-year career in golf writing can seldom be faulted.

The betting at every Open tends to favour men who have been in good form in Europe. Norman von Nida was a 6–1 choice, with a considerable gap between him and Frank Stranahan at 11–1. Thereafter, the most money was on Little and Harmon. But it was Cotton who caught the eye during the pre-qualifying, his pair of 69s approached only by Daly's 69, 71, and Roberto's 72, 68. The first-round leaders, however, were Charlie Ward, Sam King and Flory van Donck, all on 69. They were followed by Roberto de Vicenzo and Frank Jowle on 70, while Cotton, von Nida and Reg Horne were handily placed a stroke further away.

The next day, with King George VI, a keen golfer and tennis player, in his gallery, Henry Cotton went out and won the Open. The Muirfield record of 67 had stood since 1929 and was Walter Hagen's 67, equalled by Alf Perry in 1935. This was Cotton's card:

3, 4, 5, 3, 4, 4, 3, 4, 3 (33);   4, 4, 4, 3, 4, 3, 3, 4, 4 (33)

He began with a long putt for a birdie and had his only flaw on the 382-yard third, perhaps the simplest hole on the course, when he three-putted. On the fourteenth, he was dead with a putt from some 30 yards and on the next celebrated with a birdie putt of near cricket-pitch length. On the last his putt for a 65 lipped out. I always felt that Henry was a far better putter than either the public or the player himself believed. The problem was that he *looked* uncomfortable on the greens and changed his stance or putter frequently. There was, too, the contrast with the ease, efficiency and accuracy of his play through the green. Above all, he had good nerve and no one ever accused Henry of giving up.

With this round, Henry had opened up a four-stroke gap on 137, followed by Ward and King (14), Arthur Lees and van Donck (142) and then at 143 Alf Padgham, who had set an early target, von Nida, Daly and Roberto de Vicenzo.

On the final day, all went well for Henry over the opening holes, as he parred the first four. Suddenly, he began dropping shots, one at each of the next five holes to the turn and on the second half added two more bogeys. In a matter of minutes, Sam King, still three strokes behind after Henry's shakey outward 39, caught him with three, four to Cotton's pair of fives. Then the pendulum swung the other way as Cotton birdied the twelfth and thirteenth with 12-foot and 6-foot putts to King's par and bogey. The lead of three was back and was maintained to the end of the round.

There had also been a challenge from Alf Padgham, 1936 open champion. Starting six strokes behind, he played the first nine in 34 and made for home in 4, 4, 4, 2, another two under par. However, he failed to hold a superb round together, dropping shots on four of the last five holes and had the sour taste in the mouth of missing a tiny putt on the last. Nevertheless, it was still a fine 71 and he was just two shots behind the maestro, Cotton.

As the players went out for the second time that day, the position after three rounds was:

212 Cotton;  214 Padgham;  215 King, Lees, van Donck, de Vicenzo;  216 Ward (with a hole in one on the thirteenth)

Cotton and King were out early, which put them in the enviable position of being able to set a target. King played the first nine in 36 to Cotton's 37 but Henry was back to level fours after the thirteenth and, Sam King by now fallen away, faced the last hole needing a four for a 71 and a certain victory. His second shot found sand by the green and, before a packed gallery, Henry shanked his bunker shot and the ball came off the face and back into sand. A 73 was now in prospect. He got the ball out this time, to nine feet, and then holed the putt, his face thunderous as he snatched his ball from the hole. Quickly overcoming his rage, however, he left the last green hand in hand with his wife Toots.

Yet play was far from over. Alf Padgham needed a 70 to catch Henry. His 77, however, left him well out of the hunt in seventh place. A 70 was in fact the best score that day, so it had been possible for Alf to prevent what was not only a popular but an historic win. In 1937, Henry had become the first British player since the great triumvirate of Vardon, Taylor and Braid to win the Open more than once, a record that still stands. I believe that this third victory, despite Tony Jacklin's wins in both US and British Opens, means that Henry Cotton must still be considered the greatest British player at least since those early great ones. My own opinion is that he is the greatest British golfer ever.

With this final laurel on his brow, Henry withdrew from the Open Championship for several years, not returning until he could hardly be expected to win. He played a restricted programme of tournament golf after this win, not even appearing in the following year's Ryder Cup, where his presence at Ganton could well have tipped the balance of the USA's 7–5 winning margin in our favour. Yet even today, in his mid-seventies, he keeps his enthusiasm for golf, still experimenting with new designs of clubhead and shaft. And, of course, putters, a great array of them.

There is a simple illustration of this. The most prized possession in the boardroom of the PGA at the Belfry near Birmingham is the set of clubs with which Henry won the 1948 Open. Attached is a tag in Henry's own handwriting remarking that he used his driver 56 times during the championship and hit the fairway 52 of those times. 'But where', I once asked, 'is the putter?' 'Ah', came the reply, from PGA secretary Colin Snape, 'Henry visited us a couple of years or so ago and his wife Toots mentioned that he had putted particularly well with that one. Henry gave his wife a mischievous smile, winked at me and tucked it under his arm.'

*The hero of the next tale received a great deal of sympathy after the Masters was all over but he got his perspectives right saying, 'Hell, it ain't like losing a leg!'.*

# BILLY JOE GONNA DO IT
### DAN JENKINS, 1970

For sustained whoops and hollers, and all-record-breaking in Spectator Hop, Step and Jump, no Masters has ever equalled that of 1954, in which a younger Hogan was intimately involved along with Sam Snead and a crazy, chattering North Carolina amateur, Billy Joe Patton. Those were the days when tournament chairman Clifford Roberts did not edit the crowds at Augusta. They were larger in the mid and late 1950s, the biggest, trompingest galleries golf has ever known. Mary Queen of Scots doing her naked dance of the rut iron (or whatever she did to get some credit for inventing the game) could not have lured more people into Augusta than the Masters had in 1954 for the Ballad of Billy Joe.

Well, it wasn't so much a ballad as it was a slapstick whodunit. Billy Joe Patton, known only around Morganton, North Carolina, tied for the first round lead, which was unreal in itself, but then he led all alone after 36, and he hung in there five behind Hogan and two behind Snead, in third place, after Saturday. Bareheaded, bespectacled, grinning, with a faster swing than a kitchen blender, Billy Joe kept the bulk of the throng enslaved with his scrambling tactics and his comments. 'I may go for it, and I may not', he would drawl, addressing a shot. 'It all depends on what I elect to do on my backswing.'

Sundays are always psychotic at the Masters, but this one more closely resembled a South American revolution than most. Hogan and Snead, playing one hole apart, had every reason to think they were going to have their own private little tournament on Sunday, but Billy Joe, two holes ahead of them, got back in it shortly after everyone had teed off. At the sixth hole he hit a 7-iron right into the cup for the loudest hole in one in the history of Morganton, North Carolina, or Augusta, Georgia.

And all anyone could hear from the galleries during the next hour or so as Patton, Hogan and Snead began to shift the lead around, was 'Billy Joe gonna do it. He gonna *do* it.'

Everybody did it down around Amen Corner, the nickname for a cruel and scenic bend of the eleventh, twelfth and thirteenth holes. Snead three-putted himself to a 72 and 289, the highest total that ever looked like it might win. Hogan uncharacteristically hit an approach shot into the water at the eleventh for a double-bogey six and a 75 to tie Snead at 289. But while all this was happening and the hordes were running around like children at recess, Billy Joe threw the Masters so high in the air only the azalea goddesses knew where it would land. At a point when judicious play would have won it for him easily – laying up at 13 and 15 for sure pars in other words – Patton went for the greens on his second shots and landed in the water both times. To the complete horror of his followers he made a seven and a six on those holes for a 71 and missed tying by a stroke. Pars there would have given him 68 and a two-stroke victory.

The thirteenth hole provided the more important and dramatic incident, for Patton knew he was leading then, that Hogan had just made six at the eleventh. He could see, too, one presumed, that he had a nasty sidehill lie for his shot to the green with a 3-wood. He studied the shot momentarily while the crowd shouted for him to be cautious. Then he looked over at those near him, taking a wood from the bag. 'I didn't get where I am playin' safe', he said, promptly hitting the ball right into the creek bottom bordering the green.

For a moment or two there was still a glimmer of hope for Billy Joe. Walking toward the ditch Patton heard a few frantic calls and saw some members of the gallery pointing down into the high grass below the green. They were telling him the ball had not submerged quite as deep as Conrad Veidt usually took his U-boats, that perhaps it was playable. Soggy and weed-covered but playable.

Patton removed his shoes and socks, rolled up his trousers, grabbed a wedge and climbed down into the ditch. He got set once or twice for a slash at it but finally decided, amid some nervous giggles in the crowd, that it was too risky. He could take 14 or 15 slashes at the ball once he got going. So he took a penalty stroke, laid out, pitched up poorly, pitched again and required two putts for his calamitous seven.

The ballad of Billy Joe ended with him sharing a cart with Clifford Roberts the next day to follow Snead's narrow play-off victory over Hogan.

'I wouldn't play it any differently', says Patton. 'I was elated to play as well as I did. Going into those last nine holes I knew I had to take a pop at it. What if I'd played safe and lost? That wouldn't have answered anything. I didn't feel I had any lead at all with Hogan behind me. I'm talkin' about the Hogan of then. If I'd played it safe I'd always have wondered how good I really was. I'm almost delighted I lost, in fact. I might have turned pro.'

## ARRIVALS AND A DEPARTURE
### MICHAEL HOBBS, 1976

Walter Hagen said that no one remembers who came second. I am not sure he was right. For instance, in the 1939 US Open Sam Snead (though no one told him) needed just a six on the last hole to qualify for a play-off. In going for perilous shots he finished with an eight. The winner? Byron Nelson, his victory less remembered than Snead's defeat.

In the case of the 1960 US Open the winner's name has certainly survived – Arnold Palmer. He just managed to squeeze in for what seemed likely to be the first of several wins. In fact, though he later was to come close eight or nine times, the 1960 tournament remains his solitary victory, but as a result there is no question mark against his name as there is against Sam Snead's.

But to me the 1960 US Open at Cherry Hills is much more than the story of Palmer's last-round race to victory. It is also Hogan's last chance; Jack Nicklaus making his first bid; the story of what happened to poor Mike Souchak; how Jack Fleck might have done it again and thereby not gone down into golf history as the man who happened to take the Open from Ben Hogan in 1955.

It was all Souchak for the first two rounds, which he completed in 68, 67, taking only 26 putts in that first 68 and not many more in the next round. He kept on going until, on the last hole of the third round, he hooked into a pond and eventually dropped two strokes on the hole – 73. Instead of being almost as far ahead as Henry Cotton had been in the 1934 British Open, Souchak had given his pursuers cause for hope. In fact, as the final round developed, at least eight players were in contention by the halfway stage.

The round opened with Souchak on 208 (68, 67, 73), followed by two players on 211: Hogan (75, 67, 69) and the 20-year-old Jack Nicklaus (71, 71, 69), who was playing, he has said, as well then as at any time since, feeling in an ideal hitting position for all his shots.

For Palmer the round opened with a deficit of seven shots and an idea. The idea concerned the first hole. Though it was a par-four, drives travelled further in the rarified air of the Cherry Hills course in Denver and the green could be reached by the longest hitters, of which Palmer was one. But there was rough shielding the approaches to the green and other hazards paralleled the fairway: a ditch on one side, poplars and pines the other. Most of the golfers throughout the tournament had played safe by taking an iron from the tee to keep clear of the trouble to either side and to ensure they would not reach the rough just short of the green. They had only a short approach shot left anyway, so there was still a good chance of a birdie.

Palmer had been after the certain birdie and possible eagle that getting a drive through the guarding rough and on to the green would bring. As he began his final round, his driver had only brought him the sequence six, five, four. Few others were worse than level fours on it for the tournament. Never mind, Palmer was difficult to disconcert once there was an attacking, daring stroke to be played. Again he took out his driver. This time his ball did not drift into ditch or pine forest but skidded through the rough and lay clear on the putting surface.

Palmer did not, in fairy-tale style, get his eagle two but two putts and a birdie were enough to set him off on a memorable burst of scoring. At the 410 yard second he boosted his hopes further by chipping in, followed with a three on the 348 yard third and then holed a huge putt of about 15 yards on the fourth. Four holes played; four birdies. In theory he might now be only three strokes behind Souchak. He parred the fifth, had birdies on each of the next two holes and then went on to complete the outward half in 30, a scoring record for the US Open. But like Miller in the same event 13 years later, he had started far behind the leaders and had caught but not passed most of them. By the tenth, however, he was level with Souchak, and two holes later he had pulled ahead.

One of the most difficult things to do in golf is to come back. Souchak, like many others before and after him, did not succeed in doing so. In his last round he faded to a 75 and total of 283. From this point on, the championship was fought out amongst a formidable company who were all tied for the lead at some time during the homeward stretch: Ben Hogan, Jack Fleck, Jack Nicklaus, Dutch Harrison, Ted Kroll, Julius Boros and Dow Finsterwald.

Fleck's dramatic tie with Hogan in 1955 and his even more unexpected victory in the 18 holes play-off the next day had not brought him fortune and only a temporary fame. An American has to win the US Open to reach the golfer's Valhalla, but he must then go on to do more. Fleck had done little else since he had played entranced at Olympic five years before. If he were to win another Open, it would be a far different matter.

He began his chase for the title every bit as dramatically as Palmer. He too had five birdies at the first six holes and the leaders had someone else to think about. Especially Ben Hogan who must have wondered if Fleck was again to be his Nemesis, again to prevent his winning the US Open for a record fifth time.

The 48-year-old Hogan was paired with Nicklaus for the final two rounds and Hogan was giving a supreme demonstration of his mastery of manoeuvring a golf ball from tee to green. In his third round 69 he had hit the green in the regulation number of strokes every time but had holed few birdie putts.

Some great golfers have begun as good putters and have rapidly become anything from nervous to locked rigid in fright when standing over a short putt. In some cases it has seemed that the more masterful a player is with his long shots – and even approach putts – the less sure he becomes once his ball is a stride from the hole. Harry Vardon, for example, became incapable of producing a smooth stroke at the ball; Snead looked rather better but the ball all too frequently did not go into the hole until he tried a between-the-legs croquet style – and that was quickly banned by the rulers of golf. There is even a story about one US open champion who didn't putt in exhibition games. He would play his shots to the green and, once there, impassively pick up his ball. Spectators thought that he felt the humdrum business of getting the ball into the hole was too simple a matter to be worthy of a great golfer's attention. The reality was that he did not want the news to get out that he was likely to average four putts a green and sometimes jerk the ball clean off it in a nerve spasm.

Hogan had been one of the great putters, in the Hagen, Jones and Palmer class, but it had gone. In middle age you would see him practise an ingenious variety of putting strokes before addressing the ball. None of them resembled the tortured action with which, eventually, he prodded it towards the hole – after freezing over the ball for an eternity. How is it that a man like Hogan or Vardon can place a ball there or there with his tee shot and long irons into the green yet be inferior to many middle-handicap golfers once he takes putter in hand? Perhaps the answer lies in the fact that a golfer is dealing with two elements – air and earth. He can master the flight of a ball through the air. If there has been perfection of swing and judgement of wind effect, distance and perhaps even atmospheric density, the ball will fly with the trajectory and velocity his clubhead has given it. But eventually it has to come to ground and is then prey to the malignity of another element – earth. The golfer learns to accept that his ball may pitch on a slightly soft centimetre of turf and stop more quickly than he had anticipated, or land on another spot and perhaps unkindly bound on through the green. Often, indeed, fate can be with him and a shot struck too weakly may bumble on to the flag. But on the putting green few golfers will admit that a putt they have struck was lucky to dive into the hole, perhaps after being diverted by a spike mark. Very readily, however, they will complain of the 'something' that made their ball stop short of the hole, twist off the edge or divert from the line.

Over the passage of the years the number of blows from harsh fate mount up in the mind. In the end he knows, every time he putts, that some disaster lies immediately ahead. His pessimism then reaches the same level as Vardon's and Hogan's. He delays the time when he will just *have* to hit the ball by lengthily examining the line and practising his stroke before standing statuesque over the ball.

On that last afternoon of the 1960 US Open, however, Hogan at last began to make some putts, and here we had youth and age, Nicklaus and Hogan, in close pursuit of the title. For the former it would have been a glittering prize at the outset of what seemed set fair to be a great career. Nicklaus would have earned comparison with Bobby Jones as the greatest amateur of his era and the first since Johnny Goodman in 1933 (not a vintage year) to win it. For Hogan, victory would have been the fitting and well-earned final peak of a life's work devoted to striking a golf ball with ultimate purity – a record fifth US Open.

Nicklaus eagled the par-five fifth and eventually turned in 32. If he could maintain this pace Palmer would not catch him with anything worse than a 60. Nicklaus then faltered slightly, dropping a stroke to par on the eleventh, which, as a par-five, he would have hoped to birdie. Hogan continued in his by now set pattern of hitting every green in the regulation figures and then getting down in two putts – but not the single putts he needed to master the field.

At the 212 yard twelfth Hogan hit a wood to ten feet. At last he holed the putt. Nicklaus also holed for a two and this put him a stroke up on Palmer, Boros and Fleck. At the 385 yard thirteenth Hogan got his par safely but Nicklaus did not. He had pitched up to about 12 feet but three-putted and then did so once more on the next, a 470 yard par-four. Mechanically, Hogan again had a par. At the fifteenth, a par-three, he drew level with the leaders, who at this point on the course were Arnold Palmer and Jack Fleck, at four under for the championship. Hogan had single-putted from all of six or seven yards; was the worst element in his game, putting, about to take the championship from him? He had hit 32 consecutive greens and was now getting the putts into the hole.

At the sixteenth both Nicklaus and Hogan had chances for birdies, but both failed to get their putts down. They now faced perhaps the most dangerous hole on the course. The seventeenth measured 548 yards. This would normally mean that Nicklaus would have no difficulty in making the distance in two strokes, while Hogan could also expect to if he could put together two outstanding wooden-club shots. But the second shot at the seventeenth was perilous in the extreme, for the green was set on an island in a lake. The second shot could not bounce and run on to the green; it had to pitch on and stop quickly. The player needed to be using an iron for his second, and a very straight iron at that. Both decided not to hazard the championship on the one shot and played to a few yards of the lake. They would try to lay their short pitches close to the hole. Nicklaus went three or four yards past the hole, having played a safe shot that was never in danger of finding the water.

Hogan pondered his shot. He could play the simple shot that would run at least a few yards past the flag or he could hazard hitting a sand wedge at the flag, which was positioned well to the front of the green, and risk spinning back into the water. He took his sand wedge, opened the face and hit a low shot with all the backspin he could work on to the ball. It cleared the lake, pitched, and spun back into the shallows at the edge. Although he played a good shot from the water it was a six, not the four that would have left him needing a four at the last for 279 and, in probability, his fifth US Open. With that shot which he had played almost too well Hogan was finished, practically an old man as the competitive fire drained out of him. While Nicklaus went one over par on the last to finish with a five, Hogan finished with an exhausted seven.

The rest was Arnold Palmer, playing about two holes behind Hogan and

Nicklaus. After his burst of low-scoring on the outward half, he needed, as it turned out, only to par his way in if the others continued to drop shots – they all did.

After he had holed his final short putt, there was a pause of about half an hour and Palmer was champion.

This is how they finished:

280   Arnold Palmer (72, 71, 72, 65)
282   Jack Nicklaus (71, 71, 69, 71)
283   Dutch Harrison, Julius Boros, Ted Kroll, Dow Finsterwald, Mike
       Souchak (68, 67, 73, 75) and Jack Fleck
284   Ben Hogan (75, 67, 69, 73)

## HEAD-TO-HEAD
### MARK McCORMACK, 1968

The tournament, stripped to its essentials, was from the day it began until the moment the final record-breaking putt was sunk, a confrontation between the two strongest figures of the game today, Jack Nicklaus and Arnold Palmer. Only once before had they met quite on these terms, agreeing, you might say, to fight it out. That was at Oakmont in 1962. The winner then was Nicklaus, too. Seen from this viewpoint, the Open was as simple, powerful, and moving as a heavyweight championship fight.

*     *     *

Palmer was having a sensational year. By the end of May he had won a total of $99,225, far ahead of any money-winning pace in history. He had started the year with some experimental aluminium shafts in his clubs that caused much talk, and they were obviously good enough for him, but shortly before the Open he shifted back to steel. From the way he was swinging at the ball the shafts in his clubs could have been bamboo. I have never seen him playing better, and his own feeling was that were it not for his putting blowing hot and cold, his golf was almost perfection. The area of biggest improvement was in his approach shots, where he was finally developing enough finesse to bring that aspect of his game up to the standard set by the rest. It is hard to believe that Palmer – that fellow whom some people keep trying to write off as a fallen king – is playing the best golf of his career, but such is the case.

Arnold arrived at Baltusrol as the favourite for the tournament. (A month before, *Golf* magazine had listed him a 7-1 choice to win the Open, which led Arnold to remark: 'The last time I played the course I shot 81, 73. They better change the odds.') And they might have changed the odds if they had known that he had aggravated his sore right hip again. Arnold mentioned that the hip was troubling him, but he never let anyone see how much. By

Wednesday, the day before play was to begin, he had almost decided he would have to withdraw. He played a practice round that day with Nicklaus. He looked uneasy over the ball, did not swing with any verve, and was worried. The reason was the sore hip, which he feared might go out on him at any minute. By that night he was bathing the hip in witch hazel, Winnie Palmer was rubbing Ben-Gay into it, and Arnold was deciding he would give up practice for the rest of the Open week to put as little strain on the hip as possible.

Palmer had also received a putting lesson, and seemed pleased with the results. The man the advice came from was Byron Nelson. Arnold had seen Byron by the putting green and called him over for a look. 'Your stroke looks fine', Nelson told him. 'But just hesitate a little at the top of the backswing. Don't rush it.' When it comes to putting, nobody ever stops taking lessons – or asking for them. Including Nicklaus as well as Palmer.

If this had been one of Arnold's best years, it had to be ranked as Jack's worst. He was playing nowhere near his capabilities, and was now going through the process of changing his swing. After three years of hooking the ball, he had wisely decided to become a fader again. Such a changeover takes weeks, but Jack had enough time between the Masters and the Open to manage it. The tip-off that he was ready came at the Memphis Open, his last tournament before Baltusrol. He started with a 77 there, and then went 67, 67, 69. The ball was moving right to left instead of left to out-of-bounds, and Jack was satisfied with everything except, need it be said, his putting. There then occurred one of those incidents upon which golf tournaments turn. Nicklaus was on the Baltusrol putting green with his good friend Deane Beman. He asked to borrow Beman's putter, and he liked it. He suggested to Deane that Beman give it to him. Beman suggested that Jack go soak his head, but offered him one of three similar putters he had in his car. The man who went to get the putters was Fred Mueller, a friend of Beman's from Washington, DC, who just happened to have his own putter handy. It was also like Deane's. Nicklaus did not care for Beman's alternatives, but thought Fred's was just the thing, even though the head of it had been painted white, giving it distinction if not beauty. On Wednesday, using Mueller's putter – which he was calling White Fang – Nicklaus shot a practice round 62 on a US Open course. It was a stunning feat. Baltusrol was humiliated, but need not have been, for Jack's round was one of those occasional wonders that has to be accepted but need not be explained. Nobody got within five strokes of that 62 score once the tournament began.

Asked if Jack's 62 shook him up, Palmer said, 'I can't imagine how a 62 in practice could shake anybody up but Jack because he didn't have it tomorrow'.

'Well', said Jack, 'I think I'd rather have my 62 than Arnold's round today'.

The big men were ready to play for keeps.

Palmer got the opportunity to draw first blood on Thursday, thanks to a starting time that put him on the tee before half the commuters in New Jersey had faced up to their morning orange juice. This was actually an advantage, for two reasons. Arnold is an early riser. He brings to each day the vitality that he brings to a round of golf. He is anxious to get the day going because who knows how many good things might happen. With the pressure that the Open had built up in him bubbling away, the sooner he could get out and attack the course, the better. More obvious, but perhaps less important in Palmer's case, was the fact that playing early enables a golfer to putt on greens that have not yet been chewed up by the spike marks of the majority of the field.

In spite of the 'Go Arnie, Go' signs that were brandished by his Army at the first tee, the first place Arnie went was into the right rough. When he bunkered his second and missed a 15-footer for a par, I could only think of the advice that he gives to golfers in his book, *My Game and Yours,* but sometimes has trouble taking himself: play the first three holes of a round as hard as you play the last three holes. There are times when Arnold tends to start rather casually, as if he were sure he would birdie the last six holes in a row, so why get excited.

By the twelfth hole Arnold was two over par and in difficulty. For one thing, he was favouring his hip by swinging noticeably easier than is his wont. Even when his ball was in the rough – and he was in the rough a lot, missing six fairways – he went at it tenderly for fear that he might really hurt the hip and be forced to withdraw. This lack of aggression gave his swing an uncharacteristic appearance and contributed to the looseness of both his wood and iron play. It was not until he ran in a 45-foot putt for a birdie on 13 that he began to develop some enthusiasm. He followed that with a birdie on 14 and finally came in with a birdie on 18 for a 69. 'It was just one of those rounds', he said. 'Not good, not bad.' In truth, I think he had hoped to do much better, but on the other hand, he was relieved that his hip had held up.

Palmer's 69 was on the scoreboard by the time Nicklaus teed off more than four hours later, and Jack had much the same kind of round as Arnold. He missed five fairways, and, though he recovered better, his putter – white blade and all – was giving him no help. When he finished with a 71 he had made only one birdie, but when I had dinner with him that night he was much more satisfied than I thought he might be. His reasoning was that the 71 in part reflected the condition of the greens late in the day. 'You can see that most of the good scores were shot in the morning', he said. He had not missed the fairways by much, and he had confirmed his theory that even when you did miss fairways at Baltusrol, you could still hit the big greens and salvage a par, something you often cannot do on an Open course.

Friday was pressure-cooker day, and players staggered around trying to decide if the weather was as bad as the unforgettable Saturday at Congressional in 1964 when Ken Venturi needed a doctor at his side as he fought off heat exhaustion to win. Before the day was over, the Red Cross had treated 30 heat prostration victims, including five who were sent to the hospital. The heat bothered Nicklaus, but he still came up with the round he had suggested he might, as he started early and finished deftly with a 67, his lowest score ever in an Open. There was nothing sizzling about his play of the early holes, however. He hit over the first green and settled for a bogey, and then at the fourth hole he left himself a ten-footer for a par that he felt was the first putt he really had to make. A bogey here would have pushed him to three over par, which was getting too far back. He made the putt, and birdied the next hole as his game began to sharpen up. From this point on, his round could have been another one of those 62s, as he kept hitting irons within 20 feet of the stick and stroking away for birdies. All told, he made about half of his birdie tries. As he came up to 18, where he was on in two with a drive and a 2-iron, his playing partner, Bob Goalby, looked at the sopping-wet Nicklaus and said, 'You don't look like you're feeling so good, Jack'. 'And you don't either', said Nicklaus. It was a good thing they were on 18. By now it was obvious that Nicklaus was back on his old left to right game, that the transition he had been working on since Augusta was complete. 'I have not driven this well since 1962', he told me later.

Meanwhile, Palmer was having a much better day, too. Arnold loves the heat. If they held the US Open in a sauna bath, that would be fine with him. Perhaps he has never forgotten those long boyhood winters in Pennsylvania waiting for the first thaw so that he could play golf. At any rate, warmth is a special joy to him. Arnold was now hitting the ball much closer to the pin, but not sinking many putts. He posted five straight pars and then escaped serious trouble on six – 'It was a fun hole' – when he pulled a 4-wood to the left of the green behind a bunker, failed to get a tenderly hit sand wedge over the bunker, and had to use the same club again. This time he left it within ten feet of the hole, and he made the putt for a bogey. It was his last bogey of the day, as strings of pars and three birdies brought him home with a 68 and a one-stroke lead over Nicklaus. Arnold was especially pleased with his round, not because it was a 68, but because it was a very good 68 – just as on the previous day his 69 could have been considered as bad. This time he had hit 17 greens, and missed only three fairways. He had eight to ten putts that either hit the cup and spun out, or just slid past when they appeared to be going in. 'The ball was running over the edge of the hole all day', he said. What was more, the pain in his hip was down to a mere twinge, and even though he still was not practising, he was not worried about that any more. So Palmer was playing his best. Nicklaus was playing his best. And now, being the first two men in the standings, they were paired together for what was to have been an epic confrontation on Saturday.

Was to have been. What happened on Saturday is an interesting lesson in golf, as intriguing in its way as Palmer's collapse a year before when he started thinking about breaking Ben Hogan's scoring record and ended up losing the 1966 US Open to Bill Casper. Nicklaus and Palmer teed off at three o'clock on Saturday afternoon determined to beat each other. What they nearly did was arrange things so that neither one of them could win the Open. It was a classic case of playing the wrong foe.

*    *    *

Palmer and Nicklaus teed off Saturday before the biggest, most vociferous pro-Palmer gallery I can ever recall. It was excited, as well it might have been; it had a favourite, and it dearly wanted him to win. Jack is used to this. He says he has his fans, only they aren't so noisy. And he strains to be gracious about it. But this was going to be a painful day. (Lest you think Arnold was having things all his own way, I have to report the astonishing remark I overheard at the first tee, where a small boy poked his head through the layers of people, got a close look at Arnold, and came back to tell a friend, 'Palmer's not in bad shape for a man his age'. Ah, youth.)

Old not-in-bad-shape Arnold got himself in bad shape quickly enough on the first hole of his duel with Nicklaus by pulling his second shot some 60 feet to the left fringe, chipping up to within three feet, and missing the putt. It was a bad omen for the Army. Jack, meanwhile, hung his second shot on the flag, and was a little surprised when it landed 15 feet short, from where he missed the birdie. At this point, who in that gallery of twenty thousand would have thought they were not going to see a birdie for 16 more holes?

On the second hole Nicklaus was again inside of Arnold – this was to be a consistent pattern for two days – and needed a 15-footer for a birdie after Arnold got his par. Here was the shot that Jack thought would put him ahead of Arnold for the first time in the tournament. His putt looked perfect, but hit the cup and somehow slipped out, stopping 15 inches away. Then Nicklaus stepped up and missed the 15-incher. Much of the gallery was first shocked, then relieved on behalf of Arnold, and then apparently pleased. When Jack started to tap in his third putt a voice called out, 'Miss it again'.

At the fourth hole, a notorious troublemaker that is guarded by a large pond, Arnold hit what looked like a perfect 6-iron, but this par-three is much like the twelfth at Augusta. The wind swirls this way and that, and playing it too fine courts a double bogey. The pin was in front and Arnold wanted a birdie. Instead, his iron shot hung just a fraction short and dropped into the water. A hoped-for two became a double-bogey five. By the fifth hole the match – and it might as well be called a match, for the US Open did not seem to be on anybody's mind – began to look more like the finals of the New Jersey Amateur than a Nicklaus–Palmer face-off. Jack managed to get his approach within 40 feet of the cup, but Arnold went over the green, then hit a poor chip, and somehow succeeded in sinking a marvellous 25-foot putt over a hump for a par. On the next hole Jack hit a tree with his tee shot and settled for a routine bogey. Arnold bunkered his second, but came up with a beautiful explosion to save a par again. On the next hole both hit their tee shots into the rough and ... but is there any need to go on? Jack summed it all up when he turned to Arnold on the eighth tee and said, 'Let's stop playing each other and start playing the course'.

If they did, it was a tough course. When Arnold got his second shot to within 15 feet for a good birdie try at eight somebody called out, 'Sock it to 'em, Arnie'. At this point ''em' was bunkered, but made a good recovery for a par, and Palmer two-putted. Jack bogeyed ten, losing a stroke to Arnold who missed another birdie try, this one from 15 feet. On 11 Arnold hit a fine approach putt from 70 feet to make a par and Nicklaus hit a ghastly putt from 12 feet to halve the hole. On 12 Arnold returned the favour by hitting an even worse putt following an exhortation from the gallery that was perfectly in order: 'How about a couple of birdies', a spectator shouted. 'There's forty thousand people out here rooting for you.' The players ignored the suggestion, and perhaps were ignoring the belt that Winnie Palmer was wearing as well. Written on it was: 'The most important rule of all is keep your eye on the ball'.

I am not recounting this round in all of its gory detail for any sordid pleasure one might get in writing about the poor showing of the world's two finest golfers. Palmer and Nicklaus have played a lot worse many, many times and will again. In fact, they had more reason to play badly this day than they normally would. What I think is noteworthy — and part of the endless fascination of sport — is the way in which long-anticipated meetings between two arch rivals so often turn out to be anything but the outstanding performances anticipated. The strain becomes too great, and the marvellous discipline and coordination that is common to all great athletes breaks down. In this case we were seeing it happen in a US Open, and I think it said more about the hidden pressures of pro golf than if each of them had shot 67s.

But it is also true that this kind of hapless performance cannot continue forever. Sooner or later something happens to jolt the athletes back to reality. On this particular afternoon the break came on the sixteenth hole, a 214-yard par-three. By now I was suspecting that half the field had passed Palmer and Nicklaus — I knew Casper, Fleckman, and Beman had. Arnold had the honour because Jack had just succeeded in three-putting again, and he hit a fine 4-iron 15 feet from the hole. Jack answered that by flying his tee shot two feet inside of Arnold's. Each had a good birdie try. Well, Arnold hit a putt that was a travesty on the good name of golf. Somehow it wobbled in the general direction of the hole, and he got down in two for a par. Then Jack lined up his birdie putt and stroked one that made Arnold's look like the ultimate in artistry. From the moment it left the clubhead it was two feet off line and two feet long. Arnold then did something that you will probably never see again in a US Open. He turned his back on the green, bent over slightly, and started to laugh. He couldn't help it. The whole damn thing was too comic. Then he turned around with this wide smile on his face and said to Jack, 'Nice stroke'. Nicklaus grinned. The gallery grinned. You had to think it was two of the nicest guys in the world who had made it to the finals of the New Jersey Amateur.

But, I also remember thinking at the time that that ought to change the pattern. Things should be different now. And they were, though it took a minute to develop. Jack was now so concerned that he decided he would try to reach the seventeenth green – 623 yards away – in two, even though nobody had attempted this in the tournament, and nobody ever did it. He went wheeling into his tee shot and, as he said later, 'I might as well have hit it with the club cover on'. It hardly went two hundred yards. He then hit an iron over the fairway bunkers and a wonderful 8-iron within 12 feet of the hole, a shot that was not greeted with so much as a murmur of applause. But when Arnold hit a wedge within six feet, the gallery exploded with noise. Arnold walked onto the green first, to a great ovation, and then there was just the barest ripple of applause when Nicklaus walked up. But as Nicklaus stepped onto the green a loud voice boomed through the stillness, 'That's all right, Jack. I'm for you'. Once more, there was nothing to do but laugh. Arnold started it, Jack followed suit, and the whole gallery suddenly found it was laughing at itself. I don't know who that man is who shouted out his allegiance for Nicklaus, but I wonder if Jack doesn't owe him a vote of thanks, for Nicklaus rolled in his putt and had the first birdie of the day. From that point on nobody in the US Open field could have touched Nicklaus – or Palmer. Starting on that green, Nicklaus was to play 20 holes in seven under par. Palmer, even though he missed his short putt on 17, was to play his last 20 holes in two under, a pace that would normally have won him the Open.

Both Nicklaus and Palmer ended their day with birdies on 18, reaching the green in two and two-putting. The closing birdies helped, and so did the fact that the opposition had failed to make any significant move while Arnold and Jack were playing giveaway. Nicklaus finished with a 72, and I guess you would have to say he won the New Jersey Amateur one-up over Palmer, who had a 73. After talking to the press – 'I'm fortunate to be in it after such a bad round' – Nicklaus went to the practice tee. He was a lone figure there, swinging in the near darkness. And then, as lights began to come on across New Jersey, he moved over to the putting green.

\*     \*     \*

Sunday's Palmer–Nicklaus battle turned out to be what Saturday's might have been; it was wonderful golf that closed out the rest of the US Open field; it was superb competition, with the players minding their own business instead of fretting about each other, which is the way to do your best against any opponent. It had style, class, and brilliance. As I said before, Arnold's 69 was good enough to win; he thought a 69 would win. Jack's 65 was that much better.

Of the final 18 holes, there were four worthy of close attention, the second, seventh, eighth and eighteenth. Pars on the first hole were routine. On the short par-four second hole Jack tried for the second straight day to play safely into the very tight fairway with a 1-iron. But as happened Saturday, he caught the rough instead. His approach went into the left bunker and he exploded ten feet past the hole. Palmer, meanwhile, hit a perfect drive and a fine second shot about 12 feet from the cup. Arnold told me later that he had real hopes here of picking up two strokes, a birdie to Jack's bogey. But he missed the putt, as did Jack. I think Arnold had been looking for a sign that everything was going to go right for him this day, and when that putt stayed out he sensed instead that he was going to have to work hard for anything he got. It is a little thing, but it sets a mood.

Now they both hit wonderful approaches to three, and Jack got his birdie. Arnold did not. On four Jack hit it four feet from the hole for another birdie. On five he split the pin from out of the rough and made a 14-footer for his third birdie in a row. Palmer was now two strokes behind, but Arnold got one back on six when Jack went over the green and had to accept a bogey.

Then came the hole that settled the US Open. At least, Arnold thinks it did, and so do I. This 470-yard par-four is among the most difficult holes on the course, and a pin placement on the far right made it play harder this day than any other. In fact, the field averaged 4.4 strokes on it on Sunday. Both Palmer and Nicklaus hit excellent drives, and then Palmer hit the long iron of a lifetime, carrying the bunkers, dead on the flag all the way, and digging in eight feet from the cup. It was an electrifying shot. When Arnold turned and handed the club back to the caddy you could see how pleased he was. Nicklaus then hit a good shot about 22 feet above the hole. There was every reason to think Nicklaus would get his par, Palmer would get his birdie, and they would be all even again. As Palmer walked up the fairway somebody shouted, 'Come on, Arnie. Bury him!'. But then came one of those turn-around situations that every golfer knows can happen. Nicklaus made his long putt, a stroke that was firmly in the cup from the instant he hit it. Unsettled, Palmer missed his. Instead of being even. Arnold was two strokes down again.

I doubt Arnold had recovered from this disheartening reversal by the time he teed off on eight. At any rate, he hit his one really bad tee shot of the day into the right rough and behind a tree. All he could do was chip out to the fairway, and he ended up with a bogey five on this short par-four. Nicklaus, meanwhile, hit a big drive and then a fine wedge four feet from the hole for another birdie, his fifth in six holes. Now he was four strokes ahead, and Arnold was all but beaten. Jack's torrid pace eased for a moment as he took a bogey and three pars, but Arnold could not get the birdie that would have brought him back into contention. Then at 13 Nicklaus hit an approach three feet from the cup for a birdie, and at 14 he had it five feet from the hole for another one.

By now Jack, who is the USGA's favourite whipping boy on the matter of slow play, was racing down the fairways. His tournament was won, but he had to finish before the skies, which were getting more ominous by the minute, let loose a deluge. As the twosome headed into the home holes the sky was getting darker and the USGA officials were getting paler. At 17

Palmer made his first putt of the day for a birdie, which cut Jack's lead to four strokes. As Nicklaus walked to the eighteenth tee I had one of those startling recollections that come to a man. I remembered standing in almost the identical spot in 1954 when Dick Mayer came up to that tee as the apparent winner of the Open. All he needed was an easy par for the victory. There was a delay with the group ahead and Mayer was soon surrounded by photographers who asked him to step outside the ropes and pose for pictures, which he did. I remembered thinking that was not a very good idea, that it would break his concentration. When Mayer finally did swing he hit a terrible tee shot into the woods and ended up with a triple-bogey eight that let Ed Furgol win the Open.

Now Nicklaus was on the tee, but nobody was about to interrupt him. He needed a birdie to break Ben Hogan's scoring record – shades of Palmer a year before – but, as he said later, 'I came here to win, not to break records'. His choice of clubs was a very prudent 1-iron ('I felt like an idiot using it', he said later), which he came off of slightly, hitting the ball into some bare dirt down the right side of the rough. After taking a free drop because his ball was near a television cable drum, he tried to play a safe 8-iron short of a creek that crosses the fairway. This shot he hit miserably, taking his divot an inch behind the ball. Now he was still 230 yards from a green that was way above him and guarded by a trap with a very steep wall. He went for the 1-iron again, and late some evening I am going to ask him why. It seemed to me that he could have hit any wood club either onto the green, hole high to the left, or over the green and still have chipped back for the world's easiest six and a sure victory. Or he could have played short of the bunker and hit a wedge on for a cinch six. But what, I keep asking myself, if he had buried that 1-iron shot a foot deep into the high wall of that bunker. He hit the shot so hard that they might be digging for the ball yet. Which is why Nicklaus is a golfer and I am a lawyer. The shot he hit, of course, which he struck 'harder than I know how', was perfect. It cleared the bunker by a scant couple of feet and stopped 22 feet short of the hole.

As Nicklaus came up to the eighteenth green with the thunderstorm about to break, there was a great din of applause. It was sincere and heartfelt, for it is the way of sports fans to appreciate achievement. Many of their sentiments may have been with Arnold, but he had been beaten, and now the entire gallery was paying enthusiastic tribute to Nicklaus for his fine victory. And Jack paid them back in kind by running in the putt for a 65 and the 275 total that broke Hogan's record by a stroke.

With that the rains came, and the best golf tournament of 1967 was a memory.

# CARNOUSTIE, 1968
## PETER THOMSON, 1969

Casper was soon showing signs of stress. He began in that quick fire manner of his as usual, but there was a clear anxiety in his rhythm. His drives began to cut. By the time he passed the fifth hole he had written down three fives and all those once per year experts were nodding, 'he's gone; Casper's crashed'. Logically there was no reason at all why he should be out of the race. If anything his frightful start could have helped.

At least it had lifted from his shoulders the burden of leading. But such events shatter not only the score, they pound the stomach and weaken the knees. Only a robot could be impervious to such a setback! Even so, only one man was doing much better. Charles beside him had a horrible six at the third and Nicklaus just ahead of him in the last pair with Player dropped strokes to par on the sixth and par-three eighth.

Player in his uniform of black, set about his task with his usual intensity. Sometimes it works and sometimes it doesn't, but this day he passed hole after hole with tradesman-like efficiency and a certain amount of help. At the fourth, like most people, he aimed up the wider adjacent fifteenth fairway, only to slice it wide into the right hand rough up against the temporary picket fence. His ball found a nasty lie but relief from the fence was permissible. He summoned the red-rosetted R and A official, asked the pairing to witness and was able to drop some yards away on clearer ground from whence he hit it on the green. A fortunate break had saved him a stroke at least. However he had trouble at the next into wind and missed the green. Here he dropped a stroke but retrieved it downwind at the long sixth where he passed the centre trap safely and thrashed it home to the green edge.

Parring seven, eight and nine he found himself in the lead. Casper had slid back three behind, Charles, although he stood ahead of Casper by a stroke trailed by two and Nicklaus also out on 38 had four strokes to make up. Jacklin suicided at the seventh where he attacked with the driver and pulled it over the fence. His second ball also went wide into deep rough and three putts added up to eight.

Brewer crept closer. I had visions of this fine player pulling it off until at the crucial moment he ran a long putt six feet by and missed the return. Player missed the gap on the tenth fairway, played short of the burn, pitched over and two-putted. In so doing he lost a stroke to Nicklaus and Casper who each found the fairway. Charles took five. All missed long birdie putts at the eleventh where the hole was tucked away in the right hand front corner within eight feet of the edge – virtually inaccessible like the fourth. Each parred the next in four but Player missed the short thirteenth and dropped another stroke. Nicklaus was now within two strokes and Casper and Charles one. The Spectacles would decide the issue.

Nicklaus, grinning now, knows that it is between he and the South African.

(He had his caddy, Jimmy Dickinson dawdle behind at the twelfth to see the Casper–Charles scoreboard. After Jimmy told him of their collapse. Gary Player buttonholed the caddy: 'If Jack wants to know how others are going, OK. Tell him. But don't let me hear. I don't want to know.')

The fourteenth (the Spectacles) is long and disturbing. Jack Nicklaus has belted his drive out to the right, over the crowd rope and into a clump of trees. Player is smack in the middle of the fairway. Like ghouls the crowd scampers to examine Jack Nicklaus's trouble. Arriving there, Nicklaus says he has been lucky. He has room to swing and the ball is sitting up in a clearing with a shot to the green. A flustered official darts between the crowd-packed Nicklaus and the waiting Player. 'I want the fence down', Nicklaus tells the referee, and steps are taken immediately to take it down. The wind is blowing in our faces and it is getting cold. Gary Player is rubbing his hands, looking ahead at the two giant mounds that obscure the green from his sight. Nicklaus emerges and says to him: 'It's all right' (meaning his shot). 'In a manner of speaking', he adds half to himself.

'Are you waiting for me, or am I waiting for you?'

Player shrugs and the official says it is Nicklaus's shot. Nicklaus glares at the ground in front of him, and takes a 3-wood from Jimmy. There is muttering in the crowd. 'A 3-wood!' There is a bursting noise from the undergrowth and a gasp. The Big Bear has smacked his wood right over to the green two hundred yards away, to land just past in the rough.

Player gets set up after his long wait. The feet shuffle and waggle into position. The toes move up and down. The mouth suddenly tightens and becomes, in the right corner, at the final moment before the backswing, an ugly, pained, scowl. The arms are straight, the left elbow almost over-straight to bend inwards. There is a final twitch of the right knee and the ball is off! It flashes towards the Spectacles – where Henry Cotton and some officials are standing – over them, and towards the hidden green. A great roar from the stand by the green goes up. The spaniel eyes of Player look imploringly at them. Cotton dances up and down on the grassy mound, wild with excitement, holding his arms three feet apart!

Player strides forward in a hurry, carrying his 3-wood. The excitement is fantastic. He now has a hundred yards to go. Now 50 yards and then he sees his ball, lying waiting, not a yard from the hole. He takes off the check cap, showing flattened down crew-cut and grins. The crowd is screaming and roaring at him. That is the shot, they are saying, that has just won the Open ... Nicklaus, 15 yards from the green, chips from the rough, but not very well. However, he gets his birdie four.

Gary Player lines up his putt, wipes his ball with his hands, picking tiny pieces of dirt from it that even the careful Alf, his caddy, has missed. He puts it down, rocks a little on his heels, and drops it in. For an eagle three. On the fifteenth his shot to the green has left him a six-footer. He has played three shots, and Nicklaus, 45 feet away, two.

Player's eagle has put him three ahead of Nicklaus and the big man knows he has to hole his shot to have any chance at all now. A swallow flits about the green. Nicklaus makes only his par, Player has an eight-foot putt for his. He is again being finickety with his ball, closely examining it, wiping it, then finally and carefully placing it. While Nicklaus wanders off to chat to an American journalist, Player gets over the ball and putts. And it's in! Another roar. 'Yeeees!' cries the crowd.

Player brings his clenched fist down, eyes closed, mouth clenched as if in anger; but it is in glorious, almost unbelievable relief. Then he bows his head, and he prays. ('I try to work with God as a partner in life', Player said later.) On the 243 yard par-three sixteenth Player bunkers his drive on the right of the green, while Nicklaus's great drive is sitting pretty in the middle. They stride towards the green and Player asks Nicklaus: 'What are you trying to do to me, man?'. Nicklaus glances across at the South African: 'Hell, what have you been trying to do to me? I'm trying to beat you, that's all!'

Player was at a distinct disadvantage at the sixteenth because of its length. Two hundred and forty three yards was just about his limit with the driver against the wind. On top of that the target – ridiculously small. He carefully armed himself at address, drew his elbows in close to his sides, hunched his shoulders and drew back with all his vigour; but again he came down ever so slightly on the inside which sent his right shoulder rotating in a circle more horizontal than perfect and his ball tailing a degree right into the nearer of the two yawning traps guarding the green. Here was danger staring him in the face.

Nicklaus was by now in a desperate position much the same as he found himself in at Oak Hill. Unless Player fell on his face, he would certainly lose if he couldn't pull off something phenomenal like a two, three, three finish.

One can't help feeling about Nicklaus that all things are possible, but the thought of his uninspired putting up to then cast heavy doubt on his chances of getting up. So it was all the more electric when he teed off an immense 3-wood that rose high into the wind as straight as a howitzer would send it, and pitched full beside the flag and settled down just 20 feet past. Now Nicklaus, who carefully stepped out that hole in practice, claims it is nearer 270 to the back of the green than the 243 as the card reads. In most circumstances it would have been a winning shot, allowing that he holed the putt and unnerved his opponent. In the event he not only missed the putt but failed to affect Player in any way noticeable. Player replied with a classic explosion from the sand that landed like a parachutist a mere six feet away and stuck.

Player is an expert at bunker play. He told someone of the press tent he had actually holed out 11 times from bunkers since last March! Even allowing that the ball lay favourably in the trap and that the flag was at or about the perfect range for a full swing explosion, it was a very brave shot. That he left the putt short on the lip, judging he was rolling downhill when he wasn't, was unjust, but it made up for his previous one where he was a trifle lucky. That Nicklaus had gained one made his situation serious, but not critical. Unless something drastic happened to him, he was still most likely to win.

Meanwhile, Casper, who since the ninth had regained his composure with a run of four pars, came to grief with a six at the Spectacles where just ten minutes earlier Player had gained his three. Neither could Charles mount the necessary punch to make better than five of it, and this hole spelt death to both of them. Casper had come to the end of a shattering, soul-destroying two days of watching his well-earned lead of four steadily leak away, under the fearsome pursuit of Nicklaus and Player and the steady nagging of Charles who was ever under his nose. His wonderful round of Thursday had only earned him the unenviable role of the fox, to be hounded for the rest of the long chase home.

Had the position been reversed, had he been one of the hunt, I have no doubt in my mind he would have been a challenging force to be reckoned with. One only has to recall his memorable running down of Palmer at San Francisco three years ago, to picture what he might have done from behind. He was the unlucky one of this Open.

Player played the only possible club at the seventeenth, the 3-iron, which landed him safely across the first line of the burn and short of the second. Nicklaus with nothing to lose now and needing a three as a second last hope, let go with all his might downwind with the driver. He carried over the second loop of the burn easily, bounced hard and came to rest no more than a hundred yards short of this 458 yards hole dead in front!

There is something funny about the distance of some of his colossal drives that tickles everyone to laugh. Arthur Koestler in his *Art of Creation* explained this uncontrollable reaction as: 'The sudden bisociation of an idea – provided that the narrative, the semantic pipeline, carries the right kind of emotional tension. When the pipe is punctured and our expectations are fooled, the now redundant tension gushes out in laughter.'

Even for those of us whose expectations are no longer fooled, the effect of witnessing one of Nicklaus's big hits is still the same. Personally, I never feel much prompted to applaud, for the awe inspiring power unleashed is not, somehow, associated with skill. I would clap my hands red to see a little pint-size, squeeze it out that far. But from the stature and weight of Nicklaus you *expect* something hefty.

Yet there is more to Big Jack's massive hits than sheer heavyweight brawn. By now in his career he is also eminently straight. Watching him through the US and British Opens this year convinces me there is no one straighter from the tee. More than that he shows every indication of knowing exactly what he is doing. His swing is not classic or pretty, nor is there much attractive about the rhythm. It is not loose and fluid like Snead's, nor lazy and smooth like Jules Boros, yet it is authoritative and stern, not at all coarse and savage. (A little of the man himself.) Nicklaus's drives are large scale from a large size golfer. What makes the whole thing tickling is the impression that it is so easy! Ridiculously easy.

Player's second at the second last hole with a 4-iron, was half a club short and the ball barely climbed the upslope before the green. It left him a long putt downhill and downwind of 22 yards and the distinct possibility he could take three more to hole out.

The two players, their caddies and a horde of drably-dressed scribes walked on in single file over the tiny bridge, for what seemed an interminable time and distance, forward to Nicklaus's ball. He was a good 130 yards ahead of Player's 3-iron. The stage was now set for a gripping exchange. If he could pitch close enough to get three and Player three-putt they would be all square! Nicklaus made his calculations, chose the wedge and without delay made what appeared in the air the perfect pitch. But it elected to bite into the downslope on the forward portion of the green and instead of skidding energetically along to the flag, it died, and trickled to rest, 20 woeful feet short. I didn't see what more he could have done.

Player, then on the best of terms with his Japanese-made putter, rolled his putt, perfectly judged and struck, on to the green, down the slope, across the left to right borrow, stone dead. Nicklaus missed and that was almost the end. Not quite, the final hole was fraught with trouble. Player with no real alternative, took his 3-iron again as did most of the field and fired his tee shot safely to the right, back into that loop of the burn from where he had played his second to the seventeenth. Surprisingly, from there he took his iron again, from what he later divulged was a lie unsuitable for his 3-wood. We stood stock still as into the wind it curved away towards the rough and appeared for a moment to be swallowed by a lone bunker some one hundred yards short of the burn. But it carried just far enough and disappeared into a tangled mass of knee-high rough that looked sufficiently green to be dangerous.

Nicklaus, in a final do or die effort, hit another massive, mighty drive absolutely straight and a good three hundred yards. Again one realized there was still a possibility ... what if he could hit his second within puttable distance and Player from the rough dump his into the burn ... ? Twelve thousand hearts stopped still as he fired a 3-iron the remaining two hundred yards, but from a close and bare looking lie he cut it ever so slightly and the villanous wind did the rest, swinging it into the greenside bunker 25 feet from the flag.

Three was gone but four was still on, and Player had to get across the burn on to the green to get his five and close the door. I don't know what he would have done had he found his ball lying deep in some wet, lush, knee-high grass, but what he did find caused him no hesitation. With a 6-iron, he swung full and hard, cut a bouquet of grass into the air and sent the ball with propulsion enough to carry over that dreaded water safe to the heart of the green. Barring a miracle he was home and hosed!

After his 6-iron Player, under a suddenly warm sun shining through broken cloud, takes his cap off and advances to a chorus of shouts, whistles and cheers from the packed stands.

For a moment on the green he confers with Jack Nicklaus, looking down at his ball. Nicklaus shakes his head and ambles back to the bunker. Then the referee, with a red rosette in his button-hole, walks up to Player. The turf on the green has been re-cut to change the position of the hole, and it is the slight ridge in front of him that is worrying Player. Can he do anything about it? He is told, that unlike the US rules, it has to be played as 'the rub of the green'. He cannot move or smooth. 'OK', shrugs Gary Player.

Nicklaus's bunker shot is hit and Player gets down to his putt. A long gasp comes from the crowd as it creeps just past the hole. Player trips forward in little schoolboy steps, smiling. And taps it in. He has won the British Open Championship. Jack Nicklaus is the first to walk across and shake hands with him. Player takes off his cap, breathes a long sigh of relief, and with head hanging down, nodding slowly, walks to the side of the green. Alf Fyles, his 42-year-old caddy, wraps his arms around Player, and Player, laughing now, wraps his arms around Alf and they almost kiss in the excitement. Then quietly, at the side of the green, Player has his head down, praying to the God he says is always with him on the golf course ... 'I was saying a final "Thank You"', says Gary Player.

*The Open Championship dates back to 1860, the US Open to 1895 and the PGA to 1916. The Masters, founded in 1934, is the new-comer among the majors, though one would hardly think so – there seem to be more age-old traditions at Augusta than St Andrews. Al Barkow takes the lid off this clever public relations achievement.*

## Traditions in a Hurry
### AL BARKOW, 1974

In terms of creating an aura, a mood for the pros and the galleries, the Masters tournament, now going into its fifth decade, stands at the opposite end of the spectrum from George S. May's proletarian stomps. While George May dealt in the pits, Clifford Roberts, Chancellor of the Masters, has administered out of a panelled board room. The Masters is a carefully orchestrated grand opera next to George May's Chicagoland jazz-band concert, and has not only survived, but has become one of golf's four major championships – an unwarranted eminence since it is an invitational event that brings a less than fully representative field of the best players; even more unwarranted because it has no real authority in golf.

The three true major championships in golf, the US Open, the PGA title, and the British Open, are staged by the game's leading official national organizations, while the Masters is run by a privately held corporation under the helm of an individual entrepreneur. The Augusta National Golf Club and the Masters constitute a profit-making business. Almost all its members pay annual dues and own no interest in the club or the tournament, as at George May's Tam O'Shanter. At Augusta National, though, there are no parvenus or gangsters strutting or swaggering through its simple, white wooden clubhouse. The membership list is composed of the quiet powers that are part of America's industrial-military complex. That out of these seemingly contradictory elements the Masters has achieved so high a place in American and world golf attests to its being one of the most cleverly, brilliantly promoted enterprises in sports-business history.

From its inception in 1934, the Masters had a number of things going for it. First and foremost was Bobby Jones, a revered figure and only a few years into retirement from formal competition. The event was Jones's idea, mostly – originally a casual get-together of the best American golfers to conclude the winter-tournament season and, as it happened, to kick off the summer season for the pros and most of the nation's golfers at large. The timing, early April, also brought the Masters substantial newspaper coverage, since Augusta was then a convenient stopover on the way north for sports-writers who had been covering baseball's spring training. It was a pleasant break for them before getting into the daily grind of covering the national pastime.

The newsmen reciprocated with rhapsodic prose, which was not at all undeserved. The Masters is played on a very fine golf course. It was designed by Alister MacKenzie, but with much advice and direction from Bobby Jones. Not only is the course an excellent championship test; it is set in a hilly glade that, in April, when the dogwood is abloom, is truly exquisite. The quiet of small-town Georgia, the scenery, Bobby Jones, a fresh golf season, and a good field of golfers made an irresistible package. Later there was added a soupçon of foreign players, giving the event international flavour. There was no hurly-burly, just an idyllic gambol in green fields.

Bobby Jones's main interest was his golf course. He left the administration of the tournament to his friend and co-owning partner in Augusta National, Clifford Roberts, a native of Chicago who had gone east to make his fortune in Wall Street. Roberts' credentials were a talent for detail, secrecy, and a strength of character that assured his will would be done. He also had a knack for social climbing, his greatest coup getting Dwight D. Eisenhower to join Augusta National. The beloved Ike, the nation's First Golf Nut, brought the club maximum exposure and prestige when he became president, and the Masters did not hurt for it.

Cliff Roberts has been the promotional genius behind the Masters. His first objective was to make Augusta National a paying proposition, and whether he envisioned from the start that the Masters – a title that Bobby Jones once said 'was rather born of immodesty' – would become the fourth major championship in golf will never be known. Roberts did make a lot of correct early moves toward that, though. First off, although Bobby Jones was not much interested in playing in his tournament, Roberts convinced him to come out of retirement to play in the first one. It was Jones's presence in that field, making his first competitive appearance in four years, that hyped journalistic fervour and general interest. Could the Crown Prince of Golf still be master of all he had surveyed, they asked? The answer was no. Jones finished ten strokes back of the winner, Horton Smith, and in a tie at 294 with none other than Walter Hagen, and Denny Shute. But Jones certainly got the tournament off to a fine start.

Cliff Roberts further stimulated the favour of the press by taking a line from Bob Harlow's script. He handed out free lunches and otherwise made them more comfortable than they were accustomed to being. Roberts curried the good graces of the pros early on with such subtleties as printing on the back of Masters tickets the suggestion that everyone buy their golf equipment from accredited PGA pro shops. This was important to the pros, who were trying to protect their trade against competition with commercial retail sporting-goods stores. The pros also liked not having to pay an entry fee, and the fact that everyone got some money for playing no matter where they finished in the competition.

But more than anything else, Roberts' craft lay in following the dictum that those who are after money must act as if money was the least of their concerns. Mention of it at the Masters is anathema, like saying Solzhenitsyn in the Kremlin. Attendance figures at the Masters are not made public. The purse is never announced in advance, and only in passing at the conclusion of the event. Television announcers doing the Masters are firmly instructed to make no comments over the air about the filthy stuff. Golf tradition in the Victorian manner at Augusta National, and not without the attending hypocrisy.

During Masters week, many old-time pros are seen sitting or standing around the clubhouse at Augusta National radiating the fame and glory of yesteryear. A touch of nostalgia and tradition. However, most of the old pros never thought to make this cameo appearance until Cliff Roberts began to pay them for it. Each gets $500 to be there, and a dinner early in the week. Some of the more cynical younger old pros have been picking up their check, eating and running. And under the spreading water oak in front of the clubhouse is a consortium of golf's business doyens – player agents, clothing and equipment manufacturers, golf-course architects, et cetera – busy making contacts for new deals. All are discreet enough to keep order pads in their hotels. They had better.

Anyone who tries to make hay out of an association with the Masters sticks his head in a sawmill. The pros who cash in on endorsements from a victory at Augusta cannot be stopped, of course, but when Robert Trent Jones, the famed golf-course designer, made some dramatic changes in the course, he was careful not to publicize the fact, mentioning, rather, that he worked closely with Bobby Jones and the Masters committee on the alterations. When it appeared that Robert Trent Jones was not dropping his middle name in talking about the new holes in Augusta, Trent was not banned, but neither did he get any more business out of the place.

The Masters has long been touted as the best-run tournament in golf, and it does function well. Of course, with a smaller field than customary for a pro tournament (77 in 1974, compared with 144 for an average tour event), Roberts can run the golf off with little waiting, although during the first two days of play there are often three groups waiting to play at the second, fourth, and fifth tees. Still, over the years mounds have been built around the course to afford spectators a better view of play, and as the tourney developed, restraining ropes were set up along the sides of fairways to better control the galleries and keep the fairway grass untrampled. The Masters was the first to implement such roping in the US, although it had been tried in Great Britain early in the century but discontinued as being, of all things, in bad taste. The roping, which is now common on the tour, has the pros walking through 18 grassy arenas, isolated from the press of people – an ego-satisfying piece of staging as well as one that does give more people a chance to see the shots.

The entire ambience of the Masters has evinced 'golf as it should be': the performers properly spotlighted, the golf course well groomed and challenging, the weather usually amenable, no pro-am, the purse money acceptable and practically unmentioned. The pros, for one week at least, could and do think of themselves as sportsmen, playing in a true country-club setting just as if they were members of the club and not ordinary working stiffs.

The operative word in all this is exclusivity. It's been this elegant aspect of the thing that the pros have liked best about the Masters. Cliff Roberts has held firm to the tournament's invitation-only status, and the pros who get one also get a boost for their self-regard. Nowadays, invitations are offered on a less subjective basis than in the past, but an elitist quality still pervades.

Decorum and good taste at the Masters – the smell of old money. So pervasive and intimidating has it become that the PGA would not dare raise a voice to broaden the field, and the newsmen never complain that the Masters is the only major championship at which they cannot get inside the ropes to better follow the action. As one of the younger ones has said, the Masters 'is the only championship a reporter hears', not sees, except at three locations where the top row of bleacher seats is reserved for working press. When television sports announcer Jack Whitaker, in a fit of excitement at the close of one Masters, remarked that a 'mob' had encircled the eighteenth green (this is allowed on the last day when the last group of players putts out, for the sake of tradition), he was banished for a few years from covering the event. There are no mobs at Augusta National, there are multitudes or great assemblages. Particular ticket holders are not mere gallery, they are 'preferential patrons', and when a young, very pregnant woman was once in serious need of a powder room, she was denied access to the clubhouse, the nearest port in the storm, because she did not have the proper entrance papers.

While just outside the gates of Augusta National the blacks in their ghetto are rising up against long-running injustices, inside the gates the clubhouse

servants shuffle out of *Gone With the Wind,* the black caddies are not allowed
on the course to watch play unless they are carrying a golf bag or are assigned
to cleaning up hot-dog wrappers, and in its first 38 years no black golfer had
played in the Masters. For the first 20 years or so there was no black golfer
with the record for the field, although the late Ted Rhodes had the potential.
But after Charlie Sifford won the Hartford and Los Angeles Opens in the
late 1960s, there were a number of black pros, including Charlie, who were
certainly as qualified to play in this major tournament as the 'sprinkling of
foreign players' who are invited each year, some of whom have accomplished
little more than a victory in a Thailand Open.

The Masters was lucky in that many of its early winners were recognized
players, an important factor in developing a prestige tournament. After
Horton Smith's opening victory, Gene Sarazen, in 1935, won and com-
pounded the Masters' good fortune (as well as his own) by including his
double eagle, one of those 'shots heard round the world'. Byron Nelson won
in 1937, Guldahl in 1939, when he was a world beater, and Demaret got the
first of his three in 1940. Sam Snead has won the Masters three times, Hogan
twice, and Arnold Palmer's first came in 1958, only a couple of years into
the Masters' nationally televised era. There is little need to emphasize the
value of a man of Palmer's charismatic quality winning anything while the
electronic miracle is scanning it.

Palmer's first Masters victory, however, occasioned a curious circumstance,
and is remarked on here only because the Masters has always projected itself
as keeper of sacred golfing tradition. In the last round in 1958, Arnold was
co-leader with Sam Snead at the beginning of the day's play and paired with
Ken Venturi, three shots back of Palmer. Snead faded early, but Venturi had
cut Palmer's lead to only one stroke as they came to the treacherous twelfth
hole, a par-three short in yardage but played through swirling winds to an
extremely shallow green guarded by water in front, banks and bunkers front
and back.

Venturi bounced his tee shot on 12 off the back bank and onto the green.
Palmer's tee shot plugged in the same bank. Arnold felt he should be allowed
a free lift from the embedded lie, and asked for this ruling. Arthur Lacey
was the official on the scene, and he ruled that Palmer would have to play
the ball as it lay. His judgement, he told me years later, was based on a rule
handed down at the beginning of the day by the Masters committee, which
was not working in conjunction with the PGA at the time in the rules area.
Lacey was given to understand that a player would be allowed a free lift
from an embedded lie only if his ball was on the greens or fairways. Palmer's
ball was by no means in fairway grass, as all agreed. Palmer was still not
satisfied. He understood that the USGA's 'wet-weather' rule was in effect,
which allows a free lift anywhere on the course. Lacey, being far out on the
course, had not heard of this change, if indeed it had been made.

In any case, golfers were being held up behind Palmer and Venturi, and
there was the matter of the television schedule, so rather than wait for another

official to come out to the twelfth hole, at the far end of the course, Lacey and Arnold agreed that Palmer would play from the embedded lie, then play a provisional ball from the same place, taking a preferred lie. Arnold chopped the first ball from its hole, moving it a foot or so forward, then played onto the green, and two-putted for a five. Then he played a chip from an unplugged lie and made a three. Venturi two-putted for his three and was either now leading the Masters by one stroke or still a shot behind Arnie.

Palmer then hit a superb second shot to the par-five thirteenth and holed the putt for an eagle three. Venturi resolutely knocked in a twisting short putt for a birdie to keep even with Palmer ... or go two shots behind. During the playing of the thirteenth hole, Bill Kerr, an assistant to Cliff Roberts, came out to find out what had happened at 12. Palmer explained, and Kerr unofficially concluded that Arnold was entitled to the free drop. Arnie's three on the hole, even though unofficial, got around, and a great roar went up from the gallery. Tight security by Kerr would have been appropriate here.

On the fourteenth tee, Bobby Jones and Cliff Roberts met with the players and Lacey to hear about the events at 12. Venturi claimed that Arnie's ball had actually popped out of the hole it had dug when landing and come to rest in another pockmark, which Arnie should have played from. There was no way in the world to prove this, and Jones and Roberts finally concluded that Arnie had made a three. The always-skittish Venturi, who two years before as an amateur threw away a big lead in the Masters with a last-round 80, three-putted the fourteenth, fifteenth, and sixteenth greens. Palmer went on to win by a stroke over Doug Ford and Fred Hawkins in what the Masters has come to describe as a storybook climax that saw Ford and Hawkins miss birdie putts on the last green that would have brought them ties with Arnie. No mention is made of the incident at the twelfth. Venturi finished two shots off the pace.

It was a strange incident that brought Palmer his first major victory. The press never investigated it at any length, and Arthur Lacey left the course quickly to avoid questions, knowing that the Masters committee would not want any bad publicity from the thing. The Masters' subtle management of public, press, and players held the tournament in good stead here. As someone has said, at Augusta National dogs dare not bark nor babies cry. Ken Venturi suggested to me, some years later, that Arnold got a 'homer', a decision favouring a favoured athlete. Venturi, by the way, with a long history as a tempestuous, outspoken man, does not make a cameo appearance on the front lawn of Augusta National. When I recalled the incident with Tommy Bolt, Thunder screwed up his face as if he'd just swallowed Listerine, and said only, in his particularly irritable way, 'The Maaas . . . ters. They make their own rooools.'

# THE BEST TOURNAMENT?
MICHAEL HOBBS, 1978

There are many candidates. For instance, what about the 1972 British Open, which contained both Jack Nicklaus's splendid final round and, even more dramatic, the long-fought out confrontation between the homeland hero, Tony Jacklin, and the Mexican desperado Lee Trevino, who holed long putts, chips and bunker shots on the bounce from all over the place? Or Bobby Jones playing that superb long iron from sand to defeat Al Watrous many years before? Or Palmer and Miller coming from well behind to win in the 1960 and 1973 US Opens? Or the 1977 gun-fight between Nicklaus and Watson at Turnberry . . . but my choice is the 1975 US Masters.

Central was the battle between Johnny Miller and Jack Nicklaus. For years no one had doubted that Jack Nicklaus was the best golfer in the world. He did not always win by any means, but came to every competition as the bookmakers' favourite.

In the early months of 1975, this changed. It was no longer quite so obvious that Jack Nicklaus was the best. Perhaps Johnny Miller was. In the early tournaments on the US circuit he had confirmed his unparalleled achievement in the 1973 US Open, when he shot a final-round 63, by setting a blistering pace that none could match. As he said, 'Happiness is knowing that even your poor shots are still quite good'. In golf history, only the young Horton Smith had so dominated the tour, more than three decades before.

So, there was talk of a match between Miller and Nicklaus, to establish who was the better of the two and make a lot of money for both promoter and protagonists.

Nicklaus would have none of it. He knows his golf history. In 1926 Walter Hagen had destroyed Bobby Jones in a match over 72 holes. The other side of the coin is that Hagen virtually never won a stroke-play competition if Jones was in the field. Two years later, Hagen himself was similarly put to rout by Archie Compston — and then won the British Open in a matter of days with Compston in the field. Any match or a stroke encounter proves only who was the best at a particular time and place. Nicklaus did not want the new image of being number two because of the publicity that would attend any loss to Miller.

But the battle between Miller and Nicklaus aside, there was another ingredient: the Third Man, Tom Weiskopf. He had been playing below the peaks since his 1973 victory in the British Open but in 1975 had returned to his best form. Many thought him the most talented striker in the game.

These then were the protagonists: Miller, Nicklaus and Weiskopf. True, there were others who played very well indeed. Someone else, Bobby Nichols, led with 67 after the first round; another, Hale Irwin, recorded a course-record final 64, the lowest round of the tournament. But although they came joint fourth, at no time did either seem likely to win the Masters.

Neither, after the first round, did Johnny Miller. He had been making much of the computer in his head that measured strength of wind, humidity, how much the greens were holding, and so on. He had a 75. Apparently the computer was working adequately but he consistently found himself between clubs for his second shots. Every one, he said, was either not quite a 4-iron and a few yards too long for a 5-iron, not quite a full wedge . . . and so on.

At that point Nicklaus was seven strokes ahead of him, after a 68, and one better than Tom Weiskopf. Nicklaus did better the next day with a 67. He had now built up a formidable lead on the whole field and was five shots clear of Arnold Palmer and Tom Watson, 11 ahead of Miller, who had 71, and six better than Tom Weiskopf. Apart from Nicklaus, who had been putting inexorably, Weiskopf had played the best golf of the leaders but his second-round 72 had included sixes at the par-five thirteenth and fifteenth — both guarded by water but both birdie fours for drivers with Weiskopf's length. His ball had come to rest against a pine cone on the thirteenth and at the other he found an awkward lie.

So Nicklaus was in command, with an outside chance of beating his unapproached Masters record of 271, dating back ten years.

The drama began in the third round. Perhaps Nicklaus became cautious, tried to hold what he had. Weiskopf knew he had to go for everything. Miller might as well do the same; he was out of it anyway and had made the cut only by three strokes. He could add to his reputation only by producing a couple of scintillating rounds, though they would, in all probability, still leave him off the pace.

Miller began with a par. He then birdied each of the following six holes (a record for the Augusta course as was his outward 30) and later added another at the twelfth before parring his way home. This gave him a 65. Nicklaus had dropped strokes on the first, ninth, eleventh and had only two birdies to set against his errors. He had a one-over-par 73 and was now only three ahead of Miller, who was now very much in the running.

In fact Nicklaus no longer held the lead. Weiskopf had dropped a shot at the relatively easy 360-yard third but had recorded seven birdies in his round. A 66 meant that he had gained seven shots on Nicklaus during the third day and now led the tournament by a shot. There was all to play for again. Nicklaus, shaken by the evaporation of his lead, still knew he was the best player of a final round in the world.

Throughout, Nicklaus was playing about a hole ahead of Weiskopf and Miller, and was paired with Tom Watson. He began by dropping a shot on the four hundred-yard first hole, as a result of driving into the woods. He then birdied three of the next four holes. Miller had similar results in the opening phase, dropping a shot on the third but offset this handsomely with five birdies during the first nine holes. On a graph, Weiskopf would look the best: all pars or birdies to the turn. At this stage, Nicklaus had taken 35, Weiskopf 34 and Miller 32. With three and a half completed rounds Weiskopf looked the likely winner, for he lay two ahead of Nicklaus and Miller.

But tournaments no longer seem quite like that to either the leaders or the crowd on the course. What we and they are more aware of is the position against par for the number of holes each competitor has played. Let us look at it like that for the final holes of the 1975 Masters.

On the first four holes after the turn Nicklaus played par golf, Miller dropped and gained a shot, and Weiskopf dropped one. The fourteenth looked for a while as if it had settled the tournament. Nicklaus deliberated long on his choice of club for the shot into the green on this 405-yard hole and certainly he had something absurdly lofted in his hands for a second shot to a hole of this length. He was short of the green, used a putter to come up the slope, was too bold, and his ball ran through the back. He had little chance of a four now and in fact had difficulty getting a five. Miller's troubles were more dramatic. He was in trees from the tee and hit another with his second shot. A bogey? A double bogey? Not a bit of it. Miller hit the flagstick with his third and then holed the three-feet putt. Weiskopf, on the other hand, had no trouble at all. He was two yards away in two shots and holed for a birdie. The scoreboards showed: Weiskopf – 11; Nicklaus – 10; Miller – 9.

The fifteenth at Augusta National is 520 yards long and therefore a par-four for the likes of Nicklaus, Miller and Weiskopf – except for two things. The green is fronted by water and when you have cleared that it is still very easy to run through the back. What is needed is a huge drive so that a lofted shot can be played into the green; anything of low trajectory may well fly through the green and onwards, as Nicklaus experienced in other Masters tournaments, when he reached water far behind the green.

Nicklaus hit a good drive but still had a long shot. He wanted to take a 1-iron but was hitting into a light breeze; he felt a wood was necessary to give him sufficient length. He waited for the breeze to drop. Few noticed the delay; Nicklaus always ponders every shot. Eventually the breeze slackened and Nicklaus went quickly with a 1-iron. There was no pause while he followed the flight of the ball. Nicklaus knew it was good and marched after it like a man confident of glory. His ball was flying straight for the flag and amply long enough to clear the water. It pitched and stopped towards the rear of the green. He lagged his putt towards the hole and tapped in for a birdie. Nicklaus said later that it had been the finest 1-iron shot he had hit since 1967 (referring to one that had won him the US Open). The carry had been about 230 yards, while the flag had been about 245 yards from Nicklaus.

Weiskopf followed him a few minutes later with a 4-iron which ran through the green; Miller played a 3-wood that settled down on the green but well to the right. Weiskopf chipped boldly – too boldly – and was four yards past. He marked his ball and waited for Miller to try his 12-yard putt. Miller coasted just past the hole but had his birdie four. As Weiskopf putted he knew he had to hole it not to lose the tournament. It went straight into the middle. Weiskopf – 12; Nicklaus – 11; Miller – 10.

The sixteenth is where Henry Longhurst describes the downfall of the mighty in rotund tones for the television audience. The hole measures about 170 yards and all of that, except for the green, is over water with more water to the left. There are bunkers behind the green to dissuade anyone from playing 'safe' and taking a bigger club to be sure of clearing the water. Regulars come to watch year after year, sometimes choosing their spot and staying there for hours before the first competitor is due.

Nicklaus hit his tee shot a little heavily and regarded the flight of his ball with distaste. 'Get up', he called out. It cleared the water but pitched well short of the flag and then rolled back down the slope until it was about 14 yards away from the hole. The scene now switches to his playing partner, Tom Watson, still in with a remote chance of winning. Alas poor Tom. He needed two balls in the water before he managed to persuade one onto the green. That was a seven for him and goodbye till next year. Better days at Carnoustie lay ahead.

Nicklaus looked his putt over anxiously. If he was short, his ball might run back down the slope and finish at his feet. If he was long, he would be left with a downhill putt back – and that could drift past the hole, and on and on.

Nicklaus conceals his emotions well, though of recent years he has learned to smile and wave to his gallery but when that huge putt dropped into the hole he leapt and ran across the green. Miller later said, 'I have never seen Jack jump around like that. I was happy to walk through the Bear prints.'

Weiskopf, who had just saved himself the tournament with his four-yard putt, was watching from the tee. He now had to par the hole to stay level with Jack Nicklaus. And the sixteenth had done him no good at all the previous year when he had found the water and lost to Player.

Like Nicklaus' his iron shot was heavy and only just cleared the water. He was about 40 yards from the hole though on the green. Miller came in pin high, but about 35 feet away. Weiskopf's first putt was quite good and looked as if it just might reach the hole but it did not quite make it, tailed away, and ran back and to the left. He now had a curving, uphill 18-feet putt left. Miller putted up close and tapped in; Weiskopf missed narrowly. On the course, Nicklaus stood – 12; Weiskopf – 11; Miller – 10.

Two par-fours remained, the seventeenth and eighteenth both about four hundred yards. All three drove well at the next and played approach shots with 8-irons of nearly equal quality. Nicklaus was about 15 feet away and putted like a man who does not want to give anything to the opposition. His putt never looked like going in but always looked dead. He tapped in for par.

Weiskopf's approach had run to the back of the green and he, too, putted the four yards cautiously, perhaps now a man with thoughts of holding second place. Nevertheless, his ball finished only a foot away. Miller's putt was easily the shortest of the three and he watched it curl up, across the slope – and in.

Nicklaus, about to putt on the last hole, stopped at the roar from the gallery and waited for the scoreboard to show who had holed. If Miller had, this would leave him still one behind; if Weiskopf, they would be joint leaders at – 12.

When he saw that it was Miller, he bent down again to his eight-foot putt. Again he prodded it cautiously. The ball stopped short but left him with a safe par, a final-round of 68, and a total of 276. He was content to wait it out and see if either Miller or Weiskopf could birdie the last and earn a play-off.

Miller drove safely and Weiskopf followed with the longest drive of the tournament at the eighteenth hole, about 30 yards further than anyone else had driven. Miller's approach then came in to the right-hand half of the green, a little past the hole. He would have a downhill putt of about 15 feet with a right to left borrow on it. Weiskopf's shorter approach (he needed just a 9-iron) was then punched in and it bit and spun back. He had much the same line to the hole as Johnny Miller but about half the distance.

If Miller had been able to watch television a few minutes before he would have seen Tom Watson hole almost exactly the same putt for a face-saving birdie (remember Tom's seven at the sixteenth?). But Miller's putt always looked as if it had been struck too directly at the hole. The borrow took it past the lower edge by about two inches.

Had Weiskopf learnt anything? He consulted his caddy, who told him to go for the right lip of the hole. Weiskopf struck it firmly, perhaps a little too strongly. It made for a point an inch or so to the right – and kept on going.

So Nicklaus, for the fifth time, put on the green jacket. For Weiskopf, it was that second place, jointly with Miller, that no one is supposed to remember. But we all remember how Roberto de Vicenzo lost the Masters because of signing an incorrect scorecard in 1968, while not so many remember the winner, Bob Goalby. Perhaps the 1975 Masters will live on in memory not only by the name of its winner but because of the three men who made it, in the words of Jack Nicklaus, 'The most exciting day of golf I can remember in 25 years'.

How they finished:

276   Nicklaus 68, 67, 73, 68; 277   Miller 75, 71, 65, 66; 277   Weiskopf 69, 72, 66, 70; 282   Hale Irwin and Bobby Nichols

# THE CAR PARK CHAMPION
## PETER ALLISS AND MICHAEL HOBBS, 1984

Before every Open Championship many words are expended. There are columns to be filled for some four days leading up to the event while golf magazines seem to use well-nigh half an issue. One of the main themes, of course, is: Who is going to win?

In 1979, for the first time in many years, Jack Nicklaus was not the favourite. He had at last been displaced by Tom Watson in the betting. Watson had been again busying himself in America with four tournament victories by the end of May and had tied for the US Masters before Fuzzy Zoeller took the play-off from Watson and Ed Sneed. He was to raise the US tour money-winning record by almost $100,000 with his eventual total of $462,636 and more, of course, won outside America.

In the betting, Severiano Ballesteros was also well favoured at 12-1, but the pundits, with almost one voice, felt he had little chance of winning. The Spaniard's fairly frequent wild drives were well known and it was thought that a claustrophobic course like Royal Lytham and St Annes would frustrate even his formidable skills in recovery play. Instead a far 'tidier' player, Hale Irwin, recent winner of the US Open, was thought particularly likely to win.

There was also the often expressed thought that no American had won at Royal Lytham. This was not true. A certain Robert Tyre Jones Junior's name can be seen on the trophy for the year of 1926 and he was, incidentally, followed past the post by Al Watrous, George Von Elm and Walter Hagen, all golfers of unimpeachable American nationality. That championship was the first held at Royal Lytham and St Annes and no American professional has ever won there.

The news story of the first day was the play of Bill Longmuir, who had his lowest-ever tournament round. The Open Championship was the right time to find the inspiration. He played the first nine in 29, only the fourth time this had been done for either first or second nines in a British Open. His total of 65 equalled the lowest score for an opening round, set by Neil Coles at St Andrews in 1970 (since beaten by Craig Stadler's 64 at Royal Birkdale in 1983). Longmuir had never made the top 60 on the European tour but he had won a couple of tournaments overseas, the 1976 Nigerian Open and the Southland Classic in New Zealand the same year. He birdied five holes in a row from the third to seventh, added another at the ninth and moved smoothly into the second nine with more birdies on the tenth and twelfth. Thereafter, on the more difficult run-in, he dropped two strokes.

The round gave him a three-stroke lead on the first day over Hale Irwin, who was very keen to become one of those rare birds who have won the championships of both America and Britain in the same year. Rounds under 70 were rare throughout the championship. The only others on the first day came from Irwin and his fellow American Jerry Pate.

The second day largely belonged to Severiano Ballesteros, who notched up a 65 of his own. He reached the turn in 33 and this did not really foreshadow the score that was to come. At Royal Lytham a really good score has to be made on the first nine (three of the four 29s at that time in the Open had been recorded on this nine – by Peter Thomson, Tom Haliburton and, of course, Longmuir).

It was Ballesteros's brilliant finish that brought the 65. Because of the wind direction that day, it was reckoned that the true par for the last five holes was 4, 5, 4, 5, 4. Ballesteros finished 3, 3, 4, 3, 3 and had 32 for the inward nine.

He had played with Lee Trevino, which may well have helped his cause because the Mexican American, besides speaking his own brand of Spanish, is also a great admirer of Ballesteros's play. If Lee Trevino is not going to win himself, he likes to see Severiano take first place.

After his first-round 73, Ballesteros was now right up near the top:

136 Irwin;   138 Ballesteros;   139 Longmuir;   140 Watson;
142 Nicklaus;   144 Crenshaw;   145 Aoki

Ballesteros was later to claim that his attitude to Lytham was very different from that of so much expert opinion. The many bunkers he felt were no real problem because 'I am the best bunker player'. Probably true and even more likely to be true if the player believes it. He did not consider the rough particularly severe and later claimed that he had deliberately driven into it on his practice rounds both to test it out and to see if wide positions to right or left of some of the fairways gave better lines into the green.

Another Spanish speaker had a great influence on Ballesteros. Roberto de Vicenzo had been one of the first to recognize that Ballesteros was a major talent and did indeed recommend him to Ed Barner, the American agent/entrepreneur, who was to manage him until Ballesteros turned to a Spanish friend and former airline-executive, Jorge Ceballos, several years later. De Vicenzo has often been seen with Ballesteros on practice days and an old master-young pupil relationship grew up between them.

De Vicenzo advised him to attack the course, pointing out that Jack Nicklaus's caution may well have cost him several British Opens. Though he felt Nicklaus was the man to beat, de Vicenzo had noticed that his strategy had been cautious on the practice rounds: taking the safest line from the tee rather than the one more likely to set up a birdie chance. He also felt that, with most severe trouble – particularly out of bounds – on the right, Ballesteros should work on the practice ground to shape his shots from right to left. Not much of a problem, as the Spaniard can fade and draw at will, right-handed or left-handed, on one leg or two or, for a lark, on his knees as well. I am sure it was this ability to manœuvre a ball that so captured Roberto's imagination, for he had so much of the same ability – but not the putting and chipping finesse to anything like the same degree.

Roberto gave Ballesteros one piece of general advice that is particularly inspirational: '*Tienes las manos. Ahora juega con tu corazon.*' (You have the hands. Now play with your heart.)

For the third round, Ballesteros and Hale Irwin were paired, an experience that was wearing on the American's nerves. Irwin is an exemplary player in the Peter Thomson mould: hit it onto the fairway, then onto the green and don't three-putt. Here he was confronted by a man whose philosophy that year could be summed up as: 'Hit it as far as you can, find it, get it on the green and then try to one-putt. Never mind the bunkers and the rough. You're used to them.'

Both were round in 75 on a blustery day; both still led the field:

211 Irwin; 213 Ballesteros; 214 Nicklaus, James (with his second 69); 215 Crenshaw, Byman, Davis; 216 Aoki, Norman, Longmuir, Watson; 217 McEvoy, Marsh, D. J. Clark

With the gap between them only a couple of strokes, Ballesteros struck early, holing a fine putt for a two on the first to Irwin's par-three. On the second, Ballesteros took the championship lead, parring the hole with a four while Irwin took six after half-hitting his tee shot.

The Ballesteros immortalized in this championship was at his most characteristic on the 486-yard sixth hole. With a drawn tee shot needed to this right-to-left dogleg, he hooked wildly across the fourteenth fairway. He reckoned he was some 90 yards off-line. From this unaccustomed position, it was no surprise that neither he nor his caddy had much idea which club to use for the second shot. Ballesteros hit about 50 yards through the green. He still got his par and reached the turn in 34.

The tenth, a relatively short par-four, had given Ballesteros trouble in each round. This time he was in rough short of the green in two. He played a weak third and was still not on the green. Rather uncharacteristically he chose to putt and ran it some three yards past the hole. A double-bogey threatened, but Seve holed the crucial putt that could have cost him the championship.

The thirteenth is another short four of 339 yards. De Vicenzo advised boldness as the right tactic here. Ballesteros should use his driver and attempt to carry to the green. In the first three rounds, however, he had taken an iron from the tee. On the final day he gave it every ounce. It hit a mound to the right of the green and ran into a bunker. The carry was a yard or so under three hundred yards. From there, the Spaniard's bunker shot was on the fringe, perhaps a dozen yards from the hole. On and on the putt went as he pointed his club, matador-like, at the hole. It dived in; a decisive moment indeed.

There remained the celebrated tee shot to the 353-yard sixteenth. Conventionally, the drive should be down the left of the fairway but, because of the flag position well to the left that day, Ballesteros claims he decided to play to the right – and finished in what has often been described as a car park. This gives the impression that Ballesteros must have been about as far off-line as he had been at the sixth, or had carried the clubhouse at the first and put it in the road. Yet it was hardly a car park at all, just a reserved area for BBC vehicles, little more than 30 yards from the edge of the fairway. Nevertheless, it gave certain partisan Americans the opportunity to refer to him as 'the car park champion'. From there, Ballesteros hit a sand wedge six or seven yards from the hole and got the putt. He was poised for almost certain victory.

But what had been happening to the other contenders? Hale Irwin, after his poor start, seemed to lose heart and became almost invisible in contrast to the panache of the Spaniard's play. In the end he staggered in with a 78, not after all to be one of the select band who have won both American and British championships in the same year. His card showed six fives and two sixes. Seldom can two more contrasting styles have been paired at an Open climax. The Australian Rodger Davis, playing in elegant socks displaying his name in diamonds, was at one time championship leader, having reached the turn in 32. He went in a spell of six, five, six on the fourteenth to sixteenth holes. Crenshaw also played well that last day. When he stood on the seventeenth tee he was level with Ballesteros, who at that time had five holes to go. But Ben Crenshaw took a six – and that was that. Yet another major championship had slipped from his grasp.

Ballesteros's progress was now triumphal, for here was one of the most popular winners of modern times. The British public, of course, want a British winner but Seve was easily the next best thing. He was young, handsome, smiling, a cavalier, with an almost amateurish air about him. On the seventeenth he was in his last bunker and once again was down in two strokes to save his par. In the championship as a whole, he reckons he was fifteen times in greenside bunkers and just once failed to be down in two – possibly a record.

The diagonal line of bunkers on the eighteenth fairway has dashed the hopes of many players over the years. Ballesteros, however, was rather more worried by the gorse to the right. Naturally, then, he aimed for the left rough, to avoid both hazards, played a 5-iron to the front of the green and was down in two putts to be champion by a comfortable three-stroke margin.

Said Hale Irwin, shaking his head in disbelief, 'I cannot understand how anyone can drive as badly as that and still win an Open Championship'. There was, indeed, justice in the American's criticism. In his final round, Ballesteros had found the fairway only once with his driver and only eight times in previous rounds. Yet his power and touch from the rough had proved wrong all the pundits who had thought that Lytham would yield only to the man who could keep the ball on the fairway.

*In 1986 and 1987 Seve Ballesteros threw away the chance to win three major championships; he made several errors in the 1980 Masters, but it was still a championship he dominated throughout.*

# AUGUSTA, 1980
## SEVERIANO BALLESTEROS AND DUDLEY DOUST, 1982

The opening day dawned clear and bright, with a marauding breeze, but not enough sun to warrant the white peaked cap Ballesteros wore when he appeared on the first tee at 12.12. Frankly, he looked odd. The cap, obscuring those dark, expressive eyes, muted his glamour. He wore it for reasons: to block out gallery distractions and, more cunningly, to reduce the glare of Augusta's crystalline white bunker sand. He was dressed conservatively in a white shirt and dark blue trousers. 'I feel calm in calm colours', he says. 'I don't want people to watch me the way I dress. I want people to watch me the way I play.'

As the 1979 open champion, Ballesteros was playing the star role in his pairing. His partner was Craig Stadler, 'the Walrus', a corpulent, irritable American with a drooping moustache. In past years, Ballesteros had set out, all guns blazing, aiming his big drive over the corner of a distant bunker and, perilously, played hide-and-seek with a stand of pine trees out to the right. This year, having noticed how Trevino played the hole, he settled into his stance, slightly closer than usual to the ball, aimed down the left side of the fairway and, gently swinging in an outside-inside plane, faded his drive into the middle of the fairway. A crisp pitch, two putts, and the Spaniard was away with a par.

Ballesteros was a model of wise, easy power throughout the round, missing only one fairway off the tee – in contrast to his fabled last round in the 1979 Open at Lytham where he hit only two – and when he erred he did not strike back as he might have done in the old days. He probably never played a more impressive round in his life. At the end of the day, his 66, six under par, shared the lead with the Australian David Graham, who reigned as American PGA champion, and Jeff Mitchell who, as a West Texan, ought to have played well in the wind. The favourite Watson played without distinction for a 73 and Nicklaus, troubled by the wind, scored a 74.

The weather on the second day was blissfully bright, with barely a breeze. Ballesteros was paired with Larry Nelson whom, in the 1979 Ryder Cup matches, he had called lucky to hole a long chip shot. The American team and press had made a meal of this careless remark. After Lytham, they felt, who was calling whom lucky? At Augusta, neither man would rekindle the fuel for the press. They played with friendly, mutual respect.

The Spaniard's golf that day was pure theatre. At moments it was the old Ballesteros: he jumped at the odd ball, sending it screaming off line, then punished these mistakes with great, lashing recoveries. He scored birdies off his three most hideous drives of the day, the last one worse, by acres, than his fabled 'parking lot' drive at Lytham.

The build-up to that nightmare drive began on the fifteenth when, subduing the 520-yard hole with a drive and a 3-iron, he scored a birdie. It put him nine strokes under par, three clear of his nearest pursuer, Graham, who had just reached the sixth tee. Pumped up with adrenalin, Ballesteros called for his 8-iron as he stepped on to the tee of the watery, 190-yard sixteenth. 'No', said Herrington, 'It's a little 7-iron'. Ballesteros relented and pounded his ball 80 feet past the pin, leaving himself an ugly downhill putt. As he left the tee, a nearby explosion of applause signalled Graham's birdie on the sixth green. Ballesteros three-putted to fall back to a single stroke advantage over the Australian.

Herrington was horrified by his mistake. He apologized to Ballesteros. The Spaniard, eschewing the tenet by which he always shifts the blame away from himself, replied, 'Don't worry. It was my fault.' Ballesteros was seething with himself when he reached the seventeenth tee. He snap-hooked his drive. The ball veered left, clicked through the top of a pine tree, bounced into the adjacent seventh fairway, skipped between a pair of bunkers and ran up on to the elevated seventh green. It came to rest some ten feet from the hole – the wrong hole.

Ballesteros climbed to the green where he met Graham and his playing partner, Andy North. The situation was bizarre. Here was the Spaniard, ten holes ahead of his nearest rival, on the same green. What's more, Ballesteros's ball was in Graham's direct line to the hole. 'Nice drive', said Graham. 'Would you like to play through?'. Ballesteros, embarrassed, marked his ball and, as soon as the green cleared, dropped clear without penalty. Once, twice the ball rolled away and finally Ballesteros set it in place.

He surveyed the prospect before him. Clearly, such a shot had never before been contemplated in the 46-year history of the Masters: high over the corner of a massive scoreboard, over a gigantic hump and on to a hidden green. In all, 150 yards. Crowds were cleared from behind the green. Spectators, blundering across the path of the shot, were startled to be shouted back. Many cowered, scattered. 'Are you going to make a birdie?' a fan asked. 'Yes', said Seve.

The Spaniard took a precarious footing and smashed his 7-iron shot over the edge of the scoreboard, crouched and listened. Silence. Then deafening, distant applause. Ballesteros was away, half-sprinting after it, his fans surging behind him. It was Palmer in the 1960s, all over again. 'Waa-hoo!' Then from one Southern throat came the curious drawl *'Olé!'*.

Ballesteros found the ball only 15 feet from the hole and, smooth as milk from a pitcher, he poured in the putt for the birdie he had promised. Nelson, bemused, later remembering the Spaniard, a fixed look in his eye, marching towards the final tee. 'When Seve gets going he starts walking fast, he's got different thoughts on his mind', Nelson commented. 'Seve is a rare kind of guy. He's an excitable golfer who can concentrate.'

The pyrotechnics were done for the day. Ballesteros scored an untroubled par on the finishing hole for a 69 and a midway total of 135, which put him four strokes clear of the field. In his wake, on 139, lay Graham and Rex Caldwell, a journeyman American. The two giants of the game looked lost in the crowd, Watson on 142 after another 71; Nicklaus on 145, also having returned a 71, a total that by only a single stroke escaped the 36-hole cut.

Nelson, after scoring a workaday 72 with Ballesteros, reckoned that Watson and the Spaniard were heirs-apparent to Nicklaus. He compared and contrasted these two princes of golf. 'Tom and Seve are totally different in their attitude', he said. 'Tom is more involved in technique and perfecting his swing. It's in the back of his mind to score well, sure, but what he's concerned about is hitting the ball perfectly as a means to this end. Seve is different. He just wants to shoot lower scores than anybody else.'

There had been lower 36-hole Masters scores shot than Ballesteros's – Raymond Floyd's 131 in 1976 was the lowest – but on only three occasions had players held a more commanding lead at this point: Floyd in 1976, Nicklaus in 1975 and Herman Keiser in 1946 – all were five strokes clear of their fields. The Spaniard was set fair. 'Seve is going to have to be caught', said Graham. 'I don't think he will back up'.

The Masters was now taking shape: unless someone mounted an attack and kept pressure on him, the confident Ballesteros might turn on the steam and, like a distance runner or cyclist, break away from the field. The weather, only a mild wind and enough rain to soften the green, prophesied low enough scores for such an attack to succeed. It would be a fascinating day.

Gibby Gilbert, nine strokes behind, made the first move. He birdied four of the first seven holes before Ballesteros teed off, closing the gap to five strokes. In itself, this was not worrying, for Gilbert still had the more difficult home half of the course to play. But who next might make a run at the Spaniard?

Ballesteros opened the day with rickety bogey-birdie-bogey-par then hoiked an ungainly drive, 'almost between my legs' off the fifth and straight into a stand of pines. As luck had it, the ball came to rest precisely where the ground staff had recently uprooted a tree. Only Seve could have found such a place. If on the previous day the Spaniard, after dropping off the seventh green, played a shot no man ever had played before in the Masters, his ball lay this time where no player had ever trod: in the rough in the little valley at the bottom of the sixth fairway and, as he faced the unseen and faraway fifth green, hard against a rising wall of pine trees.

Ballesteros, nearly 250 yards from the green, could not play towards it. 'Seve, maybe here you are going to take a double-bogey six', he said to himself. 'But even if you do, you're still going to be one shot ahead. Keep calm. Don't get mad.'

Calmly, Ballesteros selected a pitching wedge, opened the face flat, and with a vicious slash sent his ball climbing steeply over the trees and back into the fairway. A long pitch and two putts later and Ballesteros had a five, possibly the most satisfying bogey he had scored in his life. Nonetheless, his lead was now only two strokes from Graham, his playing partner who birdied the hole, and Caldwell.

Ballesteros is most dangerous when wounded, and on the next hole, a par-three that drops like a stone to a wildly rolling green, he nearly scored a hole-in-one. His 7-iron shot off the 190-yard hole, pitched nicely short of the flag, ran up and twitched away from the cup for an easy birdie two. He was back in command, three strokes in front; yet he had scored only one par in his six holes for the day.

In retrospect, many holes appear crucial in the winning of a tournament but none, even during what was to be an eventful final day, could have been more important to Ballesteros's Masters victory than the eighth on the third day. The eighth – where the green was remodelled by Byron Nelson; Ballesteros came into it after parring the seventh.

As the Spaniard walked towards the tee his confidence returned: glancing up at the big scoreboard he had seen that Watson almost certainly was gone. The American had bogied the eleventh, had taken a triple-bogey six on the short twelfth (by blocking his tee shot into Rae's Creek) and lay ten strokes behind him. Graham was now four back, Caldwell three.

Ballesteros cracked a big drive, 285 yards and nearly all carry. He could not see the green from his ball but, consulting his hip booklet, he reckoned the pin to be 224 metres (245 yards) away, almost all uphill. He walked forward, had a look and took a decision. He wouldn't bother shaping his shot off the mounds; he'd just fly it string-straight, covering the flag all the way. And that's what he did: struck a stupendous 3-iron, high and straight. The ball dropped light as a feather on to the green, and came to rest six feet from the hole. Seve stroked in the putt for an eagle three.

The effect of the 3-iron blow was devastating. Graham who over the past few holes had appeared to be playing slowly in an intentional attempt to break the Spaniard's pace, was shattered. He dropped a shot on the hole and was not heard of again. With that eagle to help him, Ballesteros made the turn in 35; one under par, and playing with almost unremarkable brilliance he came home in 33 for a round of 68. This put him at 203, distantly followed by the chubby American Ed Fiori, who had come in with a 69 for a 210 total. Graham, 72, was in joint third spot, along with Newton, Andy North, the 1978 US open champion, and J. C. Snead, the legendary Sam's nephew, all on 211.

The 1980 Masters seemed over bar the shouting, and the counting. With a seven-stroke lead and standing 13 under par, Ballesteros had raised prospects of a record victory. He could not only become the youngest man ever to win the Masters, being 80 days younger than Nicklaus was when he triumphed in 1963, but he could join the exalted company of Nicklaus, Francis Ouimet and Bobby Jones as the only men in history to win two or more major championships by the age of 23. Further, the Spaniard could set another record by winning by a wider margin than Nicklaus's nine strokes in 1965.

Not surprisingly, Ballesteros said he would first see to his victory before taking on other targets. Seve, no doubt about it, was stuffing the Yanks in their own back yard, and the foreign players rallied round him. From the blunt, warm-hearted Newton, who was to be paired on the final day with the Spaniard, came a surprisingly virulent defence in a broadside delivered over television.

'I've read some of the newspaper articles this week and, you know, it's almost as though you guys are waiting for Seve to blow it', snapped Newton, glaring at the camera. 'I've also heard some pretty snide, completely uncalled-for-remarks from some of the players. They say he's lucky and a "one-putt Jessie" and all that (bleep) ... America's considered to be the tops in professional golf and here comes a young 23-year-old and he's taken some of the highlight away from your superstars. But, you know, the guy's a great player and the sooner Americans realize it the better.' With that, Newton turned and went back to the putting green.

Ballesteros looked remarkably composed. 'Come to dinner', he said to a journalist from London. 'Only we don't talk about golf, OK?' He had invited eight friends to dinner, mostly Spanish, mostly male. He does not seek attention but when later he appeared in the living room of his rented house, dressed in a yellow shirt, all eyes drifted to him. Ballesteros radiated golf that night although there was only a single golfing item in the room: an antique, hickory-shafted putter which lay on the otherwise empty coffee table: a birthday gift to Seve from Rhena Barner, Ed's wife. Guests wandered by, however, and as though it was a talisman which had been blessed by genius they picked it up, waggled it and looked askance at Ballesteros.

It was a buffet dinner and towards a pretty female American journalist, much liberated, he was courtly, guiding her through the queue and putting her firmly at the head of the table. Towards Señor Jose Santiuste, the elderly gentleman to whom he had given his 1979 Open Championship ball, he was deferential. Among his fellows, he was lusty and jovial – they indulged in great teasing of accents, and made much play of *cojones,* the Spanish measure of courage.

One minute Ballesteros was joking about Spanish football – the national team had recently been thrashed by England – the next he was watching *Saturday Night Fever* on television in the den, quite outside the mainstream of conversation. Then he was gone. It was ten o'clock. He lay on his bed, the cassette ear-piece plugged into his ear, listening to the soothing words of the Barcelona psychiatrist.

It was 13 April, the fourth day, and Ballesteros and Newton appeared on the first tee prepared to drive off at 1.48 p.m. Seve started in irrepressible form. With the most delicate of pitches he birdied the first, then the third hole, to increase his lead to ten strokes.

\* \* \*

The Spaniard had played cast-iron golf since the fifth and made the turn in 33 to go 16 under par for the tournament and ten clear of Newton – and of Gilbert, who was moving down the eleventh fairway. As the young Spaniard stood on the tenth tee the low-lying holes beneath him must have looked like El Dorado.

The golden vision soon turned to dross. On the tenth green, a speedy threadbare surface, Ballesteros three-putted and Newton, with a par, closed the gap to nine strokes. Ballesteros righted himself on the eleventh, but Newton birdied. Eight strokes. The Spaniard thought – almost non-chalantly – that his chance of breaking the tournament record of 271 strokes was slipping. ¿*Y que*? So what? Augusta's twelfth is 'the most demanding tournament hole in the world', according to Nicklaus. A one-shotter at only 155 yards, it is tucked at the end of the famed Amen Corner, just over Rae's Creek, and against a tall backcloth of pine trees. Winds coming down the course glance and swirl off this backcloth, and players standing on a sheltered tee have no way of reading the air currents high above the green. A well-struck shot can abruptly hold up and drop like a stone into a bunker in front of the green or, worse, into the creek.

Year after year, Masters aspirations drown in the creek. 1980 was no exception. A triple bogey had finished Watson's hopes on the previous day and Weiskopf, en route to his 85 on the opening day, had put five balls in the creek, an all-time record, and taken 13 on the hole. The Spaniard studied the heaving pines in the distance and planned his shot; he would start his ball left and let the wind bring it into the flag.

He set himself solidly, aiming left, and took his 6-iron into the backswing. At the top of his swing a thought suddenly struck him: go straight for the pin. As his club started down, it happened: his leading hand, the left one, tightened on the grip. He fractionally let up, 'blocked-out', and the ball flew to the right.

Ballesteros watched, feeling helpless as the ball pitched into the bank, stuck, then trickled down into the creek. There was no calling it back. The Spaniard, who rarely swears, did so now. Electing to drop out of the water under one stroke penalty, Ballesteros meticulously dropped the ball over his shoulder in the correct line between the flag and the point at which the ball entered the water. He chipped to the back of the green, just to be safe, and carefully two-putted. A double-bogey five. Newton took another birdie: the three-stroke swing closed Ballesteros's gap to five strokes. It was a comfortable enough lead, but one that was moving alarmingly in the wrong direction.

Off the next, elevated tee, Ballesteros punished his drive, drawing it nicely round the dogleg. From there, he pondered the shot: 162 metres (180 yards) over Rae's Creek which at that point lay crooked in front of the green. A 4-iron? The choice struck him as dangerous; he needed more club. He called for his 3-iron. Herrington felt it was wrong but said nothing. Ballesteros thought: hit the ball softly, get control of your power again.

His decision was disastrous. Swinging unnaturally slowly, Ballesteros hit the ball 'fat': that is, he struck the turf a full two inches too far behind the ball. The clubhead dug in. The ball climbed feebly into the air, fell short of the green and skipped into the creek. Walking up the fairway, Ballesteros felt the eyes of the crowd on him; suddenly he experienced the same sense of embattlement that he had witnessed in Player on the same fairway in 1978. These people don't think I can win. I'll show them. He lifted out of the water, as he had done on the previous hole, and dropped the ball over his shoulder. The referee asked him to drop it again. This man is trying to put me off! thought Ballesteros, and he lost his temper.

'Sir', he snapped sarcastically, 'Are you sure, sir?'. Yes, the referee was sure. Ballesteros dropped again. His chip was once again safely strong but, putting back down a slope, he hit the hole and the ball snapped away. He finished it off for a bogey six – against another Newton birdie, his third on the trot – and the Spaniard's lead was down to three strokes. Meanwhile applause mushroomed up ahead: Gilbert had birdied the fourteenth hole; the American was now four strokes behind and closing in. You are stupid, Ballesteros said to himself. What are you doing? You were comfortable but now you are in trouble. You can lose this tournament. You must work hard.

Newton cracked a perfect drive up the fourteenth fairway. Ballesteros hooked his. The ball swerved left into trees. At that point, a curious incident took place as Ballesteros moved up the fairway. A spectator shouted at him, point-blank: 'Come on, Jack! Go, Jack!' The image of a rampaging Nicklaus came into the Spaniard's mind. It did not occur to him that the man might be shouting in support of Jack Newton.

'The shout was like a knife in the heart for me', Ballesteros recalls. 'I looked at the man and made a big expression in my eyes. The crowd, the referee – and now this guy. I didn't know whether people were against me or not, but that was how I felt and, let me tell you, it helped. I am like Gary Player. The more the crowd is against me, the more I want to prove something'.

Ballesteros's shot needed shaping and with a 6-iron he shaped it perfectly round a tree, over a greenside mound and into the green, 25 feet past the flag. It was a glorious stroke, one that Newton later said won the Spaniard the Masters. Ballesteros nearly ran in the putt for a birdie, but settled happily for a par. It left him three ahead of Newton and, as news drifted back, also three ahead of Gilbert, who had just birdied the fifteenth hole.

Augusta's fifteenth, a par-five of 520 yards, travels over a lumpy fairway which, just beyond the driving area, falls away to a pond in front of a sloping, elevated green. It is a fine, frightening hole, the frequent scene of competitors, trouser-leg rolled, knee-deep in water. The tee itself presents a view of half of Georgia.

Ballesteros smashed a 310-yard drive to the perfect position, the right-centre of the fairway. 'Give me a birdie and we can take it home', said his caddy. The Spaniard selected a 4-iron, an ambitious club with water just short of the green, and gave the ball a mighty lash. He hit it fat, as he had so calamitously done on the thirteenth fairway. Herrington muttered, 'Good shot, sir', which sounded strange to the Spaniard.

Herrington was right. It was a good shot, settling softly down on the green, inside Newton's ball, and some 20 feet from the pin. As Ballesteros reached the green he lifted his hand to the applause and glanced at the scoreboard. Herrington, he thought, wasn't right this time: a birdie here might not take home the title. Gilbert had birdied the sixteenth to draw within two shots of the Spaniard.

Newton putted first. His stroke, on Ballesteros's line, sped eight feet past the hole. It not only showed the Spaniard the way, it also showed the green to be dangerously fast. Accordingly, Ballesteros played a cosy tap. Even so the ball limped on and on, four feet past the hole. Newton, playing first, missed his return putt. Ballesteros put his down. A birdie, against Newton's par, lifted him four clear of the Australian, three of Gilbert. 'Give me a three-stroke lead with three holes to play', he remembered saying on the eve of the tournament, 'and I'll win the Masters'.

All that now stood between him and the title, the Spaniard felt, was the sixteenth, where water stretches nearly the whole way from tee to green. For safety, he drilled a firm 6-iron past the pin. Then he gently tapped the first putt, holed the second. 'It's finished', he said, turning to his caddy. 'The tournament is ours'.

It was. Ballesteros, keeping an eye on the scoreboard, cruised safely into port. He scored two solid pars on the home holes, to finish with 72 for the day and 275 for the tournament, three under Watson's forecast. At 23 years and four days, Ballesteros was the youngest Master of them all.

## GRAHAM'S GREAT FINISH
### HERBERT WARREN WIND, 1981

On the final round, Burns did not play as well as he did on the first three, but he could easily have won the Open. Graham, with whom he was paired, was the only one of his challengers to make a rush at him. A 35-year-old veteran of the tour, Graham had quickly moved to within a stroke of Burns with birdies on the first two holes. Burns entered the last nine holding a one-stroke lead on Graham, but lost it on the tenth, which he bogeyed after a poor tee shot. The two men were still tied as they entered the last five holes – a stretch that has long been considered one of the great finishes in golf, along with the last five holes at Hoylake, in England, and the last three holes at Carnoustie. Graham's shot-making on those five holes was so superb that I think it is worthwhile to examine his progress hole by hole.

The fourteenth, a 414-yard par-four, is one of the most difficult holes on the course. A first-class tee shot is needed to hit the bending, pinched-in fairway and then a first-class iron to hit and hold a mean, tightly bunkered green, partially hidden from view, which is separated into two distinct sections by a trough running diagonally from the front left to the back right. On the final day, the pin was in the toughest position possible – in the back left corner, just beyond and above the trough. Burns, over the green in two, saved his par with a ten-foot putt. Graham had a birdie three. He used his driver off the tee and hit the middle of the narrow fairway. On his approach, he went for the pin with a 7-iron – a very bold shot, because of the smallness of the target area and the danger implicit in missing it. The ball carried the trough by a couple of yards, landed seven feet to the left of the pin, took a little hop, and sat down. Graham worked hard on the putt and holed it with a confident stroke. He may have won the championship then and there. At any rate, he was now in the lead for the first time. He widened his margin to two strokes on the fifteenth – the dogleg par-four on which Watson had driven out of bounds on the third round. Graham hit the fairway off the tee with a 1-iron, then lofted an 8-iron that spun itself out eight feet from the pin, which was set on the right, high side of the green. After Burns had missed an only slightly longer birdie putt, Graham made his – a sidehiller that broke a foot from right to left.

On to the sixteenth – the famous Quarry Hole, a 430-yard par-four. From the low fairway, the second shot must carry across an old, worked-out quarry filled with trees, scrub, and sand to reach a plateau green that slopes up from front to back. Here Graham played two more wonderful shots – a 3-wood down the centre of the fairway, followed by a 5-iron to the flat crown of the green, the ball stopping some ten feet from the pin. He almost made that putt, too – the ball just slipped by the rim of the cup. Burns had taken a five there, so Graham's lead was now three strokes. Merion's seventeenth is a 224-yard par-three on which the golfer plays from a high tee to an undulating green hemmed in by bunkers and rough. Graham hit a crisp 2-iron that landed near the centre of the green and ended up on the collar of the green, at the back and to the right, about 20 feet from the pin. Burns was away, his ball lodged in the rough to the left of the green. From there, he pulled off a miraculous shot, chopping the ball softly onto the edge of the green and watching it trickle down the slope and into the cup for a birdie. Graham digested this calmly. He then stroked his approach putt two feet from the hole and made the short one. A lead of two strokes, one hole to play.

Many old Merion hands are of the opinion that the eighteenth, a 458-yard par-four, may well be the hardest hole on the course. The drive is blind – over the end of the quarry to an elevated fairway hidden by bushes and trees. From the championship tee, it takes a carry of 210 yards to reach the fairway, which tilts to the left towards the rough and a long line of out-of-bounds stakes. More often than not, the second shot must be played from a downhill lie, and this makes it a bit more difficult to stop it on a green that is perched at the crest of a mild slope. Burns finished with a five when he missed a putt of tap-in length. This gave him a 73 and a four-round total of 276. Graham was down the left side of the fairway with his drive and on the green, 18 feet from the pin, with his 4-iron approach. He almost holed his putt for a birdie; the ball lipped out of the cup. He was down in four for his par, a 67 for his round, and a total of 273 – a stroke above the Open record, which Nicklaus set last year at Baltusrol.

On his last round, Graham missed only one fairway off the tee – the first. He hit every green in the regulation stroke except the seventh, eighth, and seventeenth, and on those holes his approach finished on the trimmed collar of the green. The only time he faltered all day was on the fifth green, which he three-putted from 15 feet. However, Graham's golf on the taxing and precarious last five holes is what will be especially remembered in the years to come. It had been a long time since we last saw a golfer play such brilliant, forceful, technically pure shots on the final holes of the Open. Burns did not lose the championship. Graham had the courage to try to win it, and he did so by hitting the kind of iron shots that one associated with Hogan: they were struck decisively; they travelled in the right trajectory; they covered the flag; and they pulled up abruptly when they touched down on the green. It was a genuinely memorable performance.

## Pebble Beach and the Open
### Herbert Warren Wind, 1982

On Sunday, under glum skies, Nicklaus, paired with Calvin Peete, started his fourth round at 12.38 p.m. His number one son, Jackie, who is a student at the University of North Carolina, and is many inches taller than his father, was caddying for him. Nicklaus got off slowly, bogeying the opening hole, where his approach shot spun back off the green, and then missing his birdie on the second, a par-five that is reachable in two. He appeared to be completely unfazed by his disappointing start. When he is out on the golf course during a tournament, you can practically feel the fierceness and continuousness of his concentration, and yet at the same time, despite being surrounded by pulsing thousands, he seems to be not only oblivious of the pressure of the contest but more relaxed than you and I are when we get home after work and watch the news in the living room with a drink in hand. On the third, Nicklaus holed a good-sized putt across the green for a birdie three. That set him off. He birdied the fourth when he dropped a 23-footer. For the first time in the Open, he was making some putts. He birdied the par-three fifth after he stuck a 6-iron two feet from the pin. Continuing to roll, he birdied the par-five sixth by reaching the hilltop green with a drive and a 1-iron, and two-putted from 35 feet. He birdied the seventh, the precarious 110-yard par-three, playing a crisp pitching wedge 11 feet from the pin and making the putt. His surge was stopped when he bogeyed the eighth, the hole across the inlet of Carmel Bay – here his iron to the green found the rough on the right – but, thanks to that rush of five consecutive birdies, he finished the first nine four under par for the tournament. He was in the thick of it now, tied with Watson and a stroke behind Rogers, who was the leader at that moment.

In the old days, news travelled slowly on a golf course, and the reports over the grapevine were not always reliable. Today, what with a large, well-operated leader board at nearly every hole, the players know almost instantly what their rivals are up to. Watson, paired with Rogers, certainly did. By nature a much more high-strung person than Nicklaus, he had felt a little nervous when he awakened on Sunday morning. After breakfast, he played for a spell with his two-year-old daughter, Meg, whom he adores. He then dug into two Sunday papers, taking his time as he read about the federal-budget controversy and the earthquake in El Salvador. He felt somewhat less tight when he put the papers down. He and Rogers were off at 1.05 p.m., three twosomes and 27 minutes after Nicklaus. Throughout the round, Watson was two holes or a hole and a half behind Nicklaus, depending on the length of the holes they were playing. They were seldom in sight of each other.

Watson, who had started the final round four under par, turned the front nine still four under par. A bogey on the third had offset a birdie on the second. On the short seventh, he had wasted a big chance, muffing a two-and-a-half-foot putt for a birdie. This error obviously did not affect him as much as it might have, for on the eighth he made a difficult seven-footer to save his par. At this point in the round, Rogers was going through a very shaky passage, missing his pars on the ninth and tenth and, later, on the twelfth, and therewith dropping out of the race. By that time, Devlin, too, was out of it, a stout-hearted challenge by Graham was over, and the championship had become a two-man battle – Watson against Nicklaus.

In retrospect, the tenth hole looms large in Watson's eventual victory. On that 424-yard par-four that marks the end of the glittering cliffside sequence, he managed to avoid a five and, possibly, a six or seven. This significantly changed the shape that his duel with Nicklaus took. Off the tee, he hit the narrow, slanting tenth fairway – it was only 27 yards wide for the Open – but he hung his approach shot, a 7-iron, out to the right, and it found the bunker below and to the right of the green. That green is tucked close to the edge of the cliff, and if the ball had drifted a shade more it could conceivably have toppled over the cliff and down onto the beach. (Incidentally, in the distance beyond the tenth green one takes in the crescent beach of the town of Carmel, its bright white sand washed by the breaking slate-coloured waves. It is something to contemplate. It looks the way one imagines the shore at Bali Ha'i might, except that one sees few people swimming, because the water is intensely cold.) From that sunken bunker on the tenth, Watson exploded to the edge of the green, 25 feet from the cup. Then he made the putt for his four. This not only kept him four under par but boosted him into the lead, a stroke ahead of Nicklaus, who, minutes before, had three-putted the eleventh green from 20 feet.

Which player should one watch, Nicklaus or Watson? When in doubt, it is usually wise to go with the leader. I walked to the drive zone on the eleventh. This 382-yard par-four runs uphill from the tee, but Watson, pumped up by holing that big putt on the tenth, whaled his tee shot 270 yards up the fairway, at least 40 yards beyond Rogers' drive. He was on with a pitching wedge, 22 feet from the pin. As he walked with his quick strides to the green, he acknowledged the gallery's applause with his ingenuous smile. Like Nicklaus, Watson is determined to play golf his way, and his way is to approach it as a game and to show in a natural manner his appreciation of the support that the spectators give him. The keystone of Watson's personality is his invariable honesty. This somehow comes through in his facial expression, and may explain why some people get the feeling that there

is a certain vulnerability about him. It should also be noted that there is a
lot of iron in his soul, for otherwise he would never have been able to
accomplish the things he has. After studying the line of his birdie putt on
the eleventh – close to the cup, the sidehill putt would dart from left to
right – he stepped up and knocked it in. Five under par for the tournament
now, a two-stroke lead on Nicklaus. Not for long. On the par-three twelfth,
204 yards long, he left his iron shot out to the right and was bunkered. He
played what was for him only an ordinary sand shot, leaving the ball 15 feet
short of the cup. He made a rather weak try for the putt. Back to four under
par and a lead of only a single stroke on Nicklaus. Matters stood the same
way after he parred the thirteenth. His tee shot on this hole must have been
close to three hundred yards. Under tournament tension, Watson sometimes
sprays the ball into trouble, because his hitting action gets too quick, but on
this last round, swinging well within himself, he was clouting his drives a
mile and dead straight.

The fourteenth, the long par-five that swings to the right, proved to be
another critical hole. After a good drive, Watson chose to lay up with an
iron about 80 yards short of the pin, figuring that he would be able to put
more backspin on a relatively full wedge than on an abbreviated wedge flip,
and so would be able to stop the ball close to the pin, which, once again,
was situated on the high left side of the green. I could not see what kind of
lie he had, but in any event, his shot had very little spin on it and rolled 35
feet past the pin to the back edge of the green. I think it was then – as
Watson was walking to his ball – that most of us in his gallery noticed on
the leader board adjacent to the green that a red four had gone up for
Nicklaus on the fifteenth. This meant that he had birdied that hole and now
stood four under par – tied for the lead. (We learned later that Nicklaus had
holed a 15-foot putt for that birdie. The old Golden Bear is really a tough
customer down the stretch in a championship.) Watson took a shade more
time than usual reading the line of his 35-foot birdie putt on this sleek, ripple-
filled green. He hit the ball with a good-looking stroke. Halfway to the hole,
the ball seemed to pick up speed. It was still moving fast when it dived into
the middle of the cup. A terrific putt – especially in those circumstances.
Five under par now, Watson had regained his one-shot lead over Nicklaus.
Only four holes to play.

Up-and-down rounds are nothing new to Watson, but what was called for
at this stage of the Open was sure, prudent golf: do nothing fancy, keep the
ball in play, concentrate on hitting the green in the regulation number of
strokes, get down in two well-thought-out putts. On the par-four fifteenth,
Watson was letter-perfect: on in two, down in two from 20 feet. On the
sixteenth, however, the 403-yard par-four, which slides downhill as it doglegs
to the right and drops to a green shut in on both sides by trees and further
protected by immense bunkers, Watson made an almost fatal mistake. Off
the tee, he missed hitting the fairway for the first time during the round. He
started the ball off to the right, and it stayed to the right, finally plummeting

down into the recently remodelled bunker in the crook of the dogleg. This is one of the two bunkers that Sandy Tatum, remembering Jack Neville's suggestions before the 1972 Open, had asked to have fortified for the 1982 Open, so that it would more accurately fulfil Neville's wish that it be both more intimidating off the tee and more difficult to recover from. Now its front wall rose straight up three feet high, the upper two feet sodded like a Scottish bunker. Talk about irony! Watson has no more fervent admirer or devoted friend than Tatum. A contemporary of Watson's father at Stanford, Tatum has been close to Tom ever since he came West to attend Stanford. Looking gravely at this bunker after it had caught Watson's tee shot, Tatum turned to some friends in the gallery and said, 'That's what this bunker was meant to do'. On the third round, Watson's tee shot had ended up in the same bunker, but the ball had finished at the back edge, and he was able to fly his recovery shot onto the green. On this round, though, his ball lay only a foot and a half from the base of the perpendicular front wall. Attempting to go for the green was out of the question. After some thought, Watson concluded that the best he could do was to explode out sidewise onto the fairway, which he did. The ball trickled several yards down the hillside and came to rest on a fairly severe downslope. It is not easy to put backspin on a ball from a downhill lie, and, with the pin positioned only 15 feet from the low front edge of the green, which slopes down from back to front, backspin was necessary in order to stop the ball near the pin.

Watson's third, a wedge pitch of some 80 yards, landed near the pin, but the ball had no spin on it whatever, and it rolled another 55 feet on up the green. At about this time, I began to wonder whether Watson should have exploded backwards out of the bunker onto a flat stretch of fairway from which he could have played an approach with backspin. However, this was strictly second-guessing. His lie in the bunker had been such that he probably didn't have room enough to swing the club back and play that kind of shot. Anyway, from the high back edge of the sixteenth green he would be fortunate if he could escape with a five. He came through with a beautiful approach putt. He lagged the ball downhill over the skiddy surface with its subtle slide to the right, and it died barely 15 inches from the cup. He tapped in for his five. With two holes to go, he was again tied with Nicklaus at four under par. It could have been worse. If he had three-putted the fifteenth, he would have been trailing by a stroke. He walked to the seventeenth tee at about the same time that Nicklaus, to resounding applause, was walking off the eighteenth green and heading for the scorer's tent to check his card. Except for taking those three putts on the eleventh, Nicklaus had played an errorless second nine. From tee to green, he had thought his shots out painstakingly and had executed each shot the way he had meant to. If his putting had been up to his normal standard, he could easily have been a couple of strokes lower. He had made his birdie putt on the fifteenth, but then he had missed a shortish birdie putt on the fourteenth, and on each of the last three greens he had had a crack at a birdie from seventeen feet or less. In any event, he had given one more unforgettable demonstration of how a golfer should play the final round of a championship.

Watson won the Open on the seventeenth hole, just when it seemed that he might lose it there. On the final round, the back tee of this celebrated par-three was used, so the hole played its full length – 209 yards – into a moderate wind. (On the eighteenth, the wind was blowing across the fairway, off the bay. If it had been behind Nicklaus on that hole, and if he had got off a long drive, he might have tried to reach the green in two.) The seventeenth is a tester. The green is unusually wide and unusually narrow from back to front. It sits just above a very large front bunker. Beyond the green is a string of small bunkers, along with other trouble: the rocks and water on the left. You really cannot play for the right side of the green, because you then have to deal with the dangerous ridge that divides the green into two sections. In tournaments, the pin is almost always set on the left side. It was on this day – ten feet from the left fringe, about halfway between the front edge and the back edge of the green. Watson first thought he would use a 3-iron but then changed his mind and played a 2-iron. He hooked it a shade – or, to use the current expression, he 'came over' the ball, instead of hitting under and through it. The ball finished hole-high, 20 feet to the left of the pin and eight feet from the fringe of the green, in a growth of thick, resistant rough. He would also have to cope with a downhill lie. If you were standing out near the ropes on the right side of the hole, you could not see the ball. However, Watson later explained that though it was down low, it was lying on top of the grass. 'I had a good lie', he said. 'I could get the leading edge of my club under the ball.' Opening the blade of his sand wedge and cutting under and slightly across the ball, he hit an exquisite shot. The ball came up softly, about two feet high, and landed just on the edge of the green. Curving a foot and a half from left to right with the contour of the green, it rolled straight for the pin, hit it dead centre, and fell in. The moment the ball disappeared from sight, Watson threw his arms up and broke into a wild Indian dance. The spectators packed along the seventeenth, reacting almost as immediately to this sensational birdie which put Watson in the lead by a precious stroke, began jumping for joy and shouting and howling.

Under the circumstances, Watson calmed himself down quickly. By the time he stuck his peg into the ground on the eighteenth tee, he looked composed and confident, ready to wrap things up. A par-five on the 548-yard eighteenth would do it. He played the hole just the way he meant to: a 3-wood tee shot down the right side of the fairway; a 7-iron laid up in the centre of the fairway 130 yards from the green; a 9-iron that sat down pacifically 20 feet behind the pin. Watson studied the green with care. His putt was a touch downhill, and he wanted to be sure he had the speed right, so that he would leave himself the shortest of tap-ins. He had no intention of trying to hole the 20-footer, but the ball slithered into the cup. He had won the Open. He had finally won the Open. The fact that his margin of victory was two strokes was irrelevant. He had won the championship by holing his sand-wedge shot on the seventeenth when it would have been an achievement to get down in two from the rough. (I think his ball would have rolled about seven feet past the cup if it hadn't hit the pin.) That little cut pitch out of the heavy grass may well be the greatest winning shot that has been played in the Open since 1923, when Bobby Jones, tied with Bobby Cruickshank as they came to the eighteenth in their play-off for the title at Inwood, on Long Island, summoned a perfect-plus 2-iron, from a poorish lie, that rose in a high parabola over the water hazard before the green, came down on the green, and stopped six feet from the hole. The scores of the leaders in the 1982 Open: Watson, 72-72-68-70 – 282; Nicklaus, 74-70-71-69 – 284. Two strokes farther back, at 286, were Rogers, Clampett, and Dan Pohl.

Nicklaus, after walking off the eighteenth green, watched Watson's tee shot on the seventeenth on the television monitor in the scorer's tent. When he saw the ball hook into the thatchy rough, he felt that the percentages were heavily against Watson's getting down in two from there and saving his par. He turned his attention to checking his scorecard, thinking that now he would probably win the Open and that the worst that could happen was a play-off, if Watson somehow birdied the eighteenth. When Nicklaus next looked at the monitor, what he saw was Watson dancing across the green. His first reaction was that Watson's recovery had probably lipped out of the cup.

Twelve minutes or so later, when Watson walked off the eighteenth green, Nicklaus was waiting there to congratulate him. 'You little son of a gun, you're something else', he said as they shook hands. 'That was nice going. I'm really proud of you, and I'm pleased for you.' The two men have enormous respect for each other. They also like each other. In the last Ryder Cup match, they were always together. Nevertheless, it took an extraordinary sportsman to do what Nicklaus did at the conclusion of a championship that, not many minutes before, he had thought he would win. There is no other loser in sports as gracious and warm as Jack Nicklaus has shown himself to be. This quality is due in part to training he received from an exceptional father and in part to Nicklaus's own character and sense of sport. He and Watson had previously fought three memorable battles down the stretch in major championships. In the 1977 and 1981 Masters, Nicklaus, trailing at the start of the final round, had mounted valiant rallies only to see Watson fight back successfully. In the 1977 British Open, Watson and Nicklaus happened to be paired on the third round. They both shot 65s. As the two leaders, they were paired again on the fourth round. Nicklaus had a 66, Watson another 65, with Watson prevailing on the final green. I can still see Nicklaus's yellow-sweatered, bearlike arm wrapped over Watson's shoulder as they came off that last green after their two-day, head-to-head confrontation.

And I am all admiration for Watson, for having the heart and the skill to play as he did under the stress of that long last hour. Now that he has at length won the championship, I am told by the experts and roving soothsayers that we will see a more majestic Watson. That would be fine. Apart from his superior personal qualities, he is one of the purest shotmakers since Harry Vardon. At the moment, though, the 1982 Open still fills my mind. I can think of only one US Open since the Second World War that can compare with it in dramatic impact – Ken Venturi's triumph 18 years ago at Congressional, on the outskirts of Washington. The 1982 Open is something to treasure. With the lone exception of that 1977 British Open at Turnberry, when Nicklaus and Watson duelled face to face over 36 holes – a rare combination of circumstances – I don't see how a tournament can be any better than the one we were treated to at Pebble Beach. It was just about as good as golf can get.

# No Anglo-Saxon Reserve

## PETER ALLISS AND MICHAEL HOBBS, 1986

Ballesteros had not been playing well in America, but a tip during practice rounds before the Open Championship at St Andrews worked wonders. Equally important was the fact that he was back in a land where he is accorded honorary British nationality by spectators. They love the Spaniard, but only respect Watson.

Seve began with a round of professional competence rather than brilliance, the dazzle coming with his scoring around the loop. From the eighth to the twelfth, he had five threes consecutively and his only really poor play came on the feared Road hole, the seventeenth. He hit his tee shot well left, then pulled his second shot. Trying a run-up third shot he was not quite firm enough and still short of the green. He got his five, however, which is perhaps the real par for this 461-yard hole. That first day, there were just three threes, 36 par-fours and the remaining 117 in the field had fives or worse.

Watson played very steadily, his long putting looking particularly secure. Again and again he ran the ball at the hole at just the right pace, but nothing dropped for him. He was over par just once at (where else?) the seventeenth. For the record, the actual leaders were:

Bill Longmuir, Greg Norman and Peter Jacobsen 67; Ian Baker-Finch 68; Ballesteros, Tom Kite, Nick Faldo and Jaime Gonzalez 69

On the second day, the little-known Australian Baker-Finch made much more impact. Beginning at four under par, he moved to a remarkable ten under after ten holes. He kept going to the end, even parring the seventeenth, for a round of 66 and a three-stroke lead.

The seventeenth was very much a feature of both Watson's and Ballesteros's rounds as well. Seve found his second shot on the downslope at the rear of the Road bunker and failed to get out, perhaps through being over-ambitiously delicate, but his fourth shot was four feet from the hole. He got the putt.

Playing behind, Watson needed pars on the last three holes for a round of 66. He got his four on the sixteenth safely enough, but then bunkered his second shot at the seventeenth, recovered to the front right of the green and left his approach putt eight or nine feet short and missed it. When he parred the last, he had the same round as the Spaniard, a 68. This was the position:

Baker-Finch 134; Faldo, Ballesteros and Trevino 137; Longmuir 138; Wadkins, Couples, Langer and Watson 139

It was easy enough to scoff at the chances of the 23-year-old Australian, but a young player has to arrive some time. Few had heard of Walter Hagen or Gene Sarazen before they won their first US Opens or Taylor and Vardon before their first Open Championship victories. However, it certainly seemed more significant that the two favourites, Watson and Ballesteros, were in good command of their games.

Tom, in fact, played the best round of the third day of those in the competition. His 66 was matched only by Sam Torrance and an American not qualified to play on the US tour, Bill Bergin. Watson was in full and glorious flow. He did not drop a shot on the second hole, but with five birdies reached the turn in 32 and then drove to five or so yards of the hole on the 342-yard tenth for another birdie. Another followed at the twelfth, and par followed par until he reached the seventeenth, which might again turn a 66 into a 68. This time he showed a way to play the hole that made its problems seem relatively simple. He hit his tee shot down the left half of the fairway, and played for the front of the green rather than the flag. His very long approach putt was stone dead.

Ballesteros was out with Lee Trevino, whose efforts were frustrated by relatively poor putting. Although this certainly didn't apply to Ballesteros, he was gaining very little on the greens but was consistent in everything else he attempted. There was one exception. He hit an atrocious iron to the 178-yard eighth hole, finishing left and in heather some 30 to 40 yards short. A superb recovery shot made his putt for a par a formality. On the seventeenth he took his third successive five. After three rounds, he had been over par only four times. Three of those bogeys came on the seventeenth, where Watson had fared no better with five, six, and his four in the third round.

By this time the championship had all the makings of a four-horse race:

Watson and Baker-Finch    205
Ballesteros and Langer    207

The next men, Hugh Baiocchi, Lanny Wadkins and Lee Trevino were five strokes further away on 212.

On the final day the horses were quickly reduced to three. Baker-Finch's pitch to the first unluckily spun back into the burn and he took a bogey five. Another bogey followed on the fourth, with a further two shots dropped on the sixth and yet another on the seventh. He dropped four more shots in his round, but a birdie on the last enabled him to break 80.

Two of the other three did not come through the opening holes unharmed. Watson, looking far less convincing than in his previous two rounds, dropped shots at the second and fourth but repaired some of the damage with a birdie on the third. Langer, after starting with a pitch to about one foot on the first, dropped shots on the third and fifth. Ballesteros went on his steady way with four after four. At the end, there were a remarkable 16 on his card. He had fours on both the par-fives and one of the two par-threes.

His play throughout was in great contrast to his championship win at Royal Lytham in 1979 where some of his drives were quite wild. Afterwards, Seve explained that at Lytham he had driven into the rough deliberately, to avoid bunkers or secure the best line in to the flag. Perhaps. This time he claimed his main aim from the tee was to avoid the eccentric bunkering of St Andrews, and I often saw him well over to the left side of the course. However, on the Old Course a tee shot down the right almost invariably gives the best line in for the second shot, so Seve was demanding a great deal from his short game and it didn't fail him.

Watson gave up his lead on the twelfth, a hole just over three hundred yards and one of the easiest birdie opportunities you'll find at St Andrews. Watson drove into bracken on the left and had to drop out under penalty, taking a very unwelcome five. However, he came back minutes later with a birdie at the thirteenth. On the long fourteenth Ballesteros's drive just missed the Beardie bunkers. He seemed to take this as an omen of victory and, as at Lytham five years earlier, almost broke into a run in his haste to get to his ball and hit it again. Some hit this one was, a carry of some 240 yards over Hell bunker. He made it but was still some 70 yards from the hole, ran it up to 12 feet and holed the putt to draw level again with Watson. His partner Langer also had a birdie putt, but missed and fell two behind the leaders. It was 5 o'clock exactly.

Langer was to finish his round courageously, taking the brave line with his tee shots on both the sixteenth and seventeenth: down the right side of the fairway, risking going out of bounds because of a better line in to the flag and the birdies he desperately needed. Alas, they didn't come. He had to wait until the eighteenth, where he got his three – but too late.

Both Watson and Ballesteros parred the fifteenth and sixteenth, the Span-iard only a bare quarter inch away from a birdie on the sixteenth. A play-off now seemed by far the most likely result. I expected both to drop a shot on the daunting Road hole and perhaps have birdie chances on the 'easy' eighteenth (no hole is easy when a championship is within reach).

On the Road hole, Seve's record in the previous rounds was five, five, five; Tom Watson's much the same – five, six, four. It was the Spaniard to play first. His tee shot wasn't what seemed needed – well left and in the rough. Seve was disgusted. He was safe enough for a five but the Road bunker lay in wait and, if he avoided that, his line to the green was not good. At an angle, this was a narrow target. He'd probably run through and onto the road itself – not a good position to be in.

Well it all came off. Instead of playing for the front of the green and hoping to get down in two from some 30 or 40 yards, he went for the heart with a full 6-iron from a rather flying lie. His ball bit and held. He had a certain four and minutes later putted up stone dead.

But it wasn't over yet. Immediately behind, Watson hit one of the best tee shots seen all week to the ideal position down the right side, making the Road hole green as easy a target as possible. He paused before leaving the tee, asking if his shot was in bounds. Yes, it was that close, almost in the semi-rough.

Ballesteros saw where Watson's ball had finished. Mentally, he conceded the American a par-four. He would have to birdie the last and that would probably give him the championship by one stroke.

Watson now proceeded to make that result far more likely. From his ideal position, his second shot was too strong. He hit the green but his ball then careered away, down the bank, across the road and up against the wall, not much more than a foot away.

He had to improvise a shot, going well down the grip and trying to jab his ball towards the pin off the back foot. With so impossibly short a backswing, it ruled out having any feel for the shot.

He managed it well, but not well enough. His ball was on the green but ran well past the flag. His five was inevitable and gave Seve a one-stroke lead.

Ahead, the Spaniard drove well and then played a gentle pitch dead on line for the flag which stopped perhaps three yards or so short. There was a pause while Langer, after blowing kisses to the vast crowd, ran his putt in for his first birdie since the tenth, a round of 71 and a total of 278, three strokes better than Jack Nicklaus's score in the last St Andrews Championship in 1978. The German had become a man to reckon with in the major championship. He would be rewarded the following spring at Augusta.

Ballesteros by now knew that a birdie three would give him the title, barring a miracle or two. He still had to avoid three-putting, however, for that would have him in a tie with Langer. He mustn't be overbold and miss a short one coming back.

His putt was perfect for pace all the way – but not for line. It always looked as if it was going at the right lip. So it was, but that gentle pace meant that his ball toppled in.

Joy unrestrained. Seve thrust his right arm again and again and yet again skywards, no Anglo-Saxon reserve in the gestures at all, and part of the reason why he is such an exciting player to watch.

But just possibly it wasn't all quite over. Ian Baker-Finch, now struggling to break 80 and feeling almost an intruder in these great events, and Tom Watson had still to finish. Watson did make a show of it. He needed a two to tie, and before he played his pitch to the green walked all the way up first. His ball was good for line but over the flag. It was all over, one of the greatest championships of the past several years. As Seve said in his improving English: 'I feel very exciting'. He certainly was.

# BEAM ME UP, SCOTTY!
## ANDY TOTHAM, 1987

So what do you mean the wrong man won? Scott (who's he?) Simpson plays the round of his life to defeat family favourite Tom Watson by one stroke and suddenly all we hear is a load of claptrap about the Olympic course maintaining its tradition of putting the best man second. Three times the tree-infested, tortuous Olympic Club of San Francisco has played host to the US Open, they moaned. And three times the big name has not walked away with the big prize.

Unknown Jack Fleck saw off Ben Hogan in 1955, Billy Casper did likewise to dear Arnie Palmer in 1966 and now, born-again Christian Scott Simpson does the dirty over our Tom to beat him at the death and deny the proper conclusion to his comeback bid. What an outrage! Politely they applauded Mr Simpson's victory. He got the customary standing ovation from the thousands around the eighteenth green. But there could be no disguising the underlying current among the majority of golf fans, officials and reporters. 'Why did it have to happen again?' But hold on! Make no mistake the right man did succeed this time just as he has done in past Olympic Opens.

'It' happened again for one good reason. Scott Simpson found the courage, the skill and the tenacity when it mattered most. Playing to rock-hard greens of variable pace, from fairways which declined to hold the ball, from rough which was more choking than the Boston Strangler and in the pressure-pot turmoil of the US Open in front of 25,000 boisterous spectators and millions on television, he held his game together while others could not. No. That's not quite right. Victory didn't come to Scott Simpson. With eight men within one shot of the lead at the turn in the final round he went out and grabbed victory by the throat with birdies at 14, 15 and 16 – a hat-trick we should all take our hats off to. Add to that three days of stubborn, controlled play beforehand with rounds of 71, 68, 70 (to add to the closing 68) and one of the best sand saves you are ever likely to see – a downhill lie to a glass-like seventeenth green in round four – and you can see just what made Scott great.

'I can't ever remember playing that well down the home stretch before', said Simpson after victory was secure. 'The key thing was making all those big putts. I putted the best I have ever done. I was trying to get them up and they just kept going in. When I made those three birdies I just knew it was going to be my day.' Oh yes and he had a little good fortune too. In the final round a bunker shot wrapped itself in the cloth of the flagstick and dropped to within two feet of the hole to enable him to rescue par. But who would deny him that?

Mr Simpson's main problem it seems was not so much his golf but his non-plussed reaction to winning. No one is asking him to be a stand-up comic, but please, a little enthusiasm would not have gone amiss. His Christian faith had kept him steady over the closing holes he revealed in monotonous tones immediately after the final round was over. 'I am a Christian and that is probably the most important thing in my life. I was not afraid whether I was going to win or not. Because of my faith in God I was able to stay cool because I knew I was secure no matter what happened. It has always been a dream to win it but I never really felt I was good enough to win the US Open.' (A faint glimpse of a smile at this point.)

Simpson's win was worth $150,000 plus untold riches in commercial ventures as US open champion. The prize money took his year's earnings to more than $450,000, top of the US money list. Victory automatically gave him a place in the US Ryder Cup team for Muirfield Village too. 'I was going to skip the British Open', he revealed, 'but now I guess I'll go.' Simpson, 31, married with two children and playing out of Hawaii had three tour victories to his name before Olympic including this year's Greater Greensboro Open. His career earnings now stand at more than $1.6 million.

Strangely, and in the same placid, comatose tones, he said that he had not realized he was in a winning position until after the sixteenth hole. 'I didn't look at the leaderboards all day until then so I didn't know how I was doing,' he said. 'I resisted the temptation because when I have looked up at the boards in tournaments before I got caught up and forgot what I was doing. I must admit when I did look up I was surprised that Tom was still hanging on in there and I wasn't further ahead.'

Stirring stuff indeed! In spite of his excellent deeds on the course, it is a shame that his experience in winning could not inspire him to greater enthusiasm. Scott Simpson in victory looked just like another faceless pro who had won just another tour event. As one reporter commented: 'Did he not realize what he had done?' Indeed, his wittiest quote was unintentional, when he said: 'My aim was just to live up to the way the Lord said to play golf'. (He didn't cite the specific chapter and verse.) Simpson did confess to a little devilishness though when Watson hit his 45-foot putt on the last hole to force a play-off. 'I have to admit I was hoping it wouldn't go in', said Simpson. Unsmiling and unglamorous he may be, but, as the 87th US open champion, Scott Simpson certainly had the last laugh. So much for the winner then. What about those that followed?

However the man himself may view it, for many the 1987 US Open will best be remembered as the Open where Watson came back. It had been four long years since his last Major win and although he didn't quite make it this time, he came close enough to prove that the game that once beat them all is still there. In the end his 45-foot putt to force a play-off on the seventy-second hole fell just two inches short. It was that close. That agonizing.

Watson opened with a 72 and followed it with a breathtaking, five-under 65. 'One of the best ten rounds of my career', he said. He felt on the verge of something good. 'I have heard everything about why I was in a slump', the sandy-haired Kansan declared. 'I've heard all sorts of rumours, that I'm an alcoholic, and that I am getting divorced and that I am giving up golf and so on. None of it is true. That's just people I guess but they don't know

what they are talking about.' From there Watson let his clubs do the talking
with a third round 68 which put him in the lead with rookie tour pro Keith
Clearwater whose 64 on Saturday equalled the 21-year-old course record.
Clearwater sadly fell away with a 79 on the last day. Watson hung in there.

On the eve of the last round Watson said: 'I am nervous. I am going to
play a round of golf tomorrow that is probably one of the most important
in my career. I know that and you all know that.' He went out on that last
nail-biting day and gave it his best shot. He fell short. By those two dramatic
inches. 'I had to win today to prove to myself that I was back', he declared
afterwards. 'Finishing second was no good. I can't complain though. I made
too many mistakes early on. Scotty hit the shots he had to hit to win. All
credit to him. I felt a little of the old magic coming back', he said and then
added, as if in warning: 'There is a lot of golf in Tom Watson yet. A lot of golf.'

Watson's inability to win can best be put down to his inability to master
Olympic's famed 'quake corner'. Holes two to five are regarded as the
toughest stretch on the course. On both Saturday and Sunday Watson had
dropped three shots by the time he walked off the fifth green. The shivers
had got him. He was never to recover. Simpson's winning total of 277, three
under par and Watson's 278 were the only figures in red at the end of the
week – a feat Greg Norman had described as 'highly improbable'. Four shots
behind came Seve. Ah yes! Seve who had threatened all week but whose
putter failed him most over the crucial holes. With seven to play he was tied
second but two three-putts bade him goodbye.

On the practice days he had told reporters: 'I am hitting my driver as
straight as my putter right now', leaving us all to guess on the accuracy of
both. By the seventeenth on the final round we knew. A downhill birdie
putt stopped some seven feet short. 'That was embarrassing', the Spaniard
said later. With rounds of 68, 75, 68 and 71 for a third-placed cheque of
$46,000 he seemed not too downcast. There were no histrionics as in the
Masters when he had left the course in tears. 'I feel I had a very reasonable
chance to win but my putting was not as good as it was supposed to be. But
I must be positive and how I played today will help me in the future', he
said. 'I didn't have any momentum like in the past. My putting was not the
best part of my game and to win the US Open you have to putt well.'

Putting. Now that brings us to the greens and the condition of the Olympic
course in general. It was primed to USGA rules. The fairway was faster than
some British greens, being cut to five sixteenths of an inch. First cut in the
rough (a six-foot wide strip) was to two inches, with the rough thereafter
being four inches long. But the Olympic grass is of a kind unfamiliar to
Britain. Long, sinewy, thick and damned tough even just a few feet off the
greens. When players of the calibre of Norman and Ballesteros say they have
no lie in the rough it's a fair indication of how score-destroying and mind-
destroying that grass is. Joked one groundsman: 'I went by with the mower
today in the practice round and Andy Bean gave me a standing ovation'.
The greens, too, caused immense difficulties all week, especially the sloping

seventh, seventeenth and eighteenth putting surfaces where speeds approached Mach II. Finally, even the USGA had to concede and water was applied to slow them down.

The seventeenth hole came in for most attack. A par-five for the members it was made into a long par-four for the US Open. But the bone-hard fairway proved nigh impossible to hold. Said Bernhard Langer: 'I feel the seventeenth is the worst hole I have ever played in any Open. It is a terrible hole.' The severely sloping eighteenth green brought oohs and aaahs from the galleries all week too. For example, Tom Kite's three-foot down-hiller missing and rolling 25 feet past the hole. All agreed the course was tough. Tough and testing to the limit. Tom Watson summed up the mood: 'We don't play courses like that every week and I am glad because we would all be bumbling idiots if we did. Once a year is enough.'

So what else did we have at Olympic? We had the cream at the top from the first off with Ben Crenshaw shooting 67, and the first seven players on day one, including defending champ Ray Floyd, Langer, Nakajima and southern Africans Nick Price and Denis Watson, representing four of the world's five continents. We had the prospect of a dream finish with Jack Nicklaus shooting a second round 68 to join Watson at the top of the leaderboard. Nicklaus faded after that. We had unlikely Larry Mize threatening to complete stage two of an unlikely Grand Slam (he led with eight holes to play). We had Greg Norman spending more time among the eucalyptus trees and never looking likely to win – even though he did drive the 288 yards, uphill seventh hole.

We had a mime artist in 'knickers' with no clubs doing impressions of Payne Stewart. Stewart himself, a pre-tournament favourite, played like he had no clubs as well. He missed the cut. Seventy-seven players out of 156 did not! We had the unforgettable sight of Tommy Nakajima's ball lodging 75 feet up a tree on the eighteenth and a small boy climbing up to try and find it. He didn't and Nakajima took six to end his challenge.

We had rounds of inspiration from Craig Stadler, Senior Tour player Dale Douglass, Mark Wiebe, Bob Eastwood, Lennie Clements, Curtis Strange, Keith Clearwater, Mac O'Grady and Bernhard Langer. None could maintain his challenge. And finally we had that battle royale, not this time between Edward and Mrs Simpson, but between Tom and Mr Simpson. And we all know who won that!

When it was all over and the crowds who had packed the eighteenth hole since 7 a.m. had gone home, the Olympic Club was left with an estimated $1 million profit, and Scott Simpson was left with a valuable piece of golfing silverware, it was generally agreed that a good time had been had by all.

San Francisco has the Pope and Madonna to look forward to later this summer but everyone agreed that the 87th US Open would be a hard act to follow. And the lasting memory? Tom Watson. Ball two inches from the seventy-second hole. Tears in his eyes. The roar of the crowd. The lump in the throat. Welcome back Tom!

# COURSES

*Golf architecture began when a group of influential golfers decided on good positions for greens and chose their favourite routes to get there. They made use of the most natural golfing landscape – the links of the eastern seaboard of Scotland. There they found the hollows and plateaus which are ideal as sites for greens. Dunes provided the main hazards and the paths that sheep and goats followed became their fairways.*

*Allan Robertson was probably the first course designer. Because of his fame as the best player of his time, he was asked to visit and lay out the routes of golf courses. All trace of his work has long since disappeared and after his death in 1859, Old Tom Morris became the most respected adviser.*

*Neither of these men considered changing the land they found, other than to recommend the placing of a bunker here and there. It was only when golf moved inland that earth-moving, though on a small scale, began. Golf-course designers were no longer content to choose the way an existing piece of land should be used. Increasingly they shaped it, often imitating the natural features of linksland. The first man to make a success of the job was Willie Park.*

*I have begun with two pieces which talk about the nature of golf courses and go on to give considerable space to the Old Course at St Andrews. Though it may not be the best course in the world, it was the most influential in the way its features were imitated.*

## BARREN AND RANK
### SIR WALTER SIMPSON, 1887

The grounds on which golf is played are called links, being the barren sandy soil from which the sea has retired in recent geological times. In their natural state links are covered with long, rank benty grass and gorse. These get worn away by sheep and golfers, and short springy sandy turf is disclosed. The part of the links thus worn is the course. Links are too barren for cultivation; but sheep, rabbits, geese, and professionals pick up a precarious livelihood on them.

## NATURAL GOLF
### SIR GUY CAMPBELL, 1952

Nature was their architect, and beast and man her contractors. In the formation and overall stabilization of our island coastlines, the sea at intervals of time and distance gradually receded from the higher ground of cliff, bluff and escarpment to and from which the tides once flowed and ebbed. And as during the ages, by stages, the sea withdrew it left a series of sandy wastes in bold ridge and significant furrow, broken and divided by numerous channels up and down which the tides advanced and retired, and down certain of which the burns, streams and rivers found their way to sea.

As time went on these channels, other than those down which the burns, streams and rivers ran, dried out and by the action of the winds were formed into dunes, ridges, and knolls, and denes, gullies and hollows, of varying height, width and depth. In the course of nature these channel-threaded wastes became the resting, nesting and breeding places for birds. This meant bird droppings and so guano or manure, which, with the silt brought down by the burns, streams and rivers, formed tilth in which the seeds blown from inland and regurgitated from the crops of the birds germinated and established vegetation. Thus eventually the whole of these areas became grass-covered, from the coarse marram on the exposed dunes, ridges and hillocks, and the finer bents and fescues in the sheltered dunes, gullies and hollows, to the meadow grasses round and about the river estuaries and the mouths of the streams and burns. Out of the spreading and intermingling of all these grasses, which followed, was established the thick, close-growing, hard-wearing sward that is such a feature of true links turf wherever it is found.

On these areas in due course and where the soil was suitable, heather, whins, broom and trees took root and flourished in drifts, clumps, and coverts; terrain essentially adapted to attract and sustain animal life. Nature saw to this. First came the rabbits or 'cunninggis' as an ancient St Andrews charter describes them; and after the 'cunninggis' as naturally came the beasts of prey, followed inevitably by man.

This sequence had a definite effect on these wastes or warrens. In them the rabbits bred and multiplied. They linked-up by runs their burrows in the dunes and ridges with their feeding and flocking grounds in the straths and sheltered oases flanked and backed by whins and broom. The runs were then gradually worn into tracks by foxes, and man the hunter in his turn widened the tracks into paths and rides. Generations later when man the sportsman, having adopted golf as a pastime, went in search of ground suitable for its pursuit, he found it waiting for him, in these warrens, almost ready to hand. In form it was certainly primitive but it supplied lavishly what today are regarded as the fundamental and traditional characteristics of golfing terrain.

The rides leading from one assembly place to another made the basis of each fairway; the wild and broken country over which the rides threaded their way provided the rough and hazards – rough and hazards that would now bring a blanch to the faces of the most accurate and phlegmatic of our 'professors', and the sheltered *enclaves* used by the 'cunninggis' for their feeding halls and dancing floors presented the obvious sites for greens.

Shortly the original layout of nature, interpreted and completed by beast and man, not only hall-marked golf as a point-to-point game, but from then on became the blue-print and sealed pattern for every links and course constructed by intention: indeed it remains today the ideal of all quality design.

# Innocent Enjoyment

## JAMES BALFOUR, 1887

Having played golf on these links for somewhere about 45 years, it has occurred to me to note for my own amusement some of the changes that have taken place during that time in this, one of the most fascinating of all athletic games.

\*   \*   \*

When I first visited St Andrews there were only a few resident gentlemen who played, and some occasional strangers from a distance, from Mussel-burgh, Leith, and Perth. The custom then was to meet in the small Union Parlour in Golf Place about 12 o'clock, and arrange the matches. Parties at once proceeded to play, and if the match was finished two or three holes from home they immediately turned and played their second round, taking a glass of ginger beer at the fourth or Gingerbeer hole. If, however, they finished their first round, they came into the Union Parlour only for ten minutes; did not sit down to lunch, but took very slight refreshment, and finished the second round a little after four. The dinner hour was then five.

How different now, when matches are made a week, or even a fortnight, in advance; when places are taken early in the morning, and a man is kept with a record to start each in his turn, and so prevent disputes about the order of play; when play is begun a little after nine, and 50 or 60 matches start between that hour and 12; when parties have to wait a quarter of an hour for one another at the High Hole; when an hour or an hour and a half is devoted to lunch, and the second rounds are not begun till between two and half-past three! The dinner hour is half-past seven, to give time to have a putting match on the ladies' links with the fair and enthusiastic devotees of the game!

The links belong to Mr Cheape, the proprietor of the neighbouring estate of Strathyrum. Their length is nearly two miles, and their breadth at the broadest part about $2\frac{2}{5}$ths of a mile. In some distant geological epoch they must have been submerged by the sea, but they are now protected from its waves by high natural embankments of sand. They were originally covered with thick whins, rough grass, heather, and bents. Out of this a golf-course was formed like a narrow ribbon in the form of a shepherd's crook, over which the public have acquired a servitude of playing golf. The course is marked off by march stones.

The approximate distance of the holes from one another is as follows:

| No | Yards |
|----|-------|
| 1 | 360 |
| 2 | 450 |
| 3 | 335 |
| 4 | 375 |
| 5 | 540 |
| 6 | 370 |
| 7 | 350 |
| 8 | 150 |
| 9 | 300 |

$$3230$$
$$2$$
$$1760) \overline{6460} (3 \text{ miles}$$
$$5280$$
$$\overline{1180}$$

Or $3\frac{3}{4}$ miles.

The length of the course as the crow flies is thus $3\frac{3}{4}$ miles; but following the ball in a zigzag way, the distance walked is generally considered to be about five miles. The course is marvellously adapted to the game. It used to be flanked by high whins for the greater part of its extent, and these formed an interesting hazard. The turf is smooth and fine; the subsoil is sandy; the surface sometimes undulating and sometimes flat. There are beautiful level putting-greens, while the course is studded with sand-pits, or bunkers, as golfers call them. These, with the ever-recurring hazards of whin, heather, and bent all combine to give endless variety, and to adapt the links at St Andrews for the game of golf in a way quite unsurpassed anywhere else. If there be added to its golfing charms the charms of all its surroundings – the grand history of St Andrews and its sacred memories – its delightful air – the song of its numberless larks, which nestle among the whins – the scream of the sea-birds flying overhead – the blue sea dotted with a few fishing-boats – the noise of its waves – the bay of Eden as seen from the high hole when the tide is full – the venerable towers and the broken outline of the ancient city; and in the distance the Forfarshire coast, with the range of the Sidlaws, and, further off, the Grampian hills, it may be truly said that, probably, no portion of ground of the same size on the whole surface of the globe has afforded so much innocent enjoyment to so many people of all ages from two to 89, and during so many generations.

The changes that have taken place on the course during these 45 years have been very considerable. First of all, the course is much wider. Formerly there was only one hole on each putting-green, and players played to the same hole both going out and coming in. The party first on the green had

the right to finish the hole before the match from the opposite direction
came up. This naturally kept the course narrow, but when players began to
multiply it was found to be inconvenient, and now it would be impossible.
To obviate this it was resolved to have two holes on each putting-green, one
of them being played to on going out and the other on coming in; or rather
there were two distinct putting-greens parallel to one another, and a hole in
each. This was virtually making two courses all along the links – one for
playing out and the other for coming in; thus the breadth of the course for
golfing was gradually increased, till now it is about two-thirds broader than
it used to be. This was probably unavoidable, owing to the increased number
of players, but it has taken away much of the interest of the game.

*   *   *

The links are far more carefully kept than they used to be. Tom Morris
superintends this with great assiduity, and he has two men under him who
are constantly employed in keeping the bunkers at the proper size, in filling
up rabbit-scrapes or other holes, and in returfing places which have given
way. The putting-greens also, instead of being left in their natural state as
formerly, are now carefully rolled with a heavy roller, – mowed with a
machine, – and watered in dry weather from a well that has been sunk near
each of them. The putting is made smoother and better, and much truer.

A separate teeing-ground has also been provided at each hole, which
preserves the putting-greens from being broken by the tee strokes. A wooden
box filled with sand for the tee, and placed at the teeing-ground, is a novelty
and an additional refinement.

## DEVOID OF NATURAL OBSTACLES
### J. H. TAYLOR, 1943

It may be acceptable if I give my impression of St Andrews on the occasion
of my first visit there, an impression first received as I drove along the road
skirting the links in a rickety buggy, late at night from Cupar, accompanied
by Sandy Herd whose mother kindly put me up for a few days. This was a
disappointment, which my further acquaintance the next morning failed to
remove. Since my early days at Westward Ho!, I had learned to look upon
St Andrews as being something majestically grand and awe-inspiring, where
the ancient and traditional home of the game had found a fitting environment.
I saw nothing but a long, narrow expanse of ground that appeared to be
devoid of any natural obstacles, if one excepted the whins on the right-hand
side going out and a few which impinged at a hole or two on the left coming
in. There were no carries from the tees. It looked as if one could hit the ball
hard on the top from most of them, and provided it was hard enough would
trundle along and would run as far, to almost the length of a well hit drive,
without meeting any obstruction.

It was confusing, and it didn't seem right when directed by the sapient and autocratic caddy to drive directly away from what appeared to be the straight line to the hole and aim at the wee red hoose or on to the spire of the auld kirk when a shorter cut seemed highly desirable. The eighth, ninth and tenth holes, which form the curve of the Shepherd's Crook, were, I thought, simple affairs, and it was not until one faced the playing of the short eleventh, the High Hole with Strath and other bunkers in front and the Eden behind, that here perhaps was something worthy. Even the terrors of the High Hole defeated themselves. The cautious and timid player could and often did push his shot away to the right to make sure of his four, whilst the more courageous would find himself trapped in Strath or swallowed up by the Eden beyond. Many a medal and championship round has been ruined at the High.

Certainly, the tee shot at the Long Hole In was a teaser. Between the Beardies on the left and the out of bounds boundary wall on the right was little room to spare, but if the drive were hit reasonably straight one had not much to fear. The second shot at the Long called forth the directive qualities embodied in the spire of the auld kirk. One was counselled to play it at an acute angle to the left to escape the perils of Hell bunker – I later saw Gene Sarazen, the American, lose a splendid chance of winning the championship of 1933 by taking a fearful risk in its bowels – as one zigzagged the way to the hole.

The Corner o' the Dyke hole, the sixteenth, was rendered dangerous by the fact that the drive had to be steered to the left of the Principal's Nose bunker and away from the railway on the right. This done, the shot up to it was plain sailing. The Stationmaster's Garden I found to be a misnomer. Instead of a garden, if one were bold and courageous enough, one had to carry a black looking erection of a wood shed. There were but few players who tried. The gutty ball of those days imposed severe carrying limitations. The more discreet used to sneak around to the left and I was one of them, for failing to carry the shed meant out of bounds and the beginning of a hole whose sting lay in its finish even if one had successfully overcome its initial difficulty. The Road hole at St Andrews is the most discussed hole in the world. There are many players who call it foul and many more perhaps who consider it to be the finest example of a golf hole to be found anywhere. There must be something unique about it to call for this divergence of opinion.

*Bobby Jones's feeling of puzzled dislike for St Andrews eventually changed to admiration. Sam Snead thought the land was not good enough to plant beet on. Over the years many players (including James Balfour) have regretted that the course has become easier. Since the 1920s others have deplored the fact that the greens reward 'target golf' and the running approach is no longer needed. Bill Mehlhorn, a good American professional of the 1920s expressed this opinion in the interview which follows.*

## Shooting at Steeples
### AL BARKOW, 1986

St Andrews never impressed me at all. I wondered how the devil it got such a reputation. The only reason could be on account of its age. Everything was flat, except for the little rolls on the fairways, so all the shots were blind shots. You had to shoot at a steeple five miles away.

## Atmosphere Unparalleled
### DAN JENKINS, 1970

The mystique of Muirfield lingers on. So does the memory of Carnoustie's foreboding. So does the scenic wonder of Turnberry, and the haunting incredibility of Prestwick, and the pleasant deception of Troon. But put them all together and St Andrews can play their low ball for atmosphere. To begin with, St Andrews is an old university town. Spires rise up over narrow streets littered with shops and cosy pubs. Students wearing red cloaks are bicycling around. Statues confront the stroller. An inn is here and there, and the North Sea just beyond.

There are four golf courses at St Andrews: Old, New, Eden and Jubilee, and they are all available to the public. The new course is over 70 years old. Try that on for nostalgia. But no one, of course, is ever concerned about anything but the Old. The Old Course is St Andrews, the R and A, all of those famed hazards. It is Jones, Vardon, Hagen, and Old and Young Tom Morris, and Keith Mackenzie standing on the balcony of his office in the R and A building just above the first tee surveying the entirety of the layout through a pair of mounted German submarine binoculars.

I was fortunate enough to secure lodging in the Old Course Hotel. Thus, I could walk out on my terrace and it was all there directly below me. To my left, the course stretching out to the eleventh green – the short hole, of course – and to my right, a matchless view of the eighteenth fairway leading up through the Valley of Sin with Rusacks Hotel standing there as it is supposed to be, and with the great grey edifice of the Royal and Ancient clubhouse forming a backdrop.

The Old Course has been called a lot of things because, at first glance, it looks like nothing more than a flat green city park. Some Americans have labelled it a 'third-rate municipal course', and a 'football field', but Bob Jones knew its subtleties better. It was, he said, the one course he would play forever if he could choose just one.

Two things strike the first-timer at St Andrews immediately. First, the double greens. No fewer than 14 holes share enormous putting surfaces, the second also being the sixteenth, and that sort of thing. There are two flags, naturally, and often they will be as far apart as perhaps 80 yards, with many a dip and turn between them. The erring shotmaker is apt to find the longest putts in golf at St Andrews. Secondly, the Old Course is something of a paradise for one with a chronic hook. The first nine goes straight out, you see, with all of the heather and the sea on your right. And the back nine returns, parallel, giving the hooker all of those outgoing fairways to land on.

The mystery of why no golfer has ever been able to tear apart the Old Course – 278 is the lowest a winner has shot in the British Open there – lies in the wind and the putting, and the fantastically perfect location of such hazards as Hell bunker, a deep and somewhat inescapable pit at the fourteenth, the Swilken Burn, a small brook which rushes right up against the green of the first hole and catches many a soft 9-iron, and the Valley of Sin, the cavernous lower level of the eighteenth green from which three-putts and even four-putts are commonplace.

I attacked the Old Course in the company of Ginger Johnson who had merely been caddying there for 45 years. For a few holes, he thought he had Henry Cotton again. The wind was behind and my shank, my top, my slice and my putting jerk seemed to have disappeared. Through the tenth, I was only one over par, and I said to Ginger, 'I don't know, but I think I'm bringing the Old Course to its knees'. And Ginger said, 'Aye, ya made a putt or two, sir. But now we go home into the wind.'

In rapid order, I was lost in the Elysian Fields, lost in the Beardies, trapped in Hell bunker, gouged in the Principal's Nose, over the fence, smothered in heather, and even out of bounds on an overhang of the Old Course Hotel at the Road hole. Finally, I limped up the eighteenth fairway en route to the Valley of Sin. Par for 86. 'You had a wee bit of hard luck', Ginger said. 'But it can't spoil the fact that as we cum up the eighteenth, we sense a wee bit of tradition, don't we?'

Keith Mackenzie peered down from his balcony as I walked onto the green. I putted out. One final insult: a straight-in four-footer which broke six inches. The secretary motioned me up for lunch in the R and A dining room – no smoking at all. I toured the club and reread the letter that Isaac Grainger, then the president of the USGA, had written to the R and A on the occasion of its two-hundredth birthday. He had said, in part, 'What golf has of honour, what it has of justice, of fair play, of good fellowship and sportsmanship – in a word, what is best in golf – is almost surely traceable to the inspiration of the Royal and Ancient'. I thought of those words again as I strolled back outside to stand and look at the sea, and at the town, and all across the gentle green sweep of the Old Course – the oldest course. I had been there forever.

*As the popularity of golf grew rapidly in England several courses were opened. There were many difficulties for inland golf – some courses became unplayable once the autumn rains set in; others, because of rudimentary cutting machinery, were impossible to maintain in the growing season. There was not a single good inland course until*

*Sunningdale opened shortly after the turn of the century. For 'proper' golf, those who could afford to went off to such links courses as Westward Ho!, Hoylake and St George's.*

# FULL OF HAZARD AND INCIDENT
## HORACE HUTCHINSON, 1890

At Westward Ho!, we find a course which recalls the broken, and, in parts, mountainous nature of Prestwick, Carnoustie, and North Berwick. True, we do not now play over the low lying spurs of that great ridge of sandhills known as the Alps, over whose summits we used to drive in days long past. Yet the Westward Ho! course is probably better golf today, in consequence of recent changes, than it ever was. The first three holes occupying some ground in old days unutilized, have enabled the course to be elongated, and stretched, and straightened out of its somewhat too complicated, criss-cross mazes. The new holes, though flattish, are fine golf, and the fourth hole brings us in to the country of great sand bunkers, with precipitous bluff sandy faces, and of the strong sharp rushes, which have been the features from of old of the Westward Ho! course – a course very full of hazard and of incident, where the most condign punishment visits the ball which is not perfectly played, both in point of distance and direction. This we may say is today the main characteristic of Westward Ho! – that whereas on most links it is sufficient to keep straight (there being a certain course up the whole length of which it is safe to play), at Westward Ho!, on the contrary, it is generally necessary to pick out a certain spot – not merely a certain line – to which to drive the ball. And, the ball once driven there, what a blessed reward is ours! For the lies throughout the green at Westward Ho! are better than those at any links in England or Scotland.

On the other hand, it is but just to say, having ventured upon a comparison, that there is a weakness about Westward Ho! in that the outlines of the bunkers are not sufficiently defined. Though precipitous on certain sides, these bunkers have usually as many wide mouths, belching forth wind-swept sand upon the green, as there are points of the compass. Hence, a ball which has fairly carried the bunker itself will often be found in an even worse lie, in this blown sand, than the ball that has been bungled into the heart of the bunker. Nevertheless, as a general rule, the ball that has been well struck from the tee will be rewarded with a very perfect lie, while that which has been topped will suffer a cruel fate. There is at almost every hole a carry from the tee – and the finish to the home hole, just over the burn and in front of the clubhouse, is probably the prettiest in all golf.

# A TIMELESS STRETCH OF LAND
## PAT WARD-THOMAS, 1955

It was evening, sun was over all the land and, as we looked down the links towards the pebble ridge as golfers have done for 90 years, there on the last green was a figure holding the flag for his friends, a symbol of this strong country where the years pass lightly over man and his affairs. For J. H. Taylor, last survivor of the great masters of the past, lives on sturdy and forthright as ever with the fires of an unquenchable spirit still bright behind eyes which first saw the light of Devon 84 years ago.

And talking with J. H., as on an evening four years ago, the conviction that the game of golf has changed, and not for the better, since he with Vardon and Braid bestrode the championships of a generation ago was strong once more. 'They will not get down to it', he said, and how often has one written of young players to the same effect. The age of the craftsman, who loved his art more than its rewards, has passed for ever and with it much of the true spirit of the game, which in character as a contest between man and nature is dying.

But Westward Ho! is far from dying although the gracious days of the past can never return. After five years of losing money there are signs of a returning prosperity, for an increasing profit has been made in the last two. In the professional's shop there indeed was a happy man. For S. Taggart, whose business is flourishing, whose book is full of lessons, and who never regrets for a moment leaving the North, wisely, like the good club professional he is, regards his members' interests as more important than his own playing ambitions. The club within remains one of the most friendly in experience, and no little of this is due to the secretary, A. J. Garland, and the famous Kelly, most amiable and hospitable of stewards, whose length of service to the club of more than half a century must be without parallel in the world. Only three men, and of the same family at that, have ministered to the inner needs of members in the history of the club. And succession is assured because when Kelly retires his son will take his place.

Mainly for reasons beyond the club's power to overcome, the links are no longer fashionable for championships. The ancient grazing rights, which permit sheep and cattle to wander at will, are inclined to prejudice golfers who prefer their pastures to be undisturbed and do sometimes jeopardize maintenance. The growing expense of hotels and travelling has caused committees and promoters to consider these factors more deeply than before the war. But for the ordinary golfer Westward Ho! is by no means inaccessible, accommodation is plentiful within easy range, and the course, where the artificial simply does not exist, lends itself to holiday golf more readily than most.

Although it can be a considerable test of skill, especially when the rarely absent wind is strong, for there is no false protection of trees, buildings or undulating land, it is not fearsome in the sense of long carries or lost balls in thick rough, heather, or woods. Neither is there any wearisome toiling of trolleys up and down hills. Most of the fairways are vast and spreading, but let no one think that fours will come easily because of that, for judgement of distance is of the very essence on this flat land and the greens, particularly when fast, can be most deceptive. But the land is not as flat as it seems, for the shallow hollows and runnels can produce awkward stances and tricky little shots from around the greens.

It was with a sense of relief that we saw it all again, for in this age of science, neurosis, and the welfare state, the old things, the gracious things, often are thrust aside and neglected. There have been signs of this happening in golf, especially with the increasing influence of the United States. It would, therefore, be sad if an old club and its traditions were allowed to pass. Happily this will not happen. The Royal North Devon club will continue to grace that timeless stretch of land where sea, sky and turf are as one and in 1964 will become the first seaside course in England to celebrate a hundredth anniversary.

# THE MAKING OF INLAND COURSES
## HORACE HUTCHINSON, 1919

The first architect of the inland courses, when golfers began to learn that inland courses might, in some large measure, give them the game they wanted, was Tom Dunn. He went about the country laying the courses out and as he was a very courteous nature's gentleman, and always liked to say the pleasant thing, he gave praise to each course, as he contrived it, so liberally that some wag invented the conundrum. 'Mention any inland course of which Tom Dunn has not said that it is the best of its kind ever seen.'

His idea – and really he had but one – was to throw up a barrier, with a ditch, called for euphony's sake a 'bunker', on the near side of it, right across the course, to be carried from the tee, another of the same kind to be carried with the second shot, and similarly a third, if it was a three shot hole, for the third shot. It was a simple plan, nor is Tom Dunn to be censured because he could not evolve something more like a colourable imitation of the natural hazard. A man is not to be criticized because he is not in advance of his time.

Moreover, these barriers had at least the merit that they were uncompromising. You had to be over them, or else you found perdition, and if you only hacked the ball out a little way beyond the first barrier with your first shot you could not carry the second barrier with the third. You were like a hurdle racer who has got out of his stride.

The course, constructed on these lines, on which I used to play most, from London, was Prince's at Mitcham – the most convenient of access of all, before the days of motors. I used to have great matches here with Jack White, before Sunningdale was made and he went there in charge.

Subsequently the mantle of Tom Dunn, as course constructor in chief, fell on the shoulders of Willie Park, and his ideas were more varied. He was also a good deal more thorough, more elaborate and more expensive in his dealings with the inland courses. He was the first to advocate the wholesale ploughing up of the soil of the course, and the re-sowing. He architected Broadstone, Sunningdale and a host more, and when he had finished with the Sunningdale green he had certainly produced the best thing in the way of an inland course that up to that time had been created. He did his work well, but it was not entirely or even mainly due to him that Sunningdale was so good. The soil was more light and sandy, more like the real seaside links, than that of any other inland course.

# GOLF ARCHITECTURE, USA
## CHARLES PRICE, 1962

In the middle of the 1890s, the founders of new golf clubs in the United States were almost totally ignorant of how a golf course should be shaped, since few of them had ever had an opportunity to lay eyes on a first-rate course, much less play one. More than six hundred of the nation's earliest courses had been laid out by a hack named Tom Bendelow who, almost solely on the basis of a thick Scottish burr, in 1895 quit his job as a compositor on the old *New York Herald* to hire himself out as an architectural consultant to A. G. Spalding & Bros. That year he built Van Cortlandt Park, in New York City, the first 'public links' in the country, and followed it up with some of the most abominable examples of golf landscaping ever seen, some of which he laid out in one day for a cost of $25.

Bendelow's methods were simple, to say the least. At an appropriate spot he would mark the first tee with a stake. Then he would pace off a hundred yards and stake off that spot with a simple cross-bunker. Then he would march another hundred yards and mark this location for a mound that was to be built in the shape of a chocolate drop. Then he would walk another hundred yards, more or less, and mark the location for a green. All of Bendelow's greens assumed one of two shapes: perfectly round or perfectly square. None of the greens was protected by hazards, most of them were indistinguishably flat, and all of them had to be ploughed under within a few years after they had been planted because, as anyone with a smattering of agronomy could see, they were nothing more than weed nurseries.

As a golf-course architect, Bendelow was looked upon by those who succeeded him as the Addison Mizner of the fairways, Mizner being the eccentric, amateur designer who built a palace in Palm Beach for a millionaire grocer and forgot to include a staircase. One of the first to succeed Bendelow and undo many of his mistakes was Donald Ross, of Scotland, who, beginning at the turn of the century, designed more than 250 courses while remodelling more than a hundred others. A man of vision who knew how to build permanent values into a course, Ross made up for the lack of linksland in America by shaping his greens with the variety of amoebas and terracing some of them as steeply as staircases. His fairways and greens were tightly trapped with sprawling bunkers, so logically placed and so naturally formed that they looked as though they had not been built at all but, instead, had always been there, the course somehow having been ingeniously constructed to fit them rather than the other way round. Along with many of his admirers, Ross considered his masterpiece to be the Number Two Course at Pinehurst, North Carolina, where he spent his years in retirement before his death in 1948. Among his other championship layouts were Skokie, Brae Burn, Worcester, Oakland Hills, Minikahda, Interlachen, Inverness, Scioto, Belleair, French Lick, and Whitemarsh Valley.

It is impossible to estimate how many American courses were influenced by Ross's designs, and not far behind him in number and imitators was Arthur W. Tillinghast, who designed such championship tests at Baltusrol, Winged Foot, Five Farms, and Fresh Meadows. The versatile Walter J. Travis, always looking for new phases of golf to try his hand at, took a turn at architecture by making Garden City and Westchester, in suburban New York, into two of the most penalizing courses in the East – and they had their imitations. Perhaps the crowning architectural achievement, however, came about in 1911 when old Charlie Macdonald, acting as though he had just built a watch blindfolded, opened up near Southampton, Long Island, a course that had been copied almost down to the roots from famous holes on the British Isles. With it Macdonald implied that, by comparison, all the other courses in America looked like pool tables, and, indeed, after looking at it, the designers of at least half a dozen courses elsewhere in the country tore up their plans in disgust and began anew. Macdonald called his Galatea the National Golf Links of America, as though he had intended it to be some sort of public shrine. With its neighbour, the equally socially selective Shinnecock Hills, actually it remains today, with its tiny membership, one of the two best unused courses in America.

*As the century wore on, golf course construction methods became more and more ambitious. In the USA, most of the best courses today are inland; in Britain, the links still hold pride of place.*

# ARCHITECTURAL VISIONS
## O. B. KEELER, 1929

It's a tough course, as well as a beautiful one, at Pebble Beach. Indeed, that is the impression I carry away with me from the 1929 National Amateur Championship. In the South, we have no courses suitable to compare with those architectural visions on the Monterey Peninsula, and with those I saw at Los Angeles. And even along the eastern seaboard, and on the famed black turf of the Middle West, there seems to me nothing so fine and beautiful. I honestly believe that the California courses I have seen, at Los Angeles and near San Francisco, and especially Cypress Point and Pebble Beach, on the Monterey Peninsula, are the finest golf courses in the world today.

Cypress Point is a dream – spectacular, perfectly designed, and set about with white sand dunes and a cobalt sea, and studded with the Monterey Cypress, so bewilderingly picturesque that it seems to have been the crystallization of the dream of an artist who has been drinking gin and sobering up on absinthe. And Pebble Beach is just as good, but no better. The putting surfaces . . . are the richest and finest I ever stepped on, and avoided putting on, for they are indecently fast and tricky in their breaks and slants. The courses in California are so much better than those in the rest of this country that I have no basis for comparison.

The climate, I should say, is considerably overestimated. The general landscape in Southern California especially, where the hand of man has not wielded the watering-pot, is every whit as ghastly as Arizona.

*        *        *

We have heard some quaint tales of California, and some of them are true, and some are as exaggerated as the premature reports of the death of Mark Twain. But as to golf courses, the half has not been told. The denizens of this state simply do not know how good their golf courses are.

## ALONG CARMEL BAY
### HERBERT WARREN WIND, 1985

Morse, instead of selling his prize property on the high cliffs above Carmel Bay for plush private estates, as most real-estate developers would have, reserved it for the golf course. In 1918, he made a startling decision. He did not approach either Charles Blair Macdonald or Donald Ross, the two outstanding golf-course architects in the country, or any other golf-course architect of reputation, to design his course. He entrusted this considerable responsibility to Jack Neville, a real-estate salesman who had worked for the Pacific Improvement Company and had continued with the Del Monte Properties Company. A tall, laconic man with a nice dry wit, Neville had won the California State Amateur Championship several times and was rated to be as good an amateur golfer as there was on the West Coast, but he had never built a golf course before. He set about his task with no fuss whatever. He walked the site daily, spending most of his hours mulling over how to use the extraordinary land above Carmel Bay to maximum advantage. After three weeks, he settled on the way that the holes he had in mind would be

routed. He got it absolutely right. His inspired plan went like this: the first
three holes would swing inland, and then back towards the bay. Holes four,
six, seven, eight, nine, and ten followed along the edge of the cliffs. The
fifth, a par-three framed by woods, did not. Holes 11 through 16 were inland
holes, but the seventeenth returned to the bay, and the entire left side of the
eighteenth, a long par-five, was bordered by the rocks, sand, and water of
the bay. The course was completed in 1919. The golfers who played it came
away stunned by its scenic beauty and the cornucopia of astonishing golf
shots it offered.

It is well worthwhile, I believe, to describe in some detail the eight holes
along Carmel Bay which Neville visualized and executed so brilliantly. The
first one that the golfer meets is the fourth, a par-four that is 327 yards long.
Despite its shortness, it is a worrisome hole. Along its right side, a cliff about
25 feet high drops down to a rocky beach. Since such features have a
particularly powerful subconscious effect on people wearing spiked shoes,
most golfers hook or pull their tee shot far to the left, into the rough or into
a bunker. Even if his drive stays on the left side of the fairway, the golfer
faces a touchy shot: he must feather a soft pitch just over a frontal bunker
in order to stop it on the green, perhaps the smallest of the 18 – and the
greens at Pebble Beach are smaller than those at any other of the world's
great courses.

The sixth, a par-five that measures 516 yards, presents a similar problem.
Off the tee, the golfer must avoid the right side of the fairway, for it is
bordered by a cliff that ranges from 35 to 60 feet high. Most golfers, in their
concern to avoid this hazard, again play their tee shot farther left than they
had intended to, and many drives wind up in a long trap that hugs the left
side of the fairway. This complicates matters. Approximately 350 yards from
the tee, the fairway climbs a sudden hill nearly 50 feet high, to a plateau, at
the end of which the green is situated. On a windless day, a big hitter can
reach the green in two, but for the average golfer, unless he finds the fairway
off the tee, a six is a most acceptable score. The tee on the short seventh, a
mere 110 yards, is set about five yards below the level of the sixth green but
at the edge of a cliff almost 75 feet high. When the golfer is addressing the
ball on the tee, he has no protection from the sometimes fierce winds as he
attempts to hit and hold the tiny, heavily bunkered green, far below him.
On stormy days, when the wind is buffeting the rocks just behind the green
and sending spray high into the air, a 3-iron is not too much club for a
professional. On quiet days, a pitching wedge will suffice.

After this, the course begins to get tough. In playing the eighth, where
the tee is only a short distance from the seventh green, the golfer, who has
now turned around to face inland, must produce a long, controlled drive to
reach the high land at the top of the hill that he had approached from the
opposite direction when he was playing the sixth. From the tee on this 433-
yard par-four, he takes in the cliff rising sharply along the right side of the
fairway. When he has climbed to the top of the incline – a good drive will

finish there – what may very well be the most awesome sight in golf awaits him. Here the cliff plunges straight down 150 feet or more into Carmel Bay. He sees this and also notices that up ahead the fairway jogs slightly to the left, but what transfixes his attention is the sight of the eighth green in the distance, across the waters of an inlet of the bay. The green is guarded by a cortege of five bunkers, but it actually doesn't need any of them, since it sits just beyond the continuing cliffline, approximately 50 feet high at this point. Depending on the weather, the tournament-calibre golfer, who will usually choose to lay up off the tee with a long iron or a 3-wood or 4-wood, is usually left with a carry of between 170 and 190 yards across the inlet on his second shot. The average golfer, of course, having hit a somewhat shorter or more errant drive, most times faces a longer carry on his second if he chooses to go for the green. To pull it off, he must summon nothing less than a career shot. He should give it a whirl nonetheless. After all, if he manages to get home in two he will have something to talk about for the rest of his life. On the other hand, if he is working on a tidy round and scoring well, prudence dictates that he take a long or middle iron for his second and play a conservative lay-up shot down the fairway as it begins to bend to the right and follow the curve of the inlet. He will then be in a position to hit the green with a firm pitch on his third.

The eighth leaves a golfer emotionally exhausted, but he must pull himself together quickly in order to cope with the ninth and tenth, two extremely exacting par-fours – 467 and 424 yards long, respectively – that continue southeast along the bay, which is on the right. On these two holes, the cliffs have dwindled to 30 feet, but this is enough to deter the golfer from flirting with the right side of the fairway. In addition, on both holes the fairway slopes from left to right, and, with the greens set close to the cliffs, hitting them in the regulation number of strokes in a swirling wind is no easy matter. I would guess that the eighth, ninth, and tenth constitute the most difficult succession of three par-fours in golf.

Pebble Beach has a formidable finish. The seventeenth and eighteenth return to the bay, and they can be destructive. The green on the seventeenth, a par-three that is 209 yards long from the back tee, is situated on a rocky point that juts into the bay. The eighteenth is regarded by many experts as the premier finishing hole in golf. It curves like a scimitar along the bay, which flanks the fairway on the left. Out-of-bounds stakes patrol the right side practically from tee to green. As if the hole weren't stiff enough with these constraints, there are other hazards, such as clumps of trees and bunkers, that come into play with a strategic niceness. Then, there is the wind. Some days, it blows in so ferociously off the water that experienced golfers feel that the safest course is to aim their shots out to sea and let the wind bring them back onto the fairway.

The only trouble with emphasizing the grandeur of the seaside holes at Pebble Beach is that this may promote the impression that the inland holes are rather ordinary. They are not. The opening three holes are a short par-four followed by a flat par-five and another short par-four. Though original and provocative, they present good opportunities for birdies. As a matter of fact, the trick to scoring well on Pebble Beach is to get through the first six holes a shot or two under par, for, regardless of his skill, the golfer is almost certain to give a few shots back to par over the last 12 holes. Granted, life becomes a little milder after you walk off the tenth green, but each hole on the inland stretch from the eleventh through the sixteenth requires fastidious shotmaking. On the par-four eleventh, for example, the drive must be placed on the left side of the fairway in order for the golfer to command the opening to the green on his approach. On the twelfth, a fairly long par-three, the surface of the green is hard and unreceptive, and the only way to stop a long iron or wood there is to hit the kind of shot that reaches the apex of its parabola above the green and floats down softly. On the thirteenth, a 393-yard par-four, the wide right side of the fairway beckons, but the tee shot should be played close to the large bunker on the left side, for otherwise you cannot come into the canted green from the correct angle. The fourteenth, fifteenth, and sixteenth also require knowledge and control. The greens, slippery and fast, as are all the greens at Pebble Beach, are full of quirky slopes and breaks, and you must place your tee shot – and on the par-five fourteenth your second shot as well – with a good deal of care in order to be able to stop your approach on the proper part of the green in relation to the pin, and so avoid finding yourself in a position where there is almost no escape from taking three putts. All in all, the inland holes, with their emphasis on finesse, complement the seaside holes perfectly.

# What? Only 6,500 Yards!
## MICHAEL HOBBS, 1987

The Merion club dates back to Civil War times but this doesn't mean that golf arrived here before the Apple Tree Gang started in 1888. Cricket was more the thing for sporting Philadelphians at that time. They even sent a touring side to England. It proved to have some very fine players and many thought the USA could become a leading cricketing nation. So, Merion Cricket Club it was for many years, the name not finally being dropped in favour of the word 'golf' until 1942. By then, however, golf had long been established and was the main activity from about 1900.

The first course, nine holes, was opened in the mid-1890s and a further nine were added a few years later. In 1904 and 1909, the US Women's Championship was played over it. For men, however, the arrival of the rubber core ball at the turn of the century made virtually all courses too short. The members of Merion wanted a championship lay-out. They formed a committee to consider the matter and one member, Hugh Wilson, showed such a grasp of golf architecture matters that he was asked to do the job. Like Charles Blair Macdonald in the case of the National Golf links on Long

Island, he decided to make his own pilgrimage to Britain. Beforehand, he consulted Macdonald about which courses he should see. He was away seven months and returned with notes and drawings of what had impressed him.

The 127 acres he had to work with is near the minimum for a championship lay-out and the land itself was hardly promising: thin layers of clay over rock. The ground was undulating – some might say bumpy – but did have some natural features that he made good use of, especially two brooks and a disused stone quarry. Such good use that today some consider Merion East the finest course in the USA. Two of its holes, the first and the eleventh, find a place in a book which selects the best 18 holes in the USA. No other course has more than one honoured.

In 1914, the US Amateur Championship came to Merion and saw the first appearance of a man who was to have associations with Merion right through his career which began and ended on the East Course at Merion. That man was Robert Tyre Jones Junior. He arrived as a 14-year-old with a local reputation down south in Atlanta and Georgia. Jones, playing on the West Course, which Hugh Wilson had also designed by this time, started off with a 74, phenomenal scoring for the times. He drew the crowds for the second qualifying round but subsided to an 89. This was still good enough for him to qualify. He went on to beat a former amateur champion in the first round, later going out to the defending champion, Bob Gardner.

In 1924, Jones won the first of his five US Amateurs at Merion and, six years later, his last. With this victory, he had completed the impossible feat of winning the Open and Amateur Championships of Britain and the USA in the year of 1930. That Merion win was his last. Jones felt he had done it all and retired, 13 major championships to his credit. No one has equalled his five US Amateur titles while of current players Jack Nicklaus took until 1980, late in his career, to tie Jones's four US Open titles, something also accomplished by Willie Anderson and Ben Hogan.

The US Open first came to Merion in 1934. Coming from eight strokes behind after 36 holes, there was a new champion, Olin Dutra. His total of 293 says something for the difficulty of the course. Sixteen years later, Ben Hogan tied for the championship with 287, one of the highest scores since World War II and won the play-off. It was one of his most legendary victories: Hogan had been left for dead in a car smash early in 1949 and was out of golf for nearly a year. Even by the time of the 1950 Open in June, although most conceded that Hogan was the best man in the field, just as many doubted that his legs would carry him for the 36 holes of play then needed on the final day. Hogan managed, though he nearly withdrew with cramp during the second nine of his last round. He then had to last out another 18 the following day in the play-off.

In 1971, there was a new generation of golfers and no doubt that the two outstanding players were Lee Trevino and Jack Nicklaus. It was entirely fitting that they should tie for the title, which Trevino won in the play-off over 18 holes. Their 280 for 72 holes was even par.

In 1981, however, par was beaten, this time by five players, David Graham's total being 273. His last round 67, in which he hit nearly every fairway and all the greens in regulation figures, is reckoned the equal of any round of golf ever played.

The scores I have given say something of the difficulties of Merion (Masters champion George Archer once declared that 95 per cent of the US Open field of 1971 were just not good enough to play it!). Yet it is no monster. Its length, 6,544 yards, is three hundred or more yards shorter than any other major championship course and very few tournaments indeed are played on either the US or European tours over so short a distance. When they are the winner tends to come home with an average of 66s. This has never seemed remotely in prospect at Merion. Trevino, when he first saw the course in 1971 and went out and played a few holes, thought that the key was hitting the tee shot into the fairway. Everything else was then straightforward. By the following day, he was calling Merion the hardest course he'd ever seen.

Trevino's feeling that the tee shot is vital was right – as far as it went. The rough is certainly punishing but the key is finding the right part of the fairway to ease the shot to the green. For the same championship, Jack Nicklaus planned to use his driver on only three holes. The rest of the time he felt position was far more important than length. The greens must be attacked from the right quarter. They are often small, always well defended and, for championship play, hard and very, very fast.

Most architects make their first hole a gentle introduction. This can seem to be the case at Merion. Only 355 yards long, it is certainly just 'a drive and pitch' hole but very well bunkered to either side of the fairway. The green slopes both from right to left and, more of a problem, front to rear. Later, there is an apparently absurd stretch of four more short par-fours in the space of five holes. One of these, the tenth, is only 312 yards long. Obviously the big hitters look to drive it. Twice in the 1971 Open Jack Nicklaus was not on in two!

The eleventh has seen much history. When Jones parred it in 1930 in the final he had won the US Amateur by eight and seven and completed his slam. Four years later, Gene Sarazen, leading the US Open took seven. He went on to lose the championship by a stroke. In the same event, Bobby Cruickshank hit a poor second shot which pitched into Cobb's Creek in front of the green. His ball struck a rock and bounded up into the air and onto the green. 'Thank you Lord', said Bobby, tossing his club on high. A second or two later, it felled him. Cruickshank, too, lost his championship lead. His playing partner's concentration was gone also as he collapsed in laughter.

At the finish, strong hitting rather than subtle placement and pitching is needed. At each of the last three holes the disused quarry is a feature. The sixteenth, about 430 yards, needs a second shot that carries all the way to the green and the seventeenth, over 220 yards, is easily the longest of the four par-threes, over the quarry to a green flanked by bunkers, with a swale reminiscent of the Valley of Sin at St Andrews' eighteenth. Merion's eighteenth, about 460 yards, needs 220 yards of carry to reach the fairway and the second shot is always a long iron. Needing a four to tie in 1951, Hogan hit a 1-iron to the green. That historic club was promptly stolen from his golf bag ...

Perhaps Walter Hagen made the best summation of Merion. He thought it a fair course where you believed you would break 70 'next time'. Playing past his prime in 1934 Hagen started with a 76, then got his 69. Had he got the secret? Apparently not. He finished 83, 80.

# PINE VALLEY

## ROBERT GREEN, 1985

While it's certainly not true that all great golf courses are located in grotesque surroundings, the thesis is not without foundation. Ballybunion is beside a caravan camp in an unsalubrious seaside resort, Augusta National is opposite a Piggly Wiggly store and a succession of filling stations along Washington Road, and Pine Valley is to be found in Clementon, New Jersey, a billboard-strewn and burger-bar infested town some 45 minutes across the Delaware River from Philadelphia.

Finding a jewel like Pine Valley in such a neighbourhood is as incongruous as it would be to see the Taj Mahal in the middle of Spaghetti Junction. Its name is apt – the 6,765-yard course is lined with pines (as well as oaks, firs and birches) and most holes run through a valley of trees and the fairways run a terrifying gauntlet of sand. There's more sand than on Copacabana Beach. One disheartened professional called it 'a 184-acre bunker'.

At Pine Valley there are tees, fairways and greens. There is almost no rough. Instead, there is perdition. The course is theoretically fair – the fairways are generous and the greens large where appropriate – but the penalty for missing either target is so severe that one is intimidated into doing just that. Many holes demand a long carry from the tee and the punishment for being short, left or right is frightening. Miss a green and your score can move into double figures well before you start to negotiate its fierce contours with your putter.

But though the course is so unremittingly tough and remorselessly unforgiving that even the Light Brigade might have been inclined to retreat, this is no Valley of Death. Pine Valley is beautiful. The trees and the magnificent terrain, the splendid isolation of each hole, the quietness without contrasted to the turmoil within as one seeks to conquer the mental and physical examination set by each shot – all these facets and more produce an awesome combination, a mixture of thrill and fear. Confronted by the stupendous second hole, one English visitor asked: 'Do you play this hole or do you photograph it?'.

It is also a privilege to play there. Not only does the course have a worldwide reputation unmatched by any other unexposed to regular public scrutiny via television, it is as exclusive a golf club as exists. Perhaps those with the best deal in this respect are the overseas members, who pay a nominal sum having been selected for membership because of their material contributions to the good of the game. Among them are professional Gary Player, actor Sean Connery, R and A secretary Michael Bonallack, journalist Donald Steel and Gerald Micklem. But the name of Pine Valley is not primarily known because it may be the hardest course in the world to get on. It's because it is the hardest to get round.

The Machiavelli who designed the course was George Crump, a Philadelphia hotelier and fine amateur golfer who proved himself the world's greatest amateur golf architect. He vanished into the wilderness of the pine-clad New Jersey sandhills in 1913 and by the time of his death in 1918 he had produced a masterpiece.

The criteria he laid down were followed religiously, although he received assistance from the renowned British architect, Harry Colt, and after Crump's death in 1918 Hugh Wilson, the creator of Merion, and the British firm of Colt, Mackenzie and Alison completed holes 12 to 15 on the principles Crump had enunciated.

One of Crump's original stipulations was simple and precise. He wanted 'two three-shot holes, nicely separated, and never to be reached in two'. The seventh (585 yards) has never witnessed a man putting for an eagle, while until the former US tour player Gary Groh, accomplished the feat last April, neither had the 603-yard fifteenth.

The seventh features Hell's Half-Acre, an unraked Sahara which begins 285 yards from the tee and stretches for over a hundred more. There is no way round it, only over or through it. The green is set on an island, surrounded by what is effectively one huge bunker. There is less sand on the fifteenth, but a lengthy carry over water with the drive is followed by a gradually rising and narrowing fairway to an elusive green. Miss it to the right and you may need crampons to finish the hole.

There is said to be a standing bet at Pine Valley – in fact, two. The first is that nobody can break a hundred first time out. (Personally, I believe this is harder to achieve on the second visit because one has then been made well aware of where *all* the trouble is.) The second is that nobody can complete a round 18-up on par despite a handicap of five shots a hole. A study of Pine Valley's four par-threes will tell you why.

The third measures 185 yards. One distinguished member, British businessman and golf writer Sir Peter Allen, once topped his tee shot with awful consequences. 'I took 11 on the hole without hitting another bad shot'. The fifth is 226 yards, but maybe its length is compensated for by the realization that this is the only short hole where one can miss the target and still find grass. On the other hand, it is wiser to heed the old members' saying: 'Only God can make three on the fifth'.

At 145 yards, the tenth appears a pushover on paper. However, just short of the green is a satanic pot-bunker, appropriately named something like the

Devil's Armpit. The latter word is actually lower down the anatomy, although it does begin with the same letter. Whatever one calls it, the solids doubtless hit the fan on the day an eight-handicap guest came to the tenth having played the front nine in a commendable 38. He found the sand bunker with his tee shot and recorded 38 strokes on that hole alone, a victim of an evil, optional local rule which forbids relief for an unplayable lie. One fourball once totalled 88 for the tenth, an astonishing statistic which can only be trumped by the hapless member who carded 44 shots on the wonderful but wicked 185-yard fourteenth, where the water laps against what appears to be a greenside bunker but is in fact a little beach.

Don't imagine that the par-fours are pushovers. The eighth measures a gentle 327 yards. That great writer, Bernard Darwin, once played the first seven holes in even par but picked up after nine shots on the eighth had not got him near the cup. 'It is all very well to punish a bad stroke', he later remarked, 'but the right of eternal punishment should be reserved for a higher tribunal than a green committee.'

There are alternative greens on the ninth; overshoot the left-hand one and experience on Everest is a prerequisite to retrieving the ball. A British Ryder Cup player once notched up 17 on the eleventh, another hole of under four hundred yards. A member has returned an 85 with an 11 on the fifteenth and a 12 on the sixteenth, where the drive has to clear a small desert. Sadists are fond of recalling the man who needed a bogey five at the last for an 84 and thereby to win a substantial bet that he couldn't break 90. His final tally was 97. If that is not sufficient, I should add that the 446-yard thirteenth is often heralded as the toughest par-four in America.

Though Pine Valley is so testing that the 36-hole club championship has been won with 173, it will succumb, if not to brilliance then at least to magic. A leading amateur, 'Woody' Platt, began one round by making a birdie at the first, holing his approach for an eagle at the second, aceing the third and sinking a putt for another birdie at the next. Six under par after four holes, Platt retired to the clubhouse bar, close beside the fifth tee. Though he'd been playing like God, he obviously felt a three there was beyond him. Some years later, Arnold Palmer played his first game at Pine Valley under the pressure of a bet which would earn him $200 for every stroke he was below 72. Palmer shot 68 and collected $800 towards an engagement ring for his wife, Winnie. Such is the lure of the course that in 1960 an amateur called Jack Nicklaus interrupted his honeymoon for the privilege of a round.

The course record is 64, six under par, achieved by the top American amateur, Bob Lewis, in September 1981. A month previously Lewis had been a member of the victorious American Walker Cup team at Cypress Point. This August, that same competition returns to Pine Valley, 49 years after the club hosted its one and only major international competition. The British did not win a single match in the 1936 Walker Cup. We should improve on that this time, even if victory is unlikely, but whatever else happens the amateur golfers of Great Britain and Ireland will relish the challenge of playing a course which is unequalled in its demands on every shot and where the reward for excellence is all the greater for knowing the consequences of failure. As I have indicated, Pine Valley can be distressingly penal in strokeplay. It is, however, perhaps the ultimate matchplay examination. The 18 holes at Pine Valley may well be the best, all told, anywhere. None are weak or even mediocre; they range from great to greater.

George Crump ploughed an estimated $250,000 of his own money into the creation of Pine Valley; a significant sum today, a vast fortune 70 years ago. Doubters called the project 'Crump's Folly'. That Crump never saw the completed work may lend some credence to the theory but not a lot. He bequeathed a genuine masterpiece, a Mona Lisa, to the sport.

The building of Pine Valley was demonstrably not a waste of time, even granted that Crump spent the last six painstaking years of a full and successful life on the scheme. Time is not of the essence when one is dealing with genius. After all, Michaelangelo spent eight years with brush in hand, painting 'The Last Judgement' on the altar wall of the Sistine Chapel, but nobody has ever seriously suggested he should have used a roller.

*Many players do not like the lavish use of water on so many new American courses – and elsewhere in the world, for that matter. The former US tour player, Johnny Bulla, who twice came second in the British Open is one of those players.*

## Remember the Rabbit
### AL BARKOW, 1986

I was interested in golf architecture. Donald Ross was my hero. He was over at Pinehurst, and because I asked him so many questions about golf architecture he took an interest in me. He took the time to give me answers. He explained his concepts. I remember a lot of it. Like he said, never build a trap to try to catch somebody. Always put it out to show him where not to go. Always have it where the poor player can play the hole. And always be fair. If you missed a green, he would have it so you weren't in water so the poor player could still play without taking a penalty. I was always a great believer in that. And Ross said to always make the course look like nature left it there. He was the greatest, I don't care what anybody says. I'm such a traditionalist from being around Donald that I can't stand these penalty golf courses they build now. They're always looking for how they can catch you and penalize you. But they'll change again.

## Pinehurst Revisited
### CHARLES PRICE, 1982

The Number Two Course at the country club may still be the most nearly perfect course in America. Not the toughest. Not the most scenic. But perhaps the only course in the country that does not have one hole, one green, one trap, that is not utterly in keeping with its character. You can still walk it in all its golfing majesty, since Number Two is one of the few remaining truly great courses on which carts are not allowed. And it has been almost fully restored to the original conception of Donald Ross after some West Coast desecrators tried to make it look like something you'd expect to find outside Malibu. America's master architect and a Pinehurst resident since just after the turn of the century, Ross considered Number Two to be his masterpiece. Nobody argued with him.

I had the fortunate experience of talking long hours with Donald Ross more than 30 years ago, and the unhappy experience of writing his obituary in 1948 for *The Pinehurst Outlook*. He was a strict man, with himself and everybody else, and he looked distastefully on amateurs who didn't do anything with their lives except play golf. He thought, really thought, and all those thoughts were channelled through golf. If golf can be regarded as some kind of religion among some people, then Ross regarded Pinehurst as his Vatican City.

There was and is something venerable about the place, something almost holy about its atmosphere you can't find in the newness of Palm Springs or the clutter of Palm Beach. While Pinehurst is nowhere near as greybeard as St Andrews, it still has a church quiet you won't find even there. While St Andrews has its magnificent old university, its coastline and sliver of beach, its history that predates the entire United States, Pinehurst has nothing but golf. There are some show horses trained in Pinehurst, but not even all the horsey set knows that. And now and then you'll see a couple of freaks playing tennis. But after sundown and the day's golf is over with, nobody talks about anything but golf, not politics, not religion, not even sex. Pinehurst is the total golf community, and the only one I can think of you won't be disappointed with after many years. I know I wasn't.

## THE PLEASURE PRINCIPLE
### ROBERT TYRE JONES, 1960

When I walked out on the grass terrace under the big trees behind the house and looked down over the property, the experience was unforgettable. It seemed that this land had been lying here for years just waiting for someone to lay a golf course upon it. Indeed, it even looked as though it were already a golf course, and I am sure that one standing today where I stood on this first visit, on the terrace overlooking the practice putting green, sees the property almost exactly as I saw it then. The grass of the fairways and greens is greener, of course, and some of the pines are a bit larger, but the broad expanse of the main body of the property lay at my feet then just as it does now.

I still like to sit on this terrace, and can do so for hours at a time, enjoying the beauty of this panorama.

With this sort of land, of a soft, gentle, rather than spectacular beauty, it was especially appropriate that we chose Dr Alister MacKenzie to design our course. For it was essential to our requirements that we build a course within the capacity of the average golfer to enjoy. This did not mean that the design should be insipid, for our players were expected to be sophisticated. They would demand interesting, lively golf, but would not long endure a course which kept them constantly straining for distance and playing out of sand.

There was much conversation at the time to the effect that MacKenzie and I expected to reproduce in their entirety holes of famous courses around the world where I had played in competitions. This was, at best, a bit naïve, because to do such a thing, we would have had literally to alter the face of the earth. It was to be expected, of course, that the new layout would be strongly influenced by holes which either MacKenzie or I had admired, but it was only possible that we should have certain features of these holes in mind and attempt to adapt them to the terrain with which we were working.

I think MacKenzie and I managed to work as a completely sympathetic team. Of course there was never any question that he was the architect and I his adviser and consultant. No man learns to design a golf course simply by playing golf, no matter how well. But it happened that both of us were extravagant admirers of the Old Course at St Andrews and we both desired as much as possible to simulate seaside conditions insofar as the differences in turf and terrain would allow.

MacKenzie was very fond of expressing his creed as a golf-course architect by saying that he tried to build courses for the 'most enjoyment for the greatest number'. This happened to coincide completely with my own view. It had seemed to me that too many courses I had seen had been constructed with an eye to difficulty alone, and that in the effort to construct an exacting course which would thwart the expert, the average golfer who paid the bills was entirely overlooked. Too often, the worth of a layout seemed to be measured by how successfully it had withstood the efforts of professionals to better its par or to lower its record.

The first purpose of any golf course should be to give pleasure, and that to the greatest possible number of players, with respect to their capabilities. As far as possible, there should be presented to each golfer an interesting problem which will test him without being so impossibly difficult that he will have little chance of success. There must be something to do, but that something must always be within the realm of reasonable accomplishment.

From the standpoint of the inexpert player, there is nothing so disheartening as the appearance of a carry which is beyond his best effort and which offers no alternative route. In such a situation, there is nothing for the golfer to do, for he is given no opportunity to overcome his deficiency in length by either accuracy or judgement.

With respect to the employment of hazards off the tee and through the green, the doctor and I agreed that two things were essential. First, there must be a way around for those unwilling to attempt the carry; and second, there must be a definite reward awaiting the man who makes it. Without the alternative route the situation is unfair. Without the rewards it is meaningless.

There are two ways of widening the gap between a good tee shot and a bad one. One is to inflict a severe and immediate punishment on a bad shot, to place its perpetrator in a bunker or in some other trouble which will demand the sacrifice of a stroke in recovering. The other is to reward the good shot by making the second shot simpler in proportion to the excellence of the first. The reward may be of any nature, but it is more commonly one of four – a better view of the green, an easier angle from which to attack a slope, an open approach past guarding hazards, or even a better run to the tee shot itself. But the elimination of purely punitive hazards provides an opportunity for the player to retrieve his situation by an exceptional second shot.

*In this next piece, Peter Thomson writes about the Carnoustie of the 1968 Open Championship. It is clear that he didn't like the course and it is said that Jack Nicklaus is no admirer either. Equally, there is no doubt that Carnoustie is a great links course, but one which might benefit from changes. The last championship to be held there was in 1975 when, thanks to the near windless conditions, many players scored well – Tom Watson coming through to win after a play-off with Jack Newton. Carnoustie proved to be less terrifying than people had thought.*

# UNTIDY ALLEYS
## PETER THOMSON, 1969

Carnoustie had in fact disappointed. It was dull and uninspiring, due, some said, only to the narrowing of the fairways and the positioning of the cups on the green. But I am inclined to think otherwise. In its own right Carnoustie is a great course in the sense that great things have happened there – at least I am led to believe so. (Indeed one of them I saw – as a youngster of 22 I watched Hogan win his Open which crowned his career.) But under the close scrutiny of the modern more discerning eye it looks old and decrepit. Not all courses on the seaside linksland are fine courses even though they be 7,000 yards long and windswept. To earn the highest rating a course must test all the shots and provide at the same time a chance of scoring low and frighteningly high. It must be possible to score birdies and triple bogeys.

Perhaps at Carnoustie it is because after lengthening, so many holes are neither one thing nor the other; neither fours nor fives and, as it was at the sixteenth, neither three nor four. Even the argument that its length holds no problem for the likes of Nicklaus, holds no water. Courses built for three hundred yard tee shot artists are not great courses. Carnoustie has its old fashioned quota of blind second shots. These no longer serve any purpose in championship golf.

It is difficult to define its other shortcomings. It is like looking at a painting and trying to explain what is missing. Courses like paintings are all different. Some are great and some are bad, and there are more in between. The fairway bunkering by and large is amateurish and the ones at the second and sixth perfectly ludicrous. Nor are greenside hazards very inspiring and greens themselves look more accident than design. This sounds, I know, like sour grapes, but I hope I am looking at it more objectively than that. I am a great lover of seaside links and I have consistently upheld that the greatest of seaside links are the greatest of courses.

Carnoustie could easily satisfy me with a few major renovations. Last July, mistakes were made and from these lessons should be learned. In drawing attention to them I hope they might be avoided in future and that the Open might continue to climb up to its rightful place as the world's foremost golf event. Apart from the general architecture which is so dull, I must speak out against the indiscriminate narrowing of fairways by the ruse of letting the fairway turf grow wild until it is indistinguishable from and merges with, the normal rough. To put it simply, rough should make the hole and not the other way round.

Dog-legging, off-setting of tees and such devices increase the need for judgement and clever thinking. In direct contrast, the plain shrinking of the entire length of the fairway, so that all alternatives are eliminated, robs the game of one of its important aspects – necessity to make a choice.

If golf is a test of threading one's way down narrow, alley-like avenues of untidy growth it is hardly a game. It becomes an examination. It demonstrates neither temperament nor thought. It is boring for players and spectators alike.

# PRESTWICK

## DAN JENKINS, 1970

On your left: mounds of heather and whin. Directly in front: waste. Sheer waste. Small and large clumps of it, sheltered by thin layers of fog. And the caddy hands you a driver. The fairway, presuming one is actually there, can't be more than 20 yards wide, but the caddy hands you a driver.

'*Where* is it?' I asked.

'Straightaway, sir', said Charles, who was distinguished from my caddy at Turnberry by two things. Charles wore a muffler and had his own cigarettes. 'It's just there', he said. 'Just to the left of the cemetery.'

It is asking a lot, I know, to expect anyone to believe that you can bust a drive about 250 yards on a 339-yard hole, have a good lie in the fairway, and still not be able to see a green anywhere, but this is Prestwick.

The green was there, all right, as are all of the greens at Prestwick, but you never see them until you are on them, which is usually eight or ten strokes after leaving the tee. They sit behind little hills, or the terrain simply sinks ten or 15 feet straight down to a mowed surface, or they are snuggled behind tall wood fences over which you have nothing to aim at but a distant church steeple.

You would like to gather up several holes from Prestwick and mail them to your top ten enemies. I guess my all-time favourite love-hate golf hole must be the third hole on this course. Like most of the holes at Prestwick, it is unchanged from the day in 1860 when Willie Park, Sr, shot 174 to become the first Open champion. Quite a score, I have since decided.

First of all, without a caddy, it would take you a week and a half to find the third tee. It is a little patch of ground roughly three yards wide perched atop a stream, a burn, rather, with the cemetery to your back and nothing up ahead except fine mist. Well, dimly in the distance, you can see a rising dune with a fence crawling across it – 'the Sleepers', the caddy says. But nothing more. Nothing.

'I'll be frank, Charles', I said. 'I have no idea which way to go, or what with.'

'Have a go with the spoon, sir', he said.

'The spoon?' I shrieked. 'Where the hell am I going with a spoon?'

'A spoon'll get you across the burn, sir, but it'll na get you to the Sleepers', he said.

'Hold it', I said. 'Just wait a minute.' My body was sort of slumped over, and I was holding the bridge of my nose with my thumb and forefinger. 'These, uh, Sleepers. They're out there somewhere?'

'Aye, the Sleepers', he said.

'And, uh, they just kind of hang around, right?'

'Aye', he said. 'The Sleepers have took many a golfer.'

Somehow, I kept the 3-wood in play and when I reached the shot, Charles casually handed me the 4-wood. I took the club and addressed the ball, hoping to hit quickly and get on past the Sleepers, wherever they were. But Charles stopped me.

'Not that way, sir', he said.

'This is the way I was headed when we left the tee', I said.

'We go a bit right here, sir', he said. 'The Sleepers is there just below the old fence. You want to go over the Sleepers and over the fence as well, but na too far right because of the burn. Just a nice stroke, sir, with the 4-wood.'

Happily, I got the shot up and in the general direction Charles ordered, and walking towards the flight of the ball, I finally came to the Sleepers. They were a series of bunkers about as deep as the Grand Canyon. A driver off the tee would have found them, and so would any kind of second shot that didn't get up high enough to clear the fence on the dune. A worn path led through the Sleepers, and then some ancient wooden steps led up the hill and around the fence to what was supposed to be more fairway on the other side.

It wasn't a fairway at all. It was a group of grass moguls going off into infinity. It looked like a carefully arranged assortment of tiny green astrodomes. When Charles handed me the pitching wedge, I almost hit him with it because there was no green in sight.

I got the wedge onto the green that was, sure enough, nestled down in one of those dips, and two-putted for a five that I figured wasn't a par just because the hole was 505 yards long. Charles said I had played the hole perfectly, thanks to him, and that I could play it a thousand times and probably never play it as well.

I said, 'Charles, do you know what this hole would be called in America?'.

'Sir?' he said.

'This is one of those holes where your suitcase flies open and you don't know what's liable to come out', I said.

'Aye, 'tis that', he said.

'One bad shot and you're S.O.L. on this mother', I said.

'Sir?' said Charles.

'Shit out of luck', I said.

'Aye', said Charles. 'At Prestwick, we call it the Sleepers.'

*I end with a few pieces which are critical of some trends in modern golf courses. The preparation of courses for the major championships is one such area. For the Masters at Augusta the greens may sometimes be too fast so that a downhill putt struck with what looks extreme delicacy will roll on and on – and off the green. This criticism is also made of courses used for the US Open. In Britain, the reverse is true. Links greens once famed for their speed are now usually too slow.*

*Both the USGA and the R and A have broadly similar policies for setting up their Open courses. Fairways are narrowed and balls almost on the putting greens settle well down, making a precise chip shot an impossibility. In Britain, the rough is sometimes allowed to grow like hay while in the USA the policy is to have the vegetation dense rather than long. The aim is to reward players who hit fairways, and are steady rather than enormously long. But power still pays off handsomely; when the ball settles down in dense growth, only the strongest can lash it out and on to the green.*

*But these conditions apply in the major championships; club and even tournament players meet these conditions infrequently. Water, though, is another matter – used too lavishly a course can become unplayable for the average golfer.*

# I WENT HOME
## DAVE HILL, 1977

Behind the PGA I put the US Open, the most overrated tournament in the universe. The US Open is just another tournament, except that the course is tricked up. The United States Golf Association, which sponsors the tournament, does a great job of picking courses, with a few hideous exceptions like Hazeltine, but then turns around and ruins them. It's perverse.

I couldn't believe what the USGA did to Pebble Beach [in 1972], a classic test. I barely recognized it. Pebble is one of my favourite courses on the tour – but the USGA turned a show dog into a bitch. I played out the tournament at Pebble and wished I hadn't.

The next year I went to Oakmont on the assumption that here was a course that definitely needed no doctoring ... no knee-high rough and cement-hard greens. Naïve me. I played four holes of a practice round and checked it to 'em. I went home. I didn't pick any fights or throw anything in the locker room or even criticize the USGA. The writers grilled me and I held my tongue. I simply went home. I wasn't mentally prepared to go out there and shoot 80, and that's what I would have done. There's no law that says I can't quit, and I quit. My swing had been coming along and my attitude was good and I didn't want to ruin them both. I couldn't have won the golf tournament if they'd given me a free throw on every hole. I paid my caddy $150 for the four holes and took off.

I'm a skinny little cat who has to win with style, not strength, and the game is no fun at all for me when a course is prepared like that. I don't understand it. It doesn't happen in the big events in other major sports. They don't dig chuck holes in the track for the Indianapolis 500. They don't move the goalposts back into the crowd in the Super Bowl. They don't put obstacles on the centre court at Forest Hills. They play the game the same way it's played for the rest of the season. They're content to let the best man win under normal conditions, and he will.

# PRIMITIVE COURSES
## DAVE HILL, 1977

As far as the other so-called major tournament, the British Open, goes, I don't play in it because the conditions are primitive, including most of the golf courses. In Britain, nature builds the course, not man. You're liable to find the worst trouble on a hole in the middle of the fairway, where I've always been taught you are supposed to drive the ball. If you don't like a course, you don't play as well. The idea is to play the game for fun, and if it isn't fun why play?

It's a long trip for one tournament and you have to file your entry too early.

The weather is usually abysmal. If the temperature reaches 55 degrees over there they think they're having a heat wave. The wind roars in off the ocean on those links courses and the rain lashes you, and you bundle up to survive and you can't make a decent golf swing. They play faster over there and it's no wonder – if you don't keep moving you're liable to turn into an icicle.

The weather is why the British pros for years couldn't hit the ball anywhere. They couldn't make a full swing, so they manipulated the ball with their hands. They would come over to this country and they couldn't beat Andy Gump until they'd been here five years.

I appreciate the traditions of the game but I don't have any warm spot in my heart for Britain. As far as I'm concerned we've refined the game tremendously over here and I don't get any thrills out of going back and roughing it. Give me running water every time.

Those folks are about two hundred years behind America in modernization, you know. Especially out where some of these seaside golf links are. At the 1969 Ryder Cup we were in a hotel that has something like 120 rooms, and out of those 120 rooms there are 27 private bathrooms. I was lucky – I had a private bath. Otherwise I would have used the window before I'd have headed down the hallway at 4 a.m. And that is one of the luxury hotels in the area!

The British Open is the oldest big tournament, but I don't even classify it as a major event today. The British Open probably would have died if the American stars hadn't started going over to play in it more regularly the last 15 years. Arnold Palmer saved it, but as far as I'm concerned he didn't do us any favours.

## COURSES THAT ARE HELL TO PLAY
### PETER THOMSON, 1987

You don't have to be a weatherman to notice a change in the climate. Just read Jack Renner's quote about the US Open course at Shinnecock Hills last year. 'I'll tell you what's great about Shinnecock', he said. 'No railroad ties and no greens in the middle of lakes. There are choices here, options. The modern golf course removes strategy and options from the game of golf. It's a defensive game. You just try to keep away from trouble. Here there are three or four ways to play most holes.'

Does this mean what I think it does? Have railroad ties and greens in lakes had their day? Passed out of fashion like Bermuda shorts and fins on Cadillacs? Are the cold, grey skies of depressing winter giving way to warmer days of celebration and good fun? I, for one, hope so.

The truth is, the TPC at Sawgrass and courses of that ilk are hell to play. Such courses were designed and built for the amusement of spectators, not for the pleasure of playing. They were born in commercialism as part of Commissioner Deane Beman's bold plan to make the PGA tour self-sufficient by the staging of tour events in its own stadiums. Built into these arenas are the features that make for colourful television – the horror stretches of water and wilderness, railroad ties and savage sawgrass, areas wherein it might be hoped a front-runner will come to grief to the sniggers of the multitudes watching from the high mounds. The mixture of these patterns makes for the photogenic aspect that magazines and calendars lap up, the reflection of green grass and trees in calm blue water. (Out West you can even have snow-capped mountains mirrored in the hazards.) It sells a load of real estate but has little to do with golf and, more often than not, gets in the way. What we are seeing in these courses are not practical innovations, but distortions of dimensions – not works of art but caricatures.

The whole sorry business stems on the one hand from the silly attempt to keep winning scores up at around par for four rounds, about 288. Winning scores in the early 1900s were near the three hundred mark, but they steadily declined with the advancement in clubs and balls and the tremendous improvement in course maintenance.

Winners of major championships, in this day and age, should crack the 270 mark, but for some nonsensical reason the game's authorities decided that scores should hold at the par mark. To counter low scores came the mucking about with the course, distorting its length and width, and the conversion of non-hazard areas into 'penalty zones'. The result of this misguided policy is the present-day competition for the most outrageous and bizarre.

On the other hand is the modern axiom that a golf course will sell real estate, and that the more notorious the course the higher the surrounding land prices. The trick for the developer, as devised through his architect, is to build something that is photogenically stunning, however impractical, extravagant or absurd. Never mind the golfer, that most gullible of all citizens. 'Just get us into the colour magazines', seems to be the working theory. The effect of this kind of marketing is to lead the game of golf down the garden path. By pounding out the message endlessly that golf is a gambit of tortures, and that it is somehow plebeian to play an entire round of golf with one ball, commercialism is doing a great harm to a noble sport.

These trends have been raging now for two decades or more. The consumer has had precious little say in the matter. The free market has not been in effect, he has been caught up in a mad competition of propaganda. Yet there is a ray of hope. There are signs of a change of season as a few brave professionals like Jack Renner are beginning to speak their minds. But the little man should be heard from, too. Not the land speculator or investor, but the golfer who loves the game.

As for me, when I first took to journalism, my kind but stern mentor laid down the principle that if my grandmother couldn't understand what I was writing about, it was a lousy piece of composition. I've come to carry this along into golf architecture. If my grandma can't play it, it has to be a lousy course.